金融英语证书综合考试教材
Financial English Certificate Test

MODERN FINANCIAL PRACTICES
现代金融业务（第二版）

金融英语证书考试委员会　编

经济科学出版社

图书在版编目（CIP）数据

现代金融业务/金融英语证书考试委员会编．—2版．
—北京：经济科学出版社，2010.12
金融英语证书综合考试教材
ISBN 978－7－5141－0166－9

Ⅰ．①现…　Ⅱ．①金…　Ⅲ．①金融－英语－资格考核－
教材　Ⅳ．①H31

中国版本图书馆 CIP 数据核字（2010）第 232862 号

责任编辑：周胜婷
责任校对：徐领柱
技术编辑：董永亭

现代金融业务 （第二版）

金融英语证书考试委员会　编

经济科学出版社出版、发行　新华书店经销

社址：北京海淀区阜成路甲 28 号　邮编：100142

总编部电话：88191217　发行电话：88191109

网址：www. esp. com. cn

电子邮件：esp@ esp. com. cn

印刷：北京文海彩艺印刷有限公司

装订：北京文海彩艺印刷有限公司

850×1168　16 开　24.5 印张　500000 字

2011 年 1 月第 1 版　2011 年 1 月第 1 次印刷

ISBN 978－7－5141－0166－9　定价：68.00 元

金融英语证书考试专家组名单

组　长：　金中夏　中国人民银行国际司　　　　　　　　　　　　　副司长
副组长：　李桂荣　中国人民大学外国语学院　　　　　　　　　　　教授
成　员：　张利星　中国银行业监督管理委员会国际部　　　　　　　处长
　　　　　石　莹　中国工商银行国际业务部　　　　　　　　　　　副处长
　　　　　陈海燕　中国工商银行杭州金融研修学院远程培训部　　　总经理
　　　　　侯贵峰　中国农业银行国际业务部　　　　　　　　　　　副总经理
　　　　　韩晔辉　中国银行法律与合规部　　　　　　　　　　　　高级经理
　　　　　程昆仑　中国建设银行国际业务部　　　　　　　　　　　高级副经理
　　　　　沈素萍　对外经济贸易大学英语学院　　　　　　　　　　教授
　　　　　丁志杰　对外经济贸易大学金融学院　　　　　　　　　　教授、院长
　　　　　徐进前　北京语言大学国际商学院　　　　　　　　　　　教授、副院长
　　　　　宋　玮　中国人民大学财政金融学院　　　　　　　　　　副教授

出 版 说 明

金融专业英语证书考试制度（Financial English Certificate Test，简称 FECT）是 1994 年经中国人民银行和原国家教委联合发文（银发〔1994〕107 号）批准建立的我国第一个国家级行业性外语证书考试制度，实施该考试制度的目标是为国家培养既精通现代国际金融业务、又能应用英语进行金融业务操作和管理的中高级复合型人才。为顺利实施此制度，在中国人民银行的领导下，专门设立了金融专业英语证书考试委员会及其办公室。考试委员会由中国人民银行主管副行长任主任，各主要金融机构人事教育部门负责同志参加，考试委员会办公室设在中国人民银行北京培训学院。

金融专业英语证书考试制度 1995 年试点推广，1996 年正式实施，截至 2009 年年底，全国超过 26 万人参加了金融专业英语证书各级考试，近 6 万人获得了单科或全科证书，为提高中国金融业从业人员素质起到了积极作用。

金融专业英语证书考试制度原由初级、中级、高级三个层次组成，高级考试因故一直未曾推出。为适应经济全球化和金融一体化的深入发展，2007 年 12 月举行的 FECT 考试委员会第九次工作会议提出了金融专业英语证书考试制度调整意见，并于 2008 年开始实施。调整后的金融专业英语证书制度更名为金融英语证书考试制度，由综合考试和高级考试两个层次组成，取消原中级考试。FECT 综合考试科目为《现代金融业务》；FECT 高级考试包括笔试和专业口语考试两部分，笔试科目两门（必考一门、专业选考一门）。必考科目为《现代金融理论与实务》；专业选考科目为《银行业务与管理》、《保险与证券业务》，两科任选一科。

《现代金融业务》是金融英语证书综合考试的学习用书。该教材最初由金融英语证书考试委员会 2002 年组织编写。为适应国际和国内金融业务日新月异的变化，金融英语证书考试委员会组织专家于 2006 年对教材进行了重编，参与 2006 年教材编写和审定工作的专家分工如下："中国的金融业"（第一部分）由何建雄编写，冯长甫审定；"金融机构监管"

出版说明

（第二部分）由张立星编写，李树杰审定；"中国的外汇管理"（第三部分）由林宏编写，陈建辉和张铁军共同审定；"会计"（第四部分）由林宏编写，邹勇审定；"中间业务"（第五部分）由侯贵峰编写，赵惠娟和李海燕共同审定；"信贷"（第六部分）由谢均乐和容洁共同编写，陈文君审定；"国际结算"（第七部分）由邱智坤编写，陈海燕和李昭蓉审定；"证券和期货市场"（第八部分）由戴建国编写，陈庆柏审定；"保险基础"（第九部分）由沈素萍编写，陆祖汶审定；"金融函电"（第十部分）由陈进编写，李桂荣审定。

2010 年，金融英语证书考试委员会组织专家对 2006 版教材中的错误和疏漏进行了修正，并根据国际业务的发展，对国际结算章节进行了部分改写，加入了 UCP600 的相关内容。在此，我们对参与此次教材修订的对外经济贸易大学英语学院陈庆柏教授和中国农业银行国际业务部侯贵峰副总经理表示衷心的感谢。

本教材主要内容涵盖了目前金融业务的基础知识，注重理论联系实际，具有新颖、务实、全面、准确、科学的特点，也可供金融业从业人员、大专院校财经专业学生以及其他有志于投身中国金融业的人员参考使用。

许多同志为本教材的编写和修订付出了努力。金融英语证书考试委员会常务副主任、中国人民银行沈阳分行王顺行长（原中国人民银行北京培训学院院长）多次参加专家组工作会，对教材编写和修订提出具体要求，中国人民银行北京培训学院马玉兰副院长具体组织了此次教材修订工作。考试委员会办公室全体同志在组织编写和修订、校对方面做了大量工作。王杰华教授为教材的出版付出了辛勤努力。在此，我们对为这本教材的出版做出贡献的同志一并表示衷心的感谢。

最后，我们真诚地希望本教材的读者提出宝贵意见，使这本教材越修改越好，更好地服务于读者。由于时间有限，本书的疏漏和错误之处在所难免，恳请专家和读者斧正。

金融专业英语证书考试委员会
2010 年 11 月

中国人民银行
关于实施《金融专业英语证书考试制度》的通知

（银发［1996］229 号）

中国人民银行各省、自治区、直辖市分行，政策性银行，国有独资商业银行，其他商业银行，全国性金融机构：

为适应金融业改革发展和扩大对外开放的需要，加快我国金融业与国际接轨的步伐，同时面向未来，为国家和各金融机构培养既精通现代金融知识，又能运用英语从事金融业务及管理工作的跨世纪的中、高层复合型人才，促进金融职工队伍素质的全面提高，中国人民银行与国家教委1994 年 4 月联合发出《关于建立〈金融专业英语证书考试制度〉的通知》（银发［1994］107 号），在全国试行金融专业英语证书考试制度。根据金融专业英语证书考试委员会第一次全体会议决定，1995 年 11 月 19日在北京、天津、上海、广州、佛山、深圳、呼和浩特、包头、青岛九个城市进行了初级证书考试的试点，取得了成功，受到金融系统干部职工的广泛欢迎和肯定。这项工作对全面提高金融队伍的素质具有促进作用。现决定将修订后的《金融专业英语证书考试制度》颁布施行。

该制度是国家级的行业证书制度，在中国人民银行领导管理下，由各总行、总公司组成的"金融专业英语证书考试委员会"（以下简称考试委员会）负责组织实施。考试委员会办公室设在中国金融职工教育协会秘书处。

根据考试委员会第二次全体会议决定，1996 年 5 月 19 日在全国金融系统进行金融专业英语证书（银行类初级）考试。同时，考试委员会正在抓紧（银行类）中级证书考试大纲的设计、教材选定等准备工作，计划于 1996 年 11 月在初级证书试考的城市进行中级证书的试考。从 1997年开始，全国初、中级证书考试每年进行一次。银行类高级证书考试及保险类、投资类考试也在筹划之中。有关各级各类证书考试的实施细则，考试委员会将具体部署。

中国人民银行关于实施《金融专业英语证书考试制度》的通知

　　在全国建立和实施金融专业英语证书考试制度，是一项十分重要的工作，请各行（公司）按中国人民银行办公厅 1995 年 9 月下发的《关于印发〈金融专业英语证书考试委员会第一次全体会议纪要〉的通知》（银办发〔1995〕36 号）的要求和考试委员会的有关部署，认真做好考前的各项组织工作。

　　附件：金融专业英语证书考试制度

一九九六年五月三十一日

附件

金融专业英语证书考试制度

第一条 为适应金融业改革发展和扩大对外开放的需要，加快我国金融业与国际接轨的步伐，为国家和各金融机构培养大批既精通现代金融知识，又能运用英语从事金融业务及管理工作的中、高层复合型人才，促进金融职工队伍素质的全面提高，并使金融系统职工培训工作逐步与国际接轨，特制定金融专业英语证书考试制度（Financial English Certificate Test, FECT）。

第二条 本考试制度是对金融系统专业人员的英语专业知识，尤其是国际金融方面的知识和能力进行综合性的全面测试，为扩大从事国际金融的人力资源和建立金融人才库提供依据。

第三条 金融专业英语证书考试主要面向全国金融系统（包括合资、外资银行和非银行金融机构）。凡具备一定金融专业知识和英语水平的金融从业人员以及一切有志于在金融业发展的人员都可以参加考试。

第四条 金融专业英语证书考试包括银行类、保险类、证券投资类。

第五条 金融专业英语证书分为初级、中级、高级三种程度。

初级证书考试：要求掌握一定的金融专业英语词汇量，能阅读一般金融函、电，能运用英语标准、规范地操作银行、保险等柜台业务。

中级证书考试：要求能阅读英文金融专业报刊、书籍，能运用英语处理业务函、电，进行业务操作和管理工作。

高级证书考试：要求有深厚的金融、国际金融专业知识和较高的英语阅读、书写、听说水平，能熟练地运用英语从事金融业务综合管理工作和金融理论研究工作。

第六条 上述三级证书考试每年定期举行一次，考试合格者发给相应的证书。

第七条 本考试制度是国家级的行业证书制度。证书可以作为在金融涉外业务部门从事业务或管理工作的外语水平证明。

第八条 本考试制度由金融专业英语证书考试委员会负责组织实施、确定考试科目、考试大纲、组织统一命题、实施考试、评卷、报告成绩、颁发证书等。

第九条　上述三级证书均由金融专业英语证书考试委员会统一制定颁发。

第十条　本考试制度由金融专业英语证书考试委员会负责解释、修订。

金融专业英语证书（综合考试）大纲

一、考试目的

本考试为金融英语水平综合考试，旨在测试并认定应试人员的金融英语语言水平与实际运用英语处理业务的能力。本考试的证书可作为在金融部门从事相应的涉外业务工作、参加涉外培训、职称评定和各类毕业学生进入金融部门就业等方面的参考依据。

二、考试对象

本考试的对象为金融系统（包括外资、合资银行及非银行金融机构）的从业人员及一切有志于金融事业发展的人员。

三、考试要求及范围

本考试要求应试人员具备在金融业务中较熟练地运用英语的能力。参加本考试的应试人员应掌握 7000 个基础英语及金融专业英语词汇，熟悉基本的业务概念和术语及一般的业务程序和原理，能听懂日常会话和一般的业务交谈，具有在篇章水平上运用英语基本语法知识的能力，能看懂与金融业务有关的一般文字材料，拟写一般的业务文件。

本考试涉及的业务范围主要包括：经济及金融基础知识、贸易和非贸易结算、信贷、会计、资金交易、外汇管理、保险、证券、金融监管等。

四、考试构成

本考试包括听力和笔试两部分，主要从以下方面测试应试人员运用英语处理日常金融业务的能力。

听力部分（占 30%）：包括简短会话、报告、陈述、访谈、讨论、电话通信对话、接待客户、介绍业务、提供服务等。

笔试部分（占 70%）：各种图表、备忘录、财务报表、留言、行情表、业务函电、简历、广告、业务简介等。

五、试题类型

1. 听力：分为三个部分：第一部分为针对单句的单项选择；第二部分为针对对话的单项选择；第三部分为针对短文的单项选择。

2. 笔试：分为单项选择、完形填空、判断正误、短文阅读理解（共 50%）和写作（20%）。其中写作又分为三部分：第一部分为填写表格、单证等；第二部分为翻译（汉译英或英译汉）；第三部分为按要求拟写短文（如函电、通知、留言、备忘录等）。

六、考试时间

本考试每年举行一次，时间在每年五月的第四个星期六。每次考试时间为150分钟，其中听力30分钟。

七、说明

本考试即原FECT初级证书考试，从2000年起将根据分数由高至低共划分为三个级别：A级证书、B级证书、C级证书。总体难度不增加。

根据FECT与BFT合作备忘录，BFT认可FECT的成绩，考生可在通过本考试取得级别证书后，自愿参加国家外国专家局组织的全国出国培训备选人员外语考试，取得相应的成绩后，可获相应级别的BFT证书。

Preface

This book was initiated by the Commission of Financial English Certificate Test. Although originally designed as reading materials for those preparing for "the Financial English Certificate" test, it is also intended for to benefit both practitioners and supervisors.

Textbooks on financial practices abound. However, many were written for financial environments significantly different from that in China or became outdated not long after publication. This book incorporates the current international practices with application in the Chinese background as well as its anticipated dramatic evolution in the context of China's entry into the World Trade Organization and the rapidly changing global environment.

Much of the book is devoted to the introduction of the institutional setup of the financial industry, the regulatory and supervisory standards and the foreign exchange system as the knowledge of the environment is critical to the success of financial institutions. The brief overview presented in the first part encompasses the evolution of the financial industry over the past five decades, the recent reform progress, the presence of foreign banks, the existing constraints and prospects of the sector. The part on financial supervision captures not only prudential standards and practices currently prevailing in the international financial community, but also potential changes that may significantly affect the behavior of financial institutions worldwide.

The introduction of traditional business such as commercial lending and international settlement as well as basic communication and accounting skills is complemented with an overview of intermediary business, which is becoming an increasingly important source of revenue in the industry.

This book is the result of concerted efforts of a diverse group of authors and experts, including practitioners, supervisors and the academia. These efforts would not have succeeded without the organizational and administrative support from the training center of the People's Bank of China.

While the challenges brought about to the financial sector by China's WTO membership are real, the potential opportunities cannot be taken for granted unless those working in the sector are well prepared, especially in terms of skills required to compete and succeed in the increasingly globalized and competitive environment. Indeed, this book attempts to contribute to the difficult, but determined, process of such a preparation.

He Jianxiong

Oct. 12, 2006

CONTENTS

CONTENTS

Part One

Overview of the Financial Industry in China

I. Banking Sector

1. The Evolution and Role of the Banking Sector in China

Although banks share many common features with other profit-seeking businesses, they play a unique role in the economy through mobilizing savings, allocating capital funds to finance productive investment, transmitting monetary policy, providing a payment system and transforming risks.

First, banks serve as a principal depository of liquid funds for the public. The safety and availability of such funds for transactions and other purposes are essential to the stability and efficiency of the financial system.

Second, by channeling savings to productive investments, banks play a key role in facilitating efficient allocation of scarce financial resources.

Third, banks serve to transmit the impulses of monetary policy to the whole financial system and ultimately to the real economy.

Fourth, the banking sector provides the indispensable national payment mechanism for the development of modern financial and business systems.

Fifth, the banking system as a whole reduces risks through aggregation and enables them to be carried by those more willing to bear them.

Through nearly six decades of evolution, particularly more than two decades of reform and opening up to the outside world, China's banking sector has entered a stage of vigorous development. The past few years have seen a marked acceleration of China's banking reform, particularly significant strengthening of the central bank's capacity for maintaining financial stability and macroeconomic management, substantial improvement in the management of the commercial banks, and greater openness of the banking industry.

The evolution of the Chinese banking system can be broadly divided into four phases. The establishment of the People's Bank of China (PBC) in December 1948 marked the beginning of the first phase, which was characterized by the mono-bank engaged in both policy and commercial banking operations. It was dictated by a highly centralized planned economic system.

The second phase began in 1984 when the State Council decided to make the PBC a central bank. The decision, which was made in response to the increased role of market forces in the economy, promoted diversification of financial institutions with the establishment of the four specialized banks—the Industrial and Commercial Bank of China (ICBC), the Agricultural Bank of China (ABC), the Bank of China (BOC), and the China Construction Bank (CCB), later known as the big four wholly state-owned commercial banks when distinction in their line of business became vague and the joint-equity commercial banks emerged.

The third phase began in 1993 when the State Council issued *the Decision on Financial Reform*, recognizing the urgent need for developing new financial markets, institutions and instruments. The government introduced a comprehensive package of measures aimed at restoring financial order as well as addressing the inflationary pressure and signs of overheating, particularly in the real estate sector and the stock markets.

During this period, a number of important structural measures were taken with particular significance for the banking sector. The first was the unification of the Renminbi (RMB) exchange rates and foreign exchange markets in January 1994. Second, the passage of central bank and commercial bank laws in 1995 provided a legal basis for the banking system in China. Third, the acceptance of the obligations of Article VIII of the Articles of Agreement of the International Monetary Fund in December 1996, namely commitment to RMB current account convertibility, officially removed the remaining restrictions on international payments for trade and service transactions. Fourth, the establishment of a unified inter-bank money market in 1996 facilitated better liquidity adjustment for financial institutions. Fifth, the gradual shift from direct to indirect monetary policy instruments greatly improved transmission of monetary policy and effectiveness of macroeconomic management. Finally, the segregation of banking business from securities and insurance business contributed to the stability of the financial system in a transition period characterized by massive institutional changes, inadequate regulatory resources and insufficient self-discipline.

In addition, three policy banks (the State Development Bank, the Agricultural Development Bank of China and the Export and Import Bank of China) were established in 1994 to facilitate the separation of policy banking from commercial banking operations. These policy banking institutions are playing a special role in financing major infrastructural projects and promoting agricultural development and international trade and investment.

China's accession to the World Trade Organization (WTO) ushered in a new era of the evolution of the banking system. With the Chinese economy further integrating into the world economy, China's banking sector is confronted with both unprecedented challenges and opportunities and required to adopt a number of effective measures to promote the steady development of banking. The reform since then has been focused on developing a sound and robust financial system to guard against and dissolve financial risks, cleaning up the balance-sheets of the banks, improving their ownership structure, strengthening their corporate governance, developing market infrastructure, enhancing supervisory capacity, and further opening the banking sector to foreign participants.

Through more than two decades of reform efforts, China has developed a diversified and competitive banking system: As of the end of 2005, China's banking system had three policy banks, one wholly state-owned commercial bank, 16 joint-equity commercial banks operating nationwide, 125 local commercial banks and 58 rural cooperative banks. The non-bank financial institutions mainly consists of trust and investment companies, asset management companies, securities firms, finance companies and insurance firms as well as many urban and rural credit cooperatives.

The banking sector has been playing an important role in facilitating the implementation of the stabilization and structural measures as well as sustaining strong economic growth. The macroeconomic stability and structural improvement in turn have enabled the banking sector to develop vigorously. Although capital market development is expected to speed up, banks are likely to continue playing a leading role in financing economic and technological development as well as the economic reform in the foreseeable future. In the first half of 2006, for example, banks accounted for 86.8 percent of non-financial sector financing, while the stock market, the government bond market and the corporate bond market made up 5.6 percent, 1.4 percent and 6.1 percent respectively.

2. The Reform and Functions of the Central Bank

Although a central banking system began taking shape in 1984, the transformation of the PBC into a full-fledged central bank has turned out to be a lengthy process. The PBC did not have a clear legal status until the enactment of the *Law of the People's Republic of China on the People's Bank of China* in March 1995. This law, as amended in December 2003, provides that the PBC's key functions are to conduct monetary policy, prevent and dissolve financial risks, and maintain financial stability under the leadership of the State Council. The law clearly states that the objective of the monetary policy is to maintain the stability of the currency and thereby promote economic growth.

Specifically, the PBC undertakes to formulate and implement monetary policy; issue currency and regulate its circulation; manage the official international reserves; regulate inter-bank money market, inter-bank bond market, foreign exchange market and gold market; act as fiscal agent; maintain the payment and settlement system; combat money laundering activities, and participate in international financial cooperation on behalf of the state. This law has strengthened the PBC independence by prohibiting its financing for fiscal deficits and interference in the performance of its functions by any government agency, non-government organization or individual.

The decisions of the National Financial Work Conference in November 1997 and the Ninth National People's Congress in March 1998 accelerated the reform of the PBC. Significant restructuring took place at its head office. For example, the supervisory departments were reorganized in the way that supervisory functions were consolidated and each new supervisory department was responsible for licensing, routine supervision and exit of one type of financial institutions. The PBC branch structure, which had been formerly based on administrative division, was also overhauled. Nine regional branch offices were set up. These measures were aimed at increasing the independence of the central bank and the effectiveness of monetary policy.

With the transfer of supervisory functions to the new supervisory bodies, namely China Banking Regulatory Commission (CBRC), China Securities Regulatory Commission (CSRC) and China Insurance Regulatory Commission (CIRC), the central bank's task has become more focused. The establishment of the Financial Stability Bureau, the Financial Markets Department and the Credit Information Bureau as well as the Shanghai headquarter of the PBC has indicated that greater attention has been devoted to financial stability and development of market infrastructure.

In recent years, there has been a significant improvement in the conduct of monetary policy with greater reliance on indirect policy instruments. The central bank used to rely on credit ceilings for commercial banks as a major tool for implementing monetary policy. This direct instrument has been abolished while such indirect instruments as required reserve ratio, interest rate adjustment and open market operations have emerged as major monetary policy tools. These policy instruments have helped sustain strong economic growth. As of end-June 2006, the stock of broad money (M_2) reached RMB32. 3 trillion, that of narrow money (M_1) RMB11. 2 trillion, and that of currency in circulation (M_0) RMB2. 3 trillion.

3. Vigorous Development of the Commercial Banking Sector

The role of the banking sector in the Chinese economy has increased dramatically. At the end of 2005, the total assets of the banking sector reached RMB37. 47 billion.

With its entry into the WTO, China decided to implement a phased reform of the wholly state-owned commercial banks, namely, restructuring their balance sheets, establishing corporate governance, transforming their operational mechanisms, inviting strategic investors, listing them in stock markets, and making them internationally competitive financial institutions by subjecting them to the discipline of the capital market. The financial restructuring started with the BOC and the CCB at the end of 2003, when the government recapitalized them each with USD 25 billion from the foreign exchange reserves. Recapitalization of the ICBC took place in April 2005. Remarkable progress has been made in transforming these banks. With the clarification of the ownership structure, these banks have put in place a basic framework for good corporate governance, whereby the boards of directors, the supervisory boards and the management have clear responsibilities and incentives as well as disciplines. As a result, internal control and risk management mechanisms have also been strengthened. The participation of strategic investors is expected to contribute to improving management, technology, innovation and competitiveness. The transformed banks have significantly improved their capital adequacy, profitability and other financial indicators. The CCB and the BOC have achieved great success in initial public offering (IPO) on the stock exchange. The restructuring of the Last wholly state-owned commercial bank, the ABC, is expected to start soon.

The joint-equity banks are an emerging force among the commercial banks. Their share in the banking market has been growing rapidly. They operate entirely on a commercial basis and mainly serve the local economic development in large and medium-sized cities. The development of these banks contributes to competition and efficiency in financial intermediation and thereby bringing about soundness of the banking system.

The rural banking institutions are becoming viable. Given the importance of the rural sector in the Chinese economy, the authorities have devoted great attention to improving rural financing. By the end of 2005, the central bank had issued about RMB160 billion notes to replace the non-performing loans (NPLs) of rural credit cooperatives and facilitate their restructuring. Through financial restructuring, the aggregate NPLs ratio of the rural credit cooperatives declined from 36. 9 percent at end-2002 to 12. 6 percent at end-June 2006. Consequently, their capacity for financing agricultural activities and rural development has significantly increased.

The reform of the financial system and particularly the diversification of banking institutions have triggered competition in the banking sector and improved financial services in China. Apart from the traditional deposit-taking and lending business, commercial banks now offer a broad range of intermediary services such as international settlement, bank-cards, personal banking, and financial consulting. As the economy becomes increasingly complex, there is an emerging need for developing universal banking. Its progress will, of course, depend on the supervisory capacity, market infrastructure and institutional development as well as availability of professionals with sophisticated expertise.

4. Increased Openness of the Banking Sector

The increasing presence of foreign banks has been an important aspect of banking reform in China. This will help improve the quality of regulation and information disclosure, as it will urge the domestic banks to improve their cost structure, the range and quality of their services.

From the time of China's entry into the WTO to end-May 2006, the number of foreign banking institutions operating in China increased from 177 to 264, including 14 locally incorporated foreign banks, 183 foreign bank branches and 52 sub-branches. Their total assets increased from USD 40. 1 billion to USD 96. 4 billion. Their loan reached USD 50. 17 billion and deposits amounted to USD 27. 84 billion. Until recently, foreign banking institutions were only allowed to operate in the special economic zones and coastal cities. To encourage competition from foreign financial institutions, China has expanded the areas open to foreign banking establishments to include all large cities throughout the country. The restrictions on local currency business have been substantially eased. Most of foreign banking institutions are now engaged in local currency business in 25 major cities. More than a dozen of them may now offer on-line banking services. One of the important goals of liberalizing the banking sector is to give foreign banks national treatment, that is, to subject foreign banks to the same regulatory standards as applied to the domestic banks.

Introduction of strategic investors is also an important way of opening the Chinese banking sector. The participation of foreign strategic investors in the domestic banks has improved the equity structure of the banking system.

5. Strengthened Banking Supervision

Strengthening banking supervision has become a universal task. Many countries including some advanced economies have been penalized for weak financial supervision. For China, this task is particularly relevant, as the authorities are well aware that the Chinese financial system faced with risks associated with economic transition, in addition to credit and market risks common to all countries. For instance, the magnitude and the nature of risks, the skills and institutions for risk management in an open market economy are different from those in a relatively closed and centrally planned economy. The Chinese authorities' comprehensive efforts to improve financial supervision started with the introduction of the stabilization and adjustment program in 1993. The financial crisis in Asia strengthened the authorities' resolve. The measures to strengthen banking supervision and enhance banks' capacity for prudential management include the following:

- A comprehensive risk monitoring and warning system, which focuses on the safety, liquidity and profitability of financial institutions, has been established.
- A risk-based five-category loan classification system has been phased in.
- The capital of the largest commercial banks (except the ABC) has been replenished to raise their capital adequacy ratio to the international standard.
- The responsibility for supervising the securities sector has been transferred from the PBC to CSRC. Independent insurance and banking regulatory bodies have also been established so that banking, securities and insurance industries are subjected to separate regulatory and supervisory authorities.
- Effective actions have been taken to deal with the problem institutions, including requiring them to restructure within a limited time and subjecting the insolvent ones to liquidation procedures.
- Senior executives of financial institutions have been subjected to strict fit-and-proper tests, and enforcement of penalties on those responsible for taking excessive risks or causing serious losses has been intensified. Serious offenders will be held liable to criminal charges or prohibited from doing financial business for life.
- Asset management companies have been set up to take over and dispose of part of the non-performing loans of the commercial banks.
- A nationwide credit reporting system covering individual and institutional credit information has been developed. On one hand, this is expected to improve the access of individuals and small businesses to bank loans by streamlining loan approval process. On the other hand, it will contribute to the asset quality of the banks by reducing loan delinquencies since all credit information is integrated nationwide and all credit default records are made available to potential lenders.
- The Chinese banking supervisory authorities endorse the core principles for effective banking supervision of the Basel Committee and the spirit of the new Basel Capital Accord and will adopt a phased approach to its implementation. The banks with extensive overseas branch networks (internationally active banks) will be required to implement the Accord in due course.
- An association of bankers has been established to tighten self-discipline of the

banking industry.

● Further efforts will be made to facilitate more effective market discipline. Transparency and the information disclosure of the Chinese banking industry will be brought up to international standards.

6. Prospects for Banking Sector Development

Despite all these achievements, the banking sector in China is still faced with formidable challenges. It needs to further strengthen corporate governance and internal controls, develop management information systems, improve information disclosure, and establish a deposit insurance system. These challenges call for intensified efforts on the part of the authorities in institutional building to facilitate greater enforceability of bank claims, faster market infrastructure development and better ownership structure.

Changes in the macroeconomic environment have important implications for the banking sector. The projected robust economic growth will generate strong demand for banking services on one hand, and contribute to the profitability of the corporate sector on the other hand. This will in turn enable banks to further improve their balance sheets with their better asset quality. The strengthened capacity for macroeconomic management, particularly the central bank's ability to maintain price stability, is also conducive to the healthy development of the banking industry.

Continued progress in structural reform in the financial sector will contribute to the viability of commercial banks. First, further interest rate liberalization will enhance banks' capacity for risk pricing. Second, freer cross-border capital movement will allow them to seek high returns and diversify risks on a much broader horizon. Third, greater exchange rate flexibility will facilitate expansion of foreign exchange business and foster their ability to manage foreign exchange risks. Fourth, the increased foreign presence in the banking sector is expected to help promote institutional changes, encourage financial innovation, and improve efficiency in financial intermediation. Fifth, the progress in financial legislation such as the recent passage of the new bankruptcy law will also be conducive to the healthy development of the banking sector. Last, but not the least, increased availability of professionals is also expected to add to the vigor of banking institutions in China.

In short, continued reform efforts will result in greater openness of the banking sector, integrated financial markets, increased diversification of banking institutions, strengthened competition, and improved efficiency of resource allocation.

II. Securities Sector

1. Vigorous Development of the Securities Sector

The financial markets can be classified into the following six types:

- **Capital markets**, which consist of:
  - ➤ **Stock market**, which provides financing through the issuance of shares, and enables the subsequent trading thereof. **Shares** are certificates or book entries representing ownership in a corporation or similar entity.
  - ➤ **Bond market**, which provides financing through the issuance of bonds, and enables the subsequent trading thereof. **Bonds** are written evidences of debts.
- **Commodity market**, which facilitates the trading of commodities.
- **Money market**, which provides short-term debt-financing and investment.
- **Derivatives market**, which provides instruments for the management of financial risk.
  - ➤ **Futures market**, where standardized futures contracts and options contracts on a whole range of underlying products are traded. **Options** are the right to buy or sell a financial instrument at an agreed price at some future time.
- **Insurance market**, which facilitates the redistribution of various risks.
- **Foreign exchange market**, which facilitates the trading of foreign exchange.

The capital market consists of primary and secondary markets. The **primary market** is that part of the capital market that deals with the issuance of new securities. The **secondary market** is the financial market for trading of securities that have already been issued in an initial private or public offering. **Securities** are paper certificates (definitive securities) or electronic records (book-entry securities) evidencing ownership of equity (stocks) or debt obligations (bonds). **Securities market** refers to organized exchanges plus over-the-counter markets in which securities are traded.

In this book, the term "securities sector" loosely refers to securities and futures markets. China's securities and futures markets have grown rapidly in size since the late 1970s in tandem with the market reforms and the liberalization of national economy. China's first joint-stock company went public in August 1984, and in December 1990 Shanghai Stock Exchange (SHSE) and Shenzhen Stock Exchange (SZSE) were both established. China Securities Regulatory Commission (CSRC), the national regulatory authority, was set up in Beijing in October 1992.

Following the years of remarkable achievements, sizeable markets have taken shape with enhanced market infrastructures, an improved legal framework and a unified regulatory regime. The markets have been playing an increasingly important role in optimizing allocation of resources and facilitating economic structuring and growth. It is widely believed that the markets have great potentials for further development.

There are a variety of financial products available in the markets, such as A-shares, B-shares, securities investment funds, treasury bonds, corporate bonds, convertible bonds, commodity futures, ETF, LOF and warrants.

A-shares refer to the common shares issued by the companies registered in China's mainland and traded by domestic entities or retail investors (excluding investors from Taiwan region, Hong Kong and Macau SARs) in Chinese currency.

B-shares are issued by China-registered joint-venture companies, listed on Chinese stock exchanges and denominated in Chinese currency. However B-shares are subscribed and traded in US dollars at SHSE or in HK dollars at SZSE.

Securities investment funds are pools of money that are managed by a securities investment company. They offer investors a variety of goals, depending on the fund and its investment charter. An open-end fund can be freely sold and repurchased by investors based on the closing market value for listed public securities it holds, while a closed-end fund has no regular redemption date and can only be redeemed in limited circumstances.

Bonds are commercial papers borrowing firms issue in the form of medium or long-term securities, which commit them to specific repayment dates, with either fixed or variable interest.

Treasury Bills, also known as T-bills, refer to coupon bearing government securities with a relatively longer maturity.

Convertible bonds are bonds which carry a rate of interest and give the owner the right to exchange the bonds at some stage in the future into ordinary shares according to a prearranged formula.

Commodity futures refer to contracts to supply quantities of the underlying commodity at a future date.

ETF, or **Exchange Traded Fund**, is a fund that tracks an index, but can be traded like a stock.

LOF stands for **Listed Open-ended Fund** which can be redeemed or subscribed at both stock exchanges and fund sales outlets.

Warrants refer to options to buy ordinary shares at a pre-determined exercise price.

In addition to the above-mentioned two stock exchanges, China now has three commodity futures exchanges, namely, Shanghai Futures Exchange, Zhengzhou Commodity

Exchange and Dalian Commodity Exchange, where a dozen of futures contracts are traded, mainly on agricultural products (soybean, grain and cotton, etc.) and primary products (copper, aluminum and fuel oil, etc.).

2. The Role of the Securities Sector in China

China's securities sector, as one of the fastest growing in the world, is playing an increasingly important role in promoting national economic growth. In the early 1990s, the sector was supposed to serve large state-owned enterprises (SOEs) or even to rescue them from financial difficulties. With the adoption of the modern enterprise system in 1995, many SOEs were re-organized into shareholding corporations and in consequence the majority of companies listed on China's stock exchanges were SOEs.

Since the late 1990s, however, the situation has changed as more and more private companies accessed to the securities and futures markets. Furthermore, the underlying philosophy changed since the CSRC was consolidated in 1998 as well as the Securities Law took effect in 1999. The examination and approval system as well as the quota systems for issuing securities which tended to favour SOEs were replaced by the new verification system for public offerings, which enables private companies to have an equal access to funding from the markets.

Nowadays, China's securities sector is playing at least 4 key roles. Firstly, it plays an important role in resources allocation by raising a great amount of capital for corporate growth. Secondly, it facilitates a number of companies to grow bigger and stronger by means of various restructurings. Most of the listed companies have turned into industry leaders. In particular, these companies have largely improved their corporate governance, risk control and corporate culture. Thirdly, it provides diversified investment instruments and contributes to financial-services-industry growth. After nearly two decades' development, the number of investment products has been multiplied and diversified, which provides differentiated investment choices for investors. In the meantime, the growth of securities sector contributes to deepening banking reform, financial infrastructure build-up and service enhancement. Fourthly, with the increasing international cooperation and opening-up to the outside, it provides a new channel for foreign capital to be invested in China.

III. Insurance Sector

1. Insurance and Risks

A. *What is insurance*?

Insurance is an arrangement by which one party (the insurer) promises to pay another party (the insured or policyholder) a sum of money if anything happens which causes the insured to suffer a financial loss. The responsibility for paying such losses is then transferred from the policyholder to the insurer. In return for accepting the burden of paying for losses when they occur, the insurer charges the insured a price, the insurance premium.

Consider two next-door neighbors, Bob and Steve. Both own houses worth USD 80,000, but Bob has insured his house against possible loss by fire at a premium of USD 150 while Steve has'nt. By insuring his house, Bob has been able to transfer the loss of USD 80,000 to his insurer. His financial position is therefore the same whether or not his house burns down: whatever happens all he has to pay is a premium of USD 150. Although Steve avoids paying USD 150, he has to bear the full costs of any fire. He is therefore USD 150 better off than Bob if there is no fire, but USD79,850 worse off in the event of a conflagration.

Insurance works because the insurer can collect premiums from a large group of people in similar circumstances, not all of whom will suffer losses in any one year. These premiums are then pooled together, and used by the insurer to pay losses. Losses are thus shared out among all the policyholders rather than borne solely by the unlucky few.

Nowadays insurance not only shares losses among individuals and organizations, but also spreads them over time. This is possible because in years when losses are lighter than expected, insurers can build up reserves (out of premium contributions and their investment earnings) that can subsequently be used in more difficult years.

B. Risks

Risk is present whenever human beings are unable to control or to foresee their future. Although we cannot foresee the future risk, we can, to some extent, measure it. When we toss a coin we do not know what will happen, but we can make a very good guess: we have equal chances of getting either a "head" or a "tail". We use the term risk where: although the precise future outcome is unknown, the possible alternatives can be listed (such as "heads" or "tails"); and the chances associated with those possible alternatives are also known (such as a 50 percent chance of either "heads" or "tails").

There are mainly four types of risks:

i. Fundamental and particular risk

Fundamental risk affects either society in general or groups of people, and cannot be controlled even partially by any one person. Particular risk, on the other hand, refers to those future outcomes that we can partially control and it arises from individual decisions.

ii. Pure and speculative risk

Speculative risk is present if either beneficial or adverse outcomes could stem from a specific event, whereas if possible harm is the only alternative to the present status quo the situation is one of pure risk.

C. *The relationship between risk and insurance*

Buying insurance is one method of controlling the financial aspects of the unknown future. If you buy an insurance policy, you exchange a situation of risk for one of financial certainty.

While insurance controls risk mainly by transferring the responsibility for covering losses from one person to another, it may also affect the risk directly, by influencing the chance of a loss occurring. This may happen in two opposing ways:

- Insurers may encourage policyholders to be more careful, by rewarding those whose losses are small. They may also offer advice on how to prevent losses.
- On the other hand, policyholders may either deliberately cause losses in order to obtain money from insurers, or be less careful because of the insurance protection. This behavior is termed moral hazard.

In practice, not all risks can be insured, and the insurability of a given risk depends on a number of factors:

- Losses are measurable in monetary terms.
- Only pure risks are insurable.
- The insurer must be able to collect together a sufficiently large group of separate and independent exposure units which are subject to broadly similar risks so that the Law of Large Numbers can operate effectively.
- Losses must be fortuitous.

2. Mathematic Basis

Before we introduce the basic law of mathematics in insurance and the law of large numbers, another definition needs to be given for "risk transference".

Risk transference, sometimes called "pooling", involves the transfer of risk from the individual to a pool of the insurance company's policyholders. The insurance company charges a fee, the premium (or part thereof), for accepting the risk and "pools" the premiums from a group of policyholders into a general fund to finance the claims under contract.

For example, if 10,000 policy-owners in the pool pay USD 1,000 each in annual premiums, the pool would amass USD 10,000,000 each year to cover claims resulting from losses. Should 500 members of the pool have losses during the year of USD 10,000 each, the pool would be able to reimburse the members for their losses and still accumulate a large amount of funds for later claims. In this particular case, new members would be brought into the pool and the remaining members would pay their next annual premiums to replenish the pool of funds.

The law of large numbers basically relies on the principle that the larger the pool, the more predictable the amount of losses will be in a given period. Since not all members of the pool are of the same age or in the same health condition, we can assume not all of them will be making a claim at the same time.

In fact, by recording and studying the number of claims over a very large population, the number of 62-year-old men, for example, who will die in a particular year, can be fairly predicted. This is not to say the year in which a particular person will die can be predicted. It only says that in a given year there is a high probability that X number of men who are 62 will die at that age.

Accordingly, with enough data, a statistician can comfortably predict the number of persons of a given age who will conceive a serious illness in a given year. With enough data, the statistician can assemble all of this information into tables. For deaths, the tables are called mortality tables and for sicknesses they are called morbidity tables.

All insurance is based on these two principles. A teenager commands a higher auto insurance rate because the statistical history has shown they have more accidents and the accidents are more serious than for a 40-year-old driver. Again, this is not to say there will not be instances of a 40-year-old marathon runner dying from heart troubles or other causes but, statistically, the incidences will be less for the marathon runner than for the patients who have heart disease or who smoke heavily.

3. Insurance: the Past and Present

Early methods of transferring or distributing risk were practiced by Chinese and Babylonian traders as early as in the 3rd and 2nd millennium BC respectively. Chinese merchants traveling treacherous river rapids would redistribute their wares across many vessels to limit the loss due to any single capsizing. The Babylonians developed a system which was recorded in the famous Code of Hammurabi, c. 2100 BC, and practiced by early Mediterranean sailing merchants. If any merchant received a loan to fund his shipment, he would pay the lender an additional sum in exchange for the lender's guarantee to cancel the loan should the shipment be stolen.

A thousand years later, the inhabitants of Rhodes invented the concept of the "general average". Merchants whose goods were being shipped together would pay a proportionally divided premium which would be used to reimburse any merchant whose goods were jettisoned during storm or sinkage.

The Greeks and Romans introduced the origins of health and life insurance in c. 600

AD when they organized guilds called "benevolent societies" which acted to care for the families and funeral expenses of members upon death. Guilds in the Middle Ages served a similar purpose. The Talmud deals with several aspects of insuring goods. Before insurance was established in the late 17th century, "friendly societies" existed in England, in which people donated amounts of money to a general sum that could be used in case of emergency.

Separate insurance contracts (i. e. insurance policies not bundled with loans or other kinds of contracts) were invented in Genoa in the 14th century, as were insurance pools backed by pledges of landed estates. These new insurance contracts allowed insurance to be separated from investment, a separation of roles that first proved useful in marine insurance. Insurance became far more sophisticated in post-Renaissance Europe, and specialized varieties developed.

Toward the end of the 17th century, the growing importance of London as a center for trade led to rising demand for marine insurance. In the late 1680s, Mr. Edward Lloyd opened a coffee house which became a popular haunt of ship owners, merchants, and ships' captains, and thereby creating a reliable source of the latest shipping news. It became the meeting place for parties wishing to insure cargoes and ships, and those willing to underwrite such ventures. Today, Lloyd's of London remains the leading market for marine and other specialist types of insurance, but it works rather differently than the more familiar kinds of insurance.

Insurance as we know it today can be traced back to the Great Fire of London, which in 1666 devoured 13,200 houses. In the aftermath of this disaster Nicholas Barbon opened an office to insure buildings. In 1680 he established England's first fire insurance company, "The Fire Office", to insure brick and frame homes.

Nowadays a wide variety of insurance contracts is available: transportation insurance, property insurance, pecuniary insurance, other liability insurance and personal and long-term insurance.

4. Insurance Innovation and Prospect of Insurance

There are several emerging trends in insurance industry:

A. *The integration of banking with insurance industry*

The two drives in this integration are bancassurance, which refers to the sale of insurance products through bank channels, and assurbanking, which is the system of selling bank products through the insurers' distribution channels belonging to their own banks. The causes behind this movement are: increased competition resulting from deregulation; automation that gives market-based intermediators cost advantages over traditional financial-institution-based intermediators; and government policy that gives tax advantages to insurance products offered by banks to compensate the banks for increased exposure to competitors.

B. *The strategic alliances of insurance companies*

Sometimes, through some interesting strategic alliance, insurers can meet the demands of regulators, consumers, rating agencies and financial service competitors actively and creatively. Basically, a strategic alliance strengthens a company's market offerings by forming an agreement with one or more business partners to achieve a mutually agreed-upon goal. The general business community has been forming such alliances for many years; more recently, insurers have been seeing the advantages of such alliances, too.

C. *The convergence of cyberspace with insurance*

With the phenomenal growth in the use of the internet and other electronic networks for interactions between and among individuals and firms, electronic commerce, still in its infancy, is changing the face of insurance industry. Now, firms can use computer networks for marketing and transacting business with their customers. Insurance firms have established web sites where individuals and firms can acquire information about company products and services and, in some cases, purchase products and services. The characteristics of many insurance products and services and insurance transactions make them ideally suitable for electronic commerce.

D. *The on-line application and issue of policies*

Technology now allows us to move the bulk of routine data entry and transaction processing into the field through the use of the internet which enabled on-line applications. On-line application and issuance systems will not only streamline the data entry process but will also bring added-value in the form of synchronizing all links of the data chain, that is, data entered at any point in the process can be viewed and used by other members of the chain. Forward-looking companies using internet technology and achieving lower costs will battle their more traditional counterparts, while banks seek to leverage their years of customer-service experience for the purpose of taking market share from both.

Whether the goal is to automate agency process or to eliminate the layers of brokers and agents to deal direct with customers, the cost reductions that have been achieved by automation can be passed on to the consumer, or used to justify the investment in an on-line system is so far unknown.

E. *The globalization of insurance*

Advances in technology, the interdependence of world economies, and the development of communication systems have made the world a smaller place. As the world shrinks for many industries, so does it for insurance. The globalization of the insurance industry has been accelerating as mergers and acquisitions have continued to cross country borders. During the past 20 years, however, the movement has grown in intensity, scope and visibility as a public issue.

The impact globalization has on local-national insurers is positive. When foreign insurers enter a market, they bring with them world-class product development and marketing standards that can significantly raise the awareness of consumers and force the local players to bring innovative products and raise their standards in every aspect of the sector.

Globalization has provided many benefits for the insurance industry. Over the years there has been a dramatic increase in professionalism throughout the industry as companies apply best practices developed by innovators in one market to other markets around the world. Sharing their expertise across borders that ultimately benefits both consumers and the industry as a whole has created a uniform regulatory environment. Globalization has resulted in a free flow of managerial talent across borders. Companies are moving smart managers from one market to another. This helps broaden the horizons not only of each company but also of the entire industry itself.

Notes

1. **allocation** [ˌæləˈkeiʃn] *n.* ①distributing②the act of giving something for a particular purpose

2. **channel... to...**: ①cause to go through a channel②direct money, ideas, etc. towards a particular thing or purpose

3. **be characterized by**: show the character of; give character to; mark in a special way

4. **equity** [ˈɛkwəti] *n.* ①a beneficial interest in an asset②the net assets of a company after all creditors (including the holders of "preference shares") have been paid off ③the amount of money returned to a borrower in a mortgage or hire-purchase agreement, after the sale of the specified asset and the full repayment of the lender of the money④the ordinary share capital of a company

5. **inter-bank market**: ①the part of the London "money market" in which banks lend to each other and to other large financial institutions②the market between banks in foreign currencies, including spot currencies and forward "options"

6. **liquidity** [liˈkwidəti] *n.* ①the ability of paying off debts by cash esp. , paying off current or recent debts②the extent to which an organization's assets are liquid, enabling it to pay its debts when they fall due and also to move into new investment opportunities

7. **contribute to**: ①join with others in giving help, money, etc. (to a common

cause, for a purpose) ②have a share in; help to bring about

8. **balance-sheet**: *n.* a statement of the total assets and liabilities of an organization at a particular date, usually the last day of "the accounting period"

9. **ownership** ['əunəʃip] *n.* rights over property, including rights of possession, exclusive enjoyment, destruction, etc.

10. **corporate governance**: the manner in which organizations, particularly limited companies, are managed and the nature of "accountability" of the managers to the owners

11. **enactment** [i'næktmənt] *n.* making or decreeing (a law)

12. **prevent and dissolve**: stop or hinder and bring something to an end; guard against and make something disappear

13. **open-market**: *n.* ①a situation in which companies can trade without restrictions, and prices depend on the amount of goods and the number of people buying them ②market carried out by the central bank of a country, in which it buys or sells government bonds in the same market other institutional invertors use

14. **consolidate** [kən'sɔliˌdeit] *vt, vi.* ①make or become solid or strong②unite or combine into one

15. **risk management**: the control of an individual's or company's chances of losing on an investment. Managing the risk can involve taking out insurance against a loss, hedging a loan against interest-rate rises, and protecting an investment against a fall in interest rates. A bank will always try to manage the risks involved in lending by adjusting the level of charges and interest rates to compensate for a percentage of losses

16. **public offering**: the U. S. term for "issuing a new stock publicly". The correspondent British term is "offer for sale". When a stock is issued for the first time, it is called "initial public offering (IPO)"

17. **financial intermediation**: ①all businesses serving the establishment of financial trading relationship②the collection of savings and the loaning out of the proceeds to others. For example, banks take in money as deposits and other financial products and pay it out as mortgages and other types of loans

18. **non-performing loan**: ①a loan on which the interest payments are overdue. In the USA, when interest payments are more than 90 days late they must be shown as such in the bank's accounts②Third World debts to clearing banks on which interest payments ceased in the 1980s

19. **universal banking**: banking that involves not only services related to loans and savings but also those involved in making investments in companies. Universal banking is most common in Germany, Switzerland, and the Netherlands

20. **portfolio** [pɔːtˈfəuljəu] **n.** ①the list of holdings in securities owned by an investor or institution. In building up an investment portfolio an institution will have its own investment analysts, while an individual may make use of the services of a merchant bank that offers portfolio management ②a list of the loans made by an organization. Banks, for example, attempt to balance their portfolio of loans to limit the risks

21. **insolvent** [inˈsɔlvənt] **adj.** ①not having enough money to pay what you owe ②bankrupt

22. **be liable to**: ①be subject to②have a tendency to③be likely to

23. **delinquency** [diˈliŋkwənsi] **n.** ①bad or criminal, behavior, usually of young people②wrong-doing, failing to perform a duty

24. **cross-border**: go crossing the district on either side of a boundary

25. **legislation** [ˌledʒisˈleiʃən] **n.** making laws; the law made

Questions for discussion

1. What are the main roles of banks?

2. Do you know the names of joint-equity commercial banks in China?

3. According to the revised edition of the *Law of the People's Republic of China on the People's Bank of China*, what functions does the PBC perform?

4. Can you give some examples of indirect instruments for implementing monetary policy?

5. Would you please describe the financial structuring of China's commercial banks after its access to the WTO?

6. What's the meaning of "liberalizing the banking sector"?

7. Do you know the measures taken for strengthening our banking supervision?

8. What's your viewpoint about the prospect of China's banking development?

9. What is your definition of share and bond?

10. What is the difference between the primary market and the secondary market?

11. What is the most common structure of mutual fund in the U. S. , open-end fund or closed-end fund?

12. What requirements must be fulfilled for a company to get listed on a stock exchange?

13. What is your definition of "securities"?

14. Why are risks so important to insurance business? How do you classify them?

Part Two

Supervision of Banking and Financial Institutions

I. Banking Supervision

1. Importance and Objectives of Banking Supervision

A. *The Role of Banks and Importance of Banking Supervision*

Banks are, at one level, merely corporations like manufacturing or retailing firms, operated by their management to generate profits, and their shareholders expect a reasonable return on the investment. However, it is widely recognized that banks are different from other profit-seeking businesses in that the economic and financial life of a country depends on banks in three important respects.

- Banks occupy a central place in the payments mechanism for households, government and business.
- Banks accept deposits, which are expected to be repaid in full, either on demand or at their due term; and which constitute part of society's financial assets.
- Banks in market economies play a major role in the allocation of financial resources, intermediating between depositors of surplus funds and would-be borrowers, on the basis of active judgments as to the latter's ability to repay.

Given such role of banks, they are generally subject to higher degree of financial supervision and regulation than other types of business. Strong and effective banking supervision is considered an essential component of strong economic environment, which provides a public good that may not be readily available in the marketplace. Along with effective macroeconomic policy, it is critical to financial stability in any country. While the cost of banking supervision is indeed high, the cost of poor supervision has been proved to be even higher.

On the other hand, banks are also provided with important elements of official protection. For example, the central bank usually acts as a lender of last resort to protect commercial banks against a temporary liquidity drain. This protection is an important component of the official safety net backstopping the banking system. Another major aspect of the safety net takes the form of deposit insurance fund to guarantee bank depositors that they will get their money back in the event of a bank failure.

B. Objectives of Banking Supervision

While the specifics of bank supervision vary from country to country, reflecting each country's unique historic development, the broad goals and purposes of such supervision are generally similar.

First, the key objective of supervision is to maintain stability and public confidence in the financial system.

The second goal of bank supervision is to ensure that banks operate in a safe and sound manner and that they hold capital and reserves sufficient to cover the risks that may arise in their business.

Third, a related goal is to protect depositors' funds and, if any bank should fail, to minimize the losses to be absorbed by the deposit insurance fund. Depositor protection is, of course, an important element in maintaining public confidence in the banking system and in avoiding bank runs. A strong, well-managed bank is the depositor's basic source of protection and, as just noted, fostering the development of such banks is one of the fundamental goals of bank supervision.

Nevertheless, banks do fail for one reason or another and the deposit insurance fund covers depositors' losses usually up to a certain amount per account. In view of the substantial potential for losses to the insurance fund, it is an important supervisory goal to minimize the funds loss by limiting excessive risk-taking. Thus the limit on the deposit insurance coverage also serves to minimize "**moral hazard**" on the part of depositors, that is, potential lack of caution in selecting banks as a result of deposit insurance. This goal translates into prompt intervention by the bank supervisors to ensure that a bank takes timely and effective remedial measures in emerging problem situations.

The fourth goal of bank supervision is to foster an efficient and competitive banking system that is responsive to the public need for high quality financial services at reasonable cost. Hence, the general **thrust** of banking law and regulation is to encourage competition and to prohibit monopoly and anti-competitive practices.

The fifth and final goal of bank supervision is to ensure compliance with banking laws and regulations. This is a very difficult assignment because banks are subject to a wide range of laws and regulations, covering everything from bank capital requirements and dividend limitations to consumer protection and fair employment practices.

To achieve these objectives, many countries have developed sophisticated structures of bank supervision and regulation, and bank regulators utilize a number of interrelated techniques to try to achieve their goals. These techniques range from conditions for opening new banks to procedures for dealing with failing banks. However, before we move into these specific areas, it is useful to have in mind the preconditions of effective banking supervision to gain a broader view.

C. Preconditions for Effective Banking Supervision

Effective banking supervision requires a set of preconditions (arrangements) to be in place. While these preconditions are mostly outside the direct jurisdiction of the supervisory authorities, weaknesses or shortcomings in these areas may significantly impair the effectiveness of supervision. The preconditions cover a range of areas, including:

i. Sound and sustainable macroeconomic policies

Sound macroeconomic policies are the foundation of a stable financial system. Supervisors will, however, need to react if they perceive that existing policies are undermining the safety and soundness of the banking system.

ii. A well developed public infrastructure

It comprises the following elements:

- a system of consistently enforced business laws including corporate, bankruptcy, contract, consumer protection and private property laws, which provides a mechanism for fair resolution of disputes;

- comprehensive and well-defined accounting principles and rules that command wide international acceptance;

- a system of independent audits for companies of significant size so that users of financial statements, including banks, have independent assurance that the accounts provide a true and fair view of the financial position of the company and are prepared according to established accounting principles with auditors being accountable for their work;

- an efficient and independent judiciary, and well regulated accounting, auditing and legal professions;

- well-defined rules for governing and adequate supervising of, other financial markets and, where appropriate, their participants; and

- a secure and efficient payment and clearing system for the settlement of financial transactions where counterparty risks are controlled.

iii. Effective market discipline

It depends, in part, on adequate flows of information to market participants, appropriate financial incentives to reward well-managed institutions and arrangements that ensure that investors are not insulated from the consequences of their decisions. Among the issues to be addressed are corporate governance and ensuring that accurate, meaningful, transparent and timely information is provided by borrowers to investors and creditors.

iv. Mechanisms for providing an appropriate level of systematic protection (or public safety net)

In general, deciding on the appropriate level of systematic protection is a policy question to be addressed by the relevant authorities (including the central bank), particularly where it may result in a commitment of public funds. Supervisors will also normally have a role to play because of their in-depth knowledge of the institutions involved. It is important to draw a clear distinction between this systematic protection (or safety net) role and day-to-day supervision of solvent institutions. In handling systematic issues, it will be necessary to address, on one hand, confidence risks in the financial system and contagion to otherwise sound institutions, and, on the other hand, the need to minimize the distortion of market signals and disciplines. In many countries, the framework for systematic protection includes a system of deposit insurance. Provided such a system is carefully designed to limit moral hazard, it can contribute to public confidence in the system thus limiting contagion from banks in distress.

2. Licensing Process

The first supervisory technique is the process of licensing or chartering banks. In most countries banks must acquire a charter in order to undertake banking business. By basing banking supervision on a system of licensing deposit-taking institutions (and, where appropriate, other types of financial institutions), the supervisors will have a means of identifying the banking population to be supervised and controlling entry into the banking system. The licensing process attempts to prevent destabilizing factors (such as inadequate financial resources, unqualified management, or excessive competition) from entering the banking system in the first place. Although the licensing process cannot guarantee that a bank will be well run after it opens, it has proven to be an effective method for reducing the number of unstable situations.

Bank charter is usually granted by the central bank or a separate supervisory body of a country. The actual licensing processes and scrutinizing factors considered by different chartering authorities may not be the same but usually share the following similarities:

A. *Phases of the Process*

The bank licensing process generally consists of three phases:

- an informal pre-filing stage, where staff of the chartering authorities meet with the organizing group to discuss the requirements for obtaining a bank charter, the licensing process and the feasibility of the proposal;

- the application stage, where the organizing group submits a formal application to the licensing authorities and receives preliminary approval to organize a bank; and
- the organizing stage, where the organizing group implements its preliminary approval by hiring the remainder of its management, establishing its banking premises at the proposed site, raising its capital, developing its banking systems and procedures, and finally, receiving its charter to open for business.

Of these stages, the application stage is the core of the bank licensing process.

B. *Factors Evaluated by the Chartering Authorities*

In evaluating a charter application, the chartering authorities generally considers four factors:

- the bank's prospects for future earnings (i. e. , whether it will be successful and profitable);
- the qualifications of the bank's proposed management;
- the adequacy of the bank's capital structure; and
- the convenience and needs of the community to be served by the bank.

Regulators attempt to ensure that these factors are covered by requiring an organizing group to submit the following as part of the charter application:

- an operating plan;
- personal and financial information on the proposed management for background investigations;
- pro forma financial statements and projections for the proposed bank; and
- information on the demand for banking products and services and existing competition in the target market.

In granting a bank charter, supervisors in most countries require the bank's shareholders to satisfy minimum application standards (i. e. paid-up capital, etc.) as market-entry ticket. The establishment of a bank in China shall meet the following requirements:

- having its statute in compliance with law;
- having the minimum registered capital defined by the law;
- having directors and senior managers with expertise and professional experience commensurate with their positions; and
- having the required business premise, safety measures and other facilities relevant with the business thereof.

The supervisors in examining the application for the establishment of a bank may also take into account the need for economic growth and the competition of the banking industry.

C. Basel Committee's Requirements on Bank Licensing

The Basel Committee on Banking Supervision (Hereinafter referred to as the Basel Committee) is a committee of banking supervisory authorities, which was established by the central bank Governors of the G10 countries in 1978. It is currently made up of senior representatives of banking supervisory authorities and central banks from 13 countries. In September 1997, the Basel Committee published Core Principles for Effective Banking Supervision, which were revised and reissued in 2006 to reflect the changes that have occurred since 1997 in banking supervision and regulation in individual countries.

The Core Principles are a framework of minimum standards for sound supervisory practices and are considered universally applicable. According to Principle 3, the licensing process, at a minimum, should consist of assessment of the ownership structure and governance of the bank and its wider group, including the fitness and propriety of Board members and senior management, its strategic and operating plan, internal controls and risk management, and its projected financial condition, including its capital base. Where the proposed owner or parent organization is a foreign bank, the prior consent of its home country supervisor should be obtained.

3. Arrangements for Ongoing Banking Supervision

A. Risks in Banking

Banking, by its nature, entails taking a wide array of risks. Banking supervisors need to understand these risks and be satisfied that banks are adequately measuring and managing them. From a supervisory perspective, risk is the potential that events, expected or unanticipated, may have an adverse impact on the bank's capital or earnings. The key risks facing banks are discussed below.

i. Credit risk

A major type of risk that banks face is credit risk or the failure of a counterpart to perform according to a contractual arrangement. This risk applies not only to loans but also to other on-and-off-balance-sheet exposures such as guarantees, acceptances and securities investments. Serious banking problems have arisen from the failure of banks to recognize impaired assets, to create reserves for writing off these assets, and to suspend recognition of interest income when appropriate.

ii. Market risk

Two specific elements of market risk are foreign exchange risk and interest rate risk.

Banks face a risk of losses in on- and off-balance sheet positions arising from movements in exchange rates. Established accounting principles cause these risks to be typically most visible in a bank's trading activities. Banks act as "market-makers" in foreign exchange markets by quoting rates to their customers and by taking open positions in foreign currencies. The risks inherent in foreign exchange business, particularly in running open foreign exchange positions, increase during periods of instability in exchange rates.

Interest rate risk refers to the exposure of a bank's financial condition to adverse movements in interest rates. This risk impacts both the earnings of a bank and the economic value of its assets, liabilities and off-balance-sheet instruments. The primary forms of interest rate risk to which banks are typically exposed are: (1) repricing risk, which arises from timing differences in the maturity (for fixed rate) and repricing (for floating rate) of bank assets, liabilities and off-balance-sheet positions; (2) yield curve risk, which arises from changes in the slope and shape of the yield curve; (3) basis risk, which arises from imperfect correlation in the adjustment of the rates earned and paid on different instruments with otherwise similar repricing characteristics; and (4) optionality, which arises from the express or implied options imbedded in many bank assets, liabilities and off-balance sheet portfolios.

Although it is a normal part of banking, excessive interest rate risk can pose a significant threat to a bank's earnings and capital base. Managing this type of risk is of growing importance in sophisticated financial markets. Special attention should be paid to this risk in countries where interest rates are being deregulated.

iii. Liquidity risk

Liquidity risk arises from the inability of a bank to accommodate decreases in liabilities or to fund increases in assets. When a bank has inadequate liquidity, it cannot obtain sufficient funds, either by increasing liabilities or by converting assets into cash promptly, at a reasonable cost, thereby affecting profitability. In extreme cases, insufficient liquidity can lead to the insolvency of a bank.

iv. Operational risk

The most important types of operational risk involve breakdowns in internal controls and corporate governance. Such breakdowns can lead to financial losses through error, fraud, or failure to perform in a timely manner or cause the interests of the bank to be compromised in some other way, for example, by its dealers, lending officers or other staff exceeding their authority or conducting business in an unethical or risky manner. Other aspects of operational risk include major failure of information technology systems or events such as major fires or other disasters.

v. Legal risk

Banks are subject to various forms of legal risks, including inadequate or incorrect legal advice or documentation that may result in unexpected decline in the value of assets or unexpected increase in the value of liabilities. In addition, existing laws may fail to resolve legal issues involving a bank; a court case involving a particular bank may have wider implications for banking business and incur costs to it and many or all other banks; and, laws affecting banks or other commercial enterprises may change. Banks are particularly susceptible to legal risks when entering new types of transactions and when the legal right of a counterpart to enter into a transaction is not established.

vi. *Reputation risk*

Reputation risk arises from operational failures, failure to comply with relevant laws and regulations, or other sources. Reputation risk is particularly damaging for banks since the nature of their business requires maintaining the confidence of depositors, creditors and the general marketplace.

The risks inherent in banking must be recognized, monitored and controlled, and supervisors play a critical role in ensuring that bank management does this. From supervisor's point of view, the existence of risk is not necessarily reason for concern. Likewise, the existence of high risk in any area is not necessarily a concern, so long as the management exhibits the ability to effectively manage that level of risk. Therefore, one task of supervisors is to decide whether the risks a bank undertakes are warranted. Generally, a risk is warranted when it is identified, understood, measured, monitored and controlled. It should be within the bank's capacity to readily withstand the financial distress that such risk could cause. When risks are unwarranted (i. e. , not understood, measured, controlled or backed by adequate capital to support the activity), supervisors must communicate to the management and the directorate the need to mitigate or eliminate the excessive risks.

B. *Key Prudential Issues*

An important part of the supervisory process is the authority of supervisors to develop and utilize prudential regulations and requirements to control the banking risks. These may be qualitative and/or quantitative requirements. Their purpose is to limit imprudent risk-taking by banks. These requirements do not supplant management decisions but rather impose minimum prudential standards to ensure that banks conduct their activities in an appropriate manner. The dynamic nature of banking requires that supervisors periodically assess their prudential requirements and evaluate the continued relevance of existing requirements as well as the need for new requirements.

Prudential requirements cover a broad spectrum of banking activities and play an important part in assuring the effectiveness of the supervisory process. Of which, there are five key areas where the extensive prudential policies have been implemented by bank regulators of most countries, these are capital adequacy, risk concentration, asset quality, liquidity and internal controls.

i. Capital adequacy

Capital is at the top of any bank supervisor's list. The most basic form of capital is equity capital, which is the shareholder's financial interest or net worth. Equity capital serves several purposes: it provides a permanent source of revenue for the shareholders and funding for the bank; it is available to bear risk and absorb losses; it provides a base for further growth; and it gives the shareholders reason to ensure that the bank is managed in a safe and sound manner. Minimum capital adequacy ratios are necessary to reduce the risk of loss to depositors, creditors and other stakeholders of the bank and to help supervisors pursue the overall stability of the banking industry.

According to the Basel Committees Core Principles, supervisors in each individual country set prudent and appropriate minimum capital adequacy requirements and encourage banks to operate with capital in excess of the minimum. When it appears appropriate due to the particular risk profile, uncertainties regarding the asset quality, risk concentrations or other adverse characteristics of a bank's financial condition, considerations of requiring higher than minimum capital ratios are encouraged. If any bank's capital ratio falls below the minimum, banking supervisors will act to ensure that it has a realistic plan to restore the minimum in a timely fashion, or may consider putting additional restrictions on the bank's operations.

a. The 1988 Basel Accord

The Basel Committee reached an agreement for risk-based international capital standards in 1988 (widely known as the 1988 Capital Accord and hereinafter referred to as the Accord), which calls for international **convergence** of capital measurement and capital standards in 12 developed countries. Nowadays more than 100 countries have also adopted the Capital Accord or something very close to it. The Accord addresses two important elements of a bank's activities: (1) different levels of credit risk inherent in its balance sheet and (2) off-balance-sheet activities, which can represent a significant risk exposure.

The Accord defines what types of capital are acceptable for supervisory purposes and stresses the need for adequate levels of "core capital" (in the Accord this capital is referred to as tier one capital) consisting of permanent shareholders' equity and disclosed reserves that are created or maintained by appropriations of retained earnings or other surplus (e. g. share premiums, retained profit, general reserves and reserves required by law). Disclosed reserves also include general funds that meet the following criteria: (1) allocations to the funds must be made out of after-tax retained earnings or out of pre-tax earnings adjusted for all potential tax liabilities; (2) the funds and movements into or out of them must be disclosed separately in the bank's published accounts; (3) the funds must be available to a bank to meet losses; and (4) losses cannot be charged directly to the funds but must be taken through the profit-and-loss account. The Accord also acknowledges other forms of supplementary capital (referred to as tier two capital), such as revaluation reserves, general provisions, **hidden reserves** and **hybrid** capital instruments.

The Accord assigns risk weights to on- and off-balance-sheet exposures according to broad categories of relative riskiness. The framework of weights has been kept as simple as possible with only five weights being used: 0, 10%, 20%, 50% and 100%.

The Accord sets minimum capital ratio requirements for internationally active banks of 4% tier one capital and 8% total capital (tier one plus tier two) in relation to risk-weighted assets. These requirements are applied to banks on a consolidated basis. It must be stressed that these ratios are considered a minimum standard and many supervisors require higher ratios or apply stricter definitions of capital or higher risk weights than set out in the Accord.

The risk-based capital standard plays a central role in the supervision of banks. The capital standard is in fact the **triggering** mechanism for increasingly severe supervisory action in the event that a bank slips below the minimum required level of capital. If any bank is significantly undercapitalized, it will be subject to supervisory action in the form of a capital directive which will prohibit the payment of cash dividends and could involve a wide range of supervisory actions, for example, to submit a plan to restore its capital to a more appropriate level and, in the interim, to comply with a variety of supervisory restrictions on the growth of its assets, the opening of new offices or the expansion into new businesses. In addition, the authorities can place further restrictions on such things as the salaries of senior officers, if deemed necessary. If conditions are bad enough, they can even require the sale or termination of particular activities, the dismissal of directors or senior officers, or force a merger of the bank with another institution.

b. Basel II

The Basel Committee issued, in July 2006, a comprehensive version of International Convergence of Capital Measurement and Capital standards: A Revised Framework, commonly known as Basel II, which intends to replace the 1988 Accord. The new framework is intended to align regulatory capital requirements more closely with underlying risks, and to provide banks and their supervisors with several options for the assessment of capital adequacy.

Basel II is more extensive and complex than the 1988 Accord, which is a natural reflection of the advancement and innovations in the financial marketplace and the need for a more risk-sensitive framework. Basel II is structured around three mutually reinforcing pillars that allow banks and supervisors to evaluate properly the various risks that banks face.

The three pillars are: minimum capital requirements, which relates to the minimum capital requirements each bank must hold to cover its exposure to credit, market and operational risk; supervisory review process, which is concerned with supervisory reviews that aim to ensure that a bank's capital level is sufficient to cover its overall risk; and market discipline, which relates to market discipline and details minimum levels of public disclosure.

- Pillar 1—minimum capital requirements

Pillar 1 sets out minimum capital requirements as they relate to credit, market and operational risk. Under Basel Ⅱ, banks must maintain a minimum eight percent of capital to risk-weighted assets.

In this context, capital is subdivided into the following areas:

- **Tier 1 capital** is core capital, that is, common shares, plus non-cumulative perpetual preferred shares, plus disclosed reserves, less goodwill.
- **Tier 2 capital** consists of undisclosed, asset revaluation, and general provisions (general loan-loss) reserves, as well as hybrid debt capital instruments, and subordinated term debt.

A third category of capital, **Tier 3 capital**, was added in the 1996 Amendment to the Capital Accord but can only be used to meet a proportion of a bank's capital requirements for market risk. It consists of short-term subordinated debt instruments bearing specified characteristics. Core capital must represent at least 50 percent of the bank's total capital base. It follows, then, that Tier 2 capital cannot exceed 50 percent of the capital base.

Pillar 1 provides banks with a choice between two broad methodologies for calculating their capital requirements for credit risk. One option is to measure credit risk in a standardized manner, supported by external credit assessments such as those provided by credit rating agencies. This Standardized Approach adopts a so-called "building block" approach for interest-rate related and equity instruments which differentiates capital requirements (charges) for specific risk from those for general market risk. The alternative methodology, which is subject to the explicit approval of the bank's supervisor, allows banks to use their own internal rating systems. The Internal Models Approach enables a bank to use its proprietary in-house method which must meet the qualitative and quantitative criteria set out by the Basel Committee and is subject to the explicit approval of a bank's supervisory authorities.

- Pillar 2—The Supervisory Review Process

The supervisory review process aims to ensure that banks assess their capital adequacy positions relative to their overall risks, and that supervisors review and take appropriate actions in response to those assessments. Supervisors may require banks to hold capital in excess of minimum regulatory capital ratios or take other remedial measures such as strengthening **pertinent** risk management or other practices. If higher ratios are required, supervisors will need to intervene if capital falls below these levels.

Pillar 2 requires that banks perform stress tests to estimate the extent to which their IRB capital requirements could increase during a stress scenario. The results of such tests should be used by banks and supervisors to ensure that banks hold sufficient capital buffers.

- Pillar 3— Market Discipline

Pillar 3 sets out disclosure requirements which will allow market participants to assess key pieces of information on the scope of application, capital, risk exposures, risk assessment processes, and hence the capital adequacy of the institution. It also discusses the role of materiality of information, frequency of disclosures and the issue of proprietary or confidential information.

ii. *Risk Concentration*

Concentration of risk and large exposures is one of the major supervisory concerns. Large exposures to a single borrower, or to a group of related borrowers are a common cause of banking problems in that they represent a credit risk concentration. Large concentrations can also arise with respect to particular industries, economic sectors, or geographical regions or by having sets of loans with other characteristics that make them vulnerable to the same economic factors (e. g., highly-leveraged transactions).

Banking supervisors in many countries set prudential limits to bank exposures to single borrowers, groups of related borrowers and other significant risk concentrations. These limits are usually expressed in terms of a percentage of bank capital and, although they vary, 25% of capital is typically the most that a bank or banking group may extend to a private sector non-bank borrower or a group of closely related borrowers without specific supervisory approval. Newly-established or very small banks may face practical limits on their ability to diversify, necessitating higher levels of capital to reflect the resultant risk.

In addition, supervisors monitor the bank's handling of concentrations of risk and may require that banks report to them any such exposures exceeding a specified limit (e. g., 10% of capital) or exposures to large borrowers as determined by the supervisors. In some countries, the aggregate of such large exposures is also subject to limits.

iii. *Asset Quality*

Asset quality is the most important factor in determining a bank's creditworthiness. Asset quality directly affects the provisioning decisions which largely determine the level of profits. In turn, the profit stream will affect capital ratios and the solvency of each bank. Asset quality and adequacy of provisions are therefore the major areas to which banking supervisors should pay particular attention. They need to be fully aware of the asset quality of individual banks and to be satisfied that adequate provisions have been maintained for problem assets.

For the purposes of monitoring bank's asset quality and assessing its adequacy of bad debt provisions, various banking regulatory bodies in countries/regions such as Singapore, Malaysia, Korea, Hong Kong, Philippines, Indonesia and Australia have adopted some form of risk-based loan/asset classification system. Most of such systems are modeled after the system adopted by the supervisory authorities of the United States.

Under the loan classification system, criteria used to assign credit quality ratings are primarily based upon the degree of risk and the likelihood of orderly repayment, and their effect on a bank's safety and soundness. Loans and advances (credits) are classified into the following categories:

a. Pass

Credits in this category are those where borrowers are currently meeting their commitments (pay in due time) and full repayment of interest and principal is not in doubt.

b. Special mention

A special mention extension of credit is defined as having potential weaknesses that deserve management's close attention. If left uncorrected, these potential weaknesses may, at some future date, result in the deterioration of the repayment prospects for the credit or the institution's credit position. These credits pose elevated risk, but their weakness does not yet justify a substandard classification. Borrowers may be experiencing adverse operating trends (declining revenues or margins) or all ill-proportioned balance sheet (e. g. , increasing inventory without an increase in sales, high leverage, tight liquidity). Adverse economic or market conditions, such as interest-rate increases or the entry of a new competitor, may also support a special-mention rating. Non-financial reasons for rating a credit exposure as special mention include management problems, pending litigation, an ineffective loan agreement or other material structural weakness, and any other significant deviation from prudent lending practices.

c. Substandard loans

Substandard credits are inadequately protected by the current paying capacity of the obligors or of the collateral pledged, if any. Credits classified "substandard" must have well-defined weaknesses that **jeopardize** the liquidation of the debt. They are generally characterized by current or expected unprofitable operations, inadequate debt service coverage, inadequate liquidity, or marginal capitalization. Repayment may depend on collateral or other credit risk **mitigation**. For some substandard assets, the likelihood of full collection of interest and principal may be in doubt; such assets should be placed on non-accrual basis.

Although substandard assets in the aggregate will have a distinct potential for loss, an individual asset's loss potential does not have to be distinct for the asset to be rated "substandard".

d. Doubtful loans

Credits classified "doubtful" have all the weaknesses of substandard loans with the added characteristic that the weakness make collection or the liquidation in full, on the basis of currently existing facts, conditions and values, is highly questionable and improbable. A doubtful credit has a high probability of total or substantial loss, but because of specific pending events that may strengthen the asset, its classification as loss is deferred. Doubtful borrowers are usually in default, and lack adequate liquidity or capital, as well as the resources necessary to remain as an operating entity. Pending events can include mergers, acquisitions, liquidations, capital collateral, and refinancing. Generally, pending events should be resolved within a relatively short period and the ratings will be adjusted based on the new information. Because of high probability of loss, non-accrual accounting treatment is required for doubtful credits.

e. Loss loans

Credits in this category are considered uncollectible and are of so little value that their continuance as bankable assets is not warranted. This classification does not mean that the asset has absolutely no recovery or salvage value, but rather that it is not practical or desirable to defer writing off this basically worthless asset even though partial recovery may be effected in the future.

With loss assets, the underlying borrowers, often in bankruptcy, have formally suspended debt repayments, or have otherwise ceased normal business operations. Once an asset is classified "loss", there is little prospect of collecting either its principal or interest. When access to collateral, rather than the value of the collateral, is a problem, a less severe classification may be appropriate. However, banks should not maintain any asset on the balance sheet if realizing its value would require long-term litigation or other lengthy recovery efforts. Losses are to be recorded in the period as an obligation that becomes uncollectible.

In addition to loans, balances due from banks, acceptances and bills of exchange held, as well as commitments and contingent liabilities which subject a bank to credit risk are also classified in the same way in order to give a better picture on asset quality. Some countries have gone one step further to stipulate the loan loss provisioning level required for different categories of loans, e. g. 25% for substandard loans, 50% for doubtful loans and 100% for loss loans. The objective of loan classification system is to help identify potential problem assets that may have an adverse bearing on the financial position of a bank.

In China, guidance for the five-category loan classification system is set out in the *Guideline on Risk-based Loan Classification* issued by the People's Bank of China in 1999 and updated in December 2001, during which time the system was operated on a trial basis. It took full effect on January 1, 2002. On April 25, 2002, the People's Bank of China issued a *Guideline on Loan Loss Provision requiring* all banking institutions in China to maintain adequate provisions.

iv. Liquidity

Banks need adequate liquidity to meet their obligations when they fall due, especially where the timing and amount of the commitment are uncertain, and to maintain confidence of depositors and shareholders. The major obligations in this context are demands for withdrawals from sight deposits, time deposits, and commitments to lend on a specific date, unutilized overdraft facilities and inter-bank settlements. Banks may provide for liquidity in the following ways:

- Hold cash or near-cash assets;
- Appropriate cash flows from maturing assets, via assets portfolio management; and
- New deposits may be attracted and monies could be borrowed in the money markets.

Banking regulation requires every bank to maintain a minimum liquidity ratio of "liquid assets" to "qualifying liabilities". Every bank is required to maintain a liquidity ratio of not less than 25% in each calendar month, calculated on the basis of the sum of its liquid assets and the sum of its qualifying liabilities for each working day of the calendar month concerned.

The liquidity ratio is calculated by comparing liquid assets that mature within one month to qualifying liabilities that fall due in one month. A bank's balance sheet typically consists of liabilities that are short-term and assets that are long-term, to ensure that banks could meet their obligations when they fall due. Good management of liquidity is important. Furthermore, to cater for the possibility of a sudden liquidity squeeze or other shocks that may place strains on the bank's balance sheet, a cushion of liquidity is essential.

However, maintaining a high level of liquidity at all times are costly. Banks have to run acceptable level of maturity mismatch to generate profits. Therefore, a suitable balance between liquidity and profitability has to be maintained.

v. Internal Controls

A system of effective internal controls is a critical component of bank management and a foundation for the safe and sound operation of banking organizations. Such a system helps to ensure that goals and objectives of a banking organization will be met, that the bank will achieve long-term profitability targets, and maintain reliable financial and managerial reporting, that risks in banking activities are effectively identified, understood, measured, monitored and controlled to an acceptable level, that the bank will comply with laws and regulations as well as policies, plans, internal rules and procedures, and that the bank will decrease the risk of unexpected losses or damage to the bank's reputations.

Internal control consists of five interrelated elements: (1) management oversight and the control culture; (2) risk recognition and assessment; (3) control activities and segregation of duties; (4) information and communication, and (5) monitoring activities and correcting deficiencies.

- Management oversight and the control culture

The board of directors should have responsibilities for approving and periodically reviewing the overall business strategies and significant policies of the bank, understanding the major risks run by the bank, setting acceptable levels for these risks and ensuring that senior management takes the steps necessary to identify, measure, monitor and control these risks, approving the organizational structure and ensuring that senior management is monitoring the effectiveness of the internal control system. The board is ultimately responsible for ensuring that an adequate and effective system of internal control has been established and maintained.

Senior management should have responsibilities for implementing strategies and policies approved by the board, developing processes that identify, measure, monitor and control risks incurred by the bank, maintaining an organizational structure that clearly assigns responsibilities, authority and reporting relationships, ensuring that delegated responsibilities are effectively carried out, setting appropriate internal control policies and monitoring the adequacy and effectiveness of the internal control system.

The board of directors and senior management are responsible for promoting high ethical and integrity standards, and for establishing a culture within the organization that emphasizes and demonstrates to all levels of staffs the importance of internal controls. All staffs at a banking organization need to understand their role in the internal controls process and be fully engaged in the process.

- Risk Recognition and Assessment

An effective internal control system requires that the material risks that could adversely affect the achievement of the bank's goals should be recognized and continually assessed. This assessment should cover all risks facing the bank and the consolidated banking organization (that is, credit risk, country and transfer risk, market risk, interest rate risk, operational risk, legal risk and reputation risk). Internal controls may need to be revised to appropriately address any new or previously uncontrolled risks.

- Control Activities and Segregation of Duties

Control activities should be an integral part of the daily activities of a bank. An effective internal control system requires that an appropriate control structure should be set up, with control activities defined at every business level. These should include: top level reviews, appropriate activity controls for different departments or divisions, physical controls, checking for being compliance with exposure limits and follow-up on non-compliance, system of approval and authorizations, and a system of verification and reconciliation.

An effective internal control system requires that there should be appropriate segregation of duties and that staffs are not assigned conflicting responsibilities. Areas of potential conflicts of interests should be identified, minimized, and subject to careful, and independent monitoring.

- Information and Communication

An effective internal control system requires that there should be adequate and comprehensive internal financial, operational and compliance data, as well as external market information about events and conditions that are relevant to decision making. Information should be reliable, timely, accessible, and provided in a consistent format. An effective internal control system also requires that there should be reliable information systems in place that cover all significant activities of the bank. These systems, including those that hold and use data in an electronic form, must be secure, monitored independently and supported by adequate contingency arrangement. Finally, an effective internal control system requires effective channels of communication to ensure that all staff fully understand and adhere to policies and procedures affecting their duties and responsibilities and that other relevant information is reaching the appropriate staffs.

- Monitoring Activities and Correcting Deficiencies

The overall effectiveness of the bank's internal controls should be monitored on an ongoing basis. Monitoring of key risks should be part of the daily activities of the bank as well as periodic evaluations by the business lines and internal audit. There should be an effective and comprehensive internal audit of the internal control system carried out by operationally independent, appropriately trained and competent staff. The internal audit function, as part of the monitoring of the system of internal controls, should report directly to the board of directors or its audit committee, and to the senior management. Internal control deficiencies, whether identified by business line, internal audit, or other control staffs, should be reported in a timely manner to the appropriate management level and addressed promptly. Material internal control deficiencies should be reported to senior management and the board of directors.

- Evaluation of Internal Control Systems by Supervisory Authorities

Supervisors should require that all banks, regardless of size, should have an effective system of internal controls that is consistent with the nature, complexity, and risk inherent in their on- and off- balance-sheet activities and that responds to changes in the bank's environment and conditions. In those instances where supervisors determine that a bank's internal control system is not adequate or effective for that bank's specific risk profile (for example, does not cover all of the principles contained in this document), they should take an appropriate action.

C. *Methods of Ongoing Banking Supervision*

Supervision requires the collection and analysis of information. This can be done on- or off-site. An effective supervisory system will use both means. In some countries, on-site work is carried out by examiners or by qualified external auditors, while in some others exists a mixed system of on-site examinations and collaboration between the supervisors and the external auditors.

Regardless of their mix of on-site and off-site activities or their use of work done by external accountants, banking supervisors usually have regular contact with bank management and a thorough understanding of the institution's operations. This may take the form of prudential meetings held between supervisor and bank, and/or tri-party meetings held among supervisors, bank and the bank's auditors to discuss regularly all significant issues and areas of their business. Review of the reports of internal and external auditors is also an integral part of both on-site and off-site supervision, and the various factors considered during the licensing process are periodically assessed as part of ongoing supervision.

i. *Off-site Surveillance*

Off-site surveillance is one of the key techniques of bank supervisors which relies heavily on the data that banks submit in their regulatory reports.

a. Objectives

There are three key objectives of off-site surveillance. The first is to identify banking institutions that, while currently basically healthy, may face problems in the short or medium term. Through forward-looking surveillance techniques, the supervisors can address problems before they become unmanageable. Surveillance is particularly important in countries where on-site examinations are generally spaced apart by a year or even longer, and the potential for problems to develop and expand between bank examinations is great.

The second major objective is to monitor very closely banking institutions already identified as having significant problems. This improves the supervisor's ability to prevent existing problems from growing. It also provides the supervisors with the information necessary, on a continual basis, to help the institution work through the problems.

The third objective is to assess broad patterns and trends in the banking sector. It is particularly important for bank supervisors to be cognizant of nationwide economic trends in order to be able to develop policy positions that are both relevant and beneficial.

b. Information Requirements

To conduct surveillance work effectively, regulators rely on a number of sources of information. The primary information sources are financial statements and reports prepared by the bank. The most important of them, for surveillance purposes, are the bank regulatory reports, or the statistical returns as so called in countries like the United Kingdom. This information must be verified periodically through onsite examinations or external audits. Banking supervisors need to ensure that each bank maintains adequate accounting records drawn up in accordance with consistent accounting policies and practices that enable the supervisors to obtain a true and fair view of the financial condition of the bank and the profitability of its business.

Another vital source of information for surveillance analyst is the information obtained from field examiners. Examiners sometimes uncover issues in the course of an examination that are then passed to surveillance staff to explore more in depth.

Regulators also maintain direct contact with the institutions themselves in order to stay abreast of their activities. This is done particularly through meetings with the management on a regular basis to discuss performance. On occasion, analysts may also obtain information from contacts at the institutions that may be of supervisory concern.

Regulators also utilize other reports, such as monetary policy reports submitted to the central bank which include, for example, weekly reports of condition for the largest banks in the country. Surveillance analysts also scrutinize banks' quarterly and annual reports that are issued under the **auspices** of the securities regulatory authorities.

Finally, the surveillance analysts review secondary market information to learn more about developments at banks. Analyzing market data, such as stock price movements relative to a peer index, or debt instrument yield spreads over an index (e. g. , spreads over U. S. Treasury securities) , can provide extremely beneficial insights as to how the markets view the performance and condition of an organization. Other important sources of secondary information include reports and assessments by debt and equity analysts employed by banks and investment banks, and analyses and ratings by the rating agencies.

c. Analyzing Tools

Assimilating all of these data and producing coherent analyses requires the right kinds of tools to assist analysts in their monitoring efforts. Some countries use uniform bank performance report (UBPR), which is computer-generated and presents the data in a format that allows the in-house analyst to assess the bank's condition. It provides detailed financial ratios about four key areas of a bank's financial condition. "Acceptable" ratios for these measures may vary among types of banks and among banks in different countries. These ratios are:

- Capital adequacy measures, including risk-based capital and leverage ratios;
- Asset quality indicators, such as the ratio of past-due loans to total loans or concentration measures (e. g. , the ratio of real estate loans to total loans);
- Earnings measures, such as income-to-total-assets and income-to-equity ratios; and
- Liquidity measures, such as the deposit-to-loan ratio.

Another type of tool involves electronic screens that highlight outlier banks. For example, the principal screen the U. S. Federal Reserve uses is a computer-based statistical model, which attempts to estimate a bank's composite examination rating based on the most current information available from regulatory reports and past examinations. The model highlights those institutions that appear to have suffered the most significant deterioration in financial condition.

Other tools include analytic tables to pull together information on small groups of highly visible banks from regulatory reports, bank press releases, stock price results, examination findings and rating agency publications. These tables provide a different focus comparing with that of the standardized reports for a selected group of banks. In addition, various market tables are also developed to show changes in bank stock prices over time and compare movements in bank stock prices among peers and relative to market indices.

d. The Role of In-house Analysts

The surveillance staff reviews and analyzes the information produced through the available tools and sources described above to determine which bank appears most likely to have serious problems. This analysis is critical because some institutions that appear to have problems may, upon further investigation, be considered otherwise. On the other hand, analysts may determine that an institution is problematic even if at first glance it does not appear to exhibit signs of weakness. A second responsibility of the in-house monitoring staff is to identify and report trends and patterns in the banking sector.

In addition, in-house analysts must coordinate closely with the examination staff. In-house staff notifies examiners immediately of banks that appear to be potentially problematic, so that an appropriate follow-up action can be taken.

For banks that are identified as having problems, the in-house staff initiates a special monitoring program. This program includes keeping a close watch on the performance and condition of problem institutions through increased reporting and frequent meetings. It also involves developing comprehensive plans to help banks work through their problems. Finally the in-house staff must work closely with field examiners to ensure that banks comply with those plans.

In conclusion, in-house monitoring is a vital part of the overall supervisory process. It requires analytical expertise to interpret large amounts of raw data that may not be informative by themselves. In-house monitoring provides a necessary complement to on-site examinations by enabling supervisors to track the condition of institutions on an ongoing basis in today's volatile markets. It also allows supervisors to focus efforts on problem banks without detracting from ongoing examinations responsibilities.

Aside from information on individual institutions, in-house analysis presents the supervisor with a broader perspective on issues and trends in the banking sector. This perspective is critical for developing rational bank regulatory policies and for identifying emerging problems in the banking sector that may have adversely systemic consequences.

ii. On-site Examination and the Role of External Auditors

On-site examinations remain to be an indispensable tool of banking supervision. The banking supervision agency normally establishes clear internal guidelines related to the frequency and scope of examination. Only through an actual presence in a bank can a supervisor gain the detailed knowledge of the bank's operations, controls and management that is needed to reach an informed judgment about the bank's overall financial condition and its compliance with banking laws and regulations. To be specific, on-site examinations provide the supervisors with a means of verifying or assessing a range of matters including:

- the overall operations and condition of the bank;
- the accuracy of reports received from the bank;
- the adequacy of the bank's risk management systems and internal control procedures;
- the quality of the loan portfolio and adequacy of loan loss provisions and reserves;
- the competence of the management;
- the adequacy of accounting and management information systems;
- issues identified in off-site or previous on-site supervisory processes; and
- bank adherence to laws and regulations and the terms stipulated in the banking license.

Banking supervisors recognize that banking is a business of taking risks in order to earn profit and assumes varied and complex risks that warrant a risk-oriented supervisory approach. Consequently, bank regulators in many countries have adopted risk-based approach to supervise banks. Under this approach, supervisors do not attempt to restrict risk-taking but rather determine whether banks identify, understand and control the risks they assume.

In the following paragraphs, we introduce ways the U. S. regulators (mainly the Federal Reserve and the OCC) implement on-site examinations on banks to see what the processes are and where the main focusing area is.

a. The on-site examination process

During an on-site examination, the examiners carefully evaluate a number of critical areas including the bank's strength of capital and loss reserves, its overall risk exposure, particularly asset quality, the quality of its management, including internal control procedures, and earnings and liquidity. Examiners rate the bank in each of these critical components and develop an overall composite rating that summarizes the bank's condition.

The conduct of an on-site examination requires significant preparation. In planning an examination, examiners review the report of the prior examination as well as available information on the bank's performance since that time to determine if problems or weaknesses have surfaced during examinations. For a medium-sized bank, it usually takes at least a week or two to assign the examination team and prepare for the examination. The examiner-in-charge is responsible for developing the main focal points for investigation by the examination team.

As an example, the focus of an examination of a medium-sized bank experiencing some difficulty might be:

- Asset quality, since credit quality deterioration is more often than not the source of the problem;
- The adequacy of capital, with a special focus on the sufficiency of the loan loss reserve and methodology employed;
- Corrective actions that have been taken to date by the management to address the weaknesses or issues identified by the bank supervisors, accountants or internal audit staff;
- Overall effectiveness of the bank's internal control, risk management and leadership;
- Potential for loss of public confidence in the bank and the bank's contingency funding and liquidity plans; and
- Further corrective actions needed to put the bank on the road to recovery.

When the examination begins, the team is divided into smaller groups that specialize in specific aspects of the examination—the six principal areas reviewed are capital, asset quality, management, earnings, liquidity and sensitivity to market risk. Special attention is also focused on the bank's internal audit and control procedures, which are highly critical to a successful operation. At the conclusion of the examination, each of these areas is rated by the examiners on a scale of one to five, where "1" represents the highest or best rating and "5" the lowest.

After evaluating the six critical areas of the bank through separate ratings, a composite CAMELS rating ranging from 1 to 5 is established to provide an overall judgment of a bank's financial condition and soundness, whereas "C" stands for Capital adequacy, "A" for Asset quality, "M" for Management, "E" for Earnings, "L" for Liquidity and "S" for Sensitivity to market risk.

Under the CAMELS rating system, banks rated "1" are sound in every aspect, while those rated "5" are likely to fail in the absence of immediate and substantial corrective action and external support. The composite is not determined by calculating a simple average of the separate components. Rather, it is the result of a comprehensive assessment by the examiner-in-charge of the overall condition of the bank. The composite includes additional considerations, such as the bank's competitive position, including its future prospects and trends in its financial performance. Thus, the summary rating provides a broad measure of the examiner's findings regarding a bank's overall financial condition and immediate prospects.

The ROCA system rates four areas: **R**isk management, **O**perational controls, **C**ompliance and **A**sset quality. The system places the highest priority on risk management, which enables examiners (1) to incorporate the principles of supervision by risk into the federal branch or agency evaluation, and (2) to recognize how management (both local and at the head office), policies, processes and practices affect the current and future condition of the bank. The operational controls include internal controls and internal/external audit activities. The compliance rating reflects compliance with safety and soundness regulations, as well as consumer regulations, for federal branches and agencies offering products covered under consumer laws. The evaluation of asset quality helps examiners to assess the effectiveness of credit risk management. It is also an indication of the value of the federal branch's or agency's asset base in the event of liquidation. The asset quality rating depends on the volume of problem assets while the adequacy of credit administration is included in the risk management rating.

The ROCA composite rating indicates whether, in the aggregate, the operation of the branch may present supervisory concerns and the extent of any concerns. While the individual component ratings will be taken into consideration in arriving at the branch's overall assessment, the composite rating should not be considered merely as arithmetic average of the individual components.

One of the most crucial elements of on-site examination is the assessment of the bank's asset quality, since it is one of the most fundamental considerations in determining the financial condition of a bank. How well a bank executes the credit review process will likely determine the ongoing financial health of that bank. Therefore, we now turn to focus on the supervisor's credit review process to see how the asset quality of a bank under examination is ascertained.

b. Asset quality assessment

A timely and accurate assessment of asset quality is central to the examination process and critical to the final judgment as to a bank's overall financial condition. Not surprisingly, examiners devote the largest portion of their time during an examination to the review and analysis of the many different dimensions of the bank's credit-granting process. The procedures used during the course of this review will vary according to the bank's size and general condition, but the basic principles of analysis and judgment used by examiners are applied consistently across all institutions.

To reach an informed judgment on the general soundness of a bank's credit or lending business, examiners must evaluate all facets of its lending program. The four stages of the evaluation process are:

- A careful review and assessment of the bank's written lending policies. These policies reflect the lending strategies and philosophy of both bank management and the board of directors, and determine the types and sizes of loans the bank will make, the types and sizes of borrowers that will be accommodated, and how bank management expects its loan function to determine the creditworthiness of prospective borrowers;

- An evaluation of the bank's lending procedures and the quality of internal operating controls, and management's adherence to those procedures and controls;

- A detailed review and financial analysis of the individual borrowers who make up a bank's portfolio; and

- An assessment of the adequacy of the bank's loan loss reserves, that is, the adequacy or reasonableness of the reserves relative to the risks identified in the portfolio.

Loan policies and procedures

Lending policies set general guidelines for total loan volume relative to bank assets and capital. They also set limits on the total exposure allowed for different types of industries or borrowers. The policies outline the credit approval process and criteria for granting loans, the collateral requirements, documentation standards and repayment terms. And, finally, the loan policies set the specifics for each loan officer's lending authority and responsibilities.

The examiners look for evidence that the bank's lending standards require the borrower to furnish complete, current financial statements and other appropriate documentation (e. g. , tax returns), that the bank has its own internal credit rating system that incorporates assessments made by the lending officers, and that the bank has an independent monitoring system to verify the accuracy of the internal ratings. If the bank's loan policies appear to be sound in concept, examiners seek to determine if the policies are being adhered to faithfully. This means that all the elements of the credit decision process should be documented in the loan file, with a clear indication of the factors that led to the approval of the loan. Examiners seek to determine the extent to which actions taken by lending officers are regularly monitored and evaluated by both credit administration and the bank's independent loan review function.

A key ingredient of a good lending function is a strong and independent credit administration department. This department's functions require independent analysts charged with the review and analysis of borrower's financial condition and prospects. The department also evaluates loan performance and adherence to loan covenants, reviews statistical data and trends in the portfolio, and identifies exceptions to policies and procedures. Much of this information is regularly shared with senior management and, where necessary, with the board of directors. The internal review should also focus on the types of credit being extended, the level of risk concentration in particular areas, the loss experience in various segments of the portfolio, and the need for changes in credit standards and guidelines.

The extent to which lending to a particular borrower or group of borrowers would raise the bank's exposure to an uncomfortable level—the concentration issue—is another important factor for the bank to consider as a part of its overall credit review and monitoring process and therefore is carefully assessed by examiners.

The credit review process

The actual credit review or loan appraisal process, that is, evaluating the quality of individual loans—is the core of the process that provides the examiner with a true picture of the condition of the bank's loan portfolio. To make a qualitative assessment regarding a bank's underlying asset quality, the examiners conduct a detailed review of the bank's outstanding loans and commitments, as well as their associated documentation files. The objective is to determine the relative financial health and creditworthiness of each borrower. Examiners will need to express a view as to the borrower's ability to repay the debt as scheduled.

The process that examiners follow entails a careful review, analysis and rating of each of the credits. The aim is to identify problem loans and emerging problem loans. Examiners will also seek to determine the extent to which weaknesses in the bank's lending policies and procedures and other basic internal controls may have contributed to the problems.

In reviewing individual credit, examiners look at a number of financial and related factors. Some of the more important ones are:

- The purpose of the loan and source (s) of repayment.

- The borrower's financial statements i. e. , the balance sheets and income statements, for at least the last three years. This information is extremely valuable for both the bank and the examiner in determining if the actual or proposed level of borrowing can be fully supported. Recent financial history and trends also help in evaluating and understanding a borrower's financial position and prospects.

- The ability of the borrower to generate a sufficient cash flow to repay the debt in accordance with the terms of the loan.

- The borrower's business history and past performance with other creditors.

- Where appropriate, whether there is adequate collateral or other forms of reliable support, such as guarantee from a financially strong and responsible third party.

Based on their review and analysis of the individual credit, the examiners estimate the degree of risk in each credit arrangement and assign a rating, i. e. , one of the pass, special mention, substandard, doubtful and loss.

To provide with a benchmark for the probable loss that the level of classified assets poses to a bank's capital resources, the examiners compute what is called "risk-weighted-classified-assets ratio". Substandard assets are weighted at 20 percent, doubtful assets at 50 percent and loss assets at 100 percent. The sum of the risk-weighted-classified assets is then divided by the bank's Tier 1 capital plus loan loss reserves. This ratio has proven over time to be fairly reliable estimate of the potential impact of problem assets on a bank's capital and loan loss reserves. This ratio represents the supervisor's principal tool for determining a bank's asset quality rating — the lower the ratio, the lower the level of risk to the bank's capital resources. Similarly, a higher ratio is presumed to indicate a higher level of risk to the bank's capital. The assets quality rating is then generally assigned to the different ranges that this ratio may cover — from a "1" asset quality rating, the strongest, for a weighted ratio below 5 percent, to a "5" rating, the weakest, for a ratio that is over 50 percent.

In assigning an asset quality rating, examiners would also consider recent trends in the portfolio relative to past due and non-performing loans, whether the problems are receding or growing and the qualitative judgments regarding the bank's loan policies and procedures and management's adherence to them. It is obvious that a "5" rating for asset quality is very severe and indicates a very serious problem that could cause a bank to fail.

From a procedural standpoint, it is not necessary for examiners to analyze every single credit on the books of the bank, since a fairly reliable picture can be obtained by analyzing the bank's largest and most important credits. In general, examiners aim to evaluate a minimum of 50 percent of the value of a bank's loan portfolio, generally the commercial loan portfolio. At banks with recognized problems, a higher level of coverage, perhaps up to 80 percent, would be sought. To achieve the appropriate level of coverage, a minimum value of a loan to an individual borrower or group of borrowers is established, and this minimum is called the "line limit". It normally would equal 1/2 percent to 1 percent of the bank's total capital funds. Once the line limit is established, examiners will read and evaluate all loans at or over that minimum amount. In addition, all previously identified problem loans and all high risk credits, including those seriously past due or **delinquent**, would also be evaluated.

In cases where bank examiners have confirmed that a bank has a well-developed and effective internal loan review function, they also employ a statistical sampling program. In this program, a random sample of credits in the bank's loan portfolio is considered; this sample is sufficiently large to provide a high degree of confidence that it is representative of the entire loan portfolio. The credits are then read and the examiners rating of each loan is compared with the bank's internal risk rating for the same credits. If the examiners' ratings agree with the bank's, then examiners will use the bank's internal risk reviews to round out their review of the bank's loan portfolio.

Adequacy of loan loss reserves

Another very important aspect of bank supervisor's on-site examination is the assessment of the adequacy of the loan loss reserves in conjunction with the evaluation of the effectiveness of the bank's reserve methodology and policies for adding to loss reserves. Examiners need to make certain that the reserves in place provide sufficient coverage for the risks in the portfolio, namely the anticipated or probable losses. As a guide, the examiners use as a reserve estimate measure a weighting system similar to the asset quality measure mentioned earlier. This measurement system provides examiners with a reference point or "comfort zone" for adequate reserve.

c. The Use of External Auditors

Depending on its use of examination staff, the banking supervisory agency may use external auditors to fulfill the above functions in whole or in part. In some cases, such functions may be part of the normal audit process (e. g. assessing the quality of the loan portfolio and the level of provisions that need to be held against it). In other areas, the supervisor may require work to be commissioned specifically for supervisory purposes (e. g. on the occurring of reports filed with supervisors on the adequacy of control systems).

Assisting supervisors in discharging their examination duties as mentioned above is only one example what auditors can do. Apart from that, banking laws in many countries require banks to appoint accountants as their external auditors. Such appointments and any subsequent changes in these appointments must be notified to the banking supervisors. Notification to the supervisors is also required where a bank decides to remove or replace its auditor, or the auditor resigns or decides not to seek reappointment on expiry of his term of office.

The primary objective of an audit of a bank by an external auditor is to enable the auditor to express an opinion as to whether the published financial statements of the bank give a "true and fair view of " the bank's financial position and the results of its operation for the period for which such statements are prepared. The auditor's report is normally addressed to the shareholders, but is used by many other parties, such as depositors, creditors and supervisors. The auditor's opinion helps establish the credibility of the financial statements.

iii. Supervision on a consolidated basis

An essential element of banking supervision is the ability of the supervisors to supervise the consolidated banking organization. This includes the ability to review both banking and non-banking activities conducted by the banking organization, either directly or indirectly (through subsidiaries and affiliates), and activities conducted at both domestic and foreign offices. Supervisors need to take into account that non-financial activities of a bank or group may pose risks to the bank. Supervisors need to decide which prudential requirements will be applied on a bank-only (solo) basis, which ones will be applied on a consolidated basis, and which ones will be applied on both bases. In all cases, the banking supervisors must be aware of the overall structure of the banking organization or group when applying their supervisory methods, and have the ability to coordinate with other authorities responsible for supervising specific entities within the organization's structure.

4. Dealing with Weak Banks

A. *Definition of a weak bank*

A weak bank is one whose liquidity or solvency is or will be impaired unless there is a major improvement in its financial resources, risk profile, strategic business direction, risk management capabilities and/or quality of management. Weak banks do not occur overnight. Problems that seem to emerge rapidly are often the sign of financial or managerial weakness that have been allowed to persist for some time. These problems can rapidly become a major concern to a supervisor if minimum prudential requirements are not met and viability is threatened.

B. Symptoms and causes of bank problems

It is important to distinguish between the symptoms and causes of bank problems. The symptoms of weak banks are usually poor asset quality, lack of profitability, losses of capital, reputation problems, and/or liquidity problems. The different symptoms often emerge together. Experiences from several countries indicate that liquidity problems have seldom occurred alone and their emergence has generally been one aspect of broader difficulties. While banking difficulties usually result from a combination of factors, they have become evident as credit problems in the majority of cases. This should not be surprising given that lending has been and still is the mainstay of banking business. More often than not, credit losses stem from weaknesses in management control and credit risk management systems. In particular, it is often true that management and control processes have not been sufficiently robust to prevent poor lending practices, excessive loan concentrations, excessive risk taking, overlap of existing policies and procedures, and fraud and criminal activities and self-dealing by one or more individuals.

Apart from credit risk, a bank's weakness may also stem from other risks, including interest rate risk, market risk, operational risk and strategic risk. These risks are not new, although historically they have been less important in accounting for banks failures than credit risk. Some of these risks may become more important for banks. For example, operational risk will come into greater focus as banks make use of more sophisticated systems, new delivery channels and outsourcing arrangements that increase the bank's reliance and exposure to third parties. At the same time, the increase in one type of risk is often compensated by a reduction in another type of risk-securitization of assets, for example, increases operational and legal risk but reduces credit risk. Banks should also benefit from improved techniques and instruments for risk reduction.

Weak banks in the past, contributed to or exacerbated financial crises. Equally, external factors such as negative macroeconomic shocks (including a currency crisis, a weak sector; inadequate preparation for financial sector liberalization, etc.) may also lead to problems for banks. External factors may not overwhelm a well-managed and financially sound bank but will certainly expose deficiencies in management and control in weaker banks.

C. Principles for dealing with weak banks

A central objective of supervision is to maintain stability and confidence in the financial system, thereby reducing the risk of loss to depositors and other creditors. In dealing with weak banks, this objective translates itself into supervisory actions aimed at preserving the value of the bank's assets with minimal disruption to its operations (i. e. maintaining the economic entity), subject to minimizing any resolution costs. In certain cases, it may well be that the bank as a legal entity should cease to exist.

The guiding principles for a supervisor when dealing with weak banks include the following:

- Speed. If not dealing with the problems promptly, the problems of a weak bank will have grown rapidly thus making the eventual resolution efforts more difficult and more expensive, with the possibility of becoming more widespread and systemic.

- Cost-efficiency. A least cost criterion should guide the supervisor when making choices between alternative actions consistent with achieving the supervisory objectives.

- Flexibility. The legislation should permit the supervisor to exercise discretion in the deployment and timing of supervisory tools.

- Consistency. Consistent and well-understood supervisory actions will not distort the competitive environment. Such an approach will also minimize confusion and uncertainty in times of crisis. Similar problems in different banks, large or small, private or state-owned, should receive similar treatment.

- Avoiding moral hazard. Supervisory action should not create incentives for banks to act in a manner that incurs costs which they do not have to bear entirely.

- Transparency and cooperation. Inadequate or incorrect information from the bank increases uncertainty for everyone involved. It can lead to misplaced supervisory action and add to the costs of solving the problems.

D. *Corrective actions*

Corrective actions are those actions required to deal with deficiencies and change the behavior in a weak bank. They can be implemented voluntarily by the bank under the supervisor's informal oversight or, if necessary, via formal supervisory intervention. Under normal circumstances, it is the responsibility of the Board of Directors and senior management of the bank, and not of the supervisor, to determine how the bank should solve its problems. However, should the bank engage in unsound banking practices or breach statutory or other key supervisory duties, the supervisor should have powers to compel the bank to take necessary remedial action and a statutory responsibility to ensure that the remedial action taken is appropriate. At the extreme, supervisors should have powers to close the bank.

In order to formulate a plan of corrective action, there has to be an assessment of the nature and seriousness of the weakness. An on-site assessment is usually the most efficient way of identifying the full extent and nature of the problems facing a bank. An essential part of the assessment is to determine the bank's present and expected liquidity and capital position and evaluate the bank's contingency plans. In assessing the prospects of insolvency, there has been an assessment of the fair value of the bank's net assets.

Typically, supervisors are willing to use informal methods and less intrusive and corrective action in cases where the bank's problems are less serious. If the bank faces more serious problems, or in the absence of cooperation by the bank, the supervisor may have to take formal actions to ensure compliance with its recommendations. Depending on domestic regulations, this will involve the issue of some form of supervisory or enforcement notice outlining the actions the bank and management must take and the time frame for acting. It could also involve cease and desist orders requiring the bank and/or management to stop engaging in a specified practice or violation. More severe corrective actions should be considered if there is an increased danger of insolvency. In such cases, the supervisor may impose a sale and payment prohibition on the bank to prevent or limit the dissipation of assets.

E. *Resolution issues and exit*

i. Resolution techniques

- Resolution plans. While a weak bank may be required to reorganize its operations as a corrective action, if insolvency is imminent, the bank may be required to carry out a radical business on a sound footing in the short term. Far-reaching restructuring may be the only solution for large and complex institutions that are unlikely to find partners with the financial resources to carry through a merger or acquisition.

- Mergers and acquisitions. When a bank cannot on its own resolve its weaknesses, it should consider a merger with, or acquisition by, a healthy bank. This is a private sector resolution technique. Arrangement for a merger or acquisition (M&A) should take place early before assets dissipate in value. Acquirers should have sufficient capital to meet the costs of the new bank and a management capable of protecting and implementing a reorganization program. Full and accurate information should be provided by the weak bank to all potential acquirers, although this may have to provide sequentially and under strict confidentiality agreements. In countries where the law permits, this could be done in cooperation with the supervisors.

- Purchase-and-assumption transactions. If a private sector M&A is not forthcoming or cannot be arranged, a purchase and assumption (P&A) transaction may be considered. A P&A transaction is one where a healthy institution or private investor purchases some or all of the assets and assumes some or all of the liabilities of a failed bank. P&A transactions in most countries require withdrawal of the bank license and the commencement of resolution proceedings by the liquidator. The acquiring bank purchases assets of the failed bank but not its charter.

- Bridge bank. A bridge bank is a resolution technique that allows a bank to continue its operations until a permanent solution can be found. The weak bank is closed by the licensing authorities and placed under liquidation. A new bank, referred to as a bridge bank, is licensed and controlled by the liquidator. The liquidator has discretion in determining which assets and liabilities are transferred to the bridge bank. Those assets and liabilities that are not transferred to the bridge bank remain with the liquidator. A bridge bank is designed to bridge the gap between the failure of a bank and the time when the liquidator can evaluate and market the bank in such a manner that allows for a satisfactory acquisition by a third order to submit their offers while at the same time permitting uninterrupted service to bank customers. A bridge bank transaction is most commonly used when the failed institution is usually large or complex or when the deposit insurer or the government believes there is value to be realized or costs minimized, but does not have a ready solution other than a payoff.

ii. Use of public sector monies in resolution

Public funds for the resolution of weak banks may be considered in potentially systemic situations, including the risk of loss or disruption of credit and payment services to a large number of customers. Government support may take the form of financial inducement to facilitate a resolution measure discussed in the above section.

Alternatively, the government may offer solvency support to a weak bank to allow it to remain open for business, which may take the form of a direct capital injection, loans provided by the government to the bank, or the purchase of troubled assets by asset management companies created expressly for this purpose or other institutions whose losses are covered by the government.

F. Closure of the bank: Depositor pay-off

If no investor is willing to step in to rescue the bank, the repayment of depositors and the liquidation of the bank's assets are unavoidable. In countries with a deposit insurance scheme, closure of the bank is also the right decision where a depositor pay-off is less costly than other resolution measures.

II. Securities Supervision

1. Importance and Objectives of Securities Supervision

The securities and futures markets are vital to the growth and strength of market economies as they support corporate initiatives, finance the exploitation of new ideas and facilitate the management of financial risk. Further, since retail investors are placing an increasing proportion of their money in securities investment funds and other collective investments, the markets have become central to individual wealth and retirement planning.

Sound and effective regulation and, in turn, the confidence it brings is important for the integrity and development of the markets. Sound domestic markets which are now increasingly being integrated into a global market are necessary to the strength of a developed domestic economy and domestic markets. Securities regulators, at both the domestic and international levels, shall be guided by a constant concern for investor protection. Consistently high regulatory standards and effective international cooperation will not only protect investors but also help to reduce systemic risk.

Increasingly globally-integrated-financial markets pose significant challenges to the regulation of securities and futures markets. Therefore, in a globally integrated environment regulators must be in a position to assess the nature of cross-border conduct if they are to ensure the existence of fair, efficient and transparent markets.

There are three core objectives of securities regulation:

- The protection of investors;
- Ensuring that markets are fair, efficient and transparent;
- The reduction of systematic risk.

The three objectives are closely related and, in some respects, overlap. Many of the requirements that help to ensure fair, efficient and transparent markets also provide investor protection and help to reduce systemic risk. Similarly, many of the measures designed for reducing systematic risk provide protection for investors. Further, matters such as thorough surveillance and compliance programs, effective enforcement and close cooperation with other regulators are necessary to give effect to all the above-mentioned three objectives.

2. Securities Supervision in China

A. *Regulatory Regime*

In China, the securities and futures markets are supervised by the CSRC with the frontline disciplining supports from self-regulatory organizations (SROs) which regulate, with varying degrees of effectiveness, the activities of their members. In October 1992, the State Council Securities Committee (SCSC) and its executive arm — the CSRC were established and mandated to regulate China's securities and futures markets. In 1998, the SCSC was disbanded with all functions being transferred to the CSRC which ever since has become the sole competent regulator supervising nationwide markets.

The top executive body of the CSRC is composed of one Chairman, several Vice-Chairmen and Assistant Chairmen. The Commission has over a dozen of departments and several affiliate centers. Headquartered in Beijing, the CSRC has an extensive network of 36 regional bureaus located throughout China's provinces, municipalities, autonomous regions and key cities, in addition to 2 supervisory offices in Shanghai and Shenzhen respectively.

The SROs primarily include the Securities Association of China (SAC), China Futures Association (CFA), 2 stock exchanges and 3 commodity futures exchanges. A financial futures exchange is expected to come into existence in late 2006.

The SAC (founded on August 28, 1991) and CFA (established on December 29, 2000) are non-profit SROs with a legal person status subject to joint guidance, supervision and administration of the CSRC and the Ministry of Civil Affairs. These SROs' major functions are:

- to ensure the enforcement of laws and regulations governing securities/futures;
- to safeguard the legitimate rights and interests of members and report to the authorities the suggestions and requests of members;
- to formulate rules governing its members, organize professional trainings and facilitate exchange of ideas among members;
- to supervise and inspect members' professional conduct and impose disciplinary sanctions on any member that violates articles of association and self-regulatory rules.

An **exchange** is a self-regulatory legal person or legal entity that provides the site and facilities for centralized securities trading and supervises the trading activities. Each exchange has a general assembly of members and board of governors. The former is the highest authority while the board of governors is the executive body with a chairman and vice chairman. At present, both stock exchanges and futures exchanges are under the supervision of the CSRC. The major functions of an exchange include:

- providing the site and facilities for securities/futures trading;
- formulating business rules;
- accepting listing applications and arranging listing issues;
- organizing and supervising the activities of securities/futures trading;
- supervising the conduct of the members and listed companies;
- administering and disclosing market information.

B. *Major Functions & Powers of the CSRC*

The CSRC is mandated to perform the following functions in Chinese securities and futures markets:

- Study and formulate policies, strategies, regulations, rules and measures;
- Regulate securities and futures markets, and supervise the senior executives and

daily operations of securities companies;

- Regulate the offering, trading, custody and settlement of equities, convertible bonds, the bonds issued by securities firms and other related securities; supervise the securities investment funds; authorize the listing of corporate bonds; and supervise trading activities of listed bonds;
- Regulate the listing, trading and settlement of domestic futures contracts;
- Supervise the conducts of listed companies and their shareholders;
- Supervise securities and futures exchanges, SAC and CFA;
- Regulate the registrations and settlement companies and clearing houses; license and supervise market intermediaries; license and supervise the fund custodian business in collaboration with the banking authorities;
- Supervise overseas offerings and listings by domestic enterprises;
- Supervise market information services;
- License related market intermediaries and supervise their business activities in collaboration with competent authorities;
- Investigate and take legal actions against violating persons or parties;
- Engage in international liaison and cooperation with relevant overseas regulators and industrial bodies.

III. Insurance Supervision

1. Rationale for Regulation of the Insurance Industry

A. *Vested in the public interest rationale*

The first rationale for the regulation of insurance is that it is an industry that is vested in the public interest. Insurance, like banking, is pervasive in its influence and failures in this field can affect persons other than those directly involved in the transaction. Individuals purchase insurance to protect themselves against financial loss at a later time, and it is important to the public welfare that the insurer promising to indemnify the insured for future losses fulfills its promises.

The "vested in the public interest" rationale for regulation of the insurance industry holds that the insurance industry, like any other business holding vast sums of money in trust for the public, should be subject to government regulation because of its fiduciary nature.

B. *Destructive competition rationale*

The second rationale for the regulation of insurance is that competition in some fields of insurance, if left unregulated, could become destructive. The basic danger in the insurance industry is the possibility that in vying for business, companies may underestimate future losses and suffer failures as a result.

2. Goals of Insurance Regulation

The function of insurance regulation is to promote the welfare of public by ensuring fair contracts at fair prices from financially strong companies. The "market failures" that insurance regulation is intended to correct were insolvencies and unfair treatment of insureds by insurers. In short, the dual goals of regulation were solvency and equity.

3. Areas Regulated

A. *Licensing of companies*
The power to license insurance companies guarantees the control of the formation of new companies. In effect, when a company is licensed, the commissioner certifies the company with regard to its financial stability and soundness of operation methods.

B. *Examination of companies*
Every licensed insurer is supposed to submit an annual report to the commissioner of insurance. In addition to the annual report, a periodic inspection of each insurance company conducting business is made by the commissioner.

C. *Insurer insolvencies*
Clearly, a primary focus of insurance regulation is on insurer's solvency. Indeed, it has been argued that this should be the primary function of regulation. Regulatory interest in insurer's solvency is concerned with the early detection of potential insolvencies and prevention of consumer-suffering when insolvencies occur.

D. *Regulation of rates*
The original rationale for regulation of insurance rates was that such regulation was needed to achieve the dual goals of regulation (solvency and equity). To the extent that the insurer's promise depends on the price it charges for these promises, it was felt that these rates must be subject to government control. The regulation of insurance rates requires that the rates should be adequate, but not excessive and not unfairly discriminatory.

Adequacy is the primary requirement. The rates, with interest income from investments, must be sufficient to pay all losses as they occur and cover all expenses connected with the production and servicing of the business.

In addition to being adequate, the insurance rates must not be excessive. Insurance has been regarded as a product that is essential to the well-being of society's members, and insurers may not take advantage of this need to realize unreasonable returns.

Finally, insurance rates must not discriminate unfairly. The emphasis in this require-ment is on unfairness, since the very nature of insurance rates requires some degree of dis-crimination. By not being unfairly discriminatory, we mean that the insurance company may not charge a significantly different rate for two clients with approximately the same degree of risk. Any variation in rates charged must have an actuarial basis.

E. *Regulation of reserves*

Because insurers operate on the unusual plan of collecting in advance for a product to be delivered at some time in the future, insurance laws require specific recognition of the insurer's fiduciary obligations, that is reflected as liabilities in insurers' financial state-ments.

F. *Investments*

To a large extent an insurer's promise to pay the insared depends on the value of its in-vestments. There fore those investments must be sound and profitable.

G. *Policy forms*

Since the insurance policy is a contract, by its very nature it is technical. In most ca-ses, the customer asked to purchase it becomes a party to such a contract without fully un-derstanding its content. Because insurance contracts are complicated, they must be ap-proved by the regulatory authorities to ensure that the insurance-buying public will not be mistreated as a result of unfair provisions. In addition, the solvency of the insurers must be protected against unreasonable commitments they might make under stress of competition.

H. *Competence of agents*

Because of the technical complications in the insurance product, it is particularly im-portant that those selling insurance understand the contracts they propose to offer to the pub-lic and the laws under which they will operate and meet continuing education requirements.

I. *Unfair practices*

An insurer might be sound financially and yet indulge in practices that are detrimental to the public, such as unfairly discriminating against the insured or engaging in sharp claim practices, which should be supervised and regulated.

Notes

1. **moral hazard**: moral hazard is the asymmetric information problem that occurs after the financial transaction takes place, when the borrower of a loan or the seller of a security may have incentives to hide unfavorable information and engage in activities that are undesir-able for the lender of the loan or the purchaser of the security

2. **thrust** [θrʌst] *v.* ① push with sudden impulse or with force ② impose (thing) forcibly on, enforce acceptance of (thing) on. *n.* sudden or forcible push; forward force exerted by propeller or jet, etc.

3. **impair** [imˈpεə] *vt.* hurt, injure

4. **insulate** [ˈinsjuleit] *vt.* isolate, cut ties with (thing)

5. **contagion** [kənˈteidʒən] *n.* spreading of disease by bodily contact, or disease so transmitted

6. **entail** [inˈteil] *vt.* necessitate or involve unavoidably

7. **supplant** [səˈplɑːnt] *vt.* take the place of, e. g. by underhand means

8. **convergence** [kənˈvɔːdʒəns] *n.* coming together or towards the same point, approaching from different directions

9. **hidden reserve**: undisclosed reserve or undeclared superannuation fund, i. e. intentionally undervaluing assets or revaluing assets to result in difference between the balance sheet and its actual value

10. **hybrid** [ˈhaibrid] *n.* offspring of two animal or plants of different species or varieties, thing composed of diverse elements

11. **trigger** [ˈtrigə] *n.* movable device for releasing spring or catch and so setting mechanism (e. g. that of gun) in motion. vt. set (action or process) in motion, initiate

12. Tier 3 capital allocated for market risk plus Tier 2 capital allocated for market risk are limited to 71. 4 percent of a bank's measure for market risk. (see Timothy W. Koch Scott MacDonald: ***Bank Management*** 5th Edition. , South -Western, 2003, page 189)

13. **pertinent** [ˈpɔːtinənt] *a.* relevant to the matter in hand, or to the point

14. **jeopardize** [ˈdʒepədaiz] *vt.* endanger

15. **trail** [treil] *vt.* draw or be drawn along behind, or drag somebody along wearily

16. **cater for**: to supply food, meals, amusement for somebody or organization

17. **be cognizant of**: to recognize something, or to know something

18. **scrutinize** [ˈskrutinaiz] *vt.* close investigation ir examination into details

19. **auspices** [ˈɔːspisiz] *n.* help, donation

20. **assimilate** [əˈsimileit] *v.* to become similar to; to absorb or to be absorbed into the body or mind

21. **facet** [ˈfæsit] *n.* one aspect of problem etc. ; one side of many-sided cut thing

22. **recede** [riˈsiːd] *vi.* go or shrink back or further off; to slope backwards; to decline in force or value etc.

23. **delinquent** [diˈliŋkwənt] *a.* committing an offence; failing in a duty

24. **exacerbate** [eksˈæsə(ː)beit] *vt.* make (pain, anger etc.) worse

25. **intrusive** [in'tru:siv] *a.* force or coming uninvited or unwanted

26. **imminent** ['iminənt] *a.* about to happen

Questions for discussion

1. In what aspects do the banks differ from other profit-seeking businesses?

2. What are the objectives of banking supervision?

3. What risks might the commercial banks have to face?

4. What are the implication of credit risk, market risk, liquidity risk and operational risk?

5. At what levels does the Basel Accord set the minimum capital ratio requirements for internationally active banks?

6. Why was the Tier 3 capital raised and adopted by Basel Ⅱ?

7. Around what pillars is the Basel Ⅱ structured?

8. What categories can the loan and advances be divided into according to their risk degree and repayment likelihood?

9. What "acceptable" ratios does the UBPR require the commercial banks to comply with?

10. Say something about the abbreviation CAMEL's implication and its ratings for the bank's financial condition and soundness.

11. What is the primary objective that the commercial banks need the external auditor to perform its functions?

12. What are the guiding principles for a supervisor to deal with the weak banks?

13. What resolution techniques can be chosen by the weak banks?

14. In what case will there be delisting of securities in China?

15. What does the supervision over the listed companies focus on?

Appendix: The Core Principles

The Core Principles are a framework of minimum standards for sound supervisory practices and are considered universally applicable. The Committee drew up the Core Principles and the Methodology as its contribution to strengthening the global financial system. Weaknesses in the banking system of a country, whether developing or developed, can threaten financial stability both within that country and internationally. The Committee believes that implementation of the Core Principles by all countries would be a significant step towards improving financial stability domestically and internationally and provide a good basis for further development of effective supervisory systems.

The Basel Core Principles define 25 principles that are needed for a supervisory system to be effective. The Principles relate to: ①

Principle 1 – Objectives, independence, powers, transparency and cooperation: An effective system of banking supervision will have clear responsibilities and objectives for each authority involved in the supervision of banks. Each such authority should possess operational independence, transparent processes, sound governance and adequate resources, and be accountable for the overall exercise of its duties. A suitable legal framework for banking supervision is also necessary, including provisions relating to authorization of banking establishments and their ongoing supervision; powers to address compliance with laws as well as safety and soundness concerns; and legal protection for supervisors. Arrangements for sharing information between supervisors and protecting the confidentiality of such information should be in place.

Principle 2 – Permissible activities: The permissible activities of institutions that are licensed and subject to supervision as banks must be clearly defined and the use of the word "bank" in names should be controlled as far as possible.

Principle 3 – Licensing criteria: The licensing authority must have the power to set criteria and reject applications for establishments that do not meet the standards set. The licensing process, at a minimum, should consist of an assessment of the ownership structure and governance of the bank and its wider group, including the fitness and propriety of Board members and senior management, its strategic and operating plan, internal controls and risk management, and its projected financial condition, including its capital base. Where the proposed owner or parent organisation is a foreign bank, the prior consent of its home country supervisor should be obtained.

Principle 4 – Transfer of significant ownership: The supervisor has the power to review and reject any proposals to transfer significant ownership or controlling interests held directly or indirectly in existing banks to other parties.

Principle 5 – Major acquisitions: The supervisor has the power to review major acquisitions or investments by a bank, against prescribed criteria, including the establishment of cross-border operations, and confirming that corporate affiliations or structures do not expose the bank to undue risks or hinder effective supervision.

Principle 6 – Capital adequacy: Supervisors must set prudent and appropriate minimum capital adequacy requirements for banks that reflect the risks that the bank undertakes,

---

① Further definitions and explanations of the content of the Principles are provided in the document Core *Principles Methodology.*

and must define the components of capital, bearing in mind its ability to absorb losses. At least for internationally active banks, these requirements must not be less than those established in the applicable Basel requirement.

Principle 7 – Risk management process: Supervisors must be satisfied that banks and banking groups have in place a comprehensive risk management process (including Board and senior management oversight) to identify, evaluate, monitor and control or mitigate all material risks and to assess their overall capital adequacy in relation to their risk profile. These processes should be commensurate with the size and complexity of the institution.

Principle 8 – Credit risk: Supervisors must be satisfied that banks have a credit risk management process that takes into account the risk profile of the institution, with prudent policies and processes to identify, measure, monitor and control credit risk (including counterparty risk). This would include the granting of loans and making of investments, the evaluation of the quality of such loans and investments, and the ongoing management of the loan and investment portfolios.

Principle 9 – Problem assets, provisions and reserves: Supervisors must be satisfied that banks establish and adhere to adequate policies and processes for managing problem assets and evaluating the adequacy of provisions and reserves.

Principle 10 – Large exposure limits: Supervisors must be satisfied that banks have policies and processes that enable management to identify and manage concentrations within the portfolio, and supervisors must set prudential limits to restrict bank exposures to single counterparties or groups of connected counterparties.

Principle 11 – Exposures to related parties: In order to prevent abuses arising from exposures (both on balance sheet and off balance sheet) to related parties and to address conflict of interest, supervisors must have in place requirements that banks extend exposures to related companies and individuals on an arm's length basis; these exposures are effectively monitored; appropriate steps are taken to control or mitigate the risks; and write-offs of such exposures are made according to standard policies and processes.

Principle 12 – Country and transfer risks: Supervisors must be satisfied that banks have adequate policies and processes for identifying, measuring, monitoring and controlling country risk and transfer risk in their international lending and investment activities, and for maintaining adequate provisions and reserves against such risks.

Principle 13 – Market risks: Supervisors must be satisfied that banks have in place policies and processes that accurately identify, measure, monitor and control market risks; supervisors should have powers to impose specific limits and/or a specific capital charge on market risk exposures, if warranted.

Principle 14 – Liquidity risk: Supervisors must be satisfied that banks have a liquidity management strategy that takes into account the risk profile of the institution, with prudent policies and processes to identify, measure, monitor and control liquidity risk, and to manage liquidity on a day-to-day basis. Supervisors require banks to have contingency plans for handling liquidity problems.

Principle 15 – Operational risk: Supervisors must be satisfied that banks have in place risk management policies and processes to identify, assess, monitor and mitigate operational risk. These policies and processes are commensurate with the size and complexity of the bank.

Principle 16 – Interest rate risk: Supervisors must be satisfied that banks have effective systems in place to identify, measure, monitor and control interest rate risk in the banking book, including a well defined strategy that has been approved by the Board and implemented by senior management; these should be appropriate to their size and complexity.

Principle 17 – Internal control and audit: Supervisors must be satisfied that banks have in place internal controls that are adequate for the size and complexity of their business. These should include clear arrangements for delegating authority and responsibility; separation of the functions that involve committing the bank, paying away its funds, and accounting for its assets and liabilities; reconciliation of these processes; safeguarding the bank's assets; and appropriate independent internal audit and compliance functions to test adherence to these controls as well as applicable laws and regulations.

Principle 18 – Abuse of financial services: Supervisors must be satisfied that banks have adequate policies and processes in place, including strict " know-your-customer" rules, that promote high ethical and professional standards in the financial sector and prevent the bank from being used, intentionally or unintentionally, for criminal activities.

Principle 19 – Supervisory approach: An effective banking supervisory system requires that supervisors develop and maintain a thorough understanding of the operations of individual banks and banking groups, and also of the banking system as a whole, focusing on safety and soundness, and the stability of the banking system.

Principle 20 – Supervisory techniques: An effective banking supervisory system should consist of on-site and off-site supervision and regular contacts with bank management.

Principle 21 – Supervisory reporting: Supervisors must have a means of collecting, reviewing and analyzing prudential reports and statistical returns from banks on both a solo and a consolidated basis, and a means of independent verification of these reports, through either on-site examinations or use of external experts.

Principle 22 – Accounting and disclosure: Supervisors must be satisfied that each bank maintains adequate records drawn up in accordance with accounting policies and practices that are widely accepted internationally, and publishes, on a regular basis, information that fairly reflects its financial condition and profitability.

Principle 23 – Corrective and remedial powers of supervisors: Supervisors must have at their disposal an adequate range of supervisory tools to bring about timely corrective actions. This includes the ability, where appropriate, to revoke the banking license or to recommend its revocation.

Principle 24 – Consolidated supervision: An essential element of banking supervision is that supervisors supervise the banking group on a consolidated basis, adequately monitoring and, as appropriate, applying prudential norms to all aspects of the business conducted by the group worldwide.

Principle 25 – Home-host relationships: Cross-border consolidated supervision requires cooperation and information exchange between home supervisors and the various other supervisors involved, primarily host banking supervisors. Banking supervisors must require the local operations of foreign banks to be conducted to the same standards required of domestic institutions. The Core Principles are neutral with regard to different approaches to supervision, so long as the overriding goals are achieved. The Principles are not designed to cover all the needs and circumstances of every banking system. Instead, specific country circumstances should be more appropriately considered in the context of the assessments and in the dialogue between assessors and country authorities.

National authorities should apply the Principles in the supervision of all banking organizations within their jurisdictions. [1] Individual countries, in particular those with advanced markets and institutions, may expand upon the Principles in order to achieve best supervisory practice.

A high degree of compliance with the Principles should foster overall financial system stability; however, this will not guarantee it, nor will it prevent the failure of individual banks. Banking supervision cannot, and should not, provide an assurance that banks will not fail. In a market economy, failures are part of risk-taking.

The Committee stands ready to encourage work at the national level to implement the Principles in conjunction with other supervisory bodies and interested parties. The Commit-

---

[1] In countries where non-bank financial institutions provide deposit and lending services similar to those of banks, many of the Principles set out in this document would also be appropriate to such non-bank financial institutions. However it is also acknowledged that some of these categories of institutions do not necessarily have to be supervised in the same manner as banks as long as they do not hold, collectively, a significant proportion of deposits in a financial system.

tee invites the international financial institutions and donor agencies to use the Principles in assisting individual countries to strengthen their supervisory arrangements. The Committee will continue to collaborate closely with the IMF and the World Bank in their monitoring of the implementation of the Committee's prudential standards. The Committee is also committed to further enhancing its interaction with supervisors from non-G10 countries.

Part Three

The Foreign Exchange
System of China

I. Overview

The foreign exchange control has been in place since the establishment of the People's Republic of China. Before 1979, due to severe lack of foreign exchange resources, the foreign exchange control was strictly enforced. Since the introduction of the economic reform and the policy of opening to the outside world, China's highly centralized foreign exchange control system has been greatly changed, resulting in less state intervention and greater role of market forces in line with the evolution of the socialist market economy. The reform of Chinese foreign exchange system accelerated in 1994 with the introduction of conditional current account convertibility, unification of exchange market and adoption of a market-based managed floating exchange rate. On November 27, 1996, China formally lifted all remaining current account restrictions and became an Article VIII member of the International Monetary Fund. The payment in transfer of foreign exchange for international transactions under current account was no longer subject to the government control or restriction.

The controls over capital account transactions have also been gradually liberalized. Foreign exchange administration of overseas investment was reformed to encourage domestic enterprises to go abroad. Qualified foreign institutional investors (QFII) were permitted to invest in domestic capital market within specified quota after being approved by the authorities in 2002. Insurance companies were permitted to use their own foreign exchange to invest in international capital market in 2004. External debt administration of Chinese-funded and foreign-funded banks was unified. The controls over the market access for foreign-funded financial institutions were lifted gradually. Multinational corporations were allowed to conduct internal operation of foreign exchange funds among their domestic member companies or between their domestic member companies and their overseas ones. Controls over cross-border capital transfers by individuals were loosened. Administration of foreign exchange from overseas direct investment was improved.

On July 21, 2005, RMB exchange rate regime was changed to a managed floating system with a reference to a basket of currencies. Non-financial institutions were permitted to participate in inter-bank spot foreign exchange market. RMB forward and swap contracts were permitted to trade. Foreign banks were permitted to do forward trade. On January 4, 2006, OTC trade was introduced in inter-bank spot foreign exchange market.

In order to improve foreign exchange administration and maintain strong balance of payments position, China promulgated the Regulations on Foreign Exchange Administration on January 29, 1996. The State Administration of Foreign Exchange (SAFE) is the agency responsible for foreign exchange administration. The SAFE has a similar branch structure similar to that of the PBC, China's central bank. The Bank of China remains the principal foreign exchange bank. Other banks and financial institutions, including affiliates of non-resident banks, may handle designated transactions with the approval of the SAFE.

Foreign exchange includes the following means of payments and assets denominated in a foreign currency that can be used for international settlement:

- Foreign currencies, including banknotes and coins;
- Payment vouchers denominated in foreign currency, including negotiable instruments, bank certificates of deposit and certificates of postal savings;
- Securities denominated in foreign currency, including government bonds, corporate bonds and stocks;
- Super-national currencies such as Special Drawing Rights and the Euro; and
- Other assets denominated in foreign currency.

The state implements a reporting system for balance of payments statistics. All entities and individuals involved in foreign exchange transactions that directly affect balance of payments must report data for compilation of balance of payments statistics. Foreign currency is prohibited from being circulated and shall not be quoted for pricing or settlement.

II. Exchange Arrangement

The Chinese currency is the Renminbi (RMB). After the dual exchange rates were unified in 1994, China adopted a managed floating exchange rate regime based on market supply and demand. During the Asian financial crisis period, China narrowed the floating band of the RMB exchange rate so as to curb deterioration of the crisis. Actually, improving the RMB exchange rate formation mechanism by giving full play to the market is always an unswerving objective of China. From July 21, 2005 onwards, China started the implementation of a managed floating exchange rate regime based on market supply and demand with a reference to a basket of currencies. The main content of this round of reform include the following three aspects:

First, change of the exchange rate adjustment method. A managed floating exchange rate regime was adopted . The exchange rate of RMB is no longer pegged to the US dollar; instead, it is floated according to supply and demand of the market with a reference to a basket of currencies. A "basket of currencies" here refers to some major currencies which are selected to form a currency basket endowed with corresponding weights according to the actual performance of China's external economy. The exchange rate of RMB is managed and adjusted in accordance with the economic and financial situation at home and abroad. On the basis of market supply and demand, the change of the multi lateral exchange rate indexes of RMB is calculated with a reference to the said currency basket, so as to maintain the basic stability of the RMB exchange rate at an adaptive and equilibrium level. This will help increase the flexibility of the exchange rate, curb the one-way speculation, and maintain the stability of the multi lateral exchange rate.

Second, change of parity formation and daily floating band. At the end of each business day after the market is closed, the PBC publicizes the closing price of the exchange rate on that day, which acts as the middle price for the transaction of the relevant currency against the RMB on the next business day. At the current stage, the daily floating band of the exchange rate of RMB/USD in the inter-bank foreign exchange market remains $+/-0.3\%$ of the central parity of USD/RMB publicized by the PBC, while the floating band of non-USD currencies against RMB is 3%.

Finally, adjustment of initial exchange rate. At 19 : 00, July 21, 2005, the central parity of the US dollar against the RMB was adjusted to RMB 8. 11 per USD 1. 00 as the middle price for trading among designated banks in the inter-bank foreign exchange market on the next business day, and from that time on, the designated banks could adjust the listing exchange rate for their clients. Reform of the exchange rate system of RMB focuses on the exchange rate formation mechanism instead of the quantitative change of its level. The scale of such an adjustment is mainly defined by China's trade surplus degree and the requirement of structural adjustment, with domestic enterprises' adaptability to structural adjustment being taken into consideration. On January 3, 2006, another adjustments was made in the formation of the central parity of the RMB against the US dollar, stating that the China Foreign Exchange Trading Center enquire prices from all market makers before the opening of the inter-bank foreign exchange market on each business day, and then calculates the weighted average of the remaining prices in the sample as the central rate of the RMB against the US dollar for the day, excluding the highest and lowest offers. The weights shall be determined by the China Foreign Exchange Trading Center in line with the transaction volumes of the market makers in the inter-bank foreign exchange market as well as other indicators such as the quoted prices. The designated foreign exchange banks may, on the basis of the said central rate, quote selling and buying prices of various currencies to customers at their own discretion within the specified limit of spread stipulated by the People's Bank of China.

III. Foreign Exchange Operations of Financial Institutions

Financial institutions, including designated foreign exchange banks, must be approved by the SAFE to engage in foreign exchange transactions. The authorized financial institutions are allowed to open foreign exchange accounts for their clients and conduct relevant foreign exchange operations. They are required to keep enough foreign exchange working capital in accordance with the relevant regulations on asset and liability ratios concerning their foreign exchange operations and loan loss provisions. Designated foreign exchange banks are required to use their own RMB funds to carry out business of purchases and sales of foreign exchange.

The SAFE take the responsibility of inspecting and supervising the foreign exchange business of financial institutions. Financial institutions undertaking foreign exchange operations shall submit to the SAFE their balance sheets, income statements, other financial and accounting statements and information of foreign exchange operations.

Financial institutions must apply for the termination of foreign exchange operations to the SAFE. Once the termination is approved, these financial institutions shall liquidate their foreign exchange claims and liabilities and have their licenses for foreign exchange operations revoked.

IV. Supervision of Foreign Exchange Accounts

1. Foreign Exchange Accounts with Domestic Institutions

Domestic institutions (both Chinese-funded and foreign-funded institutions) have the right to open foreign exchange accounts for current account transactions according to their own needs. If domestic institutions need to open a foreign exchange account under current account, they will first go to the local branches of SAFE to file their basic information by presenting business license (or registration certificate of mass organization) issued by the Administration of Industry and Commerce and the certificate of organzational code issued by Technology Supervision Bureau. The opening, altering and closing of a foreign exchange account under current account can go through the procedures directly at the designated foreign exchange banks. Banks should regulate the receipts and payments scope of the account. The SAFE will specify a ceiling of the account balance according to the utilization of the foreign exchange account every year.

Effective from May 1, 2006, quotas of foreign exchange in current account retained is the sum of 80 percent of foreign exchange current income and 50 percent of foreign exchange current expenditures in the previous year. The initial quota of foreign exchange retained by domestic institutions that need to open a foreign exchange account but had no foreign exchange current income and expenditures in the previous year is the equivalent of USD 500,000. The ceiling of a current account for donation, postal remittance, international contracting, international shipping and international bidding can be set at 100 percent of their foreign exchange proceeds, import and export enterprises and manufacturing enterprises with actual needs included.

Domestic institutions may retain a certain amount of foreign exchange verified by the SAFE. The amount exceeding the ceiling shall sold to a designated foreign exchange bank. Designated foreign exchange banks shall advise domestic institutions in 90 calendar days to sell foreign exchange once the balance ceiling is exceeded or report to the SAFE if the client fails to oblige in due time. The SAFE and its local branches have right to supervise the act of banks and domestic institutions.

Designated foreign exchange banks are required to formulate a unified rule for management of foreign exchange L/C (letter of credit) deposit accounts, submit it to the SAFE for record, and open foreign exchange L/C deposit accounts for risk control purpose according to the rule submitted. Foreign exchange L/C deposit accounts may not be used for any other purposes.

Individuals (both domestic and foreign residents) in China have freedom in deposit and withdrawal of foreign currencies. Individuals shall present one of their certificates of identity to open the account for deposit.

Domestic establishments may hold foreign exchange for capital account transactions as follows:

- external borrowing by domestic entities and foreign exchange loans of domestic Chinese funded financial institutions;
- foreign exchange of domestic entities for repayment of principal of domestic and external foreign exchange liabilities;
- foreign exchange of domestic entities from stock issuance;
- capital paid in foreign exchange by Chinese investors of foreign funded enterprises;

- foreign exchange remitted by overseas entities or individuals for establishing a foreign funded enterprise.

Entities may apply to the SAFE for opening a foreign exchange account for capital transactions and upon approval go through the account opening procedure at a designated foreign exchange bank. In granting such an approval, the SAFE shall verify the receipts and payments scope, operating duration and the balance ceiling of the account, and shall indicate the foregoing information in the account opening advice. Domestic entities converting funds in foreign exchange account for capital transactions are subject to the SAFE's approval.

The SAFE exercises annual inspections of foreign exchange accounts of capital transactions.

2. Overseas Foreign Exchange Accounts

Domestic entities which meet one of the following requirements may apply for opening a foreign exchange account abroad:

- expecting small amount income during a certain period of time abroad;
- expecting small amount expenditure during a certain period of time abroad;
- undertaking overseas construction projects; and
- issuing securities denominated in foreign currency abroad.

Domestic entities shall apply to the SAFE for opening an overseas foreign exchange account. The SAFE shall give a reply within 30 working days of receipts of documents and materials as required. Domestic entities with receipts and payments through an overseas foreign exchange account shall abide by regulations of the host country or region, and take effective management measures to ensure the safety of the funds in the account. Domestic entities shall use the overseas foreign exchange accounts according to the receipts and payments scope, balance ceiling and operating duration of the account verified by the SAFE, and the entities shall not lease, lend or cross use the accounts.

V. Current Account Transactions

Foreign exchange receipts of domestic institutions for current account transactions shall be repatriated home and shall not be deposited abroad without any special reasons. Foreign exchange receipts for current account transactions shall be deposited in the foreign exchange account within the retained quota or be sold to the designated foreign exchange banks in accordance with the regulations issued by the State Council on the sale, purchase, and payment of foreign exchange. Foreign exchange for current account payment and transfer may be paid from the account or be purchased from designated foreign exchange banks upon the presentation of valid documents and commercial bills.

After the foreign exchange restrictions on current account transactions were lifted in 1996, the SAFE has taken actions to verify the authenticity of foreign exchange flows in trading for preventing illegal activities such as flight of foreign exchange or fraudulent obtainment of foreign exchange. In recent years, the SAFE has taken a series of measures to reform verification system on importing and exporting in order to adapt to the development for economic and trading situations.

To enforce the repatriation of export proceeds, the SAFE and its local branches undertake to verify collection of export earnings. When exporting goods abroad, domestic export entities are required to undergo the verification procedures. The customs offices shall accept and handle declaration for export based on verification certificate within validity period. Only after no mistakes are found in the examination can customs permit clearance. After goods have been shipped out of Chinese territory, the customs shall write their opinion and stamp with "proof seal" on the verification certificate, with which the exporter goes through verification procedures. The verification procedure is completed through "Net Working Export Verification System". The enterprises can go online for the verification operations. What they will do is to send the information on verification certificate, commercial invoices and declaration form to the SAFE within 180 days of the date of customs declaration through Internet. If domestic institutions do not follow the verification procedure or send false information to the SAFE, they may not be given the verification certificate for export and the customs shall not allow the clearance.

When making import payments, with purchased foreign exchange or from their foreign exchange accounts, importers also have to go through the verification procedures. Importers shall apply with the SAFE for entering "Importer List of External Payment in Foreign Exchange" by presenting the approval issued by the Ministry of Commerce, business license issued by the Administration of Industry and Commerce, and the certificate of organizational code issued by the Technology Supervision Bureau. Importer outside of the "Importer List" may not make import payments directly in the designated foreign exchange bank. The SAFE publishes "Importer List" subject to authenticity verification to the designated foreign exchange banks according to the verification performance of importers. Importers on this list shall be subject to authenticity verification by the SAFE for at least 1 month.

Foreign exchange owned by individuals can be held at their own discretion, deposited either in banks or sold to the designated foreign exchange banks. Individuals' foreign exchange savings deposits can be withdrawn freely.

Domestic residents in China can purchase foreign exchange in the designated foreign exchange banks. However, the SAFE implement the control of annual quota. The annual quota is the equivalence of USD 50,000/person. Every Chinese resident is eligible to purchase foreign exchange at designated foreign exchange banks on the strength of the principal ID certificates after declaring the purpose of use. Foreign exchange purchases exceeding the annual quota are subject to bona fide verification by the banks according to the foreign exchange regulations.

The remittance and /or carrying of foreign exchange abroad for such income resulting from the possession of assets in China are allowed upon the presentation of the specific certifying documents at the designated foreign exchange banks. Foreign exchange assets held by Chinese residents in the form of payment vouchers, negotiable securities denominated in foreign currency etc. , may be taken or sent abroad without authorization of the SAFE.

Foreign exchange sent or carried in by foreign institutions and residents in China can be held at their own discretion, deposited or sold to the designated foreign exchange banks. Such foreign exchange can also be remitted or taken abroad upon the presentation of valid documents. Legitimate RMB income of foreign institutions and foreign residents in China may be converted into foreign currency and repatriated upon the presentation of required documents to the designated foreign exchange banks.

Individuals shall present to the customs office valid documents for carrying a large sum of foreign exchange exceeding the specified limit outside China. Individuals who carry in a large sum of money exceeding the specified limit shall report to the customs office.

VI. Capital Account Transactions

All foreign exchange receipts by domestic establishments from capital account transactions shall be repatriated, unless otherwise specified by the State Council. All foreign exchange receipts from capital transactions shall be deposited in foreign exchange accounts opened with designated foreign exchange banks in accordance with the relevant state regulations, such revenues can be also sold to a designated foreign exchange bank upon the approval by the SAFE.

1. Overseas Investment

The source of foreign exchange for overseas investment by domestic entities must be reviewed by the SAFE before the application for such investment is filed with the relevant government agencies.

Profits or other foreign exchange income of Chinese investors from their overseas invest-ment could be remitted home or kept abroad. Whenever an enterprise winds up its overseas business, the investor shall repatriate all of the assets.

2. External Borrowing in Loans

External borrowing in loans may be undertaken by the government agencies designated by the State Council, as well as financial institutions and other enterprises duly authorized by the SAFE. External borrowing in loans by foreign-funded enterprises shall be filed with the SAFE for records.

International commercial loans refer to borrowing by domestic entities from financial in-stitutions, enterprises, individuals or other economic organizations outside China territory. Export credits, international financial leasing, compensation trade repayment of foreign ex-change, foreign exchange deposits of institutions and individuals outside the Chinese territo-ry, project financing and trade financing with a maturity of more than 90 days, and foreign exchange loans in other forms are all taken as international commercial loans.

The People's Bank of China is one of the organs in charge of the examination and ap-proval of the international commercial loans for domestic entities. International commercial loans for financial institutions is subject to the provisions of the People's Bank of China on foreign exchange asset-liability ratio control over financial institutions.

A non-financial entity must satisfy the following conditions when needing international commercial loans:

- having made profits for the latest three consecutive years, being licensed for import and export and engaged in an industry encouraged by the State;
- with sound financial management;
- for a trading enterprise legal entity, its ratio of net-to-total assets shall not be lower than 15% and for a non-trading one, the ratio shall not be lower than 30%; and
- the sum of such loans borrowed and the guarantees of foreign liabilities shall not ex-ceed 50% of the foreign exchange equivalent of the net assets of the borrower or its foreign exchange earnings in the previous year.

Without the approval of the SAFE, domestic entities are not allowed to convert their foreign exchange loans into local currency for the payment of domestic liabilities.

3. External Guarantee

External guarantee may be offered by the qualified financial institutions and enterprises meeting the government requirements and approved by the SAFE.

External guarantees refer to those in the form of guarantee letters, stand-by letters of credit, promissory notes, checks and drafts, mortgages on real properties, hypothecation on movables, which are provided by domestic entities to institutions outside China or foreign-funded financial institutions inside China with the pledges that when the debtor fails to perform the contract, the guarantors shall perform the obligation of repayment. Such guarantees include:

- Guarantees for accounts under compensation trade; and
- Guarantees for engineering projects outside China.

The PBC empowers the SAFE to be responsible for the examination, approval, administration and registration of guarantees made for external liabilities.

The combined balance of guarantees made overseas, foreign exchange guarantees within Chinese territory and foreign exchange debts of a financial institution may not exceed 20 times their foreign exchange funds. The balance of guarantees provided overseas by a non-financial institution shall not exceed 50% of its net assets or its foreign exchange revenue in the previous year. Guarantors may not provide guarantee for loss-making enterprises.

4. Registration System for External Debt

The state adopts a registration system for external debt, enabling up-to-date information on the country's external debt to be collected exactly and completely so as to effectively control the size of external borrowing, raise the efficiency of using foreign funds and expedite national economic growth. All domestic entities are required to register their external debts in accordance with the regulations formulated by the State Council on monitoring statistics of external debt. The SAFE shall take the responsibility for the nationwide collection and monitoring of data on external debts and get them published on a regular basis.

The registration of external debt may be performed on a case-by-case basis or periodically. The registration certificate for external debt shall be formulated, signed and issued by the SAFE.

Debtors are required to open external debt accounts with the authorization by the SAFE for transferring their external loan from other countries to China against the Registration Certificate of External Debts. Debtors with approval to keep their external loan proceeds abroad and those whose loans do not have to be transferred to China are required to open debt service accounts by presenting their registration for external debt. Once debtors fully clear their external debts as recorded in the Registration Certificate of External Debt, banks shall cancel the external debt accounts or the debt service accounts. The debtors in turn are required to submit their Registration Certificate of External Debt to the SAFE within 15 days.

VII. Reporting of Balance of Payments Statistics

The balance-of-payments statistics are essential to macro economic management. It reflects the economic relationship of China with the outside world. In order to improve the balance-of-payments statistics, the *Regulations on Reporting of Balance of Payments Transactions* were promulgated on September 14, 1995.

The reporting of balance of payments statistics covers all economic transactions between Chinese residents and non-residents. Here the term "Chinese resident" encompasses:

- A natural person who resides in China for more than one year, excluding students, and patients who are receiving medical treatment in China as well as foreign staffs who work in embassies and consulates in China and their dependents;

- Chinese nationals who stay abroad for less than one year, Chinese students studying abroad, Chinese nationals receiving medical treatment abroad, as well as Chinese staffs who work in Chinese embassies and consulates abroad and their dependents;

- Legal entities established within the territory of China (including foreign-funded enterprises and foreign financial institutions), as well as resident institution of foreign legal entities (excluding those affiliated to official international organizations and foreign embassies and consulates); and

- Chinese government agencies, organizations and military establishments.

In accordance with the procedures set out in the *Statistics Law of People's Republic of China*, the SAFE is responsible for implementing, monitoring and examining the reporting of balance of payments statistics; compiling and publishing the statements on balance of payments and international investment positions; formulating and revising the By-Laws to these Regulations, as well as designing and issuing balance of payments report forms. All government departments shall facilitate the reporting of balance of payments statistics.

Chinese residents shall report their transactions of balance of payments in a timely, accurate, and comprehensive manner. .

The SAFE can carry out surveys or take census on transactions of balance of payments. It has the right to examine and verify the statistics reported by Chinese residents. Reporting individuals and institutions shall submit the required data and facilitate such examination and verification. The SAFE shall keep strict confidentiality for the reporters as well as the reported data, and use such data only for the purpose of compiling balance of payments. Those engaged in balance of payments data collection and compilation are prohibited from disseminating the reported data to any other institutions or individuals unless otherwise specified by the law.

VIII. Foreign Exchange Business

The lifeblood of international trade and investment is foreign exchange. No foreign transaction is possible without foreign exchange. For example, in an American shop at Macy's, the Gap, or K-Mart, many of the products offered are foreign made. Although the Americans buy these goods with dollars, the original purchase by the American department store requires foreign exchange. When Japanese securities dealers buy U. S. Treasury bonds, foreign exchange is required. Oil is priced and traded with dollars, thus, any foreign country importing oil must obtain dollars in the foreign exchange market.

1. Foreign Exchange — Some Definitions

Foreign exchange, or forex, is money in foreign currency. All foreign Currency, consistingof funds held with banks abroad, or bills or cheques, again in foreign currency and payable abroad, are termed foreign exchange. All these play a part in the relations between a bank and its customers. In the trading of foreign exchange between banks, which is the job of the foreign exchange dealer, only foreign currency held with banks abroad is concerned. For the purposes of this book, the term "foreign exchange" applies only to bank balances denominated in foreign currency.

Foreign bank notes are not foreign exchange in the narrower sense. They can be converted into foreign exchange, however, provided they can be placed without restriction on the credit of an ordinary commercial account abroad. The exchange regulations of some countries do not allow this conversion of bank notes into foreign exchange, although the operation in reverse is nearly always permitted.

A currency, whether in foreign exchange or bank notes, is usually convertible if the person holding it can convert it. In other words foreign exchange means a foreign currency which can be changed freely into another. A distinction needs to be made, however, between unrestricted convertibility and the various forms of partial convertibility. The Swiss franc, for example, is fully convertible whether the holder is resident in Switzerland or abroad regardless of whether current payments or financial transactions are involved.

Many countries, on the other hand, recognize only external, or non-resident convertibility. Until October 1979, for instance, this was still the case with the United Kingdom: if a German exporter, say, had sterling funds in a British bank, he could (and can) simply instruct the bank to convert his pounds into any other currencies and remit the proceeds abroad; but a person domiciled in Britain could not as a general rule, export capital except with the consent of the Bank of England.

Exchange regulations may also make a distinction, as far as convertibility is concerned, between funds arising from current transactions (in goods and services) and those from purely financial operations. Only the latter is subject in some degree to a restriction on convertibility. In a few countries, this distinction between commercial and financial transactions has culminated in the establishment of two tier markets. This is the case in South Africa, and has applied temporarily, for instance, to France, Italy and Belgium in recent years.

2. Banks and the Foreign Exchange Market

The banks are the natural intermediary between foreign exchange supply and demand. The main task of a bank's foreign exchange department is to enable its commercial or financial customers to convert assets held in one currency into funds of another currency. This conversion can take the form of a "spot" transaction or a "forward" operation. Banks engaged in the foreign exchange business tend inevitably to establish a uniform price range for a particular currency throughout the financial centres of the world. If at a given moment the market rate in one centre deviates too far from the average, a balance will soon be restored by arbitrage, which is the process of taking advantage of price differences in different places. It can be seen that the foreign exchange market acts as a very important regulator in a free monetary system.

Big banks and a number of local banks specializing in foreign exchange business have a foreign exchange department with the qualified dealers. But banks which merely carry out their customers' instructions and do no foreign exchange business on their own account do not really require the services of a foreign exchange expert. For these it will be sufficient to have someone with a general knowledge of foreign exchange business because his role in practice will be that of an intermediary between the customer and a bank in the foreign exchange market.

A foreign exchange dealer acquires his professional skill largely through experience. Here we should point out how important close cooperation is among a team of dealers. The group can work together smoothly only if each member is able to bring his/her own initiative into full play. We must not forget that, almost incessantly, all the dealers are doing business simultaneously on different telephones, and when large transactions are completed the rates may change, whereupon the other dealers must be brought up to date immediately. It is essential for a dealer to have the knack of doing two things one time so that he can do business on the telephone and at the same time take note of the new prices announced by his colleagues.

Professional foreign exchange dealing requires advanced technical equipment. Business is done with telephone (with many direct lines to important names) and teleprinter, depending on distance and convenience. At many modern banks, the foreign exchange department uses the Reuter's dealing system, which combines the functions of a teleprinter with those of a television screen. Spot and forward rates of the most important currencies and money market rates are displayed on a number of rate boards, remotely controlled by the chief dealers. Current quotations can then not only be used by the bank's own dealers but also transmitted electronically to other banks. Electronic data processing equipment is employed to keep track instantly of the exchange positions, and for the administrative handling of the business done. Cross rates are worked out with the help of electronic desk top calculators.

The foreign exchange market is considered the largest global financial market and, perhaps, the most efficient one. Volume traded in the market and the depth of trading has much to do with this supposition. For example, the total international trade in goods and services on an annual basis is approximately USD4.5 trillion. Another USD1 − 1.5 trillion per year can be added to this total for foreign direct investment by all countries. The global volume for portfolio investment transactions, such as equities, bonds, and derivatives, probably amounts to USD1 − 2 trillion per year. Thus, total international commercial transactions on an annual basis amount to as much as USD8 trillion per year. If annual foreign exchange market volume amounts to as much as USD250 − 300 trillion or more, the ratio of foreign exchange traded to the amount actually needed for international transactions may be as high as 30 : 1. Foreign exchange dealers, when queried by banking regulators as to why this ratio is so high, suggesting it should be closer to a 1 : 1 ratio, justify such trading volume by stating that the liquidity furnished by 30 : 1 ratio is necessary for the presence of an orderly and viable market where exchange rates are stable and volatility is minimal.

3. Foreign Exchange Quotations

How are foreign exchange rates quoted? Most countries use direct quotation, that is, the exchange rates of the domestic currency give the equivalent of a certain quantity of the foreign currency quoted (normally one hundred units, but only one unit in the case of the dollar and the sterling). There are, however, exceptions to the rule. Great Britain in earlier times did not have the decimal system, and it was theref⋯ easier to quote the value of one pound sterling in terms of the foreign currency: this method of indirect quotation is still used now even though in 1971 Great Britain also switched to the decimal system. In the

United States, at least for domestic purposes, the direct quotation is used, which means that the prices for foreign currencies are expressed in dollars; in their international foreign exchange activities, the American banks however adhere to the "European terms", which for them is indirect quotation.

"Arbitrage" in the original sense meant making a profit by taking quick advantage of price differences prevailing in different markets, a process which of course tended to make such differences disappear. Nowadays, in all major financial centres, rates for a specific currency tend to be the same everywhere. Arbitrage in the old sense is thus hardly possible anymore. Arbitrage now simply means professional business as against customer-related business.

The electronic rate board in the foreign exchange department of a large Swiss bank will thus display the rates for the dollar against the other major currencies rather than rates for foreign currencies expressed in Swiss francs. The same is true in an analogous way for banks in other financial centres.

On July 22, 2006, for instance (the date is arbitrarily chosen), exchange rates were as per the following table (we shall use these rates in the practical examples):

Currency	Bid/Offered
EUR/USD	1. 2690/93
USD/JPY	116. 18/22
USD/CHF	1. 2365/70
GBP/USD	1. 8582/87
AUD/USD	0. 7526/30
USD/CAD	1. 1382/87
EUR/JPY	147. 45/49

The above buying and selling rates are applied to dealings between banks. Slightly wider margins may be applied in transactions with clients.

If we have a quote of 1. 2690/93 for EUR/USD, the first rate is the buying rate for the Euro or the selling rate for the U. S. Dollar, while the second is the selling rate for the Euro or the buying rate for the U. S. Dollar.

Over the past few years, trading in "Cross Currencies" has increased considerably and naturally, clients and smaller banks may often wish to do business with us against currencies other than the dollar, for instance, CHF against CAD, or GBP against CAD. In such cases we have to work out the so-called "Cross Rates". At this stage we will just briefly explain how we arrive at the formula for calculating "Cross Rates".

How can we get the cross rate for CHF/CAD? First, let's work out the middle rates for

USD/CHF, USD/CAD and GBP/USD.

The result is obtained by establishing a so-called chain equation:

X CAD = CHF100,

if   CHF1. 2368 = USD1, if

USD1 = CAD1. 1385

(Thus: the product of the right hand side of the equation divided by the product of the left hand side.)

CHF100 = 100 × 1 × 1. 1385/1. 2368 × 1 = CAD92. 0520

Now let's work out the exchange rate of GBP in terms of CAD.

XCAD = GBP1, if

GBP1 = USD1. 8585, if

USD1 = CAD1. 1385

Thus,

GBP1 = 1 × 1. 8585 × 1. 1385/1 × 1 = CAD2. 1159

(You will have noted the influence the indirect quotation has on the formula!)

What are "long" and "short" positions, and how do they arise?

A bank active in international business has to maintain sufficient working balances in all major currencies for the conduct of international payments.

As a rule, current or checking accounts maintained with foreign correspondents must not be overdrawn, but in any case, if a debit balance develops, briefly and by chance, we would have to pay appropriate debit interest. Such working (credit) balances are foreign currency assets and thus "long" positions. Since these foreign currencies had to be bought with another currency — let's assume with our domestic currencies — we are automatically "short" with the respective amounts in our domestic currency, i. e. we have corresponding liabilities in Swiss francs.

Our foreign exchange position is, however, in most cases by no means identical with the working balances maintained, for a number of reasons. First, Swiss banks will often not be enthusiastic about maintaining large working balances in all major trading currencies because of the inherent exchange risk, and will therefore seek to eliminate this risk. For this purpose, instead of buying the required foreign currencies on a spot basis, we create them by means of a swap transaction, i. e. , we buy them spot but simultaneously sell them forward. Example:

We need working balances in Yen but do not want to run the exchange risk. Thus, instead of simply buying, say, Yen100 million against Swiss francs, we simultaneously sell the Yen forward; our so-called nostro account with the Japanese correspondent will thus show a credit balance of Yen100 mill. as a result of the spot purchase, but our exchange position in Yen will be zero because we have sold forward the same amount.

Money market operations can also result in "short" and "long" positions different from our working balances. Let us assume the nostro account with our Paris correspondent is long with EUR1,000,000. We now receive a EUR10,000,000 3-month deposit from a customer; we decide (for various reasons) to convert this sum into USD and place a corresponding 3-month dollar deposit. Our exchange position in EUR would thus be "short" to the tune of EUR9,000,000 (assets of EUR1,000,000 minus liabilities of EUR10,000,000), although our working balance is still EUR1,000,000.

Changes in our foreign exchange positions are of course arising continuously from our dealing activities. If we start the day with a "long" position in USD10,000,000 and later sell USD2,000,000 spot to a customer and USD3,000,000 3-months forward to a bank, our "long" position is reduced to USD5,000,000.

The bank's foreign exchange department has to keep constant track of the positions in the various currencies, which in modern trading rooms is done by computers. This so-called "dealer position" has to reflect our exposure in various currencies regardless of maturities; it has to record not only spot but also forward transactions and currency exposures resulting from money market operations (the term "risk position" is frequently used to make clear that one refers to the total position, i. e. , the one including forward positions, and not just to the spot position). On the other hand, the currency exposures are measured on a net basis. If we receive a EUR10,000,000 3-month deposit and place again a EUR10,000,000 deposits, in the balance sheet both the foreign currency liabilities and assets would increase but the dealer's position would not change because our net exposure in Euro remains unchanged.

4. Financial Instruments

A. *Spot Transaction*

Typical foreign exchange transactions involve trading of one currency for another in the spot or cash market, or forward transactions. Spot transactions involve today's prices of currency and delivery of the currency within two business days, except for Canadian dollar (CAD), which must be delivered in one day. For example: On 10 Oct. , 2006 I buy and settle value on 12 Oct. , 2006.

The "value date" given to a transaction is the date on which the money must be paid to the parties involved. For all spot, or current, exchange operations the value date is set as the second working day after the date on which the transaction is concluded (to allow for the administrative handling of the deals).

Since banks are closed on Saturdays and Sundays, spot deals made on Thursday will show Monday as value or settlement date.

It is possible, though exceptional, to conclude foreign exchange transactions for delivery one business day after conclusion of the deal (or sometimes even value same day). Such deals will however not be made at the quoted spot rates but a slightly different rates, depending on the interest rates for the currencies concerned.

B. Forward Operations

Foreign exchange can be bought and sold not only on a spot or cash basis, but also on a forward basis (for delivery on a stipulated future date). Theoretically, the forward price for a currency can be identical with the spot price. Almost always, however, the forward price in practice is either higher (premium) or lower (discount) than the spot price.

Forward transactions can serve a number of different purposes. First of all, by doing forward transactions one can cover, or hedge, an otherwise existing exchange risk, be it of a commercial (trade) or financial nature. In connection with money market (deposit) transactions, we encounter the swap operation, which is the combination of a spot purchase with a simultaneous forward sale (or vice versa). To avoid confusion when talking about forward business, dealers use the term "outright" operation when it is a single forward transaction, as against a forward transaction forming part of a swap operation. Outright deals can, as just seen, be a hedge; however, they are speculative transactions if they lack a commercial or financial background.

International trade always creates the need for forward operations, if the exchange risk is to be hedged. Let us consider the case of a Swiss importer who has bought goods in Germany, invoiced in Euro, payable in 90 days. To eliminate the risk of a significant rise of the Euro in the meantime and also to have the basis for an exact price calculation, he buys the Euro 90 days forward (outright). In the converse case a Swiss exporter knows that in three months he will receive U. S. Dollars in payment for his exports. Here again, in order to eliminate the exchange risk, he hedges by selling the U. S. Dollars three months forward (outright). Not to do these forward transactions would be equivalent to speculating, on a fall of the Euro in the first case, or a rise of the U. S. Dollars in the second case.

Currency exposures, and the need to hedge them, can also arise from a variety of nontrade operations:

- Securities investments, money market deposits, loans extended to subsidiaries abroad, direct investments, etc., if done in foreign currencies all represent foreign currency assets, the currency risk can be covered by selling the respective currencies forward.

- Borrowings in capital markets abroad, for instance, if done in foreign currencies, represent foreign currency liabilities, the inherent exchange risk can be hedged by forward purchases of the respective currencies.

In this connection, it should be noted that hedging by means of forward operations is possible even if the underlying transaction is of a medium- or long-term nature. For many currencies, forward deals of more than twelve months are difficult to arrange, but by regularly renewing, say, a twelve month forward contract at maturity, we can match the hedge with the tenor of the underlying longer term transaction. True, in such a case one only knows the cost of the hedging for the first period while the costs for the ensuing periods are not known in advance; this, however, need not be a reason for not hedging.

One normally hedges "weak" currencies against "stronger" ones, by selling the former forward, and to many people "weak" currencies are those at a discount. Yet, it has happened many times that the supposedly "weak" currency strengthened, while the supposedly "strong" one (at a premium) declined.

Examples: From February to October 1992, sterling weakened from 1. 82 to 1. 61, although the pound was always at a premium. From the end of 1992 to the beginning of 1995, the dollar strengthened against most other hard currencies despite the fact that it was constantly at a discount. In these special instances, it would have been advisable to hedge sterling against dollars (i. e. buy forward dollars).

C. *Swaps*

Swaps refer to two simultaneous inseparable contract deals, the first for spot delivery, and the second (the contrary of spot) for future delivery (in this case your position is squared).

Or, in other words, "swap" means the simultaneous purchase and sale of identical amounts of a currency for different value dates.

Swaps can be done in the following ways:

- Overnight swap (O/N) —the time difference between purchase and sale of identical amount of a currency is just within overnight;
- Tomorrow next swap—purchase some amount of a currency at value date of tomorrow and sell the same amount of the same currency on the day after;
- Spot next swap (S/N) —make a spot deal of a currency and deliver immediately and make contrary deal on the next date of the spot deal;
- Week end swap—make a spot deal of a currency and make a contrary deal to be delivered a week later;

- 1, 2, or 3 etc. months swap—make a spot deal of a currency and make 1, 2, or 3 months forward deal of the same currency.

D. Currency Options

With the transition to floating exchange rates, central banks were no longer obliged to maintain exchange rates within narrow limits as defined in the *Bretton Woods Agreement*. Continuing disequilibrium in international balance of payments can lead to increasing fluctuations in exchange rates, especially after liberalization of cross border capital movements. The need to eliminate currency risks therefore become extremely urgent. The market for foreign exchange options, set up in the early 1980s, was a decisive step in minimizing exchange rate risks and creating greater flexibility than had previously been possible with existing instruments.

Whereas a forward transaction provides the possibility of setting an exchange rate for a future foreign exchange transaction, the buyer of the option acquires the right, but not the obligation, to go ahead with the contract, i. e. , to take up the option or to allow it to expire. It is therefore possible to hedge against a currency loss as well as to benefit from any profit from a foreign exchange transaction.

The following are types of (European) foreign exchange option contracts:

i. Call option:

The right to buy a certain amount of a currency at a fixed rate (strike price) with a prearranged expiry date.

ii. Put option:

The right to sell a certain amount of a currency at a fixed rate (strike price) with a pre-arranged expiry date.

It should be noted that the right of the buyer does not imply the obligation to exercise an option.

The buyer of an option decide whether or not he will take up (call) or supply (put) the amount of a currency stipulated in the contract after he pays a premium for this right. The seller (option writer) is obliged to sell (call) or buy (put) the underlying assets after he receives the premium from the buyer and concludes the contract.

E. Futures Transactions

Futures transactions are always traded on exchanges. In order to be marketable on exchanges, futures contracts are standardized in terms of quantity, settlement dates and quotation. While currency futures have not been able to get established in Europe due to the efficient and more flexible forward exchange business, interest rate futures have achieved some significance. A lot has been heard about financial innovations over the last few years in general, and in particular, about standardized futures. In this context, numerous new products have been developed on American forward exchanges. Together with the traditional transactions in goods and metals (commodity futures), a large number of financial contracts (financial futures) exist today on various exchanges. These include futures on stocks, interest rates, currencies and stock indexes. Since November 9, 1990, contracts on stock index futures with the Swiss Market Index (SMI) as a reference have been traded on the SOFFEX (Swiss Options and Financial Futures Exchange). Within the Swiss Bank Corporation Group, interest rate and currency options are traded via SBCI Futures Inc. , New York.

Notes

1. **accelerate** [æk'seləreit] *v.* start to go faster

2. **quota** ['kwəutə] *n.* an official limit on the number or amount of sth. that is allowed in a particular period

3. **regime** [rei'ʒi:m] *n.* a particular system of management

4. **OTC**: *abbr* over the counter

5. **promulgate** ['prɔməlgeit] *v.* make a new law come into effect by announcing it officially

6. **voucher** ['vautʃə(r)] *n.* ticket that can be used instead of money for a particular purpose

7. **compilation** [ˌkɔmpi'leiʃən] *n.* process of making a book, list, etc. form a different pieces of information

8. **index** ['indeks] *n.* a system by which prices, costs etc. can be compared to those of a previous date

9. **parity** ['pæriti] *n.* equality between the units of money from two different countries

10. **ratio** ['reiʃiəu] *n.* a relationship between two amounts that is represented by a pair of numbers showing how much greater one amount is than the other

11. **unswerving** [ʌn'swə:viŋ] *adj.* firm and dependable especially in loyalty

12. **ceiling** ['si:liŋ] *n.* the largest number or amount of sth. that is officially allowed

13. **bid** [bid] *v.* ① offer to pay a particular price for goods ② offer to do work or provide services for a specific price, in competition with other offers

14. **repatriate** [ri:'pætrieit] *v.* send profits or money to one's own country

15. **bona fide** [bəunə'faidi] *adj.* true, real

16. **negotiable** [ni'gəuʃjəbl] *adj.* that can be exchanged for money

17. **maturity** [məˈtjuəriti] *n.* the time when a financial arrangement becomes ready to be paid

18. **expedite** [ˈekspidait] *v.* make a process happen more quickly

19. **domicile** [ˈdɔmisail] *v.* live

20. **culminate** [ˈkʌlmineit] *v.* reach the highest point of development

21. **deviate** [ˈdiːvieit] *v.* change what you are doing so that you are not following or expected plan idea etc.

22. **decimal** [ˈdesiməl] *adj.* a system based on the number 10

23. **analogous** [əˈnæləgəs] *adj.* similar to another situation or thing

Questions for discussion

1. What are the key points for the latest foreign exchange system reform ?

2. What does foreign exchange include ?

3. What are the requirements for domestic institutions for opening foreign exchange accounts abroad ?

4. Narrate the import and export verification procedure .

5. What does Chinese resident include ?

6. Give the definition of foreign exchange.

7. Compare direct and indirect quotations.

8. What does arbitrage mean ?

9. Give the definition of spot and forward transaction.

10. Tell the difference between forward and futures transactions.

Part Four

Accounting

I. Financial Accounting

1. Definition

Financial accounting is the system that measures business activities, processes such information into reports, and communicates these findings to decision makers. Financial statements are the documents that report on an individual's or an organization's business in monetary amounts.

Bookkeeping is a procedural element of accounting as arithmetic is a procedural element of mathematics. Increasingly, people are using computers to do much of the detailed bookkeeping work at all levels in households, businesses, and organizations of all types.

2. Users of Accounting Information

Decision makers beg for information. The more important decision, the greater the need for relevant information. Virtually all businesses and most individuals keep accounting records to aid decision making. Most of the material herein describes business situations, but the principles of accounting apply to the financial considerations of individuals as well. The following sections discuss the range of people and group who use accounting information and the decisions they make.

Individuals. People such as Melissa Roberts use accounting information in day-to-day affairs to manage their bank accounts, to evaluate job prospects, to make investments, and to decide whether to rent or to buy a house.

Businesses. Managers of businesses use accounting information to set goals for their organizations, to evaluate their progress toward those goals, and to take corrective action if necessary. Decisions based on accounting information may include which building and equipment to purchase, how much merchandise inventory to keep on hand, and how much cash to borrow.

Investors and Creditors. Investors provide the money that businesses need to begin operations. To decide whether to help start a new venture, potential investors evaluate what return they can reasonably expect on their investment. Those people who do investments monitor the progress of the business by analyzing the company's financial statements and by keeping up with its developments in the business press, for example, the *Wall Street Journal*, *Business Week*, *Forbes*, and *Fortune*. Accounting reports are a major source of information for the business press.

Before making a loan, potential lenders determine the borrower's ability to meet scheduled payments. This evaluation includes a projection of future operations, which is partly based on accounting information.

Government Regulatory Agencies. Most organizations face government regulations. For example, the Securities and Exchange Commission (SEC), a federal agency requires businesses to disclose certain financial information to the investing public. The SEC, like many government agencies, bases its regulatory activity in part on the accounting information that is received from firms.

Taxing Authorities. The amount of the tax is figured by using accounting information. Businesses determine their sales tax based on their accounting records that show how much they have sold. Individuals and businesses compute their income tax based on their recorded earnings.

Non-profit Organizations. Non-profit organizations such as churches, most hospitals, government agencies, and colleges, which operate for purposes other than to earn a profit, use accounting information in much the same way as profit-oriented businesses do. Both profit organizations and non-profit organizations deal with budgets, payrolls, rent payments, and the like all from the accounting system.

Other users. Employees and labor unions may make wage demands based on the accounting information that shows their employer's reported income. Consumer groups and the general public are also interested in the amount of income that businesses earn. For example, during times of fuel shortages consumer groups have charged that oil companies have earned "obscene profits". On a more positive note, newspapers report on "improved profit pictures" of companies as the nation emerges from an economic recession. Such news, based on accounting information, is related to our standard of living.

3. Specialized Accounting Services

Because accounting affects people in many different fields, public accounting and private accounting include specialized services.

A. *Public Accounting*

Auditing is the accounting's most significant service to the public. An audit is the independent examination that ensures the reliability of the accounting reports that management prepares and submits to investors, creditors, and others outside the business. In carrying out an audit, CPAs from outside a business examine the business' financial statements. If the CPAs believe that these documents are a fair presentation of the business' operations, the CPAs give a professional opinion stating that the firm's financial statements are in accordance with generally accepted accounting principles. Why is the audit so important? Creditors considering loans want assurance that the facts and figures the borrower submits are reliable. Stockholders, who have invested in the company, need to know that the picture of financial management is complete. In addition, government agencies need accurate accounting information from businesses.

Tax accounting has two aims: complying with the tax laws and minimizing the taxes to be paid. Because in U. S. federal income tax rates range as high as 31 percent for individuals and 34 percent for corporations, reducing income tax is an important management consideration. Tax work by accountants consists of preparing tax returns and planning business transactions in order to minimize taxes. CPAs advise individuals on what types of investments to make and on how to structure their transactions.

Management consulting is the catchall term that describes the wide scope of advice CPAs provide to help managers run a business. As CPAs conduct audits, they look deep into a business' operations. With the insight they gain, they often make suggestions for improvements in the business' management structure and accounting systems. Management consulting is the fastest growing service provided by accountants.

B. *Private Accounting*

Cost accounting analyzes a business' costs to help managers control expenses. Good cost accounting records guide managers in pricing their products and services to achieve greater profits. Also, cost accounting information shows management when a product is not profitable and therefore should be dropped.

Budgeting sets sales and profit goals and develops detailed plans for achieving those goals. Some of the most successful companies in the United States have been pioneers in the field of budgeting, Procter & Gamble and General Electric, for example.

Information systems design identifies the organization's information needs, both internal and external. By using flow charts and manuals, designers develop and implement the system to meet those needs.

Internal auditing is performed by a business' own accountants. Large organizations, Motorola, Bank of America, and 3M among them, maintain a staff of internal auditors. These accountants evaluate the firm's own accounting and management systems to improve operating efficiency and ensure that employees follow management's policies.

Financial accounting provides information to people outside the firm, for example, creditors, stockholders, government agencies, such as the SEC, and the general public.

Management accounting generates confidential information for internal decision makers, such as top executives, department heads, college deans, and hospital administrators.

4. Accounting Concepts and Principles

Accounting practices rest on certain guidelines. The rules that govern how accountants identify, measure, process, and communicate financial information fall under the heading GAAP, which stands for generally accepted accounting principles.

Generally accepted accounting principles include not only principles but also concepts and methods that identify the proper way to produce accounting information. Generally accepted accounting principles are very much like the law or a set of rules for conducting behavior in a way acceptable to the majority of people. GAAP rests on a conceptual framework written by the Financial Accounting Standards Board. The primary objective of financial reporting is to provide information useful for making investment and lending decisions. To be useful, information must be relevant, reliable, and comparable. Accountants strive to meet these goals in the information they produce. However, you need to understand the entity concept, the reliability principle, the cost principle, the going concern concept, and the stable monetary unit concept. These are basic to your first exposure to accounting.

A. The Entity Concept

The most basic concept in accounting is that of the entity. An accounting entity is an organization or a section of an organization that stands apart from other organizations and individuals as a separate economic unit. From an accounting perspective, sharp boundaries are drawn around each entity so as not to confuse its affairs with those of other entities.

Consider GM, a huge organization made up of its Chevrolet, Buick, Oldsmobile, Cadillac, and Pontiac divisions. GM management considers each division as a separate accounting entity, and the following example shows why. Suppose sales in the Oldsmobile division are dropping drastically. GM would do well to come up with an immediate solution to the problem. But if sales figures from all five divisions are treated as a single amount, then management will not even know the Company is not selling enough Oldsmobiles.

In summary, business transactions should not be confused with personal transactions. Similarly, the transactions of different entities should not be accounted for together. Each entity should be evaluated separately.

B. The Reliability (or Objectivity) Principle

Accounting records and statements are based on the most reliable data so that they will be as accurate and as useful as possible. This is the reliability principle. Reliable data are verifiable which are to be confirmed by any independent observer, and based on information that flows from activities that are documented by objective evidence. Without the reliability principle, or called the objectivity principle, accounting records would be based on whims and opinions and would be subject to disputes.

Suppose that you want to start a stereo shop and have a place for operations, you transfer a small building to the business. You believe the building is worth USD 155,000. To confirm its value, you hire two real estate professionals, who appraise the building at USD 147,000. Is USD 155,000 or USD 147,000 the more reliable estimate of the building's value? The real estate appraisal of USD 147,000 is, because it is supported by external, independent, objective observation.

C. The Cost Principle

The cost principle states that assets and services that are acquired should be recorded at their actual cost (also called historical cost). Even though the purchaser may believe the price paid is a bargain, the item is recorded at the price paid in the transaction.

Suppose your stereo shop purchases some stereo equipment from a supplier who is going out of business. Assume you get a good deal on this purchase and pay only USD 2,000 for merchandise that would have cost you USD 3,000 elsewhere. The cost principle requires you to record this merchandise at its actual cost of USD 2,000, not the USD 3,000 that you believe the equipment to be worth.

The cost principle also holds that the accounting records should maintain the historical cost of an asset for as long as the business holds the asset. Why? Because cost is a reliable measure. Suppose your store holds the stereo equipment for six months. During this period of time, prices increase, and the equipment can be sold for USD 3,500. Should its accounting value, the figure "on the books" —be the actual cost of USD 2,000 or the current market value of USD 3,500? According to the cost principle, the accounting value of the equipment remains at actual cost, USD 2,000.

D. The Going-Concern Concept

Another reason for measuring assets at historical cost is the going-concern concept, which holds that the entity will remain in operation for a foreseeable future. Most assets, such as supplies, land, buildings, and equipments, are acquired for use rather than for sale. Under the going-concern concept, accountants assume that the business will remain in operation long enough to use existing assets for their intended purpose. The market value of a price for which the asset can be sold may change many times during the asset's life. Therefore, an asset's current market value may not be relevant to decision making. Moreover, historical cost is a more reliable accounting measure for assets.

To better understand the going-concern concept, consider another alternative where an enterprise which is to go out of business. You have probably seen stores advertise a Going out of Business Sale. That means a business entity is trying to sell all its assets. In that case, the relevant measure of the assets is their current market value. However, going out of business is the exception rather than the rules themselves. And for this reason accounting records list assets at their historical cost.

E. The Stable-Monetary-Unit Concept

In the United States accountants record transactions in dollars because the dollar is the medium of exchange. British accountants record transactions in terms of the pound sterling, and in Japan transactions are recorded in Yen.

Unlike a liter, a mile, or an acre, the value of a dollar changes over time. A general rise in prices is called inflation, and during inflation a dollar will purchase less milk, less toothpaste, and less of other necessities. When prices are relatively stable — when there is little inflation — a dollar's purchasing power is also stable. The United States has experienced low rates of inflation. Most periods of American history.

Accountants assume that the dollar's purchasing power is relatively stable. The stable-monetary-unit concept is the basis for ignoring the effect of inflation in the accounting records. It allows accountants to add and subtract dollar amounts as though each dollar had the same purchasing power.

Accountants have devised ways to take inflation into account. When inflation accelerates, the FASB (Financial Accounting Standard Board) can require companies to show inflation-adjusted amounts in reports. As we continue to explore accounting, we will discuss other principles that guide accountants.

5. Accounting Equation

Financial statements tell us how a business is performing and where it stands. But how do accountants arrive at the items and amounts that make up the financial statements?

The most basic tool of the accountant is the accounting equation. This equation presents the assets of the business and the claims to those assets. Assets are the economic resources of a business that are expected to be of benefit in the future. Cash, office supplies, merchandise, furniture, land, and buildings are examples. Claims to those assets come from two sources.

Liabilities are "outsider claims", which are economic obligations, debts payable to outsiders. These outside parties are called creditors. For example, a creditor who has loaned money to a business has a claim—a legal right—to a part of the assets until the business pays the debt. "Insider claims" are called owner's equity or capital. These are the claims held by the owners of the business. An owner has a claim to the entity's assets because he or she has invested in the business. Owner's equity is measured by subtracting liabilities from assets.

The accounting equation shows the relationship among assets, liabilities and owner's equity. Assets appear on the left-hand side of the equation. The legal and economic claims against the assets—the liabilities and owner's equity—appear on the right-hand side of the equation:

ASSETS = LIABILITIES + OWNER'S EQUITY

Let's take a closer look at the elements that make up the accounting equation. Suppose you run a business that supplies meat to fast food restaurants. Some customers may pay you in cash when you deliver the meat. Cash is an asset. Other customers may buy on credit and promise to pay you within certain time after delivery. This promise is also an asset because it is an economic resource that will benefit you in the future when you receive cash from the customer. The meat supplier calls this promise an account receivable. If the promise that entitles you to receive cash in the future is formally written out, it is called a note receivable. All receivables are assets.

The fast food restaurant's promise to pay you for the meat it purchases on credit creates a debt for the restaurant. This liability is an account payable of the restaurant, which means that the debt is not formally written out. Instead the reputation and the credit standing of the restaurant and its owner back it up. A written promise of future payment is called a note payable. All payables are liabilities.

Owner's equity is the amount of the assets that remains after subtracting liabilities. We often write the accounting equation to show that the owner's claim to business assets is a residual:

ASSETS-LIABILITIES = OWNER'S EQUITY

6. Classification of Assets and Liabilities

On the balance sheet, assets and liabilities are classified as either current or long-term ones to indicate their relative liquidity. Liquidity is a measure of how quickly an item may be converted into cash. Therefore, cash is the most liquid asset. Accounts receivable are a relatively liquid asset because the business expects to collect the amount in cash in the near future. Supplies are less liquid than accounts receivable, and furniture and buildings are even less so. Users of financial statements are interested in liquidity because business difficulties often arise due to a shortage of cash. How quickly can the business convert an asset into cash and pay a debt? How soon must a liability be paid? These are questions of liquidity. Balance sheets list assets and liabilities in the order of their relative liquidity.

Current Assets. Current assets are assets that can be converted into cash, sold, or consumed during the next 12 months or within the business' normal operating cycle if longer than a year. The operating cycle is the time span during which (1) cash is used to acquire goods and services, and (2) these goods and services are sold to customers, who in turn pay for their purchases with cash. For most businesses, the operating cycle is a few months. A few types of business have operating cycles longer than a year. Cash accounts receivable and notes receivable due within a year or less are current assets. Merchandising entities have an additional current asset—inventory. This account shows the cost of goods that are held for sale to customers.

Long-term Assets. Long-term assets are all assets other than current assets. They are not held for sale, but rather they are used to operate the business. One category of long-term assets is plant assets, or fixed assets. Land, buildings, furniture and fixtures, and equipments are examples of plant assets.

Financial statement users such as creditors are interested in the due dates of an entity's liabilities. The sooner a liability must be paid, the more current it is. Liabilities that must be paid on the earliest future date create the greatest strain on cash. Therefore, the balance sheet lists liabilities in the order in which they are due. Knowing how many of a business' liabilitiesare current and how many are long-term helps creditors assess the likelihood of collecting from the entity. Balance sheets usually have at least two liability classifications, current liabilities and long-term liabilities.

Current Liabilities. Current liabilities are debts that are due to be paid within one year or within the entity's operating cycle. Notes Payable due within one year, Salary Payable, Unearned Revenue, and Interest Payable owed on notes payable are current liabilities.

Long-term Liabilities. All liabilities that are not current are classified as long-term liabilities. Other notes payable are paid in installments, with the first installment due within one year, the second installment due the second year, and so on. In this case, the first installment would be a current liability and the remainder a long-term liability.

7. The Double-Entry Bookkeeping System

There are two basic bookkeeping systems—the double entry system the single entry system. The double-entry method was perfected by the merchants of Venice during the fifteenth century and is still widely used today.

The basic principle of double-entry bookkeeping is that every transaction has a twofold effect. In other words, a value is received and a value is yielded or parted with. Both effects, which are equal in amount, must be entered completely in the bookkeeping records. Each transaction must be analyzed to determine which accounts are effected, and whether they should be increased or decreased. An entry made on the left-hand side or column of an account is called a debit, while an entry made on the right-hand side or column is called a credit. Debit, usually abbreviated as Dr. , at one time meant value received. Credit, usually abbreviated as Cr. , meant value parted with.

From the basic accounting formula, that is, assets = liabilities + owner's equity (or capital) , certain guidelines have evolved through general agreement and custom. Debiting on the left-hand side increases asset accounts, and crediting on the right-hand side decreases them. The opposite is true for liability and owner's equity accounts, which are increased on the credit side and decreased on the debit side.

Income and expense accounts represent changes in equity. Income increases owner's equity, while expenses decrease owner's equity. Income accounts are increased on the credit side and decreased on the debit side, while expense accounts are increased on the debit side and decreased on the credit side.

Expense Accounts		Income Accounts	
Dr.	Cr.	Dr.	Cr.
+	−	−	+

Anything of value that a business or an organization owns is commonly known as an asset. Asset accounts include cash (home currency and foreign currency) which is the money on hand or in the bank; furniture and fixtures; accounts receivable; claims against customers that owe money; stock or inventory; office supplies; and many others that show what the organization owns. Debts owed to creditors are known as liabilities. If money is owed to an organization or a person for things or services purchased on credit, this liability is called an account payable. Other liabilities include wages or salaries that are owed to the employees, or taxes that have not yet been paid. The value of the organization owed to the owner or owners is known as capital. Other terms used to designate capital are proprietorship, owner's equity (usually abbreviated OE), ownership, or net worth.

Since the debits and credits in journal entries (books of original entry) must always equal each other, and these balanced entries are, in turn, posted to a ledger (a book in which the financial transactions of an organization are classified), it follows that the aggregate of the debits in all the ledger accounts must be equal to the aggregate of the credits in these accounts. In other words, the ledger should always be in balance or equilibrium. This is the basic concept of double-entry bookkeeping.

There are usually two kinds of ledgers:

General ledger. It contains the controlling accounts for each of the subsidiary ledgers. A controlling account in the general ledger shows in summary form what appears in detail in the corresponding subsidiary ledger. There is often a separate controlling account for each subsidiary ledger, thus due from banks controlling account shows in summary form the totals of all the debits and credits appearing in the correspondent banks' accounts in the Due from Banks subsidiary ledgers. The balances in the general ledger for asset, liability and capital accounts become the basis for data set forth in the Balance Sheet. The balances in the income and expense accounts become the basis for data set forth in the Profit and Loss Statements.

Subsidiary Ledger. It is a ledger maintained for subsidiary accounts of a homogeneous nature. The balances of the accounts in the subsidiary ledger equal the total of the balance shown in the controlling account for the particular subsidiary ledger maintained in the general ledger. The usual subsidiary ledgers in banking business are the depositors ledger, income ledger, expense ledger, and others. In the books of × × Bank, there are some 107 accounting items, which record and reflect its entire business activities and achievements. The books are divided into four categories, that is, Asset, Liability, Joint Asset and Liability, Loss and Income.

8. Financial Statements

After the analysis of the transactions is completed, we now look at the Financial Statements, which are formal reports of financial information about the entity. The primary financial statements are the (1) balance sheet, (2) income statement, and (3) statement of cash flows.

These statements conveniently and succinctly summarize a firm's performance and its financial status at the end of each accounting period. Although they are historical in nature, the primary financial statements usually provide a good indication of what a firm's performance is likely to be during subsequent accounting periods. These clues may not be immediately evident, however. Interested users must analyze the statements carefully in order to obtain the particular information that suits their purposes.

There are several reasons why careful analysis of financial statements is necessary.

Firstly, financial statements are general purpose statements. They are prepared for use by a variety of interested parties: stockholders, short- and long-term creditors, potential investors, government agencies, and management. These different users are involved in making different types of decisions, ranging from whether to make an investment (potential owner), or whether opportunities exist for improving performance (manager), to whether the firm's activities require regulation (government agency). Each type of decision requires different information, and therefore a different analysis.

Secondly, the relationships between key figures on the income statement, on balance sheet, or on both, and the relationships between amounts on successive financial statements, are not obvious without analysis. Accordingly, knowledgeable users develop ratios and percentages that reflect meaningful relationships and that show trends from previous years.

Thirdly, users of financial statements may be interested in seeing how well a company is doing in comparison with predetermined objective standards, other companies in the industry, or alternative opportunities for investment.

To a large extent, then, amount of information one is able to draw from financial statements depends on the care and experience with which they are analyzed.

In the following sections, we will simply discuss the three primary financial statements and have a look at the specimens of the statements for each of the three.

A. Balance Sheet

The balance sheet is divided into three sections: assets, liabilities, and owner's equity. The first section identifies the types of assets owned by a firm and amounts paid for those assets. Further, it categorizes the assets as current, or short-term, and non-current, or long-term, and thus disclosing the composition of assets and their liquidity.

The liability section informs readers of the extent and nature of a firm's borrowings, and provides a measure of its financial stability. This section, together with owner's equity, indicates how an entity is financed (whether by borrowings or by owner's contribution).

Finally, the owner's equity section completes the balance sheet by identifying the portion of a firm's resources that were contributed by owner and the amount of undistributed earnings (retained earnings) a firm has had since inception. People often think that since this section represents the residual portion of the balance sheet equation—the remainder after liabilities has been subtracted from assets—it refers to the net worth of a firm. As it now stands, however, owner's equity merely shows two of the ways in which resources are brought into a firm (owner's contributions and retained earnings). The only-other source of resources is borrowings, which are included in the liability section.

A classified balance sheet is like the following one.

Mountain Land Resources, Inc. Balance Sheet as of December 31, 19 × 4and 19 × 3

Assets	19 × 4	19 × 3
Current Assets:		
Cash	USD 17, 600	USD 7, 900
Accounts Receivable (net of Allowance of Doubtful Accounts)	106, 700	104, 900
Inventory	187, 300	197, 500
Prepaid Expenses	7, 000	9, 200
Total Current Assets	USD 318, 600	USD 319, 500
Property, Plant and Equipment:		
Land (Note 1)	USD 90, 000	USD 10, 000
Plant and Equipment (at cost)	623, 200	577, 200
Less Accumulated Depreciation	(243, 900)	(223, 600)
Total Property, Plant and Equipment	USD 469, 300	USD 363, 600
Total Assets	USD 787, 900	USD 683, 100
Liabilities and Stockholders' Equity		
Current Liabilities:		
Accounts Payable	USD 72, 200	USD 71, 700
Income Taxes Payable	7, 000	1, 500
Total Current Liabilities	USD 79, 200	USD 73, 200
Long-Term Liabilities:		
Notes Payable	USD 20, 000	0
Mortgage Payable	72, 100	85, 000
Total Long-Term Liabilities	USD 92, 100	USD 85, 000
Stockholders' Equity:		
Common Stock. USD 1 Par Value (Note 1)	USD 82, 500	USD 42, 500
Paid in Capital in Excess of Par—Common Stock (Note 1)	186, 900	146, 900
Retained Earnings	347, 200	335, 500
Total Stockholders'Equity	USD 616, 600	USD 524, 900
Total Liabilities and Stockholders' Equity	USD 787, 900	USD 683, 100

Note 1 Land with a fair value of USD 80, 000 was acquired through the issuance of 40, 000 shares of common stock.

B. Income Statement

The income statement provides a measure of the success or failure of an enterprise over a specific period of time. It shows the major sources of revenues generated and the expenses associated with those revenues. It matches efforts against accomplishments over a period of operating activity and helps external users evaluate the earnings potential of a company.

Alternative titles for the income statement include earnings statement, statement of operation, and profit and loss statement. However, income statement is by far the most popular term for this important financial statement. In brief, we can say that an income statement is used to summarize the operating results of a business by matching the revenue earned during a given time period with the expenses incurred in obtaining that revenue.

A typical income statement is presented hereunder. Like the balance sheet, the income statement begins with the name of the company and the title of the report. Note also that the income statement designates the period of time covered; here it refers to "the year ended", in contrast to the balance sheet, which is "as of" a particular date. The income statement covers a period of time and the balance sheet is a record at a point in time.

Mountain Land Resources, Inc. Income Statement

For the Year Ended December 31, 19 ×4

Net Sales Revenue	USD859, 400
Other Revenues (Note 2)	7, 800
Total Revenues	USD 867, 200
Expenses:	
Cost of Goods Sold	USD 610, 100
Selling and Administrative Expenses	147, 000
Depreciation Expense	32, 100
Interest Expense	14, 200
Total Expense	USD 803, 400
Income Before Taxes	USD 63, 800
Income Taxes	27, 200
Net Income	USD 36, 600

Note 2 Gain on the sale of equipment (cost, USD 12, 300; book value, USD 500; sale price, USD 8, 300 cash)

Mountain Land Resources Statement of Retained Earnings

For the Year Ended December 31, 19 ×4

Retained Earning, January 1, 19 ×4	USD 335, 500
Add Net Income	36, 600
	USD 372, 100
Dividends Declared and Paid	24, 900
Retained Earnings, December 31, 19 ×4	USD 347, 200

C. *Statement of Cash Flows*

The statement of changes in financial position usually is designed to explain the changes in working capital, which occurred during the period. However, it may be designed to explain the changes in cash. If it is, the descriptive phrases used in the statement should clearly state that the statement is constructed to explain cash flows. For example, "Cash provided by operations" should be used instead of "Working capital provided by operations".

One of the most important phases of management's work is to manage a company's money, so that adequate cash is available to meet liabilities, pay dividends, and so on. Also, surplus amounts of money should be kept invested in assets which will contribute income to the company. Therefore, the management of a company will often require cash flow statements to assist in planning and controlling the cash flows of the company.

A cash flow statement covers a period of time and accounts for the increase or decrease in a company's cash by showing where the company got cash and the uses it made of cash during the period.

Cash flows into a company from sales and flows out for cost of goods sold and expense; and although cost of goods sold and expenses are deducted from sales on an accrual basis income statement, the resulting net income figure does not show the amount of cash generated by operations. To determine cash from operations, it is necessary to convert the item amounts on a company's income statement from an accrual basis to a cash basis.

Mountain Land Resources, Inc.   Statement of Changes in Financial Position   (Cash Basis)
For the Year Ended December 31, 19 × 4

Sources of Cash		
Operations:		
Net Income		USD 36, 600
Add: Depreciation	USD 32, 100	
Decrease in Inventory	10, 200	
Decrease in Prepaid Expenses	2, 200	
Increase in Accounts Payable	500	
Increase in Income Taxes Payable	5, 500	50, 500
		USD 87, 100
Subtract: Gain on Sale of Equipment	USD 7, 800	
Increase in Accounts Receivable	1, 800	9, 600
Total Cash from Operations		USD 77, 500
Issuance of Stock to Acquire Land		80, 000
Proceeds from Sale of Equipment		8, 300
Proceeds from Long-Term Note		20, 000
Total Sources of Cash		USD 185, 800
Uses of Cash		
Payment of Dividends		USD 24, 900
Acquisition of Land by Issuance of Stock		80, 000
Purchase of Equipment		58, 300
Reduction of Mortgage		12, 900
Increase in Cash		9, 700
Total Uses of Cash		USD 185, 800

II. Managerial Accounting

1. The Use of Break-Even Concept and C-V-P Analysis

A. The Types of Cost Behavior

In this section, we discuss the behavior of different costs, that is, whether and how they change in response to changes in operating level or volumes of activity. This analysis provides guidelines for predicting the effect of an operating decision on future profitability. These profitability guidelines can then be used to plan organizational activities and to guide and evaluate the performance of the persons working in the company. The purpose of understanding cost behavior is to make good decisions in the company's business.

There are three common cost behavior patterns: variable, fixed, and semivariable. A cost is classified into one of these categories by the way it reacts to changes in activity level. Costs that change in total in proportion to changes in activity level are called variable costs. Those that do not change in total are called fixed costs. A cost is classified as variable only if it changes in relation to the specified activity base. If it does not change in relation to that activity base, it is fixed. Semi-variable, or mixed, costs contain both variable and fixed components.

i. Variable Costs

Variable costs change in total in proportion to changes in the activity level of a firm. Examples are the costs of direct materials, which change with the number of units produced and sales commissions, which change with sales volume. In addition to sales commissions and materials, many other costs (such as labor) could also have variable cost behavior pattern. For example, if it takes 4 hours of labor to assemble a frame of a car, and each hour costs USD12, then USD48 per frame would be variable and the total labor cost would be USD48 times the number of frames produced. So we can define variable costs as the costs that vary in total proportionately with changes in activity level, within the relevant range.

ii. Fixed Costs

Fixed costs remain constant in total regardless of activity level, at least within a certain range of activity — the relevant range. Examples of fixed assets are property taxes, insurance, executive salaries, plant depreciation, and rent. Because total fixed costs remain constant as production increases the fixed cost per unit decreases. This is in contrast to variable costs, where cost per unit remains constant through changes in level of activity. So fixed costs are defined as the costs that do not vary in total with changes in activity level, at least within a relevant range.

Relevant range means the range of operating level, or volume of activity, over which the relationship between total costs and activity level is approximately linear.

iii. Semi-variable, or Mixed Costs

Semi-variable, or mixed costs are costs that contain both variable and fixed components. An example is rent that includes a fixed rental fee plus percentage of total sales. In the analysis of semi-variable cost, they are, usually, separated into variable and fixed costs.

B. Break-Even Analysis

i. The Contribution-Margin Income Statement

Cost behavior patterns are applicable to many of the concepts. To illustrate one example of their use and to serve as a bridge between this section and the next, here we describe the contribution margin income statement and then briefly show how contribution margins are used to compute break- even points.

ii. Functional Income Statement

The normal income statement which constitutes one of the financial statements of a company, is functional income statement. So functional income statement is an income statement that segregates all costs by use; it shows revenues less cost of goods sold (gross margin) less selling and administrative expenses. This approach is useful for financial reporting purposes; it provides outside readers with information about company's progress and about which functional areas are being emphasized. For management's use in the decision-making process, however, an income statement that follows a cost behavior approach, often referred to as a Contribution-Margin Income Statement, is more valuable.

iii. Contribution-Margin Income Statement

Contribution-Margin Income Statement is an income statement that separates costs according to their behavior patterns; it shows revenues less variable costs (contribution-margin) less fixed costs.

The following exhibit contrasts "contribution-margin" and "functional" income statements.

iv. Contribution- Margin

Contribution- margin is the difference between total revenues and total variable costs; it is the portion of sales revenue available to cover fixed cost. It is based on the following relationships.

Sales Revenue-Variable Cost = Contribution- Margin

Contribution- Margin-Fixed Costs = Net Income

Comparative Income Statements Contribution Margin Approach

Sales Revenue (1, 000 unit at USD 100 each)		USD 100, 000
Variable Expenses:		
Variable Cost of Goods Sold (1, 000 unit at 40 each)	USD 40, 000	
Variable Selling Expenses (1, 000 unit at 5 each)	5, 000	
Variable General and Administrative Expenses (1, 000 unit at 4 each)	4, 000	
Total Variable Expenses		(49, 000)
Contribution Margin		USD 51, 000
Fixed Expenses:		
Fixed Cost of Goods Sold	USD 10, 000	
Fixed Selling Expenses	10, 000	
Fixed General and Administrative Expenses	16, 000	
Total Fixed Expense		(36, 000)
Net Income		USD 15, 000

Functional Approach

Sales Revenue (1, 000 unit at 100 each)			USD 100, 000
Cost of Goods Sold:			
Fixed Expenses	USD 10, 000		
Variable Expenses	40, 000		
Total Cost of Goods Sold			(50, 000)
Gross Margin			USD 50, 000
Less Operating Expenses:			
Selling Expenses:			
Fixed Selling Expenses	USD 10, 000		
Variable Selling Expenses	5, 000		
Total Selling Expenses		USD 15, 000	
General and Administrative Expenses:			
Fixed General and Administrative Expenses	USD 16, 000		
Variable General Administrative Expenses	4, 000		
Total General and Administrative Expenses		20, 000	
Total Operation Expenses			(35, 000)
Net Income			USD 15, 000

v. Break-Even and Break-Even Point

If contribution margin = fixed costs, then there would be neither profit nor loss for a firm in its operation. Such a situation is called break-even.

You can understand now that break-even point is such a point of sales (or units) at which the amount of sales revenue (or the number of units sold) equals the costs; the point at which there is neither profit nor loss. Stated another way, the break-even point for either a company or a product is the point at which total sales revenue is equal to total fixed costs plus total variable costs.

Knowing the break-even level of operations is useful because it helps management determine what appropriate selling prices and production volumes are, how much to spend on discretionary fixed costs, whether, to promote or drop a product, and so on.

C. *Target Net Income*

Once a break-even point is determined, management often wants to know how many units must be sold or how much service must be performed to reach a target net income. This target usually represents an amount of income that will enable management to reach its objective: paying dividends, purchasing new plant and equipment, or paying off existing loans. Target net income can be expressed either as a percentage of revenues or as a fixed amount.

D. *Cost-Volume-Profit Analysis*

Cost-Volume-Profit (C-V-P) analysis is the technique for determining how changes in cost and volume affect the profitability of an organization. Here we will discuss how the analysis of cost behavior patterns allows management to understand the effects that changes in cost, volume, and revenue will have on profit. The techniques for studying these relationships are collectively referred to as cost-volume-profit (C-V-P) analysis. They can be used in making decisions on selling prices, production volume, levels of discretionary fixed costs, and so on.

There are three common and related ways to perform C-V-P analysis:

- The contribution-margin approach;
- The equation approach (These two approaches are simply introduced above.) and
- the graphical approach (This one is not introduced here).

So far, we can summarize what we have just read from Section I of this Chapter. C-V-P analysis helps management understand how profits change in relation to changes in sales volume, fixed costs, variable costs, and sales revenue. Although all the three common methods of C-V-P analysis are variations of the same calculation, each approach has its advantages. The graphical approach allows the simultaneous analysis of several different activity levels.

Among other things, C-V-P analysis is used to compute break-even points and target net income levels. The equation approach is especially useful in assessing how profits change when costs or revenues change.

Three limiting assumptions are

- that the sales mix is constant
- that cost and revenue behavior patterns are linear and remain constant over the relevant range
- that all costs can be categorized as either fixed or variable. When sales volumes are

relatively stable, management should always emphasize the products with the highest contribution-margin ratios.

2. Present Value and Internal Rate of Return (IRR)

Financing a business often requires resources beyond those available from current earnings. Two common ways of generating additional financial resources are:

- **equity financing**: issuing stock (by a corporation) or making additional contributions by owner (s) (in a partnership or proprietorship);
- **debt financing**: borrowing money. Because both types of financing have their advantages and disadvantages, firms usually try to reach an appropriate balance between the two. Here we discuss the debt financing.

The obligations that result from borrowing money for periods longer than one year is classified on the balance sheet as long-term liabilities. There are many different types of long-term liabilities. The most common are notes payable, mortgages payable, deferred income taxes payable, and lease obligations. We should hereafter mention some factors that affect the measurement of all long-term liability.

A. *The Concept of Present Value and Present Value Table*

Present value is the value today of an amount to be received or paid in the future; the future amount must be discounted at a specified rate of interest. Conceptually, the amount of a liability of any particular time is the present value of all future outflows of assets required to pay the liability in full. Obviously, if a liability is short-term, the present value of outflows needed to pay it is approximately equal to the stated amount of the liability. In the case of long-term liability, however, the present value of future outflows of assets needed to settle an obligation is often significantly different from the stated amount of that liability.

B. *Net Present Value*

When we evaluate an investment project, we can use the net present value method to compare all expected cash inflows associated with an investment with the current and future outflows. All cash flows are discounted to their present values giving recognition to the time value of money. For this reason, the net present value method is superior to both the payback method and the unadjusted rate of return method and has gained in popularity, especially in recent years.

In general, the net present value method involves the following three steps.

Step 1. Using a predetermined interest rate or discount factor, compute the present value of all the expected cash inflows and outflows of an investment. (Note that most present value tables assume end of year inflows and outflows.)

Present Value Tables

Table I   The Present Value of USD 1 Due in n Periods

Period	1%	2%	3%	4%	5%	6%	7%	8%	9%	10%	12%	14%	15%	16%	18%	20%	24%	28%	32%	36%
1	0.9901	0.9804	0.9709	0.9615	0.9524	0.9434	0.9346	0.9259	0.9174	0.9091	0.8929	0.8772	0.8696	0.8621	0.8475	0.8333	0.8065	0.7813	0.7576	0.7353
2	0.9803	0.9612	0.9426	0.9246	0.9070	0.8900	0.8734	0.8573	0.8417	0.8264	0.7972	0.7695	0.7561	0.7432	0.7182	0.6944	0.6504	0.6104	0.5739	0.5407
3	0.9706	0.9423	0.9151	0.8890	0.8638	0.8396	0.8163	0.7938	0.7722	0.7513	0.7118	0.6750	0.6775	0.6407	0.6086	0.5787	0.5245	0.4768	0.4348	0.3975
4	0.9610	0.9238	0.8885	0.8548	0.8227	0.7921	0.7629	0.7350	0.7084	0.6830	0.6355	0.5921	0.5718	0.5523	0.5158	0.4823	0.4230	0.3725	0.3294	0.2923
5	0.9515	0.9057	0.8626	0.8219	0.7835	0.7473	0.7130	0.6806	0.6499	0.6209	0.5674	0.5194	0.4972	0.4761	0.4371	0.4019	0.3411	0.2910	0.2495	0.2149
6	0.9420	0.8880	0.8375	0.7903	0.7462	0.7050	0.6663	0.6302	0.5963	0.5645	0.5066	0.4556	0.4323	0.4104	0.3704	0.3349	0.2751	0.2274	0.1890	0.1580
7	0.9327	0.8706	0.8131	0.7599	0.7107	0.6651	0.6227	0.5835	0.5470	0.5132	0.4523	0.3996	0.3759	0.3538	0.3139	0.2791	0.2218	0.1776	0.1432	0.1162
8	0.9235	0.8535	0.7894	0.7307	0.6768	0.6274	0.5820	0.5403	0.5019	0.4665	0.4039	0.3506	0.3269	0.3050	0.2660	0.2326	0.1898	0.1388	0.1085	0.0854
9	0.9143	0.8368	0.7664	0.7026	0.6446	0.5919	0.5439	0.5002	0.4604	0.4241	0.3606	0.3075	0.2843	0.2630	0.2255	0.1938	0.1443	0.1084	0.0822	0.0628
10	0.9053	0.8203	0.7441	0.6756	0.6139	0.5584	0.5083	0.4632	0.4224	0.3855	0.3220	0.2697	0.2472	0.2267	0.1911	0.1615	0.1164	0.0847	0.0623	0.0462
11	0.8963	0.8043	0.7224	0.6496	0.5847	0.5268	0.4751	0.4289	0.3875	0.3505	0.2875	0.2366	0.2149	0.1954	0.1619	0.1346	0.0938	0.0662	0.0472	0.0340
12	0.8874	0.7885	0.7014	0.6246	0.5568	0.4970	0.4440	0.3971	0.3555	0.3186	0.2567	0.2076	0.1869	0.1685	0.1372	0.1122	0.0757	0.0517	0.0357	0.0250
13	0.8787	0.7730	0.6810	0.6006	0.5303	0.4688	0.4150	0.3677	0.3262	0.2897	0.2292	0.1821	0.1625	0.1452	0.1163	0.0935	0.0610	0.0404	0.0271	0.0184
14	0.8700	0.7579	0.6611	0.5775	0.5051	0.4423	0.3878	0.3405	0.2992	0.2633	0.2046	0.1597	0.1413	0.1252	0.0985	0.0779	0.0492	0.0316	0.0205	0.0135
15	0.8613	0.7430	0.6419	0.5553	0.4810	0.4173	0.3624	0.3152	0.2745	0.2394	0.1827	0.1401	0.1229	0.1079	0.0835	0.0649	0.0397	0.0247	0.0155	0.0099
16	0.8528	0.7284	0.6232	0.5339	0.4581	0.3936	0.3387	0.2919	0.2519	0.2176	0.1631	0.1229	0.1069	0.0930	0.0708	0.0541	0.0320	0.0193	0.0118	0.0073
17	0.8444	0.7142	0.6050	0.5134	0.4363	0.3714	0.3166	0.2703	0.2311	0.1978	0.1456	0.1078	0.0929	0.0802	0.0600	0.0451	0.0258	0.0150	0.0089	0.0054
18	0.8360	0.7002	0.5874	0.4936	0.4155	0.3503	0.2959	0.2502	0.2120	0.1799	0.1300	0.0946	0.0808	0.0691	0.0508	0.0376	0.0208	0.0118	0.0068	0.0039
19	0.8277	0.6864	0.5703	0.4746	0.3957	0.3305	0.2765	0.2317	0.1945	0.1635	0.1161	0.0829	0.0703	0.0596	0.0431	0.0313	0.0168	0.0092	0.0051	0.0029
20	0.8195	0.6730	0.5537	0.4564	0.3769	0.3118	0.2584	0.2145	0.1784	0.1486	0.1037	0.0728	0.0611	0.0514	0.0365	0.0261	0.0135	0.0072	0.0039	0.0021
25	0.7798	0.6095	0.4776	0.3751	0.2953	0.2330	0.1842	0.1460	0.1160	0.0923	0.0588	0.0378	0.0304	0.0245	0.0160	0.0105	0.0046	0.0021	0.0010	0.0005
30	0.7419	0.5521	0.4120	0.3083	0.2314	0.1741	0.1314	0.0994	0.0754	0.0573	0.0334	0.0196	0.0151	0.0116	0.0070	0.0042	0.0016	0.0006	0.0002	0.0001
40	0.6717	0.4529	0.3066	0.2083	0.1420	0.0972	0.0668	0.0460	0.0318	0.0221	0.0107	0.0053	0.0037	0.0026	0.0013	0.0007	0.0002	0.0001		
50	0.6080	0.3715	0.2281	0.1407	0.0872	0.0543	0.0339	0.0213	0.0134	0.0085	0.0035	0.0014	0.0009	0.0006	0.0003	0.0001				
60	0.5504	0.3048	0.1697	0.0951	0.0535	0.0303	0.0173	0.0099	0.0057	0.0033	0.0011	0.0004	0.0002	0.0001						

*The value of 0 to four decimal places.

Table II   The Present Value of an Annuity of USD 1 Per Period

Using present value tables, which are given below, is very convenient for us to discount an amount of inflow or outflow in future to present value

Number of Payments	1%	2%	3%	4%	5%	6%	7%	8%	9%	10%	12%	14%	15%	16%	18%	20%	24%	32%
1	0.9901	0.9804	0.9709	0.9615	0.9524	0.9434	0.9346	0.9259	0.9174	0.9091	0.8929	0.8772	0.8596	0.8621	0.8475	0.8333	0.8065	0.7576
2	1.9704	1.9416	1.9135	1.8861	1.8594	1.8334	1.8080	1.7833	1.7591	1.7355	1.6901	1.6467	1.6257	1.6052	1.5656	1.5278	1.4568	1.3315
3	2.9410	2.8839	2.8286	2.7751	2.7232	2.6730	2.6243	2.5771	2.5313	2.4869	2.4018	2.3216	2.2832	2.2459	2.1743	2.1005	1.3810	1.7663
4	3.9820	3.8077	3.7171	3.6299	3.5460	3.4651	3.3872	3.3121	3.2397	3.1699	3.0373	2.9137	2.8550	2.7982	2.6901	2.5887	2.4043	2.0957
5	4.8884	4.7135	4.5797	4.4518	4.3295	4.2124	4.1002	3.9927	3.8897	3.7908	3.6048	3.4331	3.3522	3.2743	3.1272	2.9906	2.7454	2.3452
6	5.7985	5.6014	5.4172	5.2421	5.0757	4.9173	4.7665	4.6229	4.4859	4.3553	4.1114	3.8887	3.7845	3.6847	3.4976	3.3255	3.0205	2.5342
7	6.7282	6.4720	6.2303	6.0021	5.7864	5.5824	5.3893	5.2064	5.0330	4.8684	4.5638	4.2883	4.1604	4.0386	3.8115	3.6046	3.2423	2.6775
8	7.6517	7.3255	7.0197	6.7327	6.4632	6.2098	5.9713	5.7466	5.5348	5.3349	4.9676	4.6389	4.4873	4.3436	4.0776	3.8372	3.4212	2.7860
9	8.5660	8.1622	7.7861	7.4353	7.1078	6.8017	6.5152	6.2469	5.9952	5.7590	5.3282	4.9464	4.7716	4.6065	4.3030	4.0310	3.5665	2.8651
10	9.4713	8.9826	8.5302	8.1109	7.7217	7.3601	7.0236	6.7101	6.4177	6.1446	5.6502	5.2161	5.0188	4.8332	4.4941	4.1925	3.6819	2.9304
11	10.3676	9.7868	9.2526	8.7605	8.3064	7.8869	7.4987	7.1390	6.8052	6.4951	5.9377	5.4527	5.2337	5.0286	4.6560	4.3271	3.7757	2.9776
12	11.2551	10.5733	9.9540	9.3851	8.8633	8.3838	7.9427	7.5361	7.1607	6.8137	6.1944	5.6603	5.4206	5.1971	4.7932	4.4392	3.8514	3.0133
13	12.1337	11.3484	10.6350	9.9856	9.3936	8.8527	8.3577	7.9038	7.4869	7.1034	6.4235	5.8424	5.5831	5.3423	4.9095	4.5327	3.9124	3.0404
14	13.0037	12.1062	11.2961	10.5631	9.8986	9.2950	8.7455	8.2442	7.7862	7.3667	6.6282	6.0021	5.7245	5.46755	5.0081	4.6106	3.3616	3.0609
15	13.8651	12.8493	11.9379	11.1184	10.3797	9.7122	9.1079	8.5595	8.0607	7.6061	6.8109	6.1422	5.8474	5.5755	5.0916	4.6755	4.0013	3.0764
16	14.7179	13.5777	12.5611	11.6523	10.8373	10.1059	9.4466	8.8514	8.3126	7.8237	6.9740	6.2651	5.9542	5.6685	5.1624	4.7296	4.0333	3.088
17	15.5623	14.2919	13.1661	12.1657	11.2741	10.4773	9.7632	9.1216	8.5436	8.0216	7.1196	6.3729	6.0472	5.7487	5.2223	4.7746	4.0591	3.097
18	16.3983	14.9920	13.7535	12.6593	11.6896	10.8276	10.0591	9.3719	8.7556	8.2014	7.2497	6.4674	6.1280	5.8178	5.2732	4.8122	4.0799	3.103
19	17.2260	15.6785	14.3238	13.1339	12.0853	11.1581	10.3356	9.6036	8.9501	8.36549	7.3658	6.5504	6.1982	5.8775	5.3162	4.84354	4.0967	3.109
20	18.0456	16.3514	14.8775	13.5903	12.4622	11.4699	10.5940	9.8181	9.1285	8.5136	7.4694	6.6231	6.2593	5.9288	5.3527	4.8696	4.1103	3.112
25	22.0232	19.5235	17.4131	15.6221	14.0939	12.7834	11.6536	10.6748	9.8226	9.0770	7.8431	6.8729	6.4641	6.0971	5.4669	4.9476	4.1474	3.120
30	25.8077	22.3965	19.6004	17.2920	15.3725	13.7648	12.4090	11.2578	10.2737	9.4269	8.0552	7.0027	6.5660	6.1772	5.5168	4.9789	4.1601	3.124
40	32.8347	27.3555	23.1148	19.7928	17.1591	15.0463	13.3317	11.9246	10.7574	9.7791	8.2438	7.1050	6.6418	6.2335	5.5482	4.9966	4.1659	3.125
50	39.1961	31.4256	25.7298	21.4822	18.2559	15.7619	13.8007	12.2335	10.9617	9.9148	8.3045	7.1327	6.6605	6.2463	5.5641	4.9995	4.1666	3.125
60	44.9550	34.7609	27.6756	22.6235	18.9293	16.1614	14.0392	12.3766	11.0480	9.9672	8.3240	7.1401	6.6651	6.2482	5.5553	4.9999	4.1667	3.125

MODERN FINANCIAL PRACTICES

Step 2. Subtract the total present value of the cash outflows from the total present value of cash inflows. The difference is the investment's net present value.

Step 3. If the net present value of the investment is positive, or at least zero, the project is acceptable from a quantitative standpoint. Before the company makes the final decision on the investment project, the management should make a study on the qualitative factors involved, which are sometimes even more important than the quantitative factors.

C. *Internal Rate of Return*

Internal rate of return is the "true" discount rate that will produce a net present value of zero when applied to the cash flows of an investment. It is another method to evaluate an investment project, and also knows the time adjusted rate of return method or discounted rate of return method. It is similar to the net present value approach in that it emphasizes the profitability of investments and takes into account the time value of money. As a discounted cash flow method, it is superior either to the payback method or to the unadjusted rate of return method. Because the calculation involves discounting by "trial and error" when uneven cash flows exist, some accountants consider the internal rate of return (IRR) method more tedious than the net present value method. Some managers, however, prefer to analyze investment alternatives in terms of comparative rates of return rather than net present value.

The IRR can also be defined as the "true" discount rate that an investment yields. To help you understand this concept, we will refer to a firm's plan to purchase a new truck. The truck costs USD 6,000 and will bring the firm a cash inflow of USD 2,000 a year for four consecutive years. For the purposes of this explanation we will ignore the trucks salvage value. Like the net present value approach, the IRR method involves three steps.

Step 1. Calculate the present value factor with the following formula.

Investment cost

Annual net cash inflows = Present value factor

6,000/2,000 = 3

Note that this is also the formula for calculating the payback method.

Step 2. In Present Value Table II, find the applicable row for the life of the investment. By moving across the table, you can find the present value factor closest to the number derived in step 1. In our example, the investment's life is known to be 4 years, so find row 4 and move across the row until you come to the factor 3.0373. This is the factor for 12%. The next factor 2.9137 represents 14 percent. Since the factor 3.0000 is between these two numbers, the truck project yields between 12 and 14 percent.

Step 3. Use interpolation to find the exact internal rate of return. Interpolation is most easily visualized by setting a table as follows:

	Rate of Return (Discount Rate)	Present Value Factors	
		High and True Factors	High and Low Factors
High Factor	12%	3.0373	3.0373
True Factor		3.0000	
Low Factor	14%	...	2.9137
Differences	2%	0.0373	0.1236

Note that the high factor is associated with the low rate, and that the low factor is associated with the high rate.

To find the exact rate of return in this example, you would make the following calculation.

$$0.12 + (0.02 \times 0.0373/0.1236) = 0.1260$$

Internal rate of return = 12.6%

What we are doing is adding the proportion 0.0373/0.1236 of the 2% difference to the low rate to get the true rate. The result, 12.6%, means that if the annual savings of 2,000 were discounted at 12.6%, the net present value of the investment would be zero.

D. Using the Internal Rate of Return

To determine the value of an investment, management must compare the project's internal rate of return with the company's standard discount rate, often called the hurdle rate, or the rate that must be cleared for a project to be accepted. If the internal rate is higher than or equal to the company's hurdle rate, the project is acceptable. If the internal rate is lower than the hurdle rate, the project is usually rejected. As with any of the capital budgeting techniques, qualitative factors must still be considered before a final decision can be made.

Net present value and internal rate of return are both discounted cash flow methods. The former uses a standard discount rate to restate all cash flows in terms of present values, and then makes comparisons. The latter method calculates the investment's "true" discount rate of return and compares it with the firm's hurdle rate. Thus an appropriate standard discount rate is extremely important in capital budgeting.

III. Bank Accounting

1. Accounting Basis

Accounting basis refers to methods for recognizing revenues, expenses, assets and liabilities in accounting statements. Major bases of accounting include the accrual, cash and modified cash bases.

In accrual accounting, revenues and gains are recognized in the period when they are earned. Expenses and losses are recognized in periods when they are incurred. Accrual basis accounting is concerned with the economic consequences of events and transactions rather than with only cash receipts and cash payments. Under accrual accounting, net income does not necessarily reflect cash receipts and cash payments for a particular period of time. Accrual accounting generally provides the most accurate measure of earning, earning power, managerial performance, future cash flows etc.

Cash basis accounting recognizes only transactions involving actual cash receipts and disbursements occurring in a given period. Cash basis accounting recognizes revenues and gains when cash is received and expenses and losses when cash is paid. No attempts are made to record unpaid bills or amounts owed to or by the entity.

Under a modified cash basis of accounting, certain expenditures, but not necessarily all, are capitalized and amortized in the future. Some revenues are recognized as earned, while others await cash receipts before the revenue is recognized. The modified cash basis of accounting is essentially part cash basis and part accrual basis accounting.

Net income from operations computed according to generally accepted accounting principles (accrual basis) can be converted to cash flow from operations according to the following general procedures:

Net income from operation + Items reducing income but not using cash, such as depreciation, depletion and amortization expenses + Decreases in current assets other than cash + Increases in current liabilities-Increases in current assets other than cash-Decreases in current liabilities = Cash flow from operations.

2. Accounting Controls

Accounting controls, also called financial controls, refer to plans, procedures and records required for safeguarding assets and producing reliable financial accounts. The primary concerns of accounting controls lie with systems authorization and approval controls over assets, internal auditing procedures and other financial matters. It is the management's responsibility to establish and maintain an appropriate system of internal accounting control.

The objectives of accounting are designed to provide reasonable assurance that

- transactions are executed in accordance with management's general or specific authorization;
- transactions are recorded as necessary to permit the preparation of financial statements in conformity with generally accepted accounting principles (GAAP), and to

maintain accountability for assets;

- access to assets is permitted only in accordance with management's authorization;
- the recorded accountability for assets is compared with the existing assets at reasonable intervals and appropriate action is taken with respect to any difference. Accounting controls are important elements of a bank's internal control system, the soundness of which is vital for bank's survival. Examples of accounting controls include the following: (1) cash receipts are deposited daily; (2) cash disbursements are made by check, and (3) perpetual inventory method is used to account for property.

3. The Chart of Accounts of a Bank

A chart of accounts is a list of names and numbers of ledger accounts systematically arranged. The numbering of accounts is to indicate classifications and relationships of accounts. The classification, grouping and description of accounts should be sufficiently complete to achieve clarity of presentation.

In the chart of accounts, ledger accounts are usually arranged in the order in which they appear on the financial statements. Assets, liabilities and shareholder's equity accounts appear in the order of their listing on the balance sheet, then revenue and expense accounts are listed in the order of their listing on the profit & loss statement. This arrangement facilitates the preparation of financial statements.

The chart of accounts is generally broken down into following divisions (1) assets, (2) liabilities, (3) capital and reserves, (4) income and expenses. Some banks may prefer to further break down the income and expenses into more detailed categories as shown in the following, in order to achieve a better understanding of the contribution factors of its profit & loss figure:

Category	Account number range (For illustration purposes only)
Assets	1,000 – 1,999
Liabilities	2,000 – 2,999
Net worth/capital	3,000 – 3,999
Interest and fee income	5,000 – 5,999
Interest expense and provision for loan losses	6,000 – 6,999
Non-interest income	7,000 – 7,999
Non-interest expenses	8,000 – 8,999
Extraordinary items	9,500 – 9,599

Chart of account numbers are assigned to bank accounts according to broad categories. The chart classifications are generally prepared as follows:

- Assets are usually arranged in the order of their general liquidity;
- Liabilities are generally in the order of their demand or use;
- Income accounts are listed by sources of revenue, with the major sources listed first; and
- Types of expenses list expenses account, again in the approximate order of their size. Occasionally, some account expenses are included in the general ledger for each department or cost center, or such sub accounts may be included in a separate accrual ledger or in a separate subsidiary ledger. General ledger accounts should be limited to those accounts to meet financial and managerial reporting requirements. Titles used for general ledger accounts should be consistent with titles used in other ledgers, reports and financial statements.

The general ledger should provide methods and procedures for:

- preparing, processing and monitoring general ledger entries;
- preparing reports and financial statements required by the board of directors, management and regulatory authorities;
- supporting and confirming various compliance requirements;
- preparing cost accounting studies and profit center reports;
- maintaining and developing the computer hardware and software associated with the system; and
- recruiting, selecting and training personnel capable of operating the system at an acceptable level.

4. Account Reconciliation

A. *Reconciliation and Evaluating Procedures in General*

For companies, balance sheet accounts should be reconciled where the book balance and the financial statement balances are adjusted for such items as deposits in transit, outstanding checks, bank charges, notes collected and similar items. Since there are no open items for income and expense accounts, such account must be verified according to the nature of the accounts. Many expense account transactions can be verified during the accounts payable process. Fees and service charges accounts can use listings by customer to compare with the general ledger.

Controllers frequently use reviews of historical trends, ratios, normal balances, accruals, and activity, budget variances and similar analytical tools to evaluate financial reports and statements before they are published. Judgment and experience are required to perform this review function satisfactorily.

For banks in specific, responsibility for preparing, balancing and processing daily general ledger entries is typically placed at a bank's department or branch office. These entries provide the basis for additional processing and posting at the operational center.

Control over cash is accomplished by a variety of means, including a daily reconciliation of the cash pool by tellers, daily balance sheets and cash reports by the management, and the separation of duties to include individuals responsible for handling cash versus those who have access to the recording process or accounting records. Similar procedures are used for other general ledger accounts in addition to cash.

A bank typically generates reports that assist management in the performance of their operations, including:

- daily trial balance containing the chart of accounts numbers, the current balance, and a total of all account activity for the day;
- daily new account report, which shows the bank's new business connections for the day;
- daily overdraft report that reports the overdraft position of all accounts accepted by the bank; and
- daily significant balance change, which shows material changes in an account that is reported to the management.

For nostro and vostro accounts reconciliation, see the following paragraphs:

B. *Nostro Reconciliation in Specific*

Nostro accounts and vostro accounts. A nostro account is one opened and held with other bank, it is also called a "Due from Bank" account. A vostro account, which literally means "your account with us", is one opened with us by an other bank. It is also called a "Due to Bank" account.

Bank reconciliation statements. For nostro accounts, we receive bank statements from other banks, but in order to ascertain that the information appear on these bank statements are correct, we need to match those on our own accounting records, the so called "mirror accounts". We compare our due from bank accounts statements with those statements received from other banks and reconcile the two by listing out all the outstanding items. And this is a "Bank Reconciliation" statement.

On bank reconciliation statements, all the outstanding items will appear under "you debit, you credit, we debit, or we credit". For vostro accounts, we send out account statements to other banks instead and they will perform their own bank reconciliation.

There are certain important points to be remembered when reconciling accounts:

- The bank reconciliation statement must be balanced. Any unbalanced statements should be investigated immediately as a top priority. The longer it takes to clear, the more difficult it is. Possible reasons for unbalanced statements are missing statements, duplicated statements, reconciliation errors, etc.

- "Our balance" can be checked with account balance. "Their balance" should be checked with the statements received from correspondent banks, whether by SWIFT, mail or both.
- Balancing the bank reconciliation is only the first basic step of the reconciliation work. The most important step is to sort out the outstanding items and find out why they are outstanding.
- Any communication to the originating/operating departments to reconcile any items must be supported by signed written evidence. Usually telephone instructions should not be accepted. Any instructions to reconcile outstanding items should be judged with common sense to see if they are justified and appropriate.
- The interest credited or debited should be checked with interest statements received or request for one if not available. The debit interest exceeding a certain amount and any back value adjustment should be double checked with the originating department.
- Account reconciliation staff should be separated from those committing transactions and accounting entries should be in principle made or passed by the originating departments.
- Bank reconciliation statements should be prepared timely and reviewed by a senior officer.

The following is a sample of a bank reconciliation statement. At this stage, you are not required to know how to reconcile but to be familiar with the format of the reconciliation statements.

RECONCILIATION REPORT			
Account with: Hanna bank Account No. : xxxxxxxx-ne, 1998			
Credit Balance Statement	14,972,925.00	Debit (O/D) Balance on Statement	0.00
Credit (O/D) Our G/L Balance	0.00	Debit Our G/L Balance	14,708,897.00
Statement Debit not yet Credited to ledger	0.00	Statement Credited not yet Debited to ledger	29,725.00
Ledger Debits not yet Credited on Statement	0.00	Ledger Credited not yet Debited on Statement	0.00
Since Credited	0.00	Since Debited	234,303.00
Total	14,972,925.00	Total	14,972,925.00

Listing of outstanding items: Description.

Date of Statement or Ledger Entry	Description3. Statement credited not yet Debited to Ledger	Amount	Remarks	Date item closed
20-April-98	Draft1265	16, 345. 00		
03-May-98	AHAC	1, 510. 00		
03-May-98	AHAC	11, 861. 00		
Date of Statement or Ledger Entry	Description3. Statement Credited not yet Debited to Ledger	Amount	Remarks	Date item closed
Total		29, 725. 00		

Prepared by: Approved by:

5. Types of Income and Expenditure of a Bank

Broadly, income and expenditure for a bank can be classified into the following main areas:

- Interest income;
- Fee income;
- Other income;
- Interest expense;
- Other expenses;
- Provisions.

A. *Interest Income*

The principal source of income for the majority of banks is still the interest received on the funds that the institution has at its disposal and is able to lend out in some form. Whenever a bank lends out money it will generally charge interest to the customer. In setting the interest rate that the customer will be charged, the bank will wish to ensure that the return exceeds the costs that it incurs or has incurred. Such costs will include the interest paid to the provider of the funds (funds from depositors or from other banks) and the various administrative costs normally incurred.

If we draw an analogy between a bank and a normal industrial company, then:

Interest received represents sales or turnover;

Interest paid represents cost of sales;

Net interest income, or margin, represents gross profit, being the difference between interest received and interest paid.

B. *Fee Income*

The other main source of revenue for a bank is fee income, or called commission income. The income and expenditure analysis provided by ABC bank (in one million US dollars) may serve to illustrating this:

	1997	1996
Income		
Interest income	10, 906	8, 689
Less: interest expense	8, 653	6, 572
Net interest income	2, 253	2, 117
Commission	1, 777	929
Foreign exchange	94	113
Other income	51	160
	3, 575	3, 319
Expenditure		
Operating costs		
Personnel costs	1, 270	1, 152
Premises and equipment	574	499
Other expenditure	660	544
	2, 504	2, 195
Bad and doubtful debts		
Specific	540	517
General	50	(8)
	590	509
Total expenditure	3, 094	2, 704
Total surplus	481	615

The above table clearly highlights the importance of commission income to the ABC Bank. In 1997, it not only exceeded the "surplus" (or profit before taxation and extraordinary items) of USD481 million, but even adding back the USD590 million provision for bad and doubtful debts. This would imply that commission income is becoming increasingly important.

The increased involvement of banks in activities that results in fee income being generated has been due to the perception, sometimes misplaced, that the income is of lower risk. In these days of high capital adequacy requirements when market condition makes it difficult for a bank to increase its capital, fee income becomes increasingly important as it normally ties up less capital.

The main types of fee income are:
- Fees for foreign trade financing services;
- Fees for guarantee and performance bond facilities;
- Fees for corporate advice;
- Money transmission and clearing fees;
- Custodianship services;

- Trust administration services;
- Private placement fees;
- Investment advice fees;
- Taxation advice, etc. .

C. *Other Income*

Generally a bank can receive the following types of other income:

- Investment income;
- Income from the sale of investment;
- Trading income (for interest rate, exchange rate and equity-based products);
- Credit card fees;
- Data processing fees;
- Rental income.

There is a whole range of other forms of income that may be received by a bank, perhaps being as numerous by type as the range of bank permits. Indeed, the analysis will vary from country to country.

D. *Interest Expense*

The main expense item for a retail or wholesale bank is the cost of funding money. Typically funding takes the following forms:

- Capital maintained by the bank in its various forms as required by the central bank in accordance with the rules applying at that particular time;
- Current accounts that are in funds;
- Deposit and savings accounts; and
- Money market deposits of various types.

Income is provided to all suppliers of funds whether as dividends or as interest. This in no way differs from dividends and interest paid on capital and loans by non-banking industry companies.

Historically, current accounts used to form a useful method of funding for a bank. They were among the cheapest forms of financing since banks did not pay interest on current accounts (nowadays interest is paid on many current accounts). However, this benefit was offset by a bank not charging for the costs of running a current account, for example, the provision of checkbooks, counter facilities and funds transmission. It has been calculated that the real cost to a bank of operating a current account is 7%. Consequently, if the bank is able to earn in excess of this amount, then a profit is made.

Deposits and savings accounts can have a variety of terms, with variable or fixed interest rates, in a variety of currencies, with various rules attached to the customer's ability to withdraw funds.

Banks take money market deposits to match a short-term gap in their funding requirements and to provide themselves with additional liquidity. They are usually interest bearing
bank deposits at variable and sometimes very high interest rates. As a rule, the greater the
need of a bank, the higher the rate to be charged to them by another institution.

E. Other Expenditure

The main sources of expenditure for a bank is personnel costs, premise costs and data
processing costs, etc.

i. Personnel costs

These usually represent the largest single expenditure item for a bank. In the case of
the 1997 ABC Bank accounts they amounted to over 50% of total expenditure excluding provision charges, a fairly typical figure for a retail bank.

ii. Premises costs

Clearing banks have large branch networks, which results in heavy property expenditure. Further, banks tend to use premises to project an image to the outside world. They
tend therefore to be modern (or extremely traditional), spacious and regularly refurnished.

iii. Other costs

Banks are involved in a high volume paper-intensive market, even given the major
strides made in recent years to reduce the volume of paper that abound in the banking industry. The market also experiences great volatility and is innovative with new markets and
products requiring new applications. Accordingly the cost to a bank can be high in terms of
software, hardware and processing.

Other costs for a bank are generally in line with those for other industries, with the exception of provision, which is in itself a normal cost of the business entered into.

6. Assets and Liabilities of a Bank

A. Assets

i. Liquid assets

This item is used to describe those assets, which are continually undergoing conversion
into cash or which are close to cash and those which may be easily converted into cash if the
need arises. The key factor in determining whether an asset is liquid is whether it can be
converted into cash as required without a significant additional loss being incurred. Liquid
assets are sometimes referred to as floating assets.

Principal types of liquid assets include the following:

- Cash (including notes and coins);

- Current balances with central and other banks;
- Items in the course of collection;
- Money at call and short notice;
- Short-term money market deposits;
- Certificates of deposit;
- Government and other readily marketable securities;
- Treasury, trade and other bills;
- Bullion.

It is important for a bank to hold sufficient liquid assets to meet the demands of depositors who may seek to withdraw their funds. However, maintenance of too high a level of liquid assets could be expensive. Cash balances in particular yield no income, yet will cost the same as any other asset of the bank.

ii. Trading assets

Banks maintain a large number of trading assets of varying types, depending on the type of trading undertaken. Generally all such assets should be marked to market on a regular basis so that the results of the institution accurately reflect the actions taken and decisions made during a period. In this way a bank is different from a company in another industry. If a dealing asset goes up in value, then an institution is able to sell that asset on the market and achieve a higher price level immediately. Accordingly there would be little gain in forcing a bank to call an increase in value of a dealing asset an unrealized profit, when it could so easily be realized.

iii. Investment securities

Investment securities are an important component of a bank's balance sheet. A bank makes investment for many reasons: liquidity, risk diversification, income, regulatory requirements and others.

Generally commercial banks may invest only in those securities that are rated as "investment grade", or have bond ratings in the top four categories. Banks may invest no more than a certain percentage of its capital and surplus in this category of bonds. Investments in equity securities in some countries are prohibited.

Investment securities purchased with the intention of holding them to maturity are stated at their face value. The premiums and discounts on acquisition are amortized over the period from date of purchase to date of maturity and an appropriation thereof is included in the profit and loss account.

On the other hand, trading securities purchased for dealing purpose are stated at cost or market value, whichever is lower.

iv. Advances accounts

Advances and security represent a major balance sheet category for the majority of banking institutions. The subject of loans and advances represents the single largest class of assets for the majority of financial institutions. They are also a class of assets where the lending institution is likely to face a high level of risk, resulting in losses being incurred. Indeed the acceptance and control of the risk of loss is the key element in the potential success of a financial institution, for it is for the acceptance of risk that the institution is being remunerated.

There are a variety of different types of loan, which you may encounter or need to consider. Among them the most frequently seen are as follows:

Overdrafts. An approved overdraft is an agreed line of lending, utilizing an overdraft facility agreed in a way similar to that adopted when a loan is entered into. The customer will then be able to draw on the current account against the overdraft facility up to the limit of that facility.

Mortgage lending. Mortgage is simply any form of lending where property is used as security for a loan.

Project lending. Project financing is simply a loan made to finance individual projects. Typically the security for the project loan is provided by the projects.

Syndicated loans. A syndicated loan is provided jointly in some way by a group of lenders that would be either unable or unwilling to provide such finance individually.

Personal loans. Apart from overdrafts and other forms of long-term finance, a variety of other personal loans can be provided. These include bridging loans, revolving credit loans, mortgages and budget of other specialized accounts.

v. Accrued interest

Accrued interest represents interest accrued on money market loan and deposit, syndication loans, securities, customer loans and deposits, inter-branch taking up to current period but not received or paid until the next period. Interest is accrued up to the last day of the current period.

B. Liabilities and Shareholders Own Funds

i. Deposits, check accounts and other borrowings

These are essentially the opposite side to the giving of advances. The taking of deposits and other forms of borrowing provide the financial institution with the funds that they can lend to third parties. Banks take deposits in various forms including current accounts, retail deposits, wholesale deposits, certificates of deposits and Euro deposits, etc.

ii. Other liabilities

Trading liabilities are the other side of trading assets as discussed earlier. They normally occur when a dealer has a short position (i. e. , it has sold more of an asset than it has pur-chased) or has undertaken a matched deal (a purchase and a sale carried out at the same nominal amount to match effectively the risks arising).

Besides, banks incur normal liabilities expected in any other business, in particular relating to personnel, premises, equipment (particularly computer equipment), taxation and dividends, etc.

iii. Reserves

Banks fund themselves through a combination of capital and reserves. These funds then become the reserves of the bank and, when geared up by further borrowing from the market and support the lending activities that the institution is engaged in.

iv. Capital

In addition to reserve funds mentioned above, the capital funds of a bank usually com-prise its share capital and loan capital. In principle these are not different from the capital funds of a commercial or industrial company and are equally important in determining the volume of borrowing and business that is possible.

7. Bad and Doubtful Debts

Provisions for bad and doubtful debts are held in respect of customer outstandings (ad-vances, overdrafts, loans, bills discounted and negotiated, securities investment), inclu-ding commercial outstandings and cross-border outstandings. The provisions comprise two el-ements, specific and general. Such provisions are made against advances when credit risks or economic or political factors make recovery doubtful.

Provisions against commercial outstandings are based on an appraisal of the loan portfo-lio. Specific provisions are made where the repayment of identified loans is in doubt, and reflects estimates of the amount of the loss.

A. General Provision

The general provision relates to the inherent risk of losses which, although not sepa-rately identified, is known from the experience to be present in any loan portfolio; and to those identified loans where material uncertainty exists as to the quantum of specific provi-sions required. The amount of the general provision reflects past experience, and judgments of conditions in particular locations or trading sectors.

B. Specific Provision

Specific provisions are made for those particular loans that have been identified as bad or doubtful: its aim is to write down the value of those loans to their estimated realizable value at the balance sheet date. In determining the extent of the specific element of the provision for bad and doubtful loans, the bank needs to consider at least five factors:

- The amount of the loan and the bank's other commitments to that borrower;
- The borrower's business prospects;
- The security for the loan (if any) and how it could be realized;
- The costs that would be incurred in obtaining repayment if security or other rights had to be enforced;
- The income from the loan.

In addition, provisions are made against cross border outstanding where it is judged that countries are experiencing or may experience severe payment difficulties and doubts exist as to whether full recovery will be achieved.

Provisions are applied to write off advances when all security has been realized and further recoveries are considered to be unlikely.

The aggregate provisions which are made during the year (less amounts released and recoveries of bad debts previously written off) are charged against operating profit. Interest on advances is accrued to profit until such time as its payment is considered not possible; thereafter such interest is not included in advances or in provisions for bad and doubtful debts. Bad debts are written off in part or in whole when a loss has been confirmed.

8. Foreign Exchange Transactions

A. Banks and Foreign Exchange

A foreign exchange transaction may be described as a contract to exchange a bank balance in one currency with a bank balance in another currency at an agreed rate of exchange at a specified point of time. The three main user groups of foreign exchange markets are banks, brokers and customers.

Banks participate in the inter bank market to move large sums of money around. The underlying purpose of these transactions may be to meet some form of customer requirement for currency, perhaps as a result of a trade financing transaction or because the customer wishes to create an investment position or hedge some existing position.

Banks also enter into foreign exchange transactions to provide the market with the liquidity, for unless there is a reasonable value of transactions taking place the market will not have the ability to deal properly with true transactions. Banks also enter into transactions to take advantage of imperfections in market pricing (arbitrage) besides entering into investment positions in their own right.

B. Some Basic Concepts for Accounting of Foreign Exchange

In accounting for foreign exchange, it is necessary to define a few terms listed below:

- Natural currency: natural currency is the actual currency of the transaction.
- Local currency: local currency is the currency in use in the country of operation.
- Foreign currency: foreign currency is any currency other than local currency in the country of operation.
- Local currency equivalent: local currency equivalent is any currency translated into the local currency.
- Base currency: the base currency is only used for reporting purposes. It may, for example, be the currency of the organization's parent.

Let's now illustrate the differences among these terms by the following example:

The British branch of an American bank is selling Australian dollars to a German bank. For this example, the currencies will be referred to as follows:

Natural currency: Australian dollars

Local currency: Sterling

Foreign currency: any currency other than sterling

Local currency equivalent: Australian dollars expressed as sterling

Base currency: American dollar

C. Systems of Accounting

Accounting for foreign transactions falls into two separate phases:

- The recording of the transaction, both on the transaction date and on the value date, including the settlement of the transaction;
- The revaluation of the bank's foreign exchange exposure.

Two accounting systems can generally be used to account for foreign exchange transactions, namely, the dual currency accounting system and the multiple currency accounting system.

i. The dual currency accounting system

In dual currency system, all ledgers are maintained in local currency, with foreign currency transactions being recorded in local currency equivalents. This is achieved through the utilization of an additional memorandum column showing the natural currency. This system is used by a minority of banks, but is more commonly used by some corporate enterprises.

Although this system can cope with the physical requirements of accounting, it does not facilitate the monitoring of foreign currency exposures. Once a foreign institution took the approach of translating all foreign currencies into local currency immediately after the transaction was entered into, and the foreign currency exposure was then totally ignored, because such conversion is considered to represent the local currency equivalent. This approach totally ignores the foreign currency exposure which continues to exist, and therefore gives rise to an exchange risk, which needs to be both monitored and managed.

ii. The multiple currency accounting system

In the multiple currency accounting system, all foreign currency transactions are only in the natural currency, a separate currency ledger being maintained for each currency used. For cross currency transactions, which involve two currencies and therefore two separate ledgers, offset entries are posted to separate control accounts utilized for each currency. This is the most widely used basis for accounting for foreign currencies.

Under the multiple currency accounting system, the following accounting records are maintained:

- A separate ledger for each currency;
- Separate subsidiary ledgers for loans and deposits for each currency;
- Separate spot and forward position accounts showing unmatured deals by currency.

No local currency equivalent records are maintained. All foreign currency assets and liabilities are recorded irrespective of whether or not they have matured.

Spot and forward transactions of unmatured instruments are initially recorded on transaction date in the bank's contingent ledger. They are not posted to the general ledger until maturity date.

D. Accounting for Spot and Forward Transactions

Initially, spot and forward transactions of unmatured instruments are recorded in the contingent ledgers maintained by the bank, separately for purchases and sales and for spot and forward transactions.

It is only for the computer or the accountant when the amounts are designated as debit (unmatured purchases) or credit (unmatured sales entries). Typically contingent entries are all reversed on value date.

This is best illustrated by the following example.

ABC Bank entered into a six-month forward foreign exchange transaction with its counterpart to purchase GBP1 million for USD1. 85 million. The accounting entries would appear as follows:

- On transaction date:

Contingent ledger:

Debit: unmatched purchases GBP1m

Credit: control account GBP GBP1m

Debit: control account USD USD1. 85m

Credit: unmatched sales USD1. 85m

- On value date:

Contingent ledger:

Debit: control account GBP GBP1m

Credit: unmatched purchases GBP1m

Debit: unmatched sales USD1.85m

Credit: control account USD USD1.85m

Currency ledger:

Debit: nostro account GBP1m

Credit: exchange GBP1m

Debit: exchange USD1.85m

Credit: nostro account USD1.85m

The unmatched ledgers are for recording transactions after transaction date but before the matching is properly undertaken on value date. At this stage the transaction is fully operational. Clearly, control over this area will be obtained through the regular reconciliation of the unmatched purchase and sales ledgers, together with the balancing of the control accounts. This will ensure that any transactions, which have not been matched, are promptly identified. This represents only the start of the story of foreign exchange accounting, the more complicated calculation and accounting of foreign exchange profits will not be required at this stage but we will give a basic idea of valuation of foreign exchange in the following case.

E. The Principles of Valuation for Foreign Exchange

For accounting purposes it is necessary to measure the results of a company in either local currency, or reporting currency, or both. This requires the foreign exchange positions to be included in either local or reporting currency equivalents, taking proper account of any resulting exchange gains or losses.

The problem is then to determine the basis for valuation for such positions. The most commonly used method is normally referred to as the "buy-back" method (or the cover method). This involves valuing forward transactions at the amount for which they could be purchased or sold at the balance sheet date. Spot assets and liabilities are usually valued at the middle market spot rate on the valuation date.

It must be emphasized that the recording of foreign exchange transactions reflects the purchase (cash outflow) of one currency, in exchange for a sale (cash inflow) in another currency. The transactions themselves merely generate entries across the various nostro accounts and therefore in themselves result in neither a profit nor a loss. The second phase of foreign exchange accounting is the revaluation of remaining positions, when the profits and losses arise.

When a bank enters into a foreign exchange transaction, it increases a position in one currency and reduces a position in another. The positions in both currencies have been changed and at the point of transaction, the equivalents of the changes would be the same. However, the local currency equivalent value of the position retained will move with changes in market exchange rates.

Any series of positions that a bank maintains will be worth a sum of money in local currency equivalent. As the exchange rates when compared with local currency vary, the difference will represent a profit or loss in local currency. A revaluation account is maintained which is credited with revaluation gains and debited with revaluation losses.

9. The Cash-Flows Statement of a Bank

Assessing the amounts, timing and uncertainty of cash flows is one of the basic objectives of financial reporting. The statement that provides information needed to meet this objective is a statement of cash flow. It presents a detailed summary of all the cash inflows and outflows, or the sources and uses of cash during the period.

A. *Objectives of the Statement*

The statement's value can help meet the information needs of users including the needs for information on:

- liquidity, the nearness to cash of its assets and liabilities;
- financial flexibility, the ability to take effective actions to alter the amount and timing of future cash flows so the company can respond to unexpected needs and opportunities;
- operational capability, the ability to maintain a given level of operations.

The statement of cash flows can also help external users assess a bank's;

- ability to generate positive future cash flows;
- ability to meet its obligations and pay dividends;
- needs for external financing;
- differences between its net income and associated cash receipts and payments;
- the cash and non-cash aspects of its investing and financing transactions during the accounting period.

Cash flows are important indicators of a bank's profitability and viability. To be profitable and viable, a bank must have sufficient cash flows to make loans and investments, meet withdrawals, satisfy loan commitments and meet other cash requirements. Cash-basis information provides critical support to accrual basis accounting.

B. *Cash and Cash Equivalents*

In the cash flow statement, cash flows include "cash and cash equivalents". Cash equivalents are highly liquid short-term investment such as treasury bills, commercial papers, money market funds, etc. They must be readily convertible to known amounts of cash, and so near their maturity that they present insignificant risk of changes in value because of changes in interest rate. Generally, cash equivalents only include investments with original maturities of three months or less. The total amounts of cash and cash equivalents at the beginning and end of the period shown in the statement of cash flows shall be the same as similarly titled line items or subtotals shown in the statement of financial position as of those dates.

C. Contents of the Cash-Flow Statement

The statement of cash flows reports cash flows relating to operating, investing and financing activities of a bank:

i. Operating activities

Operating activities include all transactions and events that are not investing and financing activities. Such activities include revenues and expenses transactions associated with the sale of products or the delivery of services, e. g. , all activities that enter into the determination of net income. Operating activities for a bank could include cash flows from:

Cash receipts

- interest income
- dividend income
- fees for services
- sale of trading securities and loans acquired specifically for resale
- other receipts not classified as investing or financing activities

Cash payments

- salaries and wages
- interest
- taxes
- purchase of trading securities and loans acquired specifically for resale
- other payments not classified as investing or financing activities

ii. Investing activities

Investing activities include (1) lending money and collection of loans and (2) acquiring and disposing of investment and productive long-term assets. Bank lending activities are included in this section and not as operating activities (although bank lending is a major operating activity). A bank's investing activities could include cash flows from:

Cash receipts

- collection of loans
- sale of loans other than those acquired specifically for resale

- sale or maturity of investments
- sale of property, plant and equipment

Cash payments

- loans to customers
- purchase of loans other than those acquired specifically for resale
- purchase of investment securities
- purchase of property, plant and equipment

iii. Financing activities

Financing activities involve liability and owner's equity items and include (1) obtaining cash from creditors and repaying the amounts borrowed and (2) obtaining capital from owners and providing them with a return on their investment (dividends) or other distributions to owners, including outlays to reacquire the enterprise's equity instruments (purchase of treasury stock). Bank deposit transactions are financing activities, but not operating activities (although they are a major operating activity of banks). Cash flows from financing activities include:

Cash receipts

- receiving deposits
- issuance of equity securities (capital stock)
- issuance of debt securities (bonds, notes, mortgages)

Cash payments

- withdrawal of deposits
- redemption of debt
- payment of dividends
- purchase of treasury stock by a bank holding company

The cash-flow statement must also clearly show (1) the net increase or decease in cash and (2) a reconciliation of the beginning cash balance to the ending cash balance. In the statement the inflows and outflows for each category should be shown separately, and the net cash flows (the difference between the inflows and outflows) should be reported.

10. Budgeting

A budget is a financial plan, which is based on expected future activity and is used to control that activity. A bank's budget should be comprehensive and coordinated, and not simply a set of vague and unrealized hopes and wishes. The budget will include different types of business activities and their target income and expenditure. It acts as guidance and forms a basis for comparison with actual figures to determine the variance.

The compilation of the budget is the whole bank's work. The budget should be prepared on the consideration of its characters, location and market forecast. The budget should usually include:

- assets and liabilities: year-end balance, average balance, average rates, budget interest, income and expenses;
- commission income: transaction volumes in numbers and amounts, the rate charged and budget commission income;
- total income and total expenditure, profit & loss budget;
- budget plan for acquisition of new fixed assets;
- any other explanations or considerations.

During and at the end of the budget execution period, the actual performance will be compared with the budget to determine the variance. For large variance the reason should be investigated and actions taken whenever necessary. If large adjustments prove necessary, the budget will be revised and reported to the executive management for approval.

Appendix

The followings are the example forms of 3 financial statements and their main items used by a bank. Their figures are omitted.

Appendix 1

Midland Bank Consolidated Balance Sheet At 31, December 1996

Assets

Cash and balances at central banks

Items in the course of collection from other banks

Treasury bills and other eligible bills

Loans and advances to banks

Loans and advances to customers

Debt securities

Equity shares

Interests in associated undertakings

Other participating interests

Tangible fixed assets

Other assets

Prepayments and accrued income

Total assets

Liabilities

Deposits by banks

Customer accounts

Items in the course of transmission to other banks

Debt securities in issue

Other liabilities

Accruals and deferred income

Provisions for liabilities and charges

—Deferred taxation

—Other provisions for liabilities and charges

Subordinated liabilities

—Undated loan capital

—Dated loan capital

Minority interests

Shareholder's funds (including non-equity interests)

Called up share capital

Share premium account

Revaluation reserves Profit and loss account

Total liabilities and shareholder's funds

Memorandum items Contingent liabilities

—Acceptances and endorsements

—Guarantees and assets pledged as collateral security

—Other contingent liabilities

Commitments

W. P. urves Chairman

K. R. Whiten Chief Executive and Director

R. M. J. Orgill Deputy chief Executive Director

I. B. Marshall Secretary

Appendix 2

Midland Bank Consolidated Profit and Loss Statement For the Year Ending 31 December

Interest receivable

—Interest receivable and similar income arising from debt securities

—Other interest receivable and similar income

Interest payable

Net interest income

Dividend income

Fees and commissions receivable

Fees and commissions Payable

Dealing profits

Other operating income

Other income

Operating income

Administrative expenses

Depreciation and amortization

Operating expenses

Operating profit before provisions

Provisions

—Provisions for bad and doubtful debts

—Provisions for contingent liabilities and commitments

Amounts written off fixed asset investments

Operating profit

Profit on disposal of fixed assets and investments

Profit from associated undertakings

Profit on ordinary activities before tax

Tax on profit on ordinary activity

Profit on ordinary activities affair tax

Minority interests

Profit for the financial year attributable to shareholders

Dividends (including amounts attributable to non-equity shareholders)

Retained profit for the financial year transferred to Reserves

Earnings per ordinary share

Appendix 3

Sample Bank Statement of Cash Flows

Year ending December 31 , 1998 and 1997 in million dollars

Cash Flows from Operating Activities:

Interest received from Loans and leases

Investment securities

Federal funds sold

Trust department income

Service fees

Other income

Interest paid to depositors

Interest paid on federal funds purchased

Interest paid on capital notes

Cash paid to suppliers and employees

Income taxes paid

Net cash provided by operating activities

Cash Flows from Investing Activities:

Proceeds from sales of investment securities

Purchase of investment securities

Federal funds sold, net

Principal collected on loans

Loans made to customers

Purchase of assets to be leased

Principal payments received under leases

Capital expenditures

Proceeds from sale of capital items

Net cash used in investing activities

Cash Flows from Financing Activities:

Net increase in demand deposits and savings accounts

Proceeds from sales of time deposits

Payments for maturing time deposits

Dividends paid

Net cash provided by financing activities

Net increase /Decrease In Cash and Cash Equivalents

Cash and Cash Equivalents, Beginning

Cash and cash Equivalents, Ending

Notes

1. **Accrual** [ə'kru:əl] *n.* ① the action or process of accruing ② something that

accrues or has accrued Accrue: to accumulate or be added periodically

2. **Margin** [ˈmɑːdʒin] *n.* ①the difference which exists between net sales and the cost of merchandise sold and from which expenses are usually met or profit derived ②the excess market value of collateral over the face of a loan

3. **Salvage** [ˈsælvidʒ] *n.* ① compensation paid for saving a ship or its cargo from the perils of the sea or for the lives and property rescued in a wreck; the act of saving or rescuing a ship or its cargo; the act of saving or rescuing property in danger (as from fire) ②property saved from destruction in a calamity (as a wreck or fire); something extracted (as from rubbish) as valuable or useful

4. **Interpolation** [inˌtəːpəuˈleiʃən] *vt.* ① to alter or corrupt (as a text) by inserting new or foreign matter; to insert (words) into a text or into a conversation ②to insert between other things or parts ③ to estimate values of (data or a function) between two known values *intransitive verb*: to make insertions (as of estimated values)

5. **Amortization** [əˌmɔːtiˈzeiʃən] *n.* ① the act or process of amortizing ② the result of amortizing Amortize: ①to pay off (as a mortgage) gradually usually by periodic payments of principal and interest or by payments to a sinking fund ②to gradually reduce or write off the cost or value of (as an asset)

6. **Reconciliation** [ˌrekənsiliˈeiʃən] *n.* the action of reconciling: the state of being reconciled; Reconcile: to check (a financial account) against another for accuracy

7. **SWIFT**: *abbr* Society for Worldwide Interbank Financial Telecommunications

8. **Turnover** [ˈtəːnˌəuvə] *n.* ① movement (as of goods or people) into, through, and out of a place ② a cycle of purchase, sale, and replacement of a stock of goods; the ratio of sales for a stated period to average inventory; the amount received in sales for a stated period ③ the number of persons hired within a period to replace those leaving or dropped from a workforce; also: the ratio of this number to the number in the average force maintained

9. **Withdraw** [wiðˈdrɔː] *vt.* ① to take back or away: REMOVE ② to remove from use or cultivation ③ to remove (money) from a place of deposit ④ to turn away (as the eyes) from an object of attention ⑤ to draw (as a curtain) back or aside

10. **Bullion** [ˈbuljən] *n.* ① gold or silver considered as so much metal; *specifically*: uncoined gold or silver in bars or ingots; metal in the mass ② lace, braid, or fringe of gold or silver threads

Questions for Discussion

1. How does the accounting information system work?

2. Who need accounting information?

3. What's the importance of accounting entity principle?

4. Why do we measure transactions in monetary units?

5. What's accounting equation and how is worked out?

6. What should we be concerned about the due dates of an entity's liabilities?

7. What are the effects of income and expense on owner's equity?

8. What's the relationship between general ledger and subsidiary ledger?

9. What are the three primary financial statements and their main components?

10. What's the purpose of Statement of Cash Flow?

11. What are the three common cost behaviors? And what are their differences?

12. Why contribution-margin income statement is more valuable than functional income statement?

13. What is break-even point and it's importance?

14. What's Cost-Volume-Profit analysis for?

15. What are the two major sources for financing?

16. What's present value and net present value?

17. How is Internal Rate of Return used to measure a business' success?

18. What are chart of accounts and the major components for a bank?

19. How could a bank control its cash?

20. Why does a bank prepare reconciliation statement?

21. How could a bank earn interest income?

22. Why should a bank keep sufficient liquid assets?

23. What are the differences among natural currency, local currency, foreign currency, local currency equivalent, and base currency?

24. What does cash equivalent mean?

25. What are the three major activities included in a bank's Statement of Cash Flows?

Part Five

Intermediary Services

I. Intermediary Services

Commercial Banks perform a variety of functions. Some are central to their main role in the economy and others are peripheral. Although lending and deposit-taking have been the epicenter of commercial banking, the last few years have witnessed a general surge in both the types and the volume of bank services. This surge has been induced in part by government deregulation, but most importantly by competitive pressures.

The three main functions of commercial banks are interrelated: the creation of money accomplished through lending and investing activities, the holding of deposits and the provision of a mechanism for payments and transfer of funds. They all relate to the bank's critical role in the overall management of the flow of money and credit through the economy.

Other services are offered primarily to draw customers by providing complete money management and ancillary services through a single institution. Some of these services, such as trust management and leasing, may themselves be profitable; others may be offered solely to attract depositors to the institution.

1. Relationship between Banks and Customers

Before we come to explore these services in detail, it is necessary to discuss the relationship between banks and their customers. The discussion may help us to have a better understanding of intermediary services provided by banks. The legal contractual relationships between banks and customers could be divided into three categories:

- debtor/creditor
- principal/agent
- bailor/bailee

A. *Debtor—Creditor Relationship*

This is the basic bank-customer relationship. It arises out of the fact that the bank holds money that belongs to the customer. The money has to be repaid at some time, and therefore the bank is the debtor, while the customer is the creditor.

When, however, the customer borrows money from the bank, the position is reversed. Here the customer is the debtor, while the banker is the creditor.

An interesting point about the debtor-creditor relationship is that it is not the debtor's (i. e. the bank's) job to seek to repay the debt, but the creditor (i. e. the customer) has the responsibility to ask for the money back. This is the opposite position to the normal debtor-creditor situation.

As a financial intermediary, a bank lends to those who want to borrow and borrows from those who want to lend. However, when we are discussing the bank's intermediary services, which is the focus of this chapter, we are not referring to those lending and borrowing activities, i. e. , the relationship between the banks and their customers is not a debtor-creditor one. Primarily speaking, the relationship between a bank and its client as intermediary services is a **principal-agent** one, i. e. , the bank is acting as an agent for its client.

B. Principal—Agent Relationship

A bank, when dealing with its customer directly, has a debtor—creditor relationship. But when a third party is involved, the relationship becomes one between a principal and an agent.

The term agency refers to a relationship by agreement between two parties whereby one party (agent) agrees to act on behalf of the other party (principal). The agent is subject to the control of the principal and is a fiduciary that must act for the benefit of the principal. The agent's authority is determined by the principal. Agents generally have the authority to perform legal acts for the principal in accordance with the agency agreement.

The principal has the obligation to compensate the agent according to the agreement, reimburse the agent for reasonable expenses, indemnify the agent for duties performed on behalf of the principal, and inform the agent of risks. The agent's obligations require that the agent act in the best interest of the principal and with complete loyalty, carry out the instruction of the principal with reasonable care and skills, account to the principal, indemnify the principal for damages wrongfully caused to the principal, provide information to the principal, and not to compete or act adversely to the principal.

In services like fund transfer, clearing, trust and factoring, banks act as agents for their principals—the clients. In the following sections, we will discuss these services in detail. Before that, we shall look at the last of the three main relationships between banks and customers.

C. Bailor—Bailee Relationship

One type of bank services is to receive valuables and documents and hold them on behalf of their customers. When a bank holds these valuables in safe custody, it has to take care of the property, thus forming a bailor-bailee relationship with their customers.

A bailor is the depositor of the property. This deposit is made on the understanding that it will be returned by the bailee, or dealt with in accordance with the bailor's instructions.

A bailee receives the property and must look after it in a careful and professional manner.

Generally speaking, when banks provide services like safekeeping, they will enter into a bailor-bailee relationship.

D. Safekeeping

Banks maintain vaults and elaborate security systems to safeguard their own stores of cash, securities, and other negotiable instruments. A traditional bank service has been to make this security available to customers for the safekeeping of their valuables. These services are of two types: safe deposit boxes and safekeeping.

Safe deposit boxes are usually metal compartments stored within the bank vault and rented to customers. This arrangement gives the customer both control over access to the stored valuables and privacy. The bank protects the goods from theft or damage, and guarantees that only the customer or authorized representatives shall have access to the box. The customer's right to the privacy of the safe deposit box is guaranteed by law and the bank may open the box only by court order.

Safekeeping, by contrast, calls for the bank to exercise custodial functions over the valuables and to act as agent for the customer. Securities such as stocks and bonds are the items most commonly held under this type of arrangement. Individuals or corporations owning large amounts of securities commonly keep them in banks. Banks frequently hold securities pledged as loan collateral.

Since we have a basic understanding of the relationships between banks and customers, as well as the differences between the banks themselves as financial intermediaries and their intermediary services lets now have a closer look at these intermediary services in detail.

2. Settlement — Payments and Funds Transfer

A. Introduction

Settlement, in general, is the striking of a balance between two or more parties having mutual dealings with one another, i. e., the payment of balance by the debtor (s) to the creditor (s). The provision of a mechanism of payment and funds transfer is an important function of banks. Transferring balances among accounts is an activity that banks perform when instructed to do so — that is when the relationship between the bank and its customer is a principal-agent one.

The procedures for effecting the actual transfers of funds are undergoing rapid changes with the introduction of new technology in the storage and transfer of information. Since the introduction of money, the settlement of funds has evolved through three stages, namely cash-based, paper-based and electronic-based settlement.

i. Cash — based

Cash is still the basic form of payment today, although its use is being restricted to the "cheaper" transactions. Banks, businesses and customers have moved away from cash as a means of payment for the more expensive goods and services for a variety of reasons including:

- Security;
- Bulk carrying;
- Cost of goods and services;
- High costs of dealing with cash.

ii. Paper — based

When we discuss the paper-based settlement, we cannot do without mentioning various **Negotiable Instruments**. From a functional perspective, negotiable instruments are documents used in commerce to represent the ownership and secure the payment of money. The three main types of them are Bills of Exchange, Cheques, and Promissory Notes. We will discuss them one by one in the next section.

iii. Electronic — based

Credit card is a transitional product for the payment system, because it is semi- paper based and semi-electronic based. While the introduction of debit cards and the spread of ATMs bring us to the era of Plastic Money, smart cards (intelligent cards) are becoming more and more popular and powerful. However, people are still worrying about the security of the Electronic Network, which is an obstacle to the wide use of electronic-based payment system.

B. Negotiable Instruments

From a functional perspective, negotiable instruments are documents used in commerce to secure the payment of money. Paying large sums of money in cash is both inconvenient and, unfortunately, risky. In all cases, negotiable instruments represent a right to payment. A right is, by definition, a promise and not a tangible piece of property. So, negotiable instruments are classified as choses in action. The three main types of them are the following:

i. Bills of Exchange

A bill of exchange is an unconditional order in writing, addressed by one person to another, signed by the person giving it, requiring the person to whom it is addressed to pay on demand, or at a fixed or determinable future time, a sum certain in money, to or to the order of a specified person, or to the bearer.

Two important advantages of using bills of exchange are as follows:

- As a method of payment, they avoid the need to transfer large sums of cash, particularly from one country to another.

- The conflicting demands of buyers and sellers can be reconciled. The buyer obtains a useful period of credit if he draws the bills payable at a future date; he hopes that at that time he can resell the goods and pay the bill out of the proceeds from that sale. On the other hand, the seller has secured a sale and he has the choice of retaining the bill until it matures, or negotiating (transferring) it to one of his own creditors who is willing to take it in payment or discounting (selling) the bill for a little less than its face value, thereby obtaining immediate payment. Thus, bills both provide credit and settle debts.

ii. Cheques

A cheque is an unconditional order in writing, addressed by a person to a bank, signed by the person making it, requiring the bank to pay on demand a sum certain in money to or to the order of, a specified person or to the bearer.

The rules applicable to bills of exchange are also applicable to cheques except in the following aspects:

- Acceptance

A cheque is never accepted by the bank on which it is drawn. Hence, the rules relating to acceptance of bills do not apply to cheques.

- Negotiation

Few cheques are ever negotiated. The vast majority is paid straight into the payee's account. In practice, therefore, the rules relating to negotiation are of very limited importance in respect to cheques.

- Forged and unauthorized signatures

In certain circumstances, an order cheque bearing a forged or an unauthorised indorsement is discharged by the bank on which it is drawn. Payment by the acceptor of a bill of exchange under similar conditions does not discharge its rights and liabilities which still exist on it.

- Crossings

The rules relating to crossings are confined to cheques (and certain other instruments), while other bills cannot be crossed. Crossing is a very important feature of cheque, so we shall give it a bit more coverage.

Most cheques bear two bold parallel lines across their face. This is the crossing. A crossing is a direction to the paying bank that the money proceeds of the cheque should be paid only to another bank as agent of the payee and not directly to the payee himself. A crossing therefore restricts payment of a cheque. The two primary categories of crossings are "general" and "special".

General crossings: General crossings consist of two transverse parallel lines across the face of the cheque, with or without the words "not negotiable".

Special crossings: A special crossing consists of the name of a particular bank to which payment must be made. As the name itself is the crossing, and while they often appear, two transverse parallel lines (the essence of a general crossing) are unnecessary.

Now let's consider a special kind of negotiable instrument to which the rules of cheques also extend—**Bank Drafts.**

Bank drafts are negotiable instruments drawn payable to order by a bank as drawer on the same bank as drawee. Legally, they are not cheques because the drawer and drawee are the same person. This is so even though the draft may be drawn, as is usual, by a branch on the head office or another branch; the bank is considered as one entity for this purpose.

It goes without saying that a bank draft is as good as cash for many commercial purposes, dishonour of it being unheard of unless it is known that the presenter is not entitled to it.

iii . Promissory Notes

A promissory note is an unconditional promise in writing made by one person (the maker) to another (the payee or the holder) signed by the maker engaging to pay on demand or at a fixed or determinable future time a sum certain in money to or to the order of a specified person or to bearer.

Compared with bills of exchange, promissory notes are charactered as follows:

- While a bill is in the form of an order, a promissory note is a promise to pay.
- The drawer and drawee are the same person, which means that there are only two original parties to the transaction in the case of a promissory note.
- A promissory note is never accepted.
- The maker of promissory note is always the party primarily liable for payment. Should the payee negotiate the note by endorsement, he then becomes liable as surety for the maker's payment. Promissory notes are not commonly used in business.
- Bank notes are promissory notes issued by a bank, they differ from other promissory notes in that they are issued for certain fixed amounts, always payable to bearer and on demand. They are, of course, also legal tenders.

C. *Plastic Money*

i. *Credit Card*

A credit card is a plastic card (or its equivalent) to be used upon presentation by the cardholder to obtain money, goods, or services, possibly under a line of credit established by the card issuer. The cardholder is billed for any outstanding balance.

Credit-card customers are given a credit limit on the credit card account and can buy goods and services up to this amount. Normally, banks will set different credit lines to the different groups of cardholders. Every time the cardholder uses a credit card for purchasing, he/she must sign a sales slip in the presence of the seller, and the signature is then compared to the signature on the card. Copies of the sales slips have the details of the card and they also show the details and amount of the sale.

Each month the cardholder receives a statement from the bank which details all the transactions in the month, together with the total amount outstanding and any minimum amount that needs to be paid. When the full balance is not settled each month, the cardholder is charged a compound interest (say 0.05%) on the outstanding balance, and this is supposed to provide the bank with a main source of income (although in China, this revenue is still low because people are reluctant to run into debt). Other two major sources of credit card services are the annual fee from the cardholders and the percentage of the sales revenue as the commission paid by the seller.

The advantages of using credit cards to pay for goods and services are as follows:

- Advantages to the cardholder:

—no need to carry cash (convenience and security);

—immediate delivery of goods;

—free credit is given;

—payments can be spread; and

—free access to many valuable services (for instance, a cardholder of the Great Wall International Credit Card issued by Bank of China can enjoy many valuable services).

- Advantages to the seller:

—increased sales;

—lowered cost of dealing with large sum of cash; and

—some security such as they contact banks to check whether the card is on the blacklist.

- Advantages to the bank:

—cost-effective way of granting credit (no need for credit approval);

—extension of service to customers who are not the bank's clients; and

—revenue from the card business.

ii. Debit Card

A debit card is a plastic card enabling the cardholder to purchase goods or services, or withdraw cash, the cost of which is immediately charged to his or her bank account. Debit cards are used to activate POS (point of sale) terminals in supermarkets, gas stations and stores. Together with credit cards, they are commonly referred to simply as bank cards.

Debit cards are widely used to pay for goods and services, much more widely in China than that of credit cards. They are used in conjunction with a current bank account. The amount of the purchase is immediately debited from the account and no credit is involved, thus it's named. A comparison of the two bank cards will help us get a full picture of them.

Differences between Credit Cards and Debit Cards

	Credit Card	Debit Card
Cost	Many banks charge an annual fee. But Some don't	Free
Payment	Monthly or by installment	Immediately charged
Credit	Have a revolving credit line	No credit

iii. Smart Card (Intelligent Card)

A smart card is a secure, portable, tamper-resistant data-storage device. It is the exact size of a credit card and contains a computer with as much power as the original mini-computer. Data stored in a smart card are accessed by placing the card in (contact) or near (contactless) a smart card reader and providing the specific security access codes associated with the data desired.

More than 70 million smart cards worth USD 500 million were manufactured and distributed in 1996, and their use is doubling every year. The worldwide market for smart cards and associated smart card products and services in 1996 generated approximately USD 2 billion in sales and is growing at the rate of about 20 percent per year.

First developed in France in 1974, smart cards have since then attained various levels of sophistication, ranging from a simple prepaid card similar to a phone card, to portable electronic devices that may feature a keyboard and a liquid crystal display, like those used by a GSM telephone subscriber.

The technology of smart cards, especially its ability to store huge amount of information and to be reloaded easily and reliably, makes it greatly different from the credit cards and debit cards. Actually, in China by now, the dominant users of smart cards are not banks, but governments and commercial organizations. Few banks in China have ever issued smart cards, and its usage is still restricted compared with its possible application.

However, its tamper-resistant and portability features, along with its ability to combine on one secure processor value exchange, identity establishment, and access authorization applications, make a smart card a natural candidate for inclusion in Electronic Commerce on the Internet. With the rapid development of Information Technology and Electronic Commerce in China, smart cards will soon become one of the dominant forms of bank cards in a near future.

iv. The Development of Bank Cards in China

The first chinese bank-card was issued in 1978 by Bank of China, and it was a debit card. In 1985, Bank of China issued the first credit card in China, which is deemed to be the beginning of the bank card industry of China. After 21 years of development, there have been more than 900 million cards that have been ever issued. In June 2006, the transaction volume reached RMB757.4 billion, and the number of ATMs and POS terminals also exceeded 89 thousand and 689 thousand respectively.

However, compared with developed countries, the bank cards are still underused in China. It is reported that in United States there are 1.2 ATMs and 5 POS terminals per thousand people.

To accelerate the development of bank cards industry in China, in 1993 the central government launched the "Golden Card Project" with an aim of connecting all the cards issued by different banks. Along with the rapid economic growth of China, the usage of bank cards is bound to boost.

D. International Settlement

The payments and funds transfer mechanism can all be utilized in an international scale, especially for individuals. However, because of the complexity of international payments, some settlement mechanisms like collections, documentary credits, and etc. different from the above mentioned ones are innovated to meet the commercial demands, Since international settlement and trade financing are such important business for an international and universal bank, we have a whole chapter devoted to this topic at the latter part of this book.

Providing for a payment mechanism is a costly activity. Indeed, managing the payments mechanism can absorb up to a third of total bank costs. Cost items include wages for tellers and bookkeepers, computers and maintenance, advertising, and substantial amounts of other equipments and supplies. A large potion of employee time is spent performing the payments-mechanism function. Service charges do not cover all of these expenses.

The expansion of computerized payment systems promises to reduce the employee time and paperwork involved in transferring funds. The introduction of automatic teller machines (ATMs) has heralded the inauguration of computerized systems that permit 24 hour banking services, such as electronic withdrawal of cash from one's deposit accounts. Highly advanced ATMs offer customers such additional services as access to their mutual fund accounts, purchase or sale of stocks, payment of utility and store bills, and printouts of bank statements.

Another related electronic development has been the trend toward Internet banking based on the IT (Information Technology). Internet banking enables a customer to communicate with the bank via an Internet terminal (a computer, a mobile phone or even a TV) linked to the bank's computer. This represents another dimension of electronic funds transfer (EFT) systems, and consequently of paperless banking. Internet banking allows any customer to transact business from anywhere, at any time. It is generally viewed as the dominant delivery system of banking services in the foreseeable future. Wider use of these services will take people out of the bank, reduce the paperwork load, and drive down cost.

3. Trust Services

For a great variety of reasons, individuals or corporations may desire a reliable, outside entity to administer their assets. To meet this need, and to attract large depositors, banks offer trust services. As wealth in China has increased, the need for trust services has grown. Management of trusts involves both investing the funds for growth and carrying out specific instructions regarding them.

To better understand the trust services banks offer, we should first understand what trust is. Legally speaking, trust is a fiduciary relationship in which one person is trusted by the holder of the legal title to property, subject to an equitable obligation to keep or use the property for the benefit of the holder or a designated party.

In early times trusts had for their purpose the preservation of property in order that favored individuals or institutions might benefit from the income from the principal of the trusts or come into the possession of the principal itself. In the establishment of a trust, there are primarily three principal parties involved:

- The trustor, or party who creates the trust is also known as the settlor, grantor, or donor;
- The beneficiary, an individual or charitable organization, for whose benefit the fund is established. A beneficiary may have an interest in trust income, corpus or both; and a present interest, commencing with the trusts creation, or a future interest, commencing when a specified event occurs, or both;
- The trustee, who is charged with the management and preservation of the property that constitutes the trust estate. It can also be one or more individuals, or an

organization (e. g. a bank) , who holds legal title to property placed in trust and is responsible for administering the property for the benefit of the trust beneficiary or beneficiaries.

The various types of trusts in terms of provisions affecting distribution to the beneficiaries are the following:

- Trusts in which the income is to be periodically paid over to the trustor himself, or the wife, child, parent, or friend of the trustor, or to a charitable or other institution;

- Trusts in which the income is to be accumulated for a minor until he or she arrives at the age of majority;

- Trusts in which the principal is to be paid over to one beneficiary at a certain age (the remainderman) , the income in the meanwhile being paid to another or the same beneficiary (the life-tenant) ; and

- Trusts in which the principal is to be paid to the beneficiary upon marriage as a marriage settlement.

Trust Deposits. They are deposits made by one person as trustee for the other person. Such deposits are made under trustee account agreements executed in advance and are subject to the terms and conditions of the agreements. Despite the usual provisions in such agreements discharging the bank from payment of the withdrawals by the trustee where a trustee has both a personal account and a trustee account in the bank, the bank might become subject to constructive notice and inquiry in cases of loss to the beneficiaries through steady and large withdrawals from the trustee account to the trustee's personal account.

4. Lease

Besides providing various kinds of loans, the banks can finance the capital investment of its clients by many other ways, like leasing.

Lease is a contract granting the possession of lands, buildings, tenements, offices, machinery, or other chattels for a specified fixed or indeterminate period, for a stated consideration, usually a periodic payment known as rent or, in the case of land, ground rent. Since merely the possession and use of the property is conveyed by the owner to the user in a lease, the property reverts to the owner at the end of the term in most cases.

The lease is a flexible device for business use. Instead of tying up capital in acquisition of title to the real or personal property, the possession and use of the property may be had for the stated term in consideration of the rent or rental, which is a tax-deductible expense of doing business.

Lease classifications for financial-accounting-reporting purposes can be done on the basis of type and accounting method by lessee and lessor:

Type	Lessee	Lessor
Noncapitalized (no sale or purchase of the assets assumed)	Operating Lease	Operating Lease
Capitalized (sale or purchase of the assets assumed)	Capital Lease	Sales-type Lease Direct-financing Lease Leveraged Lease

The lessee regards a lease as a capital lease if it meets any one of the following criteria:

- The lessor transfers ownership of the property to the lessee by the end of the lease term.
- The lessee contains an option to purchase the leased property at a bargain price.
- The lease term is equal to or greater than 75 percent of the estimated economic life of the leased property.
- The present value of rental and other minimum lease payments equals or exceeds 90 percent of the fair value of the leased property less any investment tax credit retained by the lessor.

Capital lease is a fixed term lease, usually noncancelable, used by businesses in financing capital equipment. The lessor's service is limited to financing the asset, whereas the lessee pays all other costs, including maintenance and taxes, and has the option of purchasing the asset at the end of the lease for a nominated price. It is also called a full-payout lease because the lease is fully paid out (amortized) over its lifetime. A capital lease is, in substance, the purchase of an asset and the incurrence of a liability.

If none of these criteria is met, the lease is an operating lease. An operating lease is a lease written for a shorter period than the economic life of the leased asset. These leases are often written by equipment manufacturers, who are expected to take back the equipment and release it to other users. Both commercial banks and finance companies write operating leases. Operating leases are cancelable leases, meaning the equipment can be returned at any time if it becomes obsolete or is no longer needed.

A leveraged lease is a three-party lease involving a lessee, a lessor, and a long-term creditor, usually a bank or other financial institution. The long term creditor provides nonrecourse financing to the lessor. The financing provides the lessor with substantial leverage in the transaction. For instance, the lessor makes an equity investment equal to 20% of the equipment's original cost, and borrows the remaining 80% by issuing nonrecourse notes to the lenders, and writes a noncancelable lease for the equipment.

The lessor makes an assignment of the lease and lease rental payments to the lender, who is entitled to repossess the asset if the lessee happens to default. A leveraged lease is a true lease for tax purposes, because the lessor, as owner of the asset, is entitled to all of the tax benefits of ownership, including accelerated depreciation write-offs, deduction of interest payments on the bank loan, and the investment credit, if any, for purchase of the asset.

5. Factoring

Factoring is a short-term financing from the nonrecourse sale of accounts receivable to a third party, known as a factor, usually a bank-holding company or the bank itself. The factor assumes the full risk of collection, including credit losses. Factoring is most common in the garment industry, but has been used in other industries as well. There are two basic types of factoring: (1) discount factoring, in which the factor pays a discounted price for the receivables prior to the maturity date; and (2) maturity factoring, where the factor pays the client the purchase price of the factored accounts at maturity.

Factoring can be done on a notification, or a non-notification basis. The typical method in accounts receivable factoring is non-notification financing, in which the client's debtors are not notified and the client remits payments to the factor as they are received. Factoring is normally done without recourse, meaning that the factor does the credit evaluation before credit is extended and assumes the risk of nonpayment. Financing carried out on a recourse basis is called accounts-receivable financing (see Chart 5-1).

Accounts Receivable. Accounts due from customers as shown by the books of a business, but not evidenced by notes, drafts or acceptances (open book accounts).

Accounts Receivables are one of the current assets if in fact the claims represented are payable as of the date of the statement or payable in 12 months from the date of statement, pursuant to commercial accounting practice.

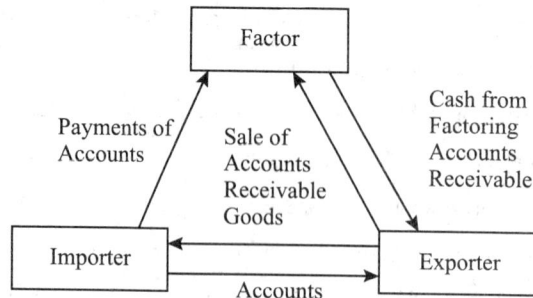

Chart 5-1

Accounts-Receivable Financing. Accounts Receivables represent a promise from customers to pay for goods sold or services rendered. Accounts Receivable Financing is a form of collateralized lending in which accounts receivables are the collateral. A bank often lends money against an agreed percentage of accounts receivables assigned to it, usually in the range of 50% – 90%. The cost of accounts receivable financing is typically higher than that associated with unsecured lending by a qualified borrower.

Accounts-receivable financing should not be confused with factoring. In factoring, a bank purchases (versus collateralized lending) selected accounts receivables from its customers at a percentage of their face value.

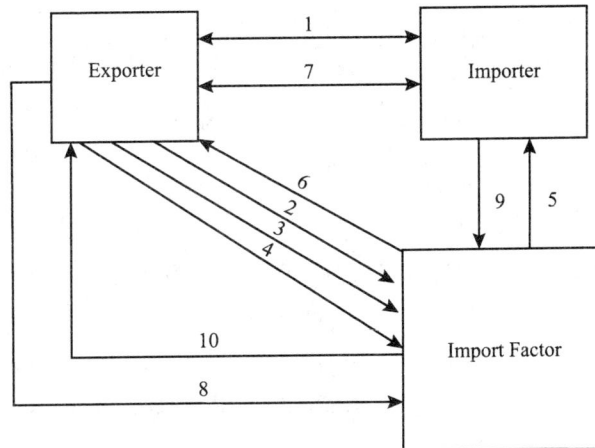

Chart 5-2 Procedures of Factoring

1. The exporter and the importer agree on the factoring settlement.
2. The exporter applies for factoring to the import factor.
3. Sign a factoring agreement.
4. Name of importer who needs credit line.
5. The import factor makes credit investigation.
6. The import factor notifies the exporter the credit line.
7. The exporter consigns goods and sends the invoice and documents to the importer.
8. The exporter presents the copy of invoice to the import factor.
9. At maturity the importer pays the import factor.
10. The import factor pays the exporter after deducting the charge.

II. Financial Markets

1. Introduction

Financial markets facilitate the lending of funds from savers to those who wish to undertake investments. Those who wish to borrow to finance investment projects sell IOUs (I owe you) to savers. Financial markets are markets for these IOUs. The various forms of IOUs are known collectively as financial instruments. Such instruments, which also are called securities, are claims that those who lend their savings have on the future incomes of the borrowers who use those funds for investment.

Now that we understand the basic function of financial markets, let's look at their structure. The following descriptions of several categories of financial markets illustrate essential features of these markets (see Chart 5-3).

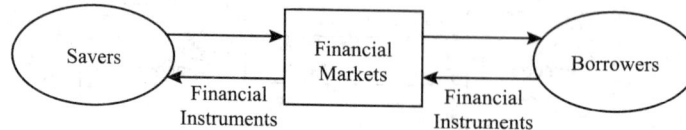

Chart 5-3

Apart from borrowing from banks, a firm or an individual can obtain funds in a financial market in two ways. The most common method is to issue a debt instrument, such as a bond or a mortgage, which is a contractual agreement by the borrower to pay the holder of the instrument fixed amounts at regular intervals (interest and principal payments) on a specified date (the maturity date). The **maturity** of debt instrument is the date when such instrument will become due for payment. A debt instrument is **short-term** if its maturity is less than a year and **long-term** if its maturity is ten years or longer. Debt instruments with a maturity between one and ten years are said to be **intermediate-term**.

The second method of raising funds is by issuing **equities**, such as common stock, which are claims to share in the net income (income after expenses and taxes) and the assets of a business. If you own one share of common stock in a company that has issued one million shares, you are entitled to one millionth of the firm's net income and one millionth of the firm's assets. Equities usually earn periodic payments (**dividends**) and are considered long-term securities because they have no maturity date.

The main disadvantage of owning a corporations equities rather than its debt is that an equity holder is a residual claimant; that is, the corporation must pay all its mature debt holders before it pays its equity holder. The advantage of holding equities is that equity holders benefit directly from any increases in the corporations' profitability or asset value because equities confer ownership rights on the equity holders. Debt holders do not share in this benefit because their dollar payments are fixed.

A **primary market** is a financial market in which new issues of securities, such as a bond or a stock, are sold to initial buyers by the corporation or government agency borrowing the funds. A **secondary market** is a financial market in which securities that have been previously issued (thus being secondhand) are resold.

The primary markets for securities are not well known to the public because the selling of securities to initial buyers takes place behind closed doors. An important financial institution that assists in the initial sale of securities in the primary market is the **investment bank**. It does this by **underwriting** securities, that is, it guarantees a price for a corporation's securities and then sells them to the public.

The New York Stock Exchange (NYSE), on which previously issued stocks are traded, is the best-known example of secondary markets, although the bond markets, in which previously issued bonds of major corporations and the U. S. government are bought and sold, actually have a larger trading volume. Other examples of secondary markets are foreign exchange markets, futures markets, and options markets. Securities brokers and dealers are crucial to a well-functioning secondary market. **Brokers** are agents of investors who match buyers with sellers of securities; **dealers** link buyers and sellers by buying and selling securities at stated prices.

When an individual buys securities in the secondary market, the person who has sold the securities receives money in exchange for the securities, but the corporation that issued the securities acquires no new funds. A corporation acquires new funds only when its securities are first sold in the primary market. Nonetheless, secondary markets serve two important functions. First, they make it easier to sell these financial instruments to raise cash; that is, they make the financial instruments more liquid. The increased liquidity of these instruments makes them more desirable and thus easier for the issuing firm to sell in the primary market. Secondly, they determine the price of the securities that the issuing firm sells in the primary market. The firms that buy securities in the primary market will pay the issuing corporation no more than the price that they think the secondary market will set for these securities. The higher the securities price in the secondary market, the higher the price that the issuing firm will receive for securities in the primary market and hence the greater the amount of capital it can raise. Conditions in the secondary market are therefore the most relevant to corporations issuing securities. It is for this reason that studies of financial market focus on the behavior of secondary markets rather than primary markets.

Another way of distinguishing markets is on the basis of the maturity of the securities traded in each market. The money market is a financial market in which only short-term debt instruments (normally maturity of less than one year) are traded; the capital market is the market in which longer-term debt (normally maturity of one year or longer) and equity instruments are traded. Money market securities are usually more widely traded than longer-term securities and so tend to be more liquid. In addition, short-term securities have smaller fluctuations in prices than long-term securities, making them safer investments. As a result, corporations and banks actively use this market to earn interest on surplus funds that they expect to have only temporarily. Capital market securities, such as stocks and long-term bonds, are often held by individuals and financial intermediaries such as insurance companies and pension funds, which have little uncertainty about the amount of funds they will have available in the future.

2. Money Market

It is no wonder that businesses have aggressively pursued alternatives to low-interest-rate bank accounts. One such alternative is provided by the money markets. This chapter carefully reviews the money markets and the securities that are traded there. In addition, we discuss why the money markets are important to our financial system.

The term money market is actually a misnomer. Money — currency — is not traded in the money market. However, because the market-securities are short-term, low-risk, and very liquid, they are close to being money in terms of their high degree of safety and liquidity, hence this name.

Money-market securities, which are discussed in detail later in this chapter, have three basic characteristics in common:

- They are usually sold in large denominations.
- They have low default risk.
- They mature in one year or less from their original issue date. Most money market instruments mature in less than 120 days.

The well-developed secondary market for money-market instruments makes the money market an ideal place for a firm or financial institution to "warehouse" surplus funds for short periods of time until they are needed. Similarly, the money markets provide a low-cost source of funds to firms, the government, and intermediaries that need a short-term injection of funds.

Most investors in the money market who are temporarily warehousing funds are ordinarily not trying to earn unusually high returns on their money market funds. Rather, they use the money market as an interim investment that provides a higher return than holding cash or money in banks. They may feel that market conditions are not right to warrant the purchase of additional stock, or they may expect interest rates to rise and hence not want to purchase bonds. Idle cash represents an opportunity cost in terms of lost interest income. The money markets provide means to invest idle funds and to reduce this opportunity cost. At the same time, the sellers of money market securities find that the money market provides a low-cost source of temporary funds.

Why do corporations and the government sometimes need to get their hands on funds quickly? The primary reason is that cash inflows and outflows are rarely synchronized. Government tax revenues, for example, usually come only at certain times of the year, but expenses are incurred all the year round. The government can borrow short-term funds that it will pay back when it receives tax revenues. Businesses also face problems caused by revenues and expenses occurring at different times. The money markets provide an efficient, low-cost way of solving these problems.

An obvious way to discuss the players in the money market would be to list those who borrow and those who lend. The problem with this approach is that most money market participants operate on both sides of the market. For instance, any large bank will borrow aggressively in the money market by selling large commercial CDs (Certificate of Deposit). At the same time, it will lend short-term funds to businesses through its commercial lending departments. Nevertheless, we can identify the primary money market players—the government, the central bank, commercial banks, businesses, investments and securities firms, and individuals—and discuss their roles.

A. *Participants of Money Market*

i. *The Government (often represented by the treasury department)*

In money market, the government is unique because it is always a supplier and demander of money market funds. The U. S. Treasury is the largest of all money market borrowers worldwide. It issues Treasury bills (often called T-bills) and other securities that are popular with other money market participants. Short-term issues enable the government to raise funds until tax revenues are received. Government also borrows from the money market to replace the maturing issues.

ii. *The Central Bank*

The central bank is the Treasury's agent for the distribution of all government securities. The central bank holds vast quantities of Treasury securities that it sells if it believes that the money supply should be reduced. Similarly, the central bank purchases Treasury securities if it believes that the money supply should be expanded. The central bank's responsibility for the money supply makes it the single most influential participant in the money market.

iii. *Commercial Banks*

Commercial banks hold a larger percentage of government securities than any other group of financial institutions. This is partly because of regulations that limit the investment opportunities available to banks. Specifically, banks are prohibited from owning risky securities, such as stocks or corporate bonds. However, there are no restrictions against holding Treasury securities because of their low risk and high liquidity.

Banks are also the major issuer of negotiable certificates of deposit (CDs), banker's acceptances, and repurchase agreements. In addition to money market securities to help manage their own liquidity, many banks trade on behalf of their customers.

Not all commercial banks deal for their customers in the secondary money markets. The ones that do are among the largest in the country and are often referred to as money center banks.

iv. Businesses

Many businesses buy and sell securities in the money markets. Such activity is usually limited to major corporations because of the large transactions involved. As discussed earlier, the money markets are used extensively by businesses both to warehouse surplus funds and to raise short-term funds.

v. Investment and Insurance Companies

• Investment Companies

Large diversified brokerage firms are active in money markets. The primary function of these dealers is to "make a market" for money market securities by maintaining an inventory from which to buy or sell. These firms are very important to the liquidity of the money market because they help ensure that both buyers and sellers can readily market their securities in both the primary market and the secondary market.

• Insurance Companies

Property and casualty insurance companies must maintain liquidity because of their unpredictable need for funds. To meet this demand, the insurance companies sell some of their money market securities to raise cash.

As to the life insurance companies, because their obligations are reasonably predictable, large money market security holdings are unnecessary. However, they must have sufficient liquidity to meet their obligations. So, they invest a portion of their cash in the money markets so that they can take advantage of investment opportunities that they may identify in the stock or bond market.

vi. Individuals

It is rare that the money market of a country allows the individuals to participate in. However, it is a common practice that an individual can have his/her money invested in the money market through the agent department of banks and investment companies, to earn a higher interest rate than just putting it in the banks.

B. Money Market Instruments

Securities with maturities within one year are referred to as **money market instruments**. A variety of money market instruments are available to meet the diverse needs of market participants. The more popular money market instruments are:

- Treasury bills
- Inter-bank market
- Commercial paper
- Negotiable certificates of deposit
- Repurchase agreements
- Banker's acceptances

i. Treasury Bills

To finance the national debt, the government issues a variety of debt securities. The most widely held liquid security is the Treasury bill, which is commonly issued by the Ministry of Finance. However, some Treasury bills, like the Treasury bill of the U. S. government, do not actually bear interest. Instead they are issued at a discount from par (their value at maturity). The investor's yield comes from the increase in the value of the security between the time it was purchased and the time it matures.

Treasury bills are attractive to investors because they are backed by the government and therefore are virtually free of default risk. Even if the government ran out of money, it could simply print more to pay them off when they mature. The risk of unexpected changes in inflation is also low because of their short-term maturity. The markets for Treasury bills in most developed countries are deep and liquid. A deep market is one with many different buyers and sellers. A liquid market is one in which securities can be bought and sold quickly and with low transaction costs. Investors in markets that are deep and liquid have little risk that they will not be able to sell their securities when they want to.

ii. Inter-bank Markets

Inter-bank markets are money markets in which short-term funds transferred (lent or borrowed) between financial institutions, usually for one day, that is, they are usually overnight investment. The interest rate for borrowing these funds is close to, but always slightly higher than, the rate that is available from the central bank.

As we all know, the central bank has set minimum reserve requirements that all banks must maintain to ensure that they have adequate liquidity. To meet these reserve requirements, banks must maintain a certain percentage of their total deposits with the central bank, which is called required reserve ratio. Banks can borrow directly from the central bank, but most prefer to borrow from other banks so that they do not alert the central bank to any liquidity problems.

iii. Commercial Paper

Commercial paper is a short-term debt instrument issued only by well-known, large and creditworthy corporations. It is typically unsecured, and the interest rate placed on it reflects the firm's level of risk. It is normally issued to provide liquidity or finance a firm's investment and accounts receivable. The issuance of commercial paper is an alternative to short-term bank loan.

An active secondary market for commercial paper does not exist. However, it is sometimes possible to sell the paper back to the dealer who initially helped to place it. In most cases, commercial paper is held until maturity by investors. Financial institutions such as finance companies and bank holding companies are major issuers of commercial paper.

Some corporations prefer to issue commercial paper rather than borrow from a bank because it is usually a cheaper source of funds. Yet, even the large creditworthy corporations that are able to issue commercial paper normally obtain some short-term loans from commercial banks in order to maintain a business relationship with them.

iv. Negotiable Certificates of Deposit (NCDs or CDs)

A negotiable certificate of deposit is a bank-issued security that documents a deposit and specifies the interest rate and the maturity date. It was firstly issued in 1961 by Citibank. Because a maturity date is specified, a CD is a term security as opposed to a demand deposit. Term securities have a specified maturity date while demand deposits can be withdrawn at any time. A CD is also called a bearer instrument. This means that whoever holds the instrument at maturity receives the principal and interest. The CD can be bought and sold until maturity.

Negotiable CDs are in large denominations. Although NCDs denominations are too large for individual investors, they are sometimes purchased by money market funds that have pooled individual investor's funds. Thus, the existence of money market funds allows individuals to be indirect investors in NCDs, making a more active NCD market. The certificate of deposit is now the second most popular money market instrument, behind only the Treasury bill.

v. Repurchase Agreements

A repurchase agreement (a repo) represents the sale of securities by one party to another with an agreement to repurchase the securities on a specified date and price. It works much the same as inter-bank market except that non-banks can participate. In essence, the repo transaction represents a loan backed by the securities. If the borrower defaults on the loan, the lender has claim to the securities. Most repo transactions use government securities, although some involve other securities such as commercial paper or NCDs. A reverse repo refers to the purchase of securities by one party from another with an agreement to sell them. Actually, a repo and reverse repo can represent the same transaction but from different perspectives.

Many non-financial institutions are active participants as well. A secondary market for repos does not exist. Some firms in need of funds will set the maturity on a repo to be the minimum time period for which they need temporary financing. If they still need funds when the repo is about to mature, they will borrow additional funds through new repos and use these funds to fulfill their obligation on maturing repos.

vi. Banker's Acceptances

A banker's acceptance is an order to pay a specified amount of money to the bearer on a given date. Banker's acceptances have been in use since the twelfth century, and are commonly used for international trade transactions. Therefore, they were not major money market securities until the volume of international trade ballooned in the 1960s.

Exporters often prefer that banks act as guarantor before sending goods to importers whose credit rating is not known. The bank therefore facilitates international trade by stamping ACCEPTED on a draft, which obligates payment at a specified point in time. In turn, the importer will pay the bank what is owed to the exporter along with a fee to the bank for guaranteeing the payment. The steps for using banker's acceptances can be summarized into the following:

- The importer requests its bank to send an irrevocable letter of credit to the exporter.
- The exporter receives the letter, ships the goods, and is paid by presenting to its bank the letter along with proof that the merchandise was shipped.
- The exporter's bank creates a time draft based on the letter of credit and sends it along with proof of shipment to the importer's bank.
- The importer's bank stamps on the time draft "accepted" and sends the banker's acceptance back to the exporter's bank so that the exporter's bank can sell it on the secondary market and have the cash before it matures.
- The importer deposits funds at its bank sufficient to cover the banker's acceptance when it matures.

Banker's acceptances are crucial to international trade. Without them, many transactions simply would not occur because the parties would not feel properly protected from losses. There are other advantages as well:

- The exporter is paid immediately. This is important when delivery time is long after shipment.
- The exporter is shielded from foreign exchange risk because the local bank pays in domestic funds.
- The exporter does not have to assess the creditworthiness of the importer because the importer's bank guarantees payment.

Because acceptances are often discounted and sold by the exporting firm prior to maturity, an active secondary market exists. They are sold on a discounted basis like commercial papers and Treasury bills.

III. Investment Banking

1. Backgrounds

Investment banks are financial institutions engaged in investment banking activities associated with securities underwriting, making a market in securities, and arranging mergers, acquisitions and restructuring.

Investment banking is a highly specialized segment of the finance industry. Its basic function is to bring together, directly through the mechanism of financial markets, ultimate savers and savings collecting institutions with those wishing to raise additional funds for investment or consumption. It also facilitates holders of accumulated wealth, held in the form of financial instruments, to reallocate their assets using financial markets in accordance with their changing evaluation of the attraction of the combination of risk/rewards/liquidity attributes of individual financial assets, compared with each other and with real assets. In performing these two basic functions those involved in investment banking act as market intermediaries.

Investment banks must be distinguished from commercial banks and other savings collecting institutions who gather and decide themselves on the allocation of savings and who act as financial intermediaries. The use of financial markets is thus at the heart of investment banking. Its development and evolution have been closely linked to the growth and expansion of financial markets (and above all capital markets), the instruments they employ and the mechanisms they use.

There is an important distinction between the activity of investment banking and the institutions that perform it. Investment banking activity can be, and is also undertaken by banks (who are financial intermediaries), provided that the respective regulatory framework allows it and individual banks (i. e. universal banks) wish to engage in it. Indeed, the history of the development of investment banking is the history of deposit and commercial banks moving into this field, subject to regulatory constraints.

A. *Who Can Offer Investment Banking Services*

Investment banking activities are undertaken by specialized and independent investment banking institutions offering all or some of the services described above, or by universal banks alongside their traditional deposit taking and loan business. The type of institution engaged in investment banking is determined by the regulatory framework within which financial institutions are free to operate at any particular time.

Broadly speaking, one can say that there are two types of regulatory framework. The first allows investment banking to be carried out by all types of commercial banks, resulting in the emergence of universal banks which, alongside commercial banking, engage in all or some types of investment banking. The second approach separates classic investment banking (i. e. underwriting) from commercial banking and sometimes also other types of investment banking activities.

B. The History of Investment Banking

There are three distinct stages in the evolution of investment banking. The first stage is concerned with classic investment banking business. It is confined almost entirely to the raising of external funds for non-financial companies and various government bodies by issuing securities on capital markets. This covers the well-known function of underwriting.

The second stage covers the expansion of investment banking into closed-end and open-ended trusts—acting as agents for the selling and buying of securities on capital markets and also dealing in them, i. e. , acting as market makers using their own funds. It then begins to include the management of funds for rich individuals, savings collecting bodies, and various closed-end and open-ended trusts which place the funds they command in instruments traded on capital, credit and money markets. Finally, there are the beginnings of participation by investment banks, on a modest scale, in industrial restructuring (i. e. mergers and amalgamations) on capital and other financial markets. During this phase, underwriting is still the main area of activity that generates the bulk of profits in the investment banking field; the remaining three groups of activities contribute a relatively modest proportion of income.

The third stage, or mature state of the evolution of investment banking is characterized, firstly, by a rapid increase in the relative importance of industrial restructuring by way of acquisitions, mergers, amalgamations and disposals linked to the emergence of an active market for corporate control. This is followed by a rapid growth in the management of funds, especially pension funds and those sponsored by investment banks in the form of open-ended funds and other types of funds held by individual and savings-collecting institutions. The final feature of this stage is direct involvement in risk pricing and transfer markets using a variety of derivatives traded on organized or unorganized markets.

C. Factors Behind the Evolution of Investment Banking

The development of investment banking is in essence linked to the development of capital markets on which its activities are centered. The growth of capital markets has, in turn, been a reflection of the interaction between underlying economic forces on the one side, and the regulatory framework on the other.

Fundamental economic forces influence the evolution of investment banking in two ways. Firstly, by increasing real per capita income and wealth they alter the nature of demand for financial services, causing ultimate savers and financial intermediaries to seek the most attractive mix of financial assets in terms of risk/rewards/liquidity attributes in relation to their preferences and constantly changing evaluation of individual financial assets. Broadly speaking, this factor leads to a rise in the demand for investment banking services, compared with services offered by commercial banks' activities. Furthermore, those wishing to obtain additional external funds for investment and/or consumption (deficit units) are able to select more easily the most appealing (i. e. least costly and most convenient) methods and financial instruments they deem suitable for their needs.

Secondly, fundamental economic forces directly and favorably affect investment banking services — all of which use and rely on financial markets (and above all capital markets) — by increasing their appeal. They achieve this by lowering relative costs and enhancing the attraction of investment banking through widening the mix of attributes associated with the products they offer, as compared with those linked to commercial banking activity. Both these influences are propelled by technological advances. Thus the economic forces improve the relative position of the demand for, and the supply of, investment banking services — in terms of cost and other attributes (underwriting by using capital markets, monitoring and disciplining by using market instruments).

The regulatory framework can either accelerate or decelerate this progress by altering the relative position of investment banking services at any particular time vis-à-vis commercial banking services. The anti-commercial bank bias can assume the form of legal separation of investment banking activities from commercial bank activities (as embodied in the Glass — Steagall Act of 1933) which was annuled in 1999, restrictions on the size of individual banks and size of individual loans, restrictions on pricing of loans, etc. The anti-investment bank bias can assume the form of prohibiting the issue of some securities on capital markets, making them very complex and expensive (as was the case in Germany) and in effect raising the relative attraction of bank loan compared with capital market instruments, to providers and users of funds.

Among the major countries investment banking is in the most developed phase in the United States and United Kingdom and in a less developed phase in Germany and Japan.

D. Investment Banks and Financial System

Investment banking enables the financial system to perform some of its basic functions better and more efficiently, and its evolution is one of the important factors propelling the development of the financial system as a whole. The fundamental functions that the financial system must perform are, firstly, to run and manage the payment clearance and settlement system; secondly, to provide liquidity; thirdly, to transfer savings from surplus units to deficit units and allocate these according to respective risk/rewards/liquidity preferences; fourthly, to monitor and discipline units using externally raised funds; and finally, to price, transfer and trade risks.

Investment banking can be said to quicken the pace of transformation of the system in that it helps to move it from a bank-orientated system, where all the five functions are performed by commercial banks by way of bilateral agreements, to the market-orientated phase, where markets play an increasing role in the performance of the last three functions and then to the phase where markets and investment banking dominate the financial system. This path of progress is economically beneficial as it reduces the resources employed to perform some of these basic functions; it betters quality in that it improves the risk evaluation, by risk sharing and risk diversifying by substituting joint market judgment based on jointly shared information for bilateral judgment; and finally by increasing scope it enhances the ability of an economy to carry more risk and to respond more rapidly to changes and to take remedial action in relation to the performance of units using externally raised funds.

When seen in this perspective, investment banking and its "marketization" involvement are propelling factors in the economic improvement and development of the financial system as a whole. Investment banking, is thus one of the crucial elements in the expansion and extension of the division of labor associated with better and more comprehensive financial information collecting, processing and communication which is at the heart of economic progress.

2. Investment Banking Activities

Because of the changing trends discussed above, investment banking today separates into three distinct kinds of activities: underwriting stocks and bonds, or the new issue of securities; transactions, including trading in the secondary market, proprietary trading for the firm's own account, and retail brokerage; and fee banking, involving activities earning a fee such as advising on mergers and acquisitions, securities and economic research, and other types of financial consulting. But simple distinctions can be difficult to maintain. Advising a client on a potential acquisition requires an investment bank to perform certain activities in the primary or secondary market, or both. Some institutions may call that activity mergers and acquisitions while others may call it corporate finance.

Since investment banking had expanded over the last fifty years, many definitions and activities that were not dreamed of fifteen years ago are now major profit center activities for many investment banks. However, the industry still maintains a traditional view of itself: Investment banking means first and foremost the underwriting of securities. Other activities are certainly important and have grown substantially, but prowess in underwriting and syndication are nevertheless the hallmark of the industry. For this reason, the activity of underwriting will be defined first here, although in the early 1990s, underwriting accounted for less than 10 percent of total revenues of investment banking on an industry-wide basis.

A. *Underwriting New Issues*

New securities by companies are usually brought to market after advice and a commitment to underwrite by an investment banking firm. Underwriting simply means that the investment banker promises to buy the securities. The investment banks help design the securities and buy it from the issuer with the intent of selling it to investors as quickly as possible. Usually, the issue is not subscribed to in its entirety by the original investment banker but is syndicated among other institutions as well. Through the syndication process, the original investment banker invites others to subscribe to a part of the issue, receiving a predetermined portion of the fees in return. The original investment banker becomes known as the lead manager of the deal. If there is more than one lead manager, the group is referred to as co-lead managers. The firm that deals directly with the company will be responsible for any syndicate formation and also for final payment on behalf of the syndicate. It is referred to as the bookrunner for the issue.

There are variations in exactly how the investment bankers subscribe to a deal and how their commitment and risk is calculated. In order to profit, the securities must be sold at a higher price than the investment bankers paid the issuer for them. The securities must be sold at the offering price if the full profit margin is to be realized—a value that has been set according to the secondary market where similar securities are already traded. The investment bankers paid that underwriting fees, so a steady market is necessary in order to sell the new issue at the desired price level. If the market weakens or the securities are difficult to sell, the investment bankers stand to lose money because they have (usually) guaranteed the discounted price to the issuer. Conversely, if the market should strengthen and investors are willing to pay more than the offering price, the investment bankers stand to gain in some cases by netting more than the expected price.

New issues of common stock come into two varieties-*primary distributions* and secondary distributions. Primaries are sales of stock that have never been issued before. There are two types of primary distributions—**initial public offerings** (IPOs) and additional floats of companies' stock that will dilute each shareholder's existing holding. Of the two, the latter are more common in the new issues market for equities since they involve offerings of shares of larger, more mature companies seeking additional equity capital. Secondary distributions are sales of stock that previously existed in some form or other forms but are too large to be accommodated on the stock exchanges. Procedures for secondaries often follow those for primaries although the offering period is much shorter and may involve a matter of hours rather than days.

The actual marketing for these issues is done by investment bankers directly to the public. On rare occasions, companies have attempted to sell their shares or bonds directly to the public, avoiding investment banking fees. Unless the company is very well known, such attempts are less than successful. The behavior of investment bankers is key to the reception of new issues and directly affects the cost of capital for a company. As a result, the choice of an investment banker is crucial for a company, and a wrong choice could affect its costs over the near term. This is true for bonds as well as for common stocks.

B. *Transactions* (*Dealing and Broking*)

On the transaction side, investment banks have become much more active in recent years. While at one time avoiding selling and trading, most investment banks have come to embrace these activities as vital to both their own needs and their clients. The most obvious place to find transaction activity is in the secondary market for issues. Some, but not all, members of a syndicate will become market makers in a new bond or over-the-counter stock. This function serves two purposes. Firstly, it facilitates trading in the instrument, providing a service for both the issuer and investor. Secondly, it allows the bank to act as dealer to make a profit on the spread charged between bid and offer prices. However, not all banks will engage in market making because it requires certain special trading skills that not all banks can develop to the same degree.

In addition to market making in the bond and stock market, another major area of trading is the trading of Derivatives. Derivatives trading has rapidly passed through several product cycles within the last ten years. Traditional options and financial futures, introduced in the early and mid-1970s, are sometimes referred to as first-generation derivatives, while interest rate swaps and currency swaps, introduced about a decade later, form the second generation. Those instruments which combine the two categories-collars, swaptions, and commodity swaps can be referred to as third-generation products. Development in the market has been so rapid that many investment banks now offer the services to their customers as well as use the products for themselves in hedging exposure risk. Some also use them for proprietary trading purposes — that is, trading for the house account.

When combined with traditional institutional services, retail brokerage provided a complement to the more traditional corporate services. By diversifying into retail, many investment banks realized that brokerage could provide additional revenues when business was good. But their general strategy is quite similar to that of commercial banks. Many of those that have adopted a full services philosophy which historically means wholesale or institutional banks that actively courted consumer deposits, have found that the retail side has helped them when the institutional side has been less profitable than anticipated. Investment bankers have assumed that a retail mix is both good business and a useful hedge against other operations.

C. Fee Banking

As a specialized area within investment banking, financial advising is somewhat nebulous and can vary in degrees. Advising companies on mergers and acquisitions (M & A), reorganizing capital structures, and advising on market timing are all part of the activity. Most often the clients are corporate, but they can also be governmental, or non-profit organizations.

Mergers and acquisitions simply mean that one company would attempt to take over another by gaining enough of its common stock for control. In the simplest sense, merger means two companies becoming one with the acquirer being in the commanding position.

Mergers come in one of several distinct forms. A **horizontal merger** brings together two companies in a similar industry—two steel companies for example. A **vertical merger** brings together two companies in related industries. A steel company taking over an energy producer such as a coal mine would be such an example. An automobile producer taking over an auto-parts manufacturer is another. In either case, the merger is designed to produce a synergy between the two companies that did not exist before. The horizontal merger should produce greater scale and efficiency, avoiding duplication of products and production. Both forms of merger bring together companies related either directly or indirectly.

Another type of merger, or takeover as the case may be, is the merger of two unrelated companies. This is known as the **conglomerate merger**—a company purposely buying another not engaged in the same business at all. This sort of merger and the companies it creates—conglomerates—were originally conceived to serve as hedge against changing economic climates.

Leveraged buyout (LBO)—the purchase of one company by another using mainly borrowed funds.

Generally, most M&A activity involves one company buying another, taking the target company out of the public marketplace. On occasion, the management of a company will itself tender for the outstanding shares of a company, accomplishing the same ends. This type of privatization is referred to as a management buyout, or MBO.

Acquisitions are either friendly or hostile, depending upon the direct reaction of the target company to the proposed bid. If management remains opposed and attempts to dissuade shareholders from accepting the offer of the acquirer, the proposed purchase price is known as a hostile offer, as opposed to a friendly offer where they agree to the terms and conditions. But it should not be assumed that all hostile bids will be successful. Target companies can mount expensive defenses to ward off unwanted suitors, although the costs can be quite high. Some of those defenses are also products of the 1980s and are equally or more famous than some of the financial engineering techniques developed during the same period.

The deals included in the general category of financial advising go far beyond merger and acquisition. Companies that go private after having been public or vice versa, spin-off operations to another company, or simply sell parts of themselves all fall under the general category. The financings too are of many variations and forms, so only generalizations can be made with any ease. And when securities are offered in a takeover or acquisition in lieu of outright cash, the deals can become very complex and difficult to value.

Investment bankers enter the picture on either side of the deal. They may be asked to represent the acquiring company or the target in the case of an acquisition or may act as advisors to any restructuring or sale of assets. As advisors, they are privy to otherwise secret information that could quickly change the price of a company's stock. Therefore, any advice given is done in the strictest confidence to avoid any conflict of interest or insider trading that may ensue as the result of leaked information.

The role of investment banks in financial advising is best seen in M & A activity, but other noncorporate areas of advising also exist. Performing essentially the same functions for nonprofit organizations and for government is one occasional area. The research function can also fit under this category, although, as noted in the Introduction, research is usually confined to individual securities or to more general macroeconomic trends in the economy. Essentially, M & A is a corporate finance function rather than one of research.

As the securities business became more and more competitive, many securities firms recognized the need of their investment clients for sound, reliable advice. As a result, "sell side" research became very popular with most firms, and almost all began offering it to clients in one form or another.

The establishment of the concept of "prudent man" investing is another driving force. A fiduciary is expected to invest clients' money in a prudent and reasonable manner in line with the clients' objectives. Investment advisors who do not follow those principles are liable for damages to their clients if pursued legally. As more and more investment advisors sought research on securities, the sell side research function became more and more important. It should also be noted that "sell side" research is distinct from "buy side" research, generated by the fund managers themselves or by outside contractors whose view may be assumed to be somewhat more distant from that of sell side analysts.

D. Prospect of Investment Banking

When looking ahead the economic factors is likely to continue to extend their influence in favor of expansion of investment banking. And changes in the financial system regulatory framework will inevitably follow them. Globalization of the world economy can be expected to lead to a rise in the relative importance of investment banking in the financial system. The attention paid to and the need to contain systemic risks are likely to accelerate this trend — placing financial markets and investment banking even more firmly at the center of finance and banking.

IV. Banking on the Internet

1. Backgrounds

Internet banking has many advantages for banks. It is much cheaper to service a customer who makes contact only by phone, interactive TV, computer or other terminals without doing the expensive branch network. Nevertheless, with Internet banking, customers do much of the basic data inputting themselves, thus further saving staff time of banks. Banks can invest the saved resources of human power and capital in utilizing the information of its customers when they are transacting, i. e. to route, analyze, and integrate data into meaningful patterns. Processed customer information is and will remain to be an invaluable asset of banks. And there is an element of self-selection by higher – earning customers— the Internet banking customers tend to be those who are relatively wealthy and generate the bank profits. These advantages therefore suggest that the Internet is regarded as an increasingly important commercial tool by a growing number of banks.

However, the risks are real and the uncertainty of outcome is still high. In fact, moving financial services to the Internet creates a totally new competitive landscape for banks. Instead of operating within clear-cut service boundaries, banks suddenly find themselves competing for customer's loyalty and liquidity. The competition from other well-established financial organizations could be increased. What's more, the competition may come from a technology provider, a tiny start up, or a telecommunications Titan as easily as from within the industry. The advent of Web-based commerce has added new layers of complexity and unpredictability to the worlds of commercial and retail banking, investment banking, back-end processors and front-end financial software providers.

Customers, too, can benefit from Internet banking but still have a number of things to worry about. For them, Internet banking is convenient, and avoids the time wasted in branches. They can manage their financial affairs anytime, anywhere and anyhow. But they have more things to worry too. Among various worries concerning the Internet banking, the first and foremost is the problem of security. And besides, many may not prefer to have every detail of their transactions recorded, which is easy to realize in Internet banking.

Here in this chapter, we will mainly discuss the backgrounds of Internet Banking, its latest development, the products and services currently available on line, and the major challenges as well as the future prospects.

Historically, banks have emphasized direct personal contact with customers, particularly for larger banking transactions. Large branch networks have been established together with complex hierarchical organizational structures that function to deliver the personal level of contact traditionally required by customers. For more than 100 years banks have relied on their extensive branch works to facilitate the requirement for personal communication. Branch networks remain an integral element for most of the major commercial banks. In many cases existing extensive branch networks continue to expand.

However, because the costs of these more traditional delivery channels have risen, banks are increasingly considering other technologically mediated solutions. The Internet is viewed as one of several important alternatives in this respect. Nevertheless, with a cultural tradition that has emphasized the dissemination and sharing of information and knowledge, the Internet has until quite recently been viewed with mistrust and suspicion by the global banking community. The Internet, with its emphasis on facilitating open communication, is essentially at variance with banking culture, which emphasizes the importance of safeguarding information in its privileged form and minimizing its perceived misuse. This cultural contrast led to an understandable initial reluctance by major banks to embrace the new opportunities that the Internet had to offer. However, from an initial position of hostility and mistrust, interest in the Internet has grown significantly over a very short period of time as banks have come to acknowledge its critical role in providing a platform for global electronic commerce. Increasingly there is a recognition that banks have to embrace this new opportunity and view it as a replacement rather than simply an alternative to some of their existing **proprietary networks.**

The disadvantages of proprietary networks and the advantages of the Internet could be put into context by considering the case of automated teller machines (ATMs) , which have become synonymous with bank automation. In most of the major industrialized countries, ATMs account for more than 50 percent of transactions involving cash acquisition from the banking system (i. e. , cash withdrawals from individual bank accounts) . ATMs have earned increasing customer acceptance and trust.

However, despite having become ubiquitous and representing a significant achievement in its own right, ATM technology networks remain costly, with single transaction costs typically from 0. 50 to 1. 00 depending on the type of network switching required. Furthermore, it has taken more than 20 years for the technology to become fully accepted by customers, and a significant number continue to depend on bank branches for all their banking transactions. The relatively high cost of ATMs reflects specific technological priorities concerned with guaranteeing the necessary level of confidence and trust on the part of customers while ensuring high levels of security in networks. At the same time, ATMs illustrate the competitive threat and opportunities presented by the Internet, which has the potential to deliver commercial transactions at a cost measured in a few cents once similar issues associated with trust and customer confidence can be successfully addressed. In other words, the emphasis on creating proprietary, directly controlled networks has been influential in establishing the current level of consumer acceptance but at the same time has created a cost structure that is now vulnerable to the vast network externalities the Internet has to offer. Commercial banks are increasingly coming to terms with the fact that the more traditional proprietary networks on which they have relied in the past are unable to deliver small value transactions at a sufficiently reduced level of cost for lack of flexibility and the requirement for non-standard computer equipment and software.

The driving forces for change appear to fall into four groups:

- The development of technology, especially on the information technology (IT).
- The attraction of lowering transaction cost and operation cost. The Internet is starting to offer alternative solutions to problems that banks continue to face in their very large communication and information management. The Internet is being actively explored as another way in which banks can reach out to new and existing customers by providing an alternative distribution channel. Furthermore, equally important has been the opportunity to facilitate further communication channels for internal communication and especially the integration of externally generated data with intra-organizational information.
- The demand of electronic commerce. Banks recognize the need to meet the new requirements being generated by commercial activities taking place on the Internet.

The resulting forms of electronic commerce are putting much stronger pressures on traditional methods of making payments and in particular forcing a comprehensive review of the still relatively labor-intensive, unautomated methods presently available for making smaller-value payments.

- The pressures from the non-bank competitors. The greater willingness to embrace the Internet opportunity has in part been a competition-based response. Non-banks are showing increasing willingness to ignore traditional boundaries between banking and non-banking services.

2. On-Line Banking Products

Initially, Web sites represented little more than electronic brochures. As a result of initiatives currently led largely by U. S. banks such as Wells Fargo and Bank of America, Web sites are being expanded to offer full banking services.

On-line banking services are those providing the ability to conduct bank transactions from the comfort of home (or office) by using a telephone, television, or personal computer. Examples of the transactions include reviewing checking and savings account balances, transferring funds among accounts, paying bills, reconciling checking accounts, ordering duplicate bank statements or new checks, viewing and downloading bank and credit card statement, opening new accounts, applying for loans, and possibly in the future taking out "cash" in the form of a smart card.

These transactions fall into three categories: basic (the need to manage the past, for example, access to bank statements and bills); intermediate (the need to manage the present, for example, funds transfer, access account-related information); and advanced (the need to manage the future, for example, download data for use with personal finance software products).

A. *Basic products and services*

Basic products and services are those involved in personal finance such as checking and savings account statement reporting and 24-hour account management. Basic services also include a growing array of home financial management services, such as household budgeting, updating stock portfolio values, and listing most recent transactions.

Internet banking, which allows consumers to avoid standing in long queues in both teller and toll-free service, as well as giving them the flexibility of doing their banking at any time, clearly has potential in the area of personal finance. In addition, on-line banking offers the industry cost cutting potential in both office expenses and physical buildings. It is estimated that processing an electronic transaction costs one-sixth of the cost of processing a check.

B. *Intermediate products and services*

They add to the basic services such offerings as account reconciliation across several products (balancing checkbooks); paying bills, status of payments, or stop-payment requests; and consumer and mortgage loan management. Increasingly, these services will be complemented by a broad array of activities such as obtaining loan application, historical performance data, prospectus download, and stock and mutual funds information.

Bill payment is by far the most mature service in this category. The on-line payment of bills was developed in the early 1980s and has become one of increasing interest to consumers. Currently, many Chinese banks offer the services of paying telephone and mobile phone bills through the telephone by the debit or credit cards.

C. *Advanced products and services*

They include stock and mutual funds trading services, foreign exchange trading and cash management, letters of credit management, tax return preparation, and other sophisticated services such as electronic submission and acknowledgment of income tax filings and payments for individuals, proprietorships, partnerships, and corporations to taxing authorities.

There is a growing push in the banking community to develop systems that support the important financial decisions people make concerning their savings including investment, retirement planning, college savings, insurance decisions, house buying and financing and refinancing, etc. These financial decisions are not new but are much more complex today than they were ten or even five years ago, because of the increase of average wealth and the reform of the social security system.

Different from those banks in the developed countries, banks in China either did not offer these services, or offered some of them to a limited group of people. This relatively low starting point could be an advantage if they directly start to offer these advanced services on the Internet. Unlike those Western banks, Chinese banks have invested little in these portfolio management services before the emergence of Internet, i. e. , the sunk cost is not significant, which makes it easier for them to establish a new service structure on the Internet.

3. The Challenging Issues in Internet Banking

There are numerous challenges facing the banking industry when they are carrying out Internet banking services. Among them, the first one, which people care most, is the provision of a secure platform for banking transactions and at the same time, protect the customers' privacy.

The second challenge is whether management has the creativity and vision to harness the technology and provide customers with the new financial products necessary to satisfy their continually changing financial needs.

The immediate question facing the banking industry is how to deliver high-quality products for the customers' convenience with high-tech, high-touch personal service for the right price. To achieve this, management has to balance the five key values that increasingly drive customers' banking decisions: simplicity, customized service, convenience, quality, and price. These values vary in levels of importance to customers, but together they represent a synergy of buying values. On-line banking will realize its full potential when the following key elements fall into place:

- The development of an interesting portfolio of products and services that are sufficiently differentiated from competitors' and create value in the eyes of the consumer.
- The creation of on-line financial supply chains to manage the shift from banks as gate-keepers to banks as gateways.
- An emergence of low-cost interactive access terminals for the home, as well as interactive home information services offered at an attractive price.
- The identification of new market segments with untapped needs such as the willingness to pay for the convenience of remote banking.
- Good customer service on the part of banks. Because technology increases the ease of switching from one bank to another, banks that do not offer superior customer service may see low levels of customer loyalty.
- The development of effective back-office systems that can support sophisticated retail interfaces. Back-office systems must be given due importance in the on-line banking area.

However, banks that wait to be adept at all of the mentioned elements before offering on-line banking services may be least likely to reap the rewards. Since on-line banking is attractive to a wealthy segment of the population initially, the banks that move first will increase their market share of the most profitable customers. And, assuming they do their job well, these first movers will have a rather effective hedge against competing services that will inevitably follow.

4. The Future Prospects of On-Line Banking

Commercial banks have historically made major investments in their branch networks. However, there are strong indications that banks around the world are taking much more innovative approaches to establishing new delivery channels for their customers. Before moving financial services to the Web, bankers have tried many other channels to deliver their services in a cost-effective way. Telephone banking, which was still a restricted and novel service in the early 1990s, has expanded dramatically in China. However, the services provided now are still far from being comprehensive, not to mention a "supermarket". Most banks in China have no more than a phone reply service, with a PIN number, allowing customers to find out their cash balance, move money between accounts, and report the loss and stop the use of their bank cards.

Just five years ago, commercial banks were indistinguishable from one another. Today, the strategic options of these banks vary much. The retail banking industry is entering a period unlike any in its history—a period of unbridled competition that will call for all the creative ingenuity, innovation, and entrepreneurial skills that bankers possess.

Banks today have reason to worry that if they do not offer on-line banking services, affluent customers will be stolen away by software companies, on-line access services, brokerages, or global entertainment companies. The current situation presents both opportunities and risks. In addition to protecting their existing franchise, financial institutions can look to on-line banking and related services to expand their product offerings and win new business.

Financial institutions must not lose sight of the fact that on-line banking is in their best interest and that it is up to them to market the idea. They need to market on-line banking as the ability to organize in an increasingly complex and confusing world. The term organization encapsulates the ideas of control, timeliness, time-savings, and easy access to more information. This is not a major shift; this is the goal customers have always had in their banking activities.

Commercial banking in its present form dates back almost 150 years. A variety of technological developments have helped to mold banking institutions but have not dramatically changed the nature of banking in substance. The Internet presents yet another challenge for banking institutions to adopt these new technologies successfully in the same way in which they became some of the most successful early adopters of computer mainframes and proprietary digital data networks. There appears to be strong evidence that after some initial delays a similar process of technological adoption is occurring. However, the explosion of bank Web sites and financial services offered on line signifies a major change of perspective.

The Internet is changing banking in a number of ways. New opportunities for low-value payment systems are emerging that could help to replace the overriding dependence on cash as a payment medium and that makes electronic payment transfer for very low-value payment prohibitive in terms of costs. Banks are adopting the Internet as an effective means for intra-organizational communication, by using a combination of Email, Web server, and groupware technologies. Similarly, commercial banks worldwide are beginning to embrace the possibilities for greater direct customer contact, with a number of banks moving to second-generation sites that provide true transactional capabilities and represent a significant extension of functionality compared with the electronic brochures that initially predominated.

There are increasing signs that the creation of Internet-based banking may ultimately have very dramatic effect on commercial banks as traditional savings intermediaries. Individuals are being offered highly cost-effective tools that can be used to manage savings and to effect payments. At the same time there is an increasingly global dimension to the changes, as a variety of geographically dispersed institutions are established, creating a vanguard of change. Future development is still uncertain. However, there are clear indications that the pace of change is accelerating and that the Internet's wide-ranging network externalities will start to create major competitive pressures first in domestic and then in international banking markets.

Notes

1. **intermediary** [ˌɪntəˈmiːdiəri] *adj.* existing or occurring between; intermediate, acting as a mediator or an agent between persons or things

2. **peripheral** [pəˈrifərəl] *adj.* related to, located in, or constituting an outer boundary or periphery; Perceived or perceiving near the outer edges of the retina

3. **surge** [səːdʒ] *v.* to increase suddenly.

4. **deregulation** [diˈregjuˌleitʃən] *n.* the activity of exerting less control over

5. **reimburse** [ˌriːimˈbəːs] *v.* to repay, to pay back

6. **indemnify** [inˈdemnifai] *v.* to compensate for one's loss

7. **elaborate** [iˈlæbərit] *adj.* containing a lot of small parts that are connected with each other in a complicated way

8. **compartment** [kəmˈpɑːtmənt] *n.* one of the parts or spaces into which an area is subdivided; a separate room, section, or chamber

9. **pledge** [pledʒ] *v.* to deposit as security; pawn

10. **collateral** [kɔˈlætərəl] *n.* property acceptable as security for a loan or other obligation

11. **tangible** [ˈtændʒəbl] *adj.* that can be valued monetarily

12. **reconcile** [ˈrekənsail] *v.* to settle or resolve; to make compatible or consistent

13. **indorsement** [inˈdɔːsmənt] *n.* signing one's name on the back of the instrument to confirm sth.

14. **transverse** [trænsˈvəːs] *adj.* situated or lying across; crosswise

15. **entity** [ˈentiti] *n.* something that exists as a particular and discrete unit

16. **entitle** [inˈtaitl] *vt.* to authorize, to gain the right to do sth.

17. **legal tenders**: the legal currency issued by the national monetary authority

18. **equivalent** [iˈkwivələnt] *n.* something that is essentially equal to another

19. **outstanding** [autˈstændiŋ] *adj.* still in existence; not settled or resolved

20. **commission** [kəˈmiʃən] *n.* a fee or percentage allowed to a sales representative or an agent for services rendered

21. **candidate** [ˈkændidit] *n.* a person who seeks or is nominated for an office, prize, or honor; one that seems likely to gain a certain position or come to a certain fate

22. **herald** [ˈherəld] *v.* to proclaim; announce

23. **inauguration** [inˌɔːgjuˈreiʃən] *n.* a formal beginning or introduction

24. **equitable** [ˈekwitəbl] *adj.* marked by or having equity; just and impartial

25. **corpus** [ˈkɔːpəs] *n.* the principal or capital, as distinguished from the interest or income, as of a fund or estate

26. **tenant** [ˈtenənt] *n.* one that pays rent to use or occupy land, a building, or other property owned by another

27. **tenement** [ˈtenimənt] *n.* a building for human habitation, especially one that is rented to tenants

28. **chattel** [ˈtʃætl] *n.* an article of personal, movable property

29. **consideration** [kənˌsidəˈreiʃən] *n.* payment given in exchange for a service rendered; recompense

30. **indeterminate** [ˌindiˈtəːminit] *adj.* not precisely determined, determinable, or established

31. **amortize** [əˈmɔːtaiz] *v.* to liquidate (a debt, such as a mortgage) by installment payments or payment into a sinking fund

32. **obsolete** [ˈɔbsəˌliːt] *adj.* no longer in use

33. **assignment** [əˈsainmənt] *n.* the transfer of a claim, right, interest, or property from one to another

34. **default** [diˈfɔːlt] *n.* failure to perform a task or fulfill an obligation, especially failure to meet a financial obligation

35. **confer** [kənˈfəː] *v.* to invest with (a characteristic, for example)

36. **alternative** [ɔːlˈtəːnətiv] *n.* the choice between two mutually exclusive possibilities; a situation presenting such a choice; either of these possibilities

37. **misnomer** [ˌmisˈnəumə] *n.* an error in naming a person or place; application of a wrong name

38. **denomination** [diˌnɔmiˈneiʃən] *n.* one of a series of kinds, values, or sizes, as in a system of currency or weights

39. **interim** [ˈintərim] *adj.* belonging to, serving during, or taking place during an intermediate interval of time; temporary

40. **synchronized** [ˈsiŋkrənaizd] *adj.* at the same time

41. **brokerage** [ˈbrəukəridʒ] *n.* The business of engaging in buying and selling sth. for clients

42. **casualty** [ˈkæʒjuəlti] *n.* an accident, especially one involving serious injury or loss of life

43. **diverse** [daiˈvəːs] *adj.* differing one from another; made up of distinct characteristics, qualities, or elements

44. **discount** [ˈdiskaunt] *v.* to deduct or subtract from a cost or price; to purchase or sell (a bill, note, or other commercial paper) at a reduction equal to the amount of interest that will accumulate before it matures

   n. a reduction from the full or standard amount of a price or debt; the interest deducted prior to purchasing, selling, or lending a commercial paper; the discount rate

45. **overnight** [ˈəuvənait] *adj.* lasting for, extending over, or remaining during a night

46. **irrevocable** [iˈrevəkəbl] *adj.* impossible to retract or revoke

47. **premium** [ˈpriːmjəm] *n.* the amount paid or payable, often in installments, for an insurance policy; the amount at which something is valued above its par or nominal value, as money or securities

48. **household** [ˈhaushəuld] *n.* a domestic unit consisting of the members of a family who live together along with nonrelatives such as servants

49. **coupon** [ˈkuːpɔn] *n.* a negotiable certificate attached to a bond that represents a sum of interest due; a detachable part, as of a ticket or advertisement, that entitles the bearer to certain benefits, such as a cash refund or a gift

50. **fluctuate** [ˈflʌktjueit] *v.* to vary irregularly; to rise and fall in or as if in waves; undulate

51. **indenture** [inˈdentʃə] *n.* a contract binding one party into the service of another for a specified term; a deed or legal contract executed between two or more parties

52. **privilege** [ˈprivilidʒ] *n.* a special advantage, immunity, permission, right, or benefit granted to or enjoyed by an individual, a class, or a caste

53. **covenant** [ˈkʌvinənt] *n.* a binding agreement; a compact

54. **discretion** [disˈkreʃən] *n.* the quality of being discreet; ability or power to

decide responsibly; freedom to act or judge on one's own

55. **liquidate** ['likwideit] *v.* to pay off (a debt, a claim, or an obligation); settle

56. **debenture** [di'bentʃə] *n.* a certificate or voucher acknowledging a debt; an unsecured bond issued by a civil or governmental corporation or agency and backed only by the credit standing of the issuer

57. **priority** [prai'ɔriti] *n.* precedence, especially established by order of importance or urgency; an established right to precedence

58. **speculative** ['spekjuˌlətiv] *adj.* bought or done in the hope of making a profit later

59. **dividend** ['dividend] *n.* a part of a company's profit that is divided among the people who have shares in the company

60. **index** ['indeks] *n.* a number or symbol, often written as a subscript or superscript to a mathematical expression, that indicates an operation to be performed on, an ordering relation involving, or a use of the associated expression

61. **Underwriting** ['ʌndəˌraitiŋ] *n.* Buying the securities from institutions and selling them to the public the price gap

62. **Merger** [məːdʒə] *n.* Two companies becoming one

63. **Acquisition** [ˌækwi'ziʃən] *n.* Purchasing, gaining, paying enough money to take over another company and controlling it

64. **Closed-end and Opened-end trusts:** Closed-end trust means the number of trust fund is fixed, it can't be expanded. In opened-end trusts, the trust fund can be extended according to market

65. **Universal banks:** *n.* Banks which can engage in all kinds of financial transactions involved in banking \ security \ insurance

66. **Amalgamation** [əˌmælgə'meiʃən] *n.* Combination, joining into together

67. **Disposal** [dis'pouzəl] *n.* Adjustment administration

68. **Pension** ['penʃən] *n.* Money paid when one is too old to work

69. **Derivative** [di'rivətiv] *n.* Those financial assets which are produced based on traditional financial assets. In financial market, many financial assets such as option and future are all derivatives

70. **US Glass Steagall legislation:** The USA's legislation in 1933 in order to separate the banking transactions from security and insurance. But in 1999, this law was annuled.

71. **Bank-orientated system:** Financial system in which banks are in dominant position the key financial channels

72. **Market-orientated:** Financial system in which monetary are allocated mainly by financial market

73. **Marketisation**: *n.* A position or a trend in which resource allocation is depended on market

74. **Fee banking**: Banking transactions that income is gained by providing services such as merger and acquisition

75. **Corporate finance**: The financial management of corporate

76. **Syndicate** ['sindikit] *n.* An organization lines on between cartel and trust v. To organize a combo to achieve a hard task. In this chapter, it means securities underwriting is shouldered by more than one bank

77. **Lead manager**: The leader of a syndicate, which is charged with organizing the syndication and assuming main responsibility

78. **Co-lead managers**: Members of a syndication who help leader manager to arrange loan or underwriting

79. **Book runner**: A member of syndication who manage finance

80. **Offering price**: The price in which the securities underwriting syndication sell securities in the market

81. **Discounted price**: The price in which securities underwriting syndication buy in

82. **Outstanding shares**: A segment shares which is over a particular threshold

83. **Fiduciary** [fi'dju:fiəri] *n.* Trustee, a person who is trusted to manage trustor's property

84. **Interest rate swap**: A transaction in which two parties agree to exchange periodic interest payments, especially when one payment is at a fixed rate and the other is at floating rate

85. **Currency swap**: A transaction in which two parties exchange periodic currency in order to avoid exchange rate risk

86. **Start up**: A new establishing company

87. **Hierarchical** [ˌhaiə'rɑːkikl] *adj.* Being separated into several degrees

88. **Proprietary** [prə'praiətəri] *adj.* Privately owned or controlled

89. **Prospectus** [prə'spektəs] *n.* A printed statement describing the details of a new issuing

90. **Proprietorship** [prə'praiətəʃip] *n.* ownership

91. **Sunk cost**: The cost which have been paid and can't be taken back

92. **Entrepreneurial** [ˌɔntrəprə'nəriəl] *adj.* Owned to entrepreneur

Questions for discussion

1. What are commercial papers?

2. List some of the banking services which show the relationship between banks and

customers as one between an agent and a principal.

3. Why cash-based settlement is not popular nowadays?

4. What are negotiable instruments? List some examples.

5. What's the function of crossings on cheques?

6. What are the differences between credit cards and debit cards?

7. What's the difference between capital lease and operating lease?

8. How is a leveraged lease operated?

9. What's the meaning of Account Receivable Financing?

10. What are the procedures of factoring?

11. Compare the primary markets and secondary markets. Which is more important? Why?

12. What are basic characteristics of money market securities?

13. List at least three influential participants of money market.

14. Why treasury bills are attractive to investors?

15. What are the features of inter-bank markets?

16. What are the differences between bonds and stocks?

17. How have NCDs become the second most popular money market instruments?

18. How are banker's acceptance operated?

19. What products does the on-line banking provide?

20. What are the challenging issues in internet banking?

Part Six

Loans

I. Definition and Categories of Loans

1. Definition

A loan is a sum of money advanced to a borrower, to be repaid at a later date, usually with interest. Legally, a loan is a contract between a buyer (the borrower) and a seller (the lender), enforceable under relevant law. The terms and conditions for repayment of a loan, including the finance charge or interest rate, are specified in a loan agreement. A loan may be payable on demand (a demand loan), in equal monthly installments (an installment loan), or it may be good until further notice or due at maturity (a time loan).

More generally, loan refers to anything given on condition of its return or repayment of its equivalent. A loan may be acknowledged by a bond, a promissory note, or a mere oral promise to repay. Because of biblical injunctions against usury, the early Christian church forbade the taking of interest. In feudal European society, loans were little needed by the great mass of relatively self-sufficient and noncommercial peasants and serfs, but kings, nobles, and ecclesiastics were heavy borrowers for personal expenditures. Merchants and other townsmen, especially the Jews, were the moneylenders, and various devices were found for circumventing the prohibition of usury. With the rise of a commercial society, restrictions on the taking of interest were gradually relaxed. Today, banks and finance companies make most loans, usually on collateral, such as stocks, personal effects, and mortgages on land and other property, or on assignments of wages. Credit unions have attained some importance in making personal loans at relatively low interest rates, and micro-credit programs and organizations, which offer small-scale loans, have been proved useful, particularly in developing countries, in helping individuals to establish small businesses.

A loan is a type of debt. All material things can be lent but this chapter focuses exclusively on monetary loans. Like all debt instruments, a loan entails the redistribution of financial assets over time, between the lender and the borrower. The borrower initially receives an amount of money from the lender, which may be paid back, usually but not always in regular installments, to the lender. This service is generally provided at a cost, referred to as interest on the debt.

Acting as a provider of loans is one of the principal tasks for financial institutions. For other institutions, issuing of debt contracts, such as bonds is a typical source of funding. Bank loans and credit are one way to increase the money supply.

Other types of debt include mortgages, credit card debt, bonds, and lines of credit. A mortgage is a very common type of debt instrument, used by many individuals to purchase housing. In this arrangement, the money is used to purchase the property. The bank, however, is given the title to the house until the mortgage is paid off in full. If the borrower defaults on the loan, the bank can repossess the house and sell it, to get their money back by the legal procedure.

2. Categories of Loans

There are various methods lenders use to categorize loans, both for internal control and for reporting lending activity to governmental agencies, for example, classification by maturity, industry, security, and type of borrower. In the United States of America, bank loans are normally classified into: (1) commercial and industrial loans to business organizations; (2) inter-bank loans, which are mostly Federal Fund transactions, from one bank to another; (3) loan participations, or loans to a single borrower shared by several banks; (4) real estate loans, which may be divided into construction loans and long-term mortgage loans; and (5) loans to consumers, such as auto loans and other forms of consumer installment credit.

In order to better understand the different categories of loans, we can divide them according to different criteria.

A. According to Maturity

By maturity, loans can be divided into two broad categories. Those with maturity of one year or less are called short-term loans while those with maturity exceeding one year are called medium- or long-term loans. Short-term loans are often used to satisfy working capital needs, to fill clients' short-term needs for financing projects within the business scope before medium- and long-term loan contracts have been performed. Examples include: preparatory funds, funding for equipment, materials and other costs covered by budget estimates, advances to meet temporary funding shortages before supporting funds are in place, and short-term loans for production and operation. Medium and long-term loans are often used to finance fixed asset investment. They are mainly used to assemble capital for infrastructure, basic industries and pillar industries as well as technology upgrading projects.

B. According to interest rate

Loans can be divided into two broad categories based on interest rate. Those with a rate of interest that varies with the market, more particularly with an agreed reference standard, e. g., the **London Inter-bank Offered Rate (LIBOR)** are called **floating rate loans**. **Fixed rate loans** generally refer to loans on which the borrower receives a predetermined and unchanging rate of interest on the principal as opposed to the non-guaranteed, variable interest rate.

C. According to Number of Lenders

According to number of lenders, loans can be divided into bilateral loans and syndicated loans. A **bilateral loan** is a loan arranged by a bank between a borrower and itself. A **syndicated loan** is a very large loan extended by a group of banks to a corporate borrower. These syndicate banks share credit information and credit risk. Syndicated loans are a modern version of the old "club loans", improved by several features of the public securities markets including distribution of risk among a number of investors. In the syndicated loan market, banks act more like underwriters and add value by structuring and distributing loans, committing capital, and servicing loans in the aftermarket. Lead arrangers can underwrite the loan or arrange it on a "best efforts" basis.

Syndicated loans are usually made at an interest rate tied to a variable rate index such as LIBOR, HIBOR or on bank certificates of deposit. The loans are often sold to investors in the secondary loan market. In recent years, institutional investors such as mutual funds became major buyers of syndicated loans.

Syndicated loans to major corporate borrowers are rated by credit rating firms such as Standard & Poor's, which uses a rating system similar to that used for corporate bonds. With the creation of a secondary market linking loan-originating banks with investors, multi-bank commercial loans may some day trade as corporate debt securities in the over-the-counter (OTC) dealer market. In contrast with highly leveraged transaction, a high-interest rate loan is extended to riskier borrowers.

D. According to Type of Borrowers

Based on types of borrowers, loans can be divided into corporate and institutional loans and personal loans. Those to borrowers that are either companies or institutions are called **corporate and institutional loans**. Those to borrowers that are individuals are called **personal loans**. The above-mentioned commercial & industrial (C&I) loans and loans to consumer are classified according to similar criteria.

C&I loans are those loans to a corporation, commercial enterprise, or a joint venture, as opposed to a loan to a consumer. C&I loans can be a source of working capital, or used to finance the purchase of manufacturing plants and equipment. These loans are generally short-term, secured by collateral pledged by the borrower or can be fully unsecured, and usually are made at flexible rates. Generally, the rate is pegged to the bank prime rate or money market rate, such as LIBOR. Many lenders also require borrowers to file periodic financial statement, usually annually, and meet other conditions, such as maintaining proper insurance on the loan collateral.

Loans to consumer, also called consumer credit, are extended to individuals for personal or household use, rather than for business. Broadly defined, consumer credit includes all forms of installment credit other than loans secured by real estate (home mortgages, for instance) plus open-end credit such as credit cards. New forms of credit, however, have blurred these distinctions; a home equity credit line is a revolving line of credit secured by real estate-a lien on the borrower's home. Many traditional forms of consumer credit, such as auto loan, have standard monthly payments-fixed repayment schedules of one to five years or more-and are made at either fixed interest rates or variable rates that are based on an index. Consumer loans fill a variety of needs: financing the purchase of an automobile or household appliance, home improvement, debt consolidation, and so on. These loans may be unsecured or secured by an assignment of title, as in an auto loan, or money in a bank account.

E. According to Nature of Common Usages

Based on the nature of common usages, loans can be divided into working capital loans and fixed asset loans. **Working capital loan** is a short-term business loan financing the purchase of income-generating assets, principally inventory. Working capital loans are generally written with lending terms requiring full payment within a specified period, such as 60 days or 90 days from the date the funds are advanced.

Fixed asset loans refer to loans granted by a bank to meet the demands of enterprises in their investments in fixed assets. Investments by enterprises in fixed assets include capital construction, technical innovation, developing and manufacturing of new products as well as related house purchase, civil engineering, purchase and installation of technical equipment, etc.

F. According to the Nature of Particular Usages

Based on the nature of particular usages, we have **real estate development loans, mortgage loans, agriculture loan, education loan, etc.**

Real estate development loans for either commercial or residential real estate development are granted to a qualified property developer. The evaluation of the particular project and the qualification of the particular developer must be taken into consideration when a bank decides whether to issue loans.

Mortgage loan for residential houses is granted to a borrower to purchase a residential house (s), for which he/she owns the proprietary, including first-hand house (s), second-hand house (s), and economical houses provided by the government.

Agriculture loans are similar to commercial & industrial loans in that short-term credit finances seasonal operating expenses. Agricultural loans are associated with planting and harvesting crops. Much like working capital loans, the proceeds are used to purchase inventory in the form of seed, fertilizer, and pesticides and to pay other production costs. Farm operators expect to pay the debt when the crops are harvested and sold. Long-term credit finances livestock, equipment, and land purchases. The fundamental source of repayment is cash flow from the sale of livestock and harvested crops in excess of operating expenses.

Education loans are made for college or vocational training expenses, often at a below market rate. In the USA, loans backed by the Student Loan Marketing Association (Sallie Mae) are 90% guaranteed for repayment of principal and interest. A guaranteed student loan (called a Stafford Student Loan, after Sen. Robert T. Stafford of Vermont) is insured by a state guarantee agency and reinsured by Sallie Mae. Repayment of a Stafford Student Loan is deferred until after college graduation.

G. Other Categories

According to different criteria, loans can be categorized into secured loans vis-à-vis unsecured loans, redeemable loans vis-à-vis irredeemable loans, interest free loans vis-à-vis interest bearing loans, commercial loans vis-à-vis government backed loans, etc.

Secured loans (in contrast with **Unsecured Loans**, which are backed only by the borrower's promise to pay) are collateralized by assignment of rights to property and a security interest in personal property or real property taken by the lender. A mortgage borrower (the mortgagor) gives the lender a mortgage in the property financed. A business loan can be secured by cash, inventory, accounts receivable, marketable securities, or other acceptable collateral. In the event the borrower fails to repay according to the original credit terms, the lender can take legal action to reclaim and sell the collateral.

Redeemable loans are loans that are repayable over a five year period, currently at a 0 interest rate, following the completion of the works. Redeemable loans are linked to property valuations before and after any works are undertaken. Irredeemable loans or no payback loans have no repayment conditions unless the property is sold within a period of 5 years after completion of the works.

When based on interest charge, loans can be divided into **interest-bearing loans** and **interest-free loans**. It is easy to understand interest-free loans vis-à-vis interest-bearing loans literally. Interest-free loans are usually used to finance special-purposed projects, low-income families, financially difficult communities and so on, e. g., interest-free loans are available for new church sites, certain minority situations, natural disaster emergencies, certain off-continent situations and intentionally integrated congregations.

The general rule on interest-free loans is that the interest is treated as a gift from the lender to the borrower. The lender is also treated as receiving the payment back from the borrower, thus producing taxable income to the lender. However, many donors to charities are interested in allowing charities to use funds interest-free, so long as the donor could re-acquire the funds if later needed. This interest-free loan allows the charity to invest the funds and use the earnings to fund the exempt purposes of the charity.

An interest-bearing loan means that the borrower must pay interest on the principle of the loan to the lender. Commercial loans are usually based on commercial terms and the interest rate is decided by the market. Compared with commercial loans, government backed loans are often used to finance projects or people supported by government policies. For example, export credit and education loans are some types of government backed loans.

3. Introduction to Major Loan Categories

A. *Working Capital Loans and Fixed Asset Loans*

It is better to understand the definitions of working capital and fixed asset first. Working capital is technically defined as the difference between current assets and current liabilities, and is also known as net working capital. Working capital is the measurement of the availability of liquid assets a company has to build its business. Generally, companies that have a lot of working capital will be more successful since they can expand and improve their operations. Companies without working capital may lack the funds necessary for growth.

The working capital of a company reflects its ability to meet its obligations as they come due, and thereby avoiding bankruptcy. Thus, the amount of working capital may influence the character and scope of the business. Working capital loans or financing are the funds usually granted to finance working capital short-falls.

It is believed in some financial sector that the financing difficulties for small businesses arises only when they seek funds for working capital (operating expenses, purchasing inventory, receivables financing). The reason, they say, unlike a loan for the acquisition of fixed assets, is that a loan for working capital is not secured.

Fixed asset is a long-term, tangible asset held for business use and not expected to be converted in to cash in the current or upcoming fiscal year, such as manufacturing equipment, real estate, and furniture or plant.

Working capital loans are used to fill clients' short-term needs for funds, for projects within the business scope before medium- and long-term loan contracts have been completed. Examples include: preparatory funds, funding for equipment, materials and other costs covered by budget estimates, advances to cover temporary funding shortages before supporting funds are in place, and short-term loans for production and operation. **Fixed asset loans** are mainly used to assemble capital for infrastructure, basic industries and pillar industries as well as technology upgrading projects.

Working capital loan has high liquidity, which is applicable to the industrial and commercial customers with medium- and short-term financing needs. Under normal circumstances, a bank makes decision as to grant, amount, term, and interest of the loans after checking customer credit standing and doing loan examination as per the loan principle of "safety, liquidity, and profitability".

When based on maturity, working capital loan can be divided into temporary working capital loan, short-term working capital loan and medium-term working capital loan:

Temporary working capital loan: The loan term is within or equal to 3 months, mainly used for the temporary funds needed in the one-time goods purchase or manufacturing or for making up the insufficiency of other payments.

Short-term working capital loan: The term is more than 3 months and less than (or equal to) one year. This type of loan is mainly used as the turnover funds in the process of production and operation of enterprises.

Mid-term working capital loan: The term is more than one year but less than (or equal to) three years, Such kind of loan is mainly used for frequently occupied funds in the process of production and operation.

The other categories of working capital loans are listed as follows:

Revolving liquidity loan: The working capital loan service is the arrangement where the lender and the borrower sign ad hoc borrowing contract, and during the term stipulated in the contract, the lender permits the borrower to draw on the loan for multiple times and repay the borrowing in batches, which the credit line is revolving.

Liquidity loan with installments: In such a working capital loan arrangement, the customer may withdraw the funds in lump sum and repay the loan by installments.

Corporate body account overdraft: It is loan approach where the bank approves a line of credit as per customer application to permit the customer directly draw within the pre-approved credit line when the customer runs shortage in its settlement account.

Fixed Asset Loans: Fixed asset loan refers to loans granted by the bank to meet the demands of enterprises in their investments in fixed assets. Investments by enterprises in fixed assets include capital construction, technical innovation, developing and manufacturing of new products as well as related house purchase, civil engineering, purchase and installation of technical equipment, etc.

Fixed asset loan is divided into long-term loan, temporary circulating loan and foreign exchange loan based on the following purposes:

Capital Construction: Infrastructure, municipal works, service facilities, new or enlarged productive projects ratified and approved by the state authorities concerned.

Technical Innovation: The technical innovation items are aimed at the expanding reproduction by the existing enterprises.

Scientific and Technological Development: Such activities involve research, manufacturing and development of new technologies and products and with regard to the transformation or application of the development results in the production field.

Other Purchases of the Fixed Assets: They refer to the direct purchases of houses or facilities not built by the enterprise itself for the use of production, storage and office building.

B. *Syndicated Loan*

i. *Concept of Syndicated Loan*

A syndicated loan is a very large loan arranged by a lead bank among a single borrower and a group of other banks that are parties to the original credit agreement. These syndicate banks share in credit information and credit risk.

A syndicated loan is a large credit, generally more than USD10 million, negotiated between a borrower and a single bank, but actually funded by several banks. The negotiating or "lead" bank wins the "mandate" from a number of competitors and underwrite a large portion of the credit and is responsible for organizing the syndication which includes inviting other banks to act as manager/co-manager in providing additional underwriting support to the credit before going to market for general syndication to the "participants". The resulting credit is governed by a single loan agreement signed by the borrower and all of the banks involved.

The syndication market has developed largely because single lenders have found it increasingly difficult to meet large borrowing requirements of corporate clients. Since syndication is usually arranged for sums ranging from USD 10 million to USD 1 billion plus, a single bank may not be able or willing to extend such a large amount because of legal lending limits, exposure, and portfolio considerations. Also, the lead bank often chooses to allow room in its credit availability for future funding opportunities to the same borrower.

Every syndication has an agent bank to administer the loans from signing to repayment. Based on the complexity of its duties, the agent bank normally receives a fee from the borrower. This fee is separate and distinct from any front-end or other fee paid to the bank. Duties of the agent include issuing advices for interest charges, processing the movement of funds, and assuring that the borrower has complied with the terms and conditions of the loan agreement.

The purpose of the syndicated loan is usually to finance a major development, a project, a temporary imbalance of payments, a major capital investment program, a project cost over-run, acquisition of a company, short-term to long-term debt conversion, or rationalization of the schedule of long-term debt repayments.

The most successful lead managers (banks) or co-lead managers in the syndication field are professionally adaptable at performing the four basic functions in a syndication, namely information memorandum preparation, documentation, syndication function and agency function. **Information Memorandum**, to be distributed to potential participants, presents a detailed analysis of the borrower, including disclosures of the borrower's past performance, projections, management and an economic analysis of the borrower's country.

Lead manager bears potential legal obligation of preventing the memorandum from fraudulent or negligent misrepresentation. It should be emphasized that the borrower has warranted and confirmed that all information is true, accurate, complete and correct and that no independent verification or judgment is given by the managers. The lead manager, in conjunction with local and international legal assistance, prepares and negotiates an acceptable loan agreement and any necessary supplemental documentation. Documentation must be acceptable to all participants in the syndication.

To perform the syndication function, a successful lead manager, in having secured a mandate from the borrower based on specific terms and conditions, must market the loan to international financial institutions in a manner that is consistent with its selldown objective. This function is inherently the most risky in circumstances where the lead bank or manager bank underwrites a substantial portion of the loan. An in-depth understanding of the market and the borrower enables the lead manager to secure a mandate based on conditions that are acceptable in the market given the competitive aspects of securing mandates today. This is the most difficult and perilous function in loan syndication.

Acting as agent, the lead manager will oversee the loan throughout its tenor and act as an advisor for both the borrower and the participants as condition precedent and requirement. representation and warranties.

ii. Fee and Cost

An arrangement fee (front-end or management fee) is normally charged for the arrangement of the loan agreement, information memorandum, syndication and signing ceremony.

This fee is split between the lead manager, managers and co-managers, depending on the distribution of the work involved, the amount of underwriting and the final takes. Front-end fees are also paid to participants to encourage them to join the syndication.

The pricing spread is added to the basic rate (usually LIBOR, or possibly SIBOR if Singapore is the denominated financial center), which is calculated from an average of rates provided by the Reference Banks. Not all participants may be able to obtain funds at this rate and may consequently incur a funding risk. It is attempted to minimize this risk by choosing reference banks representative of the whole syndicate. In determining the lending spread or margin above cost for lenders, the lead manager must consider the credit rating of the borrower; acceptability of the borrower and borrower's country to the syndication market; tenor and average life of the loan; whether there are other loans in the market or in process for that country since the comparability of transactions is a factor in how lenders allocate country lending limits; and market trends, i. e. , in which way interest rates, and lending margins, etc. are moving.

iii.   Procedure

A syndicated loan generally has to undergo the following procedures:
- development of strategy and exploration of market;
- negotiation of basic terms and conditions;
- receipt of the mandate from the borrower;
- development of time schedule and marketing strategy;
- preparation of information memorandum;
- negotiation of the loan agreement with the borrower;
- making offers to participating banks;
- negotiation of loan agreement with participating banks;
- signing the loan agreement;
- closing documentation; and
- disbursement.

The average size of a syndicated loan is approximately USD100 million. The size of loans presents too great a credit risk exposure for most individual banks. U. S. regulations limit the size of a loan to less than 15% of a bank's capital. By sharing in the financing and credit risk of many different syndicated loans, banks can achieve greater diversification, lowering their risk of failure.

Restructuring a syndicated loan of a financially distressed borrower often requires unanimous agreement of all banks. This can be costly if banks have conflicting objectives, as was the case with many sovereign syndicated loans of the 1980s.

Derivatively syndicated loans take two forms: loan sale and asset securitization. In the case of a loan sale, a bank negotiates a credit agreement with a borrower and then negotiates an agreement (called a secondary loan participation) with another investor, who buys all or part of the cash flows from the original loan agreement. This investor is exposed to the borrower's credit risk from the part of the loan that he buys, even though he is not part of the original credit agreement. In the case of asset securitization, one or more banks or non-bank lenders sell multiple loans to a "Special Purpose Corporation" or "Grantor Trust". This corporate entity holds the pool of loans as assets and finances the purchase of loans by issuing some equity but mainly debt shares to many investors.

C. *Export Credit*

Export credit is government (export credit agencies, e. g. , Export-import Bank of the United States) guaranteed lending channeled through a commercial bank to support export trade. There are two kinds of export credit: **buyer credit** and **supplier credit**.

In **buyer credit**, exporter's bank provides loans to the importer (importer's bank guarantees) or to importer's bank, which on-lends the loan to the importer to finance the partial value of the individual contract between the exporter and the importer. A buyer credit usually includes the following terms and conditions:

- The loan is arranged in support of a supply contract for capital goods and related services mainly from the country to provide loan.
- Value of financing is available for 85% of the eligible contract value. The balance must be paid in cash or with a commercial loan.
- Period of financing varies with each contract considered to be eligible and approved for financing, normally between 5 and 10 years.
- Payment of financing should be in equal half-yearly installment of principal commencing from a time determined by the export credit agency or the scope of the supply contract.
- Interest rate is fixed in accordance with Commercial Interest Reference Rates (CIRRs) which are the official lending rates of Export Credit Agencies. They are calculated monthly and are based on government bonds issued in the country's domestic market for the country's currency. In the case of the US dollar, the CIRR is based on the U. S. Treasury bond rate. CIRR rates are updated on the Monday preceding the 15th of the month and are effective on the 15th of the month.
- Commitment fee at a rate per annum is calculated from the date of signing of the loan agreement until the date of full disbursement of the loan thereunder on the amount of loan not disbursed from time to time.
- Management fee is calculated at flat on the amount of the loan.
- Credit insurance premiums as determined by the agencies are payable by the borrower or added to the supply contract value and refinanced under the term of the export

credit loan.

The procedure of buyer credit varies depending on whether the importer's bank provides guarantee or on-lends it when the loan is provided to the importer. In the first case, the following procedures are followed. (See chart below)

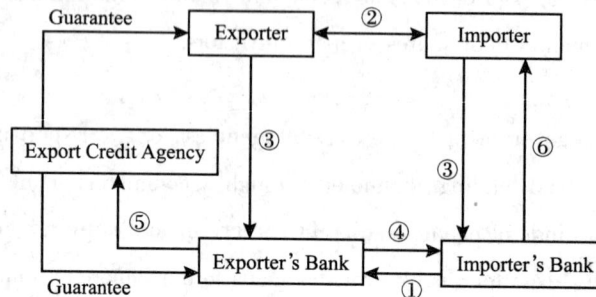

- Exporter's bank and importer's bank conclude a general agreement (frame agreement) of export credit. Importer's bank requests and exporter's bank agrees to make available the facility line pursuant to the terms and conditions of the agreement (①).
- The exporter and the importer conclude a supply contract (②).
- The exporter and the importer make an application to exporter's bank and importer's bank respectively (③).
- Exporter's bank signs an individual loan agreement with importer's bank to finance the contract after both have accepted the applications, respectively (④).
- Exporter's bank makes an application for the individual loan agreement to government's export credit agency, and the loan agreement comes into effect after the export credit agency has approved it (⑤).
- The importer's bank makes the loan to the importer (⑥).

In the second case, the following procedures are applied: (See chart below)

- The exporter and the importer conclude a supply contract (①).
- The exporter and the importer make an application to exporter's bank and importer's bank respectively (②).
- Exporter's bank signs a loan agreement with the importer, and importer's bank issues a letter of guarantee in favor of exporter's bank after they accept the applications respectively (③).
- Exporter's bank files an application for the individual loan agreement to government's export credit agency, and the loan agreement comes into effect after the export credit agency approves it (④).

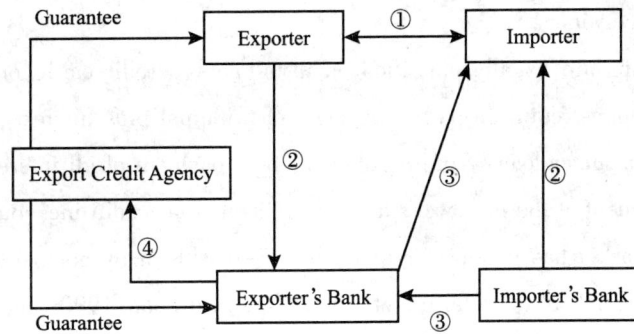

The other export credit is **supplier credit**. In supplier credit, exporter's bank provides loans to the supplier (exporter) to finance the contract with special payment terms under which importer pays for the contract goods by half-yearly installments. Such terms require the issuance of bill of exchange by the supplier for pre-acceptance by the buyer/borrower. The usual terms and conditions of supplier credit are the same as those of buyer credit. Supplier credit procedures are as follows.

- The supplier (exporter) enters into a contract with the importer for supplying goods and services. The payment terms of the contract requires the importer to pay for the goods in half-yearly installments.

- The supplier and the importer apply to supplier's bank and importer's bank respectively. Importer's bank issues a letter of guarantee in favor of the supplier after accepting the application. Supplier's bank enters into a loan agreement with the supplier. The loan agreement and the contract come into effect after the export credit agency approves them.

D. *Consumer Loans*

Non-mortgage consumer loans differ substantially from commercial and industrial loans. Their usual purpose is to finance the purchase of durable goods, although many individuals borrow to finance education, medical care, and other expenses. The average loan to each borrower is relatively small. Most loans have maturities from one to five years, are repaid in installment, and carry a fixed interest rate. In general, an individual borrower's default risk is greater that a commercial customer's. Consumer loan rate is thus higher to compensate for the greater losses.

Although most consumer loans carry fixed rates, installment payments increase their rate sensitivity so their average duration is relatively short. Long-term loans, however, may subject the bank to considerable interest rate risk. Finally, consumer loans are relatively illiquid. Banks generally cannot sell them near face value because no secondary market exists. This is slowly changing, however, as more banks attempt to securitize automobile loans and credit card receivables.

Consumer loans are usually classified as installment, credit card, or non-installment loan. Installment loans require a partial payment of principal plus interest periodically until maturity. Other consumer loans require either a single payment of all interest plus principal or a gradual repayment at the borrower's discretion, as with a credit line. Bank's share of the consumer credit market has fallen over time, but even with many competitors, commercial banks held around 38% of the total credit outstanding in the late 1990s and were the largest single holders of automobile loans, mobile home loans, and all other types (the case of USA). Non-installment loans are for special purpose in which the individual normally expects a large cash receipt to repay the debt, such as a temporary bridge loan for the down payment on a house that is repaid from the sale of the previous house.

E. *Personal Residential Mortgage Loans*

Commercial banks provide long-term mortgage loans to borrowers (consumers) to purchase houses/land. The ownership of the property remains with the mortgagee and the possession of property usually is taken by the mortgagor unless and until the occurrence of default or full repayment. Maturity of such loans is usually 30 years and the interest rates are fixed. Maximum amount of such loans is 70% of the property value, and the balance should be paid in cash as down payment. A home mortgage plan is much more than a mortgage loan. It has additional benefits. For example, the loan amount is up to 85% of the borrower's property value, and repayment periods are up to 30 years. Repayment schemes include straight-line repayment schemes, reducing balance repayment schemes, step-up repayment schemes, and fortnightly repayment option. Other financial services include home owner's overdraft, decoration loan, with a repayment period of up to three years.

F. *Overseas Fund-Raising and On-lending*

Overseas fund-raising and on-lending refer to the credit service that a bank, with the mandate from its domestic clients, raises funds overseas first from foreign export credit agencies, commercial banks, investment banks, or other financial institutions, and then on-lends the funds further to its domestic client to facilitate the importing of capital goods, technologies and relevant services.

The target customers applying for the loans include the independent legal business entities and governmental organs. Such credit service consists of two aspects, namely, overseas fund-raising and domestic on-lending. The bank plays a very important role in the whole process. On the one hand, the bank serves as the borrower and, therefore, it is bounded by the loan agreement with a foreign counterpart and is obliged to serve the principal and interests of the loan according to the repayment schedule. On the other hand, the bank possesses the right to demand repayment of the loan from its domestic client to which it has extended the overseas-raised funds.

The overseas funding can take various forms, e. g. , government loans, mixed loans, export credit, and commercial loans. The fundamental requirements and procedures are as follows:

- The project has to be approved first by relevant authorities in China, such as the State Reform and Development Commission;
- The domestic client has to issue a mandate to the bank;
- The financing has to be approved by the bank;
- The bank signs a loan agreement with its foreign counterpart while signing simultaneously an on-lending agreement with the client;
- The execution of the loan agreement.

G. Introduction to Typical Loans A typical Loans

i. Credit Line

A line of credit (also called a credit line or credit limit) is the maximum amount of money a bank will lend to an individual or a business entity without requiring additional approval. The lender determines a line of credit based largely on the individual's credit worthiness and income potential. Certain large corporations and high-profile public figures have such a substantial line of credit that they can literally borrow money against it for a lifetime. Having a line of credit is very useful for small business owners who may have to take out several loans over time to purchase equipment or upgrade their facilities. Instead of applying for one USD 25,000 bank loan, for example, a business owner with a USD 25,000 line of credit can take out a USD 5,000 loan in April, then a USD 10,000 loan in August and finally a USD 2,000 loan in December, all with prior approval from the lender. By using a line of credit, borrowers can take out just enough money for a specific expense then pay it back entirely before taking out additional funds. The amount of interest charged for each smaller loan in a line of credit can be variable. The first loan may have been taken out when lending rates were low, but the second might be affected by an upward or downward change in the prime lending rate or other factors. Banks can also charge penalty fees for late payments on all outstanding loans. Borrowers must keep track of individual loan obligations in order to keep payments on track.

Most people encounter a line of credit when dealing with credit cards or home equity loans. The credit card company establishes an upper limit on charges made by individual cardholders. This line of credit may be adjusted by customer request or by the company itself. Severe financial penalties may be levied on cardholders who borrow more money than their line of credit will allow. Credit cards do allow holders to make several purchases without seeking the approval of the lender. Home financing options may also include a line of credit based on the value of the borrower's home. This practice is often called a home equity line of credit and is a genuine temptation for cash-strapped homeowners. Similar to a second mortgage, a home equity line of credit establishes a maximum amount of money a homeowner can borrow. In the case of a second mortgage, the bank lends the entire amount of money and the borrower makes regular payments based on the balance due. A line of credit arrangement, however, allows the homeowner to borrow smaller amounts of money to pay off contractors or bills without incurring a large debt up front.

Legally, credit line is an arrangement in which a bank or vendor extends a specified amount of unsecured credit to a specified borrower for a specified time period. If the bank agreed to lend a specific amount to a borrower, and to allow that amount to be borrowed again once it has been repaid, such facility is called revolving credit line.

ii. Overdraft Facility

Overdraft is a credit facility, within a set limit, to provide working capital. The level of the facility is usually limited to the security offered.

A loan facility on a customer's current account at a bank permits the customer to overdraw up to a certain limit for an agreed period. Interest is payable on the amount of the loan facility taken up, and it may therefore be a relatively inexpensive way of financing a fluctuating requirement.

iii. Trade Finance

Trade finance means credit provided to overseas buyers, also known as export finance. Such finance is available as: supplier credit, under which an exporter allows credit terms to an overseas buyer and then arranges funds to cover these terms from a local financial institution; and buyer credit, under which a local financial institution provides funds direct to an overseas buyer or other approved borrower so that an exporter can be paid immediately after goods are shipped.

Trade finance covers a wide scope of products, including letter of credit, factoring and forfaiting. For details, please refer to the relative part of this book.

iv. Project Financing

Its defination is given by the International Project Finance Association (IPFA) as follows: The financing of long-term infrastructure, industrial projects and public services based upon a non-recourse or limited recourse financial structure where project debt and equity used to finance the project are paid back from the cash flow generated by the project.

In other words, project financing is a loan structure that relies primarily on the project's cash flow for repayment, with the project's assets, rights, and interests held as secondary security or collateral.

BOT (**Build-Operate-Transfer**) is a typical form of Project Financing. The vehicle company established specially by the sponsors carries out the construction and operation of the project, which is usually a large turnkey project and installation of industries, for a limited period, and then the operational project is transferred to the relevant state authorities, namely, a government agency. The vehicle companies in many developing countries are private ones. The BOT approach is likely to be a favorite to a government that is keen to minimize the impact on its capital budget, introduce increased efficiency from the private sector, and encourage foreign investment and introduction of new technology.

A BOT structure is normally based on a concession agreement between a government or a government agency and the vehicle company established by the sponsors to carry out the construction and operation of the project. The liabilities undertaken by the project vehicle are substantial and the vehicle itself is incorporated specifically to obtain the concession. The sponsors might be required to provide support for the vehicle's performance, by entering into the concession agreement or providing independent commitments. Conversely, the sponsors will wish to ensure that the government accepts that it might, in certain circumstances, need to give continuing support. For example, connecting infrastructure might need to be put into place and payments might need to be made for the benefits received from the project once it becomes operational.

Sponsors are likely to require assurances as to a government intention on a range of further issues, which might affect the project. While governments are unlikely to be either willing or able to fetter the future exercise of their legislative and administrative powers, sponsors might nevertheless try to ensure that adequate compensation shall be payable in the event that the government subsequently acts inconsistently with its expressed intentions and to the detriment of the project.

The government's concern is that concerned proper work of maintenance and repair is carried out in order to provide an adequate service, to meet necessary safety and other requirements and to ensure that, upon transfer at the end of the term, the government inherits an operational project and not simply a liability.

The vehicle company and sponsors are responsible for the finance of a BOT project. The risk of the finance is allocated between the parties (the vehicle company and the lender). The concession agreement is likely to affect substantially the project risk allocation and the negotiations between the relevant parties on these issues should take account of the likely response of lenders to this allocation of risk. In BOT projects the host government not only plays a much greater role than in other projects, but also might have direct contact with the lender. Since the interests of the host government and the lenders will not necessarily coincide, it is essential for the sponsors and their advisers to fully appreciate the particular requirements of all parties involved.

II. The Credit Process

Lending business of a bank involves two-level issues. One is the overall business strategy of a bank, mainly referring to the total volume and portfolio structure of loans, which is also called **Credit Planning**. The other is the **decision making of an individual lending** business, mainly taking the repayment ability of specific client or project into consideration.

The fundamental objective of lending is to make profitable loans with minimal risk. Management should target specific industries or markets in which lending officers have expertise. The somewhat competing goals of loan volume and loan quality must be balanced with the bank's liquidity requirements, capital constrains, and rate of return objectives. The credit process relies on each bank's systems and control that allow management and credit officers to evaluate risk and return trade-offs.

The credit process includes three functions: business development and credit analysis, underwriting or credit execution and administration, and credit review. Each reflects the bank's written loan policy as determined by the bank. A loan policy formalizes lending qualities and establishes procedures for granting, documenting, and reviewing loans.

1. Main Consideration in Credit Planning

A. Assets and Liabilities Management

i. Capital Adequacy Requirement

The Commercial bank is subject to the risk-based capital guidelines issued by the central bank or monetary authorities according to the Basle Accord. These guidelines are used to evaluate capital adequacy based primarily on the perceived credit risk associated with balance sheet of assets and liabilities as well as certain off-balance sheet exposures such as unused loan commitment, letters of credit, interest rate and foreign exchange derivatives.

The Bank for International Settlements (BIS) unifies Risk Class of Assets and Risk Weight of Asset issued by commercial banks in the world. All assets of commercial banks are classified into various risk assets by risk class of assets, and each class of assets is assigned a risk weight. For instance, risk weight of loans to non-sovereign companies is 100%. Risk-Adjusted Asset = Risk Weight × Asset. The risk-based capital guidelines require a minimum ratio of Tier-1 capital to risk-adjusted assets of 4% and a minimum ratio of combined Tier-1 and Tier-2 capital to risk-adjusted assets of 8%.

Loans are parts of risk-adjusted assets. Risk-adjusted assets consist of several components of assets because commercial bank requires diversified assets for adequate liquidity which is defined as having funds available at all times to meet fully and promptly all maturing liabilities, including demand deposits and off-balance sheet commitments. To control the risk of loans, the following criteria are applied:

- The advance of loan will not cause capital/ (risk-adjusted Assets) to go below 8%.
- Total Outstanding Loan/Total Deposits less than X% (75%, in China).
- Loan to individual borrower/Capital less than Y% (10%, in China).

ii. Portfolio Management

In the management of their portfolio, commercial banks emphasize the importance of asset and earnings diversification, the immediate recognition as losses of all credits judged to be uncollectible, and the maintenance of appropriate credit loss allowance.

Since all identified losses are immediately written off, no portion of allowance is specifically allocated or restricted to any individual group of loans, and the entire allowance is variable to absorb all probable credit losses inherent in the portfolio.

Credit loss experience is often expressed as the credit loss ratio of annual credit losses as a percentage of average loans. Pricing and credit policies reflect the loss experience of each particular product. Loans are generally written off not later than a predetermined number of days past due on a contractual basis. The number of days is set at an appropriate level by loan product and by the country.

In commercial lending, losses as a percentage of outstanding loans can vary widely from period to period and are particularly sensitive to economic circle.

According to portfolio risk analysis, some commercial banks in the world created "Credit Mix" (Credit portfolio). Credit Mix consists of 5 factors:

- Tenor — Term structure of loan
- Risk Rating — Risk rating of assets (loan) and borrowers (obligors)
- Industry — Appraising industry risk
- Obligor — Obligor's quality
- Concentration — Loan concentration

Portfolio management is becoming an integral part of the credit process. In the credit transaction business, process is being developed involving setting limits for obligor and industry concentrations. Each credit risk will be monitored in terms of a standard set of risk dimensions including industry codes and risk ratings.

B. Profitability and Budgetary Control

i. Profitability

The management and operation of commercial banks are responsible for revenue, investor's stock value and strengthening continually their ability to make profits. As part of revenue of commercial banks results from loans, commercial banks must consider the profitability of their credit business.

ii. Budgetary Control

The operating target of commercial banks is profit. The revenue of credit constitutes the main part of revenue of the banks. Commercial banks set up budgetary control for realizing target profit. Credit is also regulated by a control system. A budget is a predetermined statement of management policy during a given period, which sets up a standard for comparison with the result actually achieved.

Commercial banks usually establish a responsibility of budget for their credit department which must consider budgetary target, net revenue and cost. In preparation of the budget, it must incorporate the ideas of all levels of management; coordinate all the activities of the business; centralize control; decentralize responsibility on to each manager involved; act as guide for management decisions when unforeseeable conditions affect the budget; plan income and expenditure control so that maximum profitability is achieved; direct capital expenditure in the most profitable direction; ensure that sufficient working capital is available; provide a yardstick against which actual results can be compared; and show the management when action is needed to remedy a situation.

C. Liquidity Ratio

Liquidity ratio is the proportion of a financial institution's assets held in easily cashable form. This may be established as a matter of internal control or by direction from the monetary authorities, as in the case of liquidity ratios imposed on banks by the reserve bank or the central bank for prudential reasons. For a bank this is the cash held by the bank as a proportion of deposits in the bank. Liquidity of a bank can be shown in terms of its debt to loan ratio. But is the lower the debt to loan ratio, the better for a bank, or vice versa? The answer depends on the bank's risk management capability and its judgment on incoming market changes. Presently, for most of the largest Chinese banks, the debt to loan ratio stands at 60% or so. In other words, the liquidity ratio is very high. But correspondently, the operation efficiency of capital of those banks is not high. The debt to loan ratio of large banks in the US can reach about 108% and that of large banks in Europe can amount to around 88%. The higher capital operation efficiency is attributed to their much stronger risk management capabilities. If Chinese banks want to improve their efficiency, the enhancement of risk management capability will be one of the critical factors. Meanwhile, changes in the market values of assets and liabilities will affect earnings and capital. Therefore a bank's forecast of the market risk will influence its liquidity ratio as well.

D. Government's Macro-economic Policy

The banking industry plays a critical role in a country's financial system and economic development. If any country wants to build a healthy financial system and a stable, balanced economic development, a robust banking industry must be in place. For this reason, a bank's business and operation should be consistent with its government's macro-economic policy. From a government perspective, if there is over-investment in some industry or segment, the government will control this overheated industry or segment. If there are insufficient inputs in some industry or segment, and if this industry or segment is of strategic importance to either people's life or a country's development, it will be very natural for the government to try to mobilize more resources and capital there by promulgating macro-economic policy. Then the regulating authorities, in China, namely, the PBOC or the Central Bank and the CBRC will seek to use their window guidance function to confine or boost the banking industry's loan growth to a reasonable level.

Sometimes, a bank's overall loan growth goal and its loan growth aim for a specific industry are consistent with those of the regulating authorities. It means that the bank has the same judgment on the overall economic development and on a specific industry's prospect with the government. In practice, it is shown in the bank's decision on lending business, whether to increase, maintain, gradually decrease or even withdraw the loan disbursement in some industry. But sometimes, it is not the case. Because the government views the economy from a national perspective and there must be imbalance between different regions and clients. It is a kind of tradeoff between long-term interests and short-term returns, a healthy national economy and a bank's profitability. We cannot deny that there are still some high quality clients in some overheated industry. Banks can still make great profits via lending to them. But for the banking industry, the overall economic development is the cornerstone of its current and sustainable profitability. Therefore, for its lending business, a bank must take the government's macro policy into consideration, balancing with its own current loan portfolio, and adjust it in line with the government's macro policy and meet the bank's own profitability goal.

2. Basic Process of an Individual Loan

From a bank's perspective, a basic credit process consists of 5 steps, namely, loan application acceptance, investigation and assessment, review and approval, loan disbursement and post-disbursement management. See the Chart on the next page (Source: a Chinese bank's Credit Manual).

A. Application Acceptance (Business Development)

This is the first step, mainly consisting of client's application, qualification review, client's submission of materials for preliminary review. The associates of a bank to receive applications will decide whether to accept a client's loan application or not, in accordance with relevant laws, rules, regulations and their bank's credit policy.

In a more competitive environment, this phrase should be **business development**, i. e. , the process of marketing bank service to existing and potential customers. With lending, it involves identifying new credit customers and soliciting their banking business, as well as maintaining relationships with current customers and cross-selling noncredit services. Every bank employee, from tellers handling drive-up facilities to members of top management, is responsible for business development.

B. Investigation and Assessment (Credit Analysis)

This is the second step. If any client wants a bank to issue a letter of loan intent, then the bank will conduct a preliminary investigation. If the client is not qualified according to the investigation result, the application will be handed back. If the client is qualified, the bank will issue a letter of intent first, then, the bank will conduct a comprehensive investigation and assessment. If the client does not need the bank to issue a letter of intent, the bank will directly conduct a comprehensive investigation and assessment which is composed of 3 parts, namely, client assessment, business assessment, security review.

Once a customer requests a loan, bank officers analyze all available information to determine whether the loan meets the bank's risk-return objectives. Credit analysis is essentially a default risk analysis in which a loan officer attempts to evaluate a borrower's ability and willingness to repay. The areas of commercial risk analysis are generally related to the following questions:

- What risks are inherent in the operation of the business?
- What have managers done or failed to do in mitigating those risks?
- How can a lender structure and control its own risks in supplying funds?

(The key risk factors and methods of credit analysis will be introduced in the next section.)

The formal credit analysis procedure includes a subjective evaluation of the borrower's request and a detailed review of all financial statements. Credit department employees may perform the initial quantitative analysis for the loan officer. The process consists of:

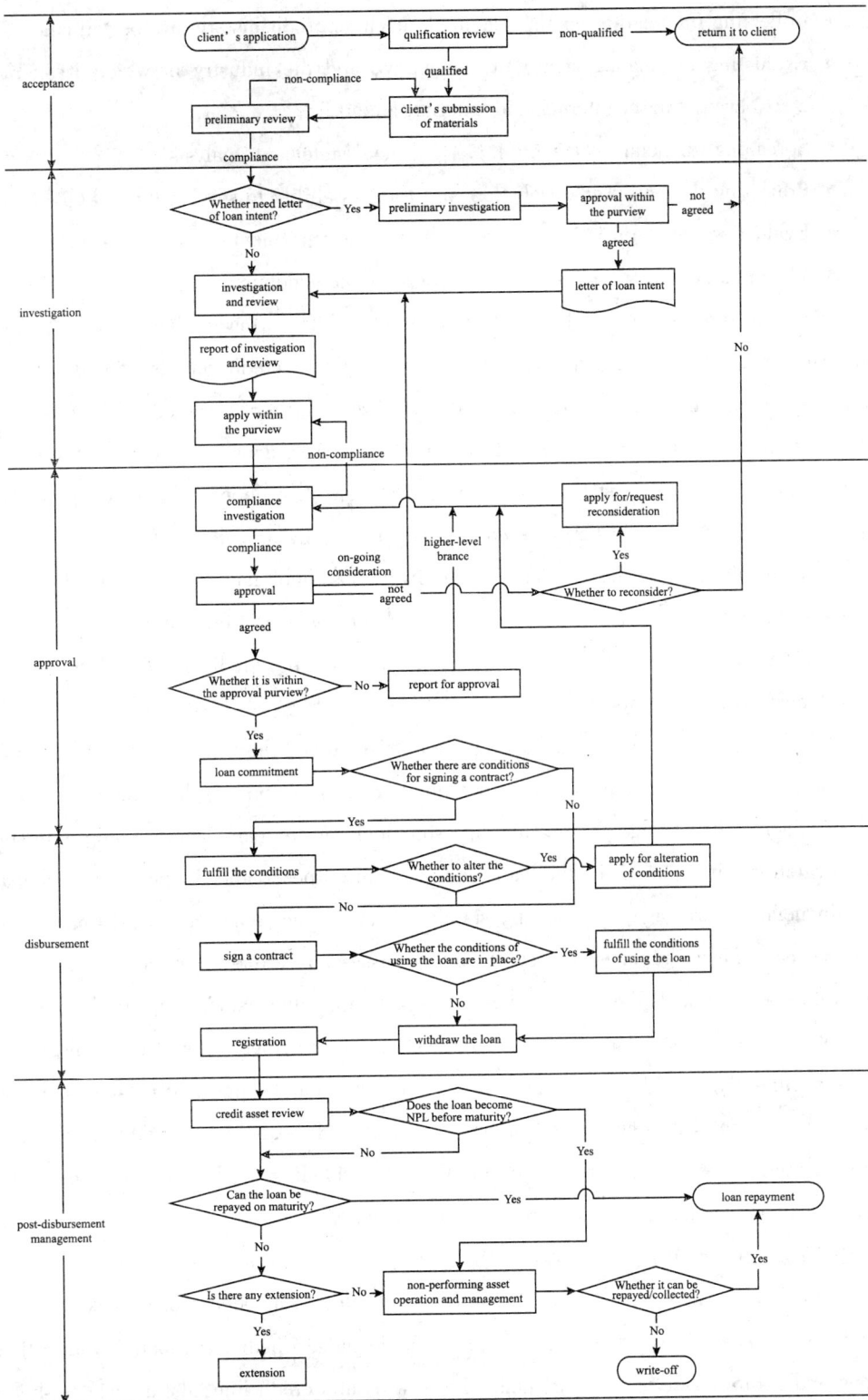

acceptance

client's application → qulification review — non-qualified → return it to client

qualified ↓

non-compliance ← client's submission of materials

preliminary review

compliance ↓

investigation

Whether need letter of loan intent? — Yes → preliminary investigation → approval within the purview — not agreed → No

No ↓ | agreed ↓

investigation and review ← letter of loan intent

report of investigation and review ↓

apply within the purview

non-compliance ↓

approval

compliance investigation ← apply for/request reconsideration

compliance ↓ | higher-level brance | on-going consideration | Yes ↑

approval — not agreed → Whether to reconsider?

agreed ↓

Whether it is within the approval purview? — No → report for approval

Yes ↓

loan commitment → Whether there are conditions for signing a contract? — No / Yes

disbursement

fulfill the conditions → Whether to alter the conditions? — Yes → apply for alteration of conditions

No ↓

sign a contract → Whether the conditions of using the loan are in place? — Yes → fulfill the conditions of using the loan

No ↓

registration ← withdraw the loan

post-disbursement management

credit asset review → Does the loan become NPL before maturity?

No ↓ | Yes

Can the loan be repaid on maturity? — Yes → loan repayment

No ↓

Is there any extension? — No → non-performing asset operation and management → Whether it can be repayed/collected? — Yes

Yes ↓ | No ↓

extension — write-off

- Collecting information for the credit file such as credit history and performance.
- Evaluating the management, the company, and the industry in which it operates i. e. , evaluation of internal and external factors.
- Spreading financial statements i. e. , financial statement analysis.
- Projecting the borrower's cash flow and thus its ability to service the debt.
- Evaluating collateral or the secondary source of repayment.
- Writing a summary analysis and making a recommendation.

The credit file contains background information on the borrower, including call report summaries, past and present financial statements, pertinent credit reports, and supporting schedules such as an aging of receivables, a breakdown of current inventory and equipment, and a summary of insurance coverage. If the customer is a previous borrower, the file should also contain copies of the past loan agreement, cash flow projections, collateral agreements and security documents, and narrative comments provided by prior loan officers, and copies of all correspondence with the customer. One of the most important aspects of lending is to determine the customers *desire to repay the loan*. Although this is critically important, it is difficult to measure. Information in the credit file will give the credit officer information on the customer's repayment history.

The credit analyst also uses the credit file data to spread the financial statements, project cash flow, and evaluate collateral. An evaluation of management, the company, and industry is also needed to insure the safety and soundness of the loan. The last step is to submit a written report summarizing the loan request, loan purpose, and the borrower's comparative financial performance with industry standards, and to make a recommendation.

The loan officer evaluates the report and discusses any errors, omissions, and extensions with the analyst. If the credit (loan) does not satisfy the bank's risk criteria, the officer notifies the borrower that the original request has been denied. The officer may suggest any procedures that would improve the borrower's condition and repayment prospects and solicit another proposal if circumstances improve. If the credit satisfies acceptable risk limits, the officer negotiates specific preliminary credit terms including the loan amount, maturity, pricing, collateral requirements and repayment schedule.

C. *Review and Approval* (*Credit Execution*)

In this step, when materials are submitted, the relevant associates of a bank will conduct a compliance review. Then the associates should judge whether the loan is within their review and approval purview. For a client with or without a credit line, the associates should refer to the credit policy of their own bank.

If the review conclusion is not an approval, relevant associates should be informed in time. If the conclusion is an approval and also is within the purview, they should also be no-tified in time. If the conclusion is on-going consideration, inform the relevant associates and ask them to fulfill the required procedures. If the conclusion is an approval but out of the purview, submit the application materials to the higher level branch or even the head office. The materials should be complete in form, accurate in data, detailed in analysis, clear-cut in opinion.

The formal credit decision can be made individually, by an independent underwriting department, or by committee, depending on a bank's organizational structure. This structure varies with a bank's size, number of employees, and the type of loan handled. A bank's board of directors normally has the final say in the matter over of which loans should be ap-proved. Typically, each lending officer has independent authority to approve loans up to some fixed amount. Junior officers at a large bank might have authority to approve loan no larger than USD 100,000, while senior lending officers might independently approve loans up to USD 500,000. *A loan committee* made up of the bank's senior loan officers often for-mally reviews larger loans. This committee reviews each step of the credit analysis as presen-ted by the loan officer and supporting analysts and makes a collective decision. Loan com-mittee meets regularly to monitor the credit approval process and asset quality problems when they arise. When required, the board of director or a directors' loan committee reviews this decision and grants final approval.

Many large banks employ a centralized underwriting department. *Centralized underwrit-ing* uses a relationship manager (RM), who sources new business and manages existing re-lationships within the portfolio. After releieving new credit requests, the RM advises the cli-ent on the required information to process the request, evaluates and prescreens the request when the information is received, and if the request has a good probability of approval and then he, will prepare the package and send it to the loan center. If the request has a remote probability of approval, the RM will advise the customer of that prospect—a de facto decline of the loan. Credit specialists in central underwriting make the final loan decision, but some banks allow for market overrides if the RM can mitigate the reasons for decline. Most large banks use computer software to quantitatively spread and evaluate the credit requests. Ap-provals from the computer system are considered one of the required signatures. The RM's signature will be the second required signature (up to officer's authority).

D. *Loan Disbursement (Credit Administration)*

Loan disbursement is the fourth step and consists of 5 components, namely, fulfilling pre-lending conditions, signing a contract, fulfilling loan using conditions, loan withdrawal and credit registration.

Once a loan has been approved, the officer notifies the borrower and prepares a **loan agreement**. This agreement formalizes the purpose of the loan, the terms, repayment schedule, collateral required, and any loan covenants. It also states what conditions would bring about default by the borrower. These conditions may include late principal and interest payments, the sale of substantial assets, a declaration of bankruptcy, and breaking any restrictive loan covenant (Please see section 5 for details). The officer then checks that all loan documentation is present and in order. The borrower signs the agreement along with other guarantors, turns over the collateral if necessary, and receives the loan proceeds.

DOCUMENTATION. A critical feature of executing any loan involves perfecting the bank's security interest in collateral. A security interest is the legal claim on property that secures payment on a debt or performance of an obligation. When the bank's claim is superior to that of other creditors and the borrower, its security interest is said to be *perfected*.

Because there are many different types of borrowers and collaterals, there are different methods of perfecting a security interest. In most cases, the bank requires borrowers to sign a security agreement that assigns qualifying collateral to the bank. This agreement describes the collateral and relevant covenants or warranties. Formal closure may involve getting the signature of a third-party guarantor on a loan agreement or having a key individual assign the cash value of a life insurance policy to the bank. In other cases, a bank may need to obtain title to equipment or vehicles. Whenever all parties sign a security agreement and the bank holds the collateral, the security interest is perfected. When the borrower holds the collateral, the bank must file a financing statement that describes the collateral and the rights of the bank and borrower. It must be signed to establish the bank's superior interest.

Losses are a normal part of lending. They can only be totally eliminated by taking no credit risk. Banks have many procedures that help limit their loss exposure. The primary strategic tool is a formal loan policy that establishes exposure limits to any single borrower or group of borrowers. Such maximum exposures will not put the bank at risk of failure if the entire exposure goes unpaid. Other specific procedures include position limits, risk rating loans and loan covenants.

E. *Post-disbursement Management* (*Credit Review*)

Post-disbursement management includes review, collection, extension of lending asset, and non-performing asset management.

The loan review effort is directed at reducing credit risk as well as handling problem loans and liquidating assets of failed borrowers. Effective credit management separates loan review from credit analysis, execution, and administration. The review process has two functions: monitoring the performance of existing loans and handling problem loans. Many banks have a formal loan review committee, independent of calling officers, that reports directly to the chief executive officer and director's loan committee. Loan review personnel audit current loans to verify that the borrower's financial condition is acceptable, loan documentation is in place, and pricing meets the return objective. If the audit uncovers problems, the committee initiates corrective action. Removing the problem may simply involve getting signatures on omitted forms or filing required documents with the state. If the borrower has violated any loan covenants, the loan is in default. The bank can then force the borrower to correct the violation or it can recall the loan. Recalling a loan is normally a last resort and done only when the borrower does not voluntarily correct the problem. It allows the bank to request full payment before repayment prospects worsen.

The problem is much more serious when the borrower's financial condition deteriorates. These loans are classified as problem loans and require special treatment. In many cases, the bank has to modify the terms of the loan agreement to increase the probability of full repayment. Modifications include deferring interest and principal payments, lengthening maturities, and liquidating unnecessary assets. Often the bank requests additional collateral or guarantees and asks the borrower to contribute additional capital. The purpose is to buy time until the borrower's condition improves. Banks often separate loan work-out specialists from traditional loan officers because they are liquidation-oriented and frequently involved in intense negotiations.

COMPARISON: TYPICAL CREDIT PROCESS OF A BANK IN AMERICA

Business Development and Credit Analysis	Credit Execution and Administration	Credit Review
■ Market research ■ Advertising, public relations ■ Officer call programs ■ Obtain formal loan request ■ Obtain Financial statements borrowing resolution, credit reports ■ Financial statement and cash flow analysis ■ Evaluate collateral ■ Loan officer makes recommendation on accepting/rejecting loan	■ Loan committee reviews proposal/recommendation ■ Accept/reject decision made, terms negotiated ■ Loan agreement prepared with collateral documentation ■ Borrower signs agreement, turns over collateral, receives loan proceeds ■ Perfect security interest ■ File materials in credit file ■ Process loan payments, obtain periodic financial statements, call on borrower	■ Review loan documentation ■ Monitor compliance with loan agreement: Positive and negative loan covenants; Delinquencies in loan payments; Discuss nature of delinquency or other problems with borrower ■ Institute corrective action: Modify credit terms; Obtain additional capital, collateral, guarantees recall loan

3. The Key Factors and Commonly Used Methods Of Credit Analysis

A. 5Cs Of Credit

Traditionally, key risk factors have been classified according to the five Cs of credit:

character, capital, capacity, conditions, and collateral.

Character refers to the borrower's honesty to repay. If there are any serious doubts, the loan should be rejected. **Capital** refers to the borrower's wealth position measured by financial soundness and market standing. Can the firm or individual withstand any deterioration in its financial position? Capital helps cushion losses and reduces the likelihood of bankruptcy. **Capacity** involves both the borrower's legal standing and management's expertise in maintaining operations so the firm or individual can repay its debt obligations. A business must have identifiable cash flow or alternative sources of cash to repay debt. An individual must be able to generate income. **Conditions** refers to the economic environment or industry-specific supply, production, and distribution factors influencing a firm's operations. Repayment sources of cash often vary with the business cycle or consumer demand. Finally, **collateral** is the lender's secondary source of repayment or security in the case of default. The bank can seize and liquidate an asset when a borrower defaults but does not justify lending proceeds when the credit decision is originally made.

B. 5Cs of Bad Credit

Golden and Walker identify the five Cs of **bad** credit, representing things to guard against to help prevent problems. These include complacency, carelessness, communication breakdown, contingencies, and competition.

Complacency refers to the tendency to assume that because things were good in the past they will be good in the future. Common examples are an over-reliance on guarantors, reported net worth, or past loan repayment success because it's always worked out in the past. **Carelessness** involves poor underwriting typically evidenced by inadequate loan documentation, a lack of current financial information or other pertinent information in the credit files, and a lack of protective covenants in the loan agreement. Each of these makes it difficult to monitor a borrower's progress and identify problems before they are unmanageable. Loan problems often arise when a bank's credit objectives and policies are not clearly **communicated**. Management should articulate and enforce loan policies, and loan officers should make management aware of specific problems with existing loans as soon as they appear. **Contingencies** refers to lenders tendency to play down or ignore circumstances in which a loan might default. The focus is on trying to make a deal work rather than identifying downside risk. Finally, **competition** involves following competitor's behavior rather than maintaining the bank's own credit standards. Doing something because the bank down the street is doing it does not mean it's good.

C. 5Ps Model

A useful framework for sorting out the facts and opinions in credit analysis is the 5Ps approach: people, purpose, payment, protection, and perspective. The 5Ps model dissects the information and focuses on risk. This enables a banker to reach a conclusion rapidly in each category and to make the final decision by weighting the categories, with people and payment normally carrying the most weight.

i. The People Factor

People should be appraised on three bases. The first is management/ownership. There should be an investigation of the principal backgrounds through the normal sources of industry, professional relationships, ownership, management ability, managers reputation, company's litigation records, and competitors. The second concerns business operations. An evaluation should be taken about operating trends, returns on equity and returns on total assets relative to those of competitors. The third is banking relationship. The company's treatment of its bankers is demonstrated by the principal's willingness and ability to repay debt as agreed, by a reasonable attitude toward disclosing appropriate financial and credit information, and by the realization that a reasonable profit for the bank is a prerequisite for a continuing relationship.

ii. The Purpose Factor

In balance sheet terms, the purpose of every bank loan can be assigned to one of three categories. The first is to support or acquire assets—current assets of seasonal nature, non-current assets or normal productive capacity. The second is to replace liabilities. Replacing liabilities can take the form of either assistance in making trade discounts, making tax payments or significantly riskier category of taking out (or "bailing out") other banks or financial institutions. The third is to replace equity. Replacing equity is a risky purpose since the effect of substituting debt or equity will substantially increase leverage. Occasionally, such a loan is appropriate, however, particularly in solving control problems of highly profitable companies.

iii. The Payment Factor

Asset conversion analysis may be made through two approaches. One is loan repayment analysis which is based on the past performance. Another is the ratio analysis. Management's policies and procedure regarding inventories and receivables should be explored. As far as inventory is concerned, it should be asked how good management's judgment of style or technology is, how the raw material, work-in-process, and finished goods mix are, whether there are control problems, when an inventory cushion and adequate insurance are provided Asset conversion loans normally are only for a limited time period. The uncertainty of the future is less than in other loans because their short tenor is more readily analyzed, and because cash flow may provide a viable longer term source of payment if asset conversion is inadequate in timing or magnitude.

Any loan which is not repaid by seasonal asset conversion is a cash flow loan which is repaid from future internally-generated funds or external funds, debt or equity, which the firm can attract. The capacity to generate internal funds depends on quality, magnitude, and trend of funds and cash from operations. Non-cash charges, principally depreciation and deferred taxes, must be analyzed as a continuing source of cash. Capital expenditures, due to inflation, technological change, and growth, will normally exceed depreciation expense and growth, and deferred taxes, just as deferred taxes arising from installment sales are usually more than offset by a higher level of receivables. With few exceptions, non-cash charges are sources of cash, which are exceeded by the related use of cash. In addition, ability to raise funds from other banks or financial institutions for replacing liability—repayment should be taken into consideration.

iv. The Protection Factor

A properly structured loan includes protection— a "second way out" in case the primary repayment source fails. Protection can be internal where the lender looks exclusively to the borrower, and external where a third party adds its credit responsibility to the borrower. Internal protection relies on capitalization, liquid (accounts receivable and inventory quality and composition), and fixed asset values. Internal protection can be either specific collateral or future cash flow if the primary source of repayment is asset conversion. External protection most commonly takes the form of guarantee, endorsement, or repurchase agreement, hypothecated collateral, etc. However, any loan based solely on the obligation of the guarantor is normally a high risky loan at the outset, because there is only one source of repayment.

v. The Perspective Factor

What are risks? Do they all make sense in risk analysis framework? How are the risks mitigated? Is the all-in with a pricing sufficient to compensate for the risk? Here the principal risk of either having business with a particular borrower or being inherent in a specific transaction should be reviewed. The analyst should assess how the risks are being mitigated, or where a risk cannot be fully covered, and why we should proceed with the proposed transaction.

The pricing and structure of a transaction are also important components of the perspective section. They are important guidelines because they affect the price and costs of products both on and off the balance sheet.

For each product and transaction, it is important to know what the credit requirements are, and whether product revenues cover the loss, the capital and the cost.

D. *Financial Ratio Analysis*

Ratios are mathematical aids used in the analysis of financial statements that simplify relationships and facilitate comparisons. Although ratios help in evaluating a firm's financial strength, they are only the starting point. They must be interpreted, and underlying data must be examined. Ratios are not a substitute for thorough research and sound thinking. This section explains the purpose and limitations of ratios, and expands on basic analytical concept, ratio calculation and interpretations.

Ratio analysis is used to compare certain factors, which may affect a company's ability to repay debt or otherwise satisfy its creditors. It provides the analyst with the tools to measure the quality and worth of assets, as well as the extent and nature of liabilities. Ratios help measure the ability of a firm's management: Does the company earn a fair return? Can it withstand downturns? Does it have financial flexibility as measured by its ability to attract additional creditor or investors?

Ratio analysis concentrates on the past rather than on the future. A company's future performance may or may not be an extrapolation of past trends. However, we can learn from its past performance about deteriorating trends, volatility, and often about management's control over these factors.

Other factors may also limit the usefulness of ratios. For example, analysis may be limited by the accounting presentation. The analysts should understand that the generally accepted accounting principles allow for flexibility and therefore, varied interpretation. Further different accounting methods distort inter-company comparisons.

A summary of types of ratios is presented below.

i. Liquidity ratios

Liquidity ratios measure the company's ability to meet short-term obligations and continue operations through the cash conversion cycle.

- **Current Ratio** (= Current Assets / Current Liabilities) is a gross measure of liquidity. Historically, analysts have viewed a current ratio of about 2.0 to be consistent with adequate liquidity. This means that firms hold twice as much cash, inventory, and accounts receivable as current liabilities coming due in the next year.

- **Quick (Acid Test) Ratio** (= Quick Assets/Current Liabilities). Quick assets are those that can be converted into cash in a relatively short time period. As such, Quick ratio is a more conservative and accurate of liquidity of the current ratio because it isolates the most liquid of the current assets. (Quick Assets = Cash + Marketable Securities + Other Short-term Investments + Trade Receivables). Please note that excluded from this ratio are other receivables, inventories, prepaid, other miscellaneous current assets.

- **Inventory Reliance** (= (Current Liabilities – Quick Assets)/Inventory) measures the percentage of inventory (at book value) which must be quick asset meeting current obligations, to the extent that it can be liquidated to meet current obligations when the quick assets have been exhausted.

ii. Activity ratios

Activity ratios measure resource utilization and examine effectiveness with which assets are employed by comparing income statement items to appropriate asset categories. They can also be used in measuring asset quality (receivables, inventory and payable turnovers, etc.):

- **Sales to Asset Ratio** indicates the efficiency that the firm's asset base produces revenue.

- **Days Accounts Receivable Collection Period** (= Accounts Receivable / average daily credit sales) indicates the average number of days required to convert accounts receivable into cash.

- **Inventory Turnover** (= Cost of Goods Sold / Inventory) represents the number of times at a given level of inventory turnovers per given accounting period.

Working Capital Turnover (= Net Sales / Working Capital) indicates demand on capital in supporting sales growth. A high or rising ratio might indicate the need for longer term funding.

iii. Leverage Ratios

Leverage ratios indicate the mix of the firm's financing between debt and equity and potential earnings volatility resulting from debt financing. The greater is a firm's level of debt, the higher are its fixed interest payments and the more likely it is to generate insufficient earnings (cash flow) to cover debt payments, thus, the greater is a firm's leverage, the more volatile its net profit (or losses) because certain sales are required to cover fixed interest charges.

Leverage = Total Liabilities / Net Worth

　　　or = Senior Liabilities / Capital Funds

Leverage = Total Liabilities / Tangible Net Worth

　　　or = Senior Liabilities / Tangible Capital Funds

Senior Liabilities equal to total liabilities less subordinated debts. Capital Funds are stockholders' equity (net worth) plus subordinated debts while Tangible Capital Funds are Capital funds less intangibles. Whenever there is outstanding subordinated debt, the simple debt/net worth ratio must be replaced with, or supplemented by, the Senior Liabilities/Capital Funds or Senior Liabilities/Tangible Capital Funds ratio.

From the bank's point of view, leverage ratios vary from conservative (highest calculated leverage) to liberal (lowest calculated leverage). The most conservative leverage ratio shows the most debt and least net worth. Therefore, the total liabilities/tangible net worth ratio will produce the highest leverage and thus be the most conservative because all liabilities are included. On the net worth side, equity has been reduced by the intangible assets on the balance sheet. Intangible assets do not necessarily yield cash, so it is more conservative to subtract these assets from net worth. Conversely, the senior liabilities/capital funds ratio would show less leverage because only senior liabilities are shown as debt, and net worth has been augmented by the amount of subordinated debt outstanding.

iv. Profitability Ratios

Profitability ratios measure management's ability to maximize revenues, control expenses and improve profitability. Basic profitability ratios include the firm's return on equity (ROE = Net Income/Equity), return on assets (ROA = Net Income/Assets), profit margin (PM), asset utilization (AU or asset turnover), and sales growth rate.

- **Net Margin** (= Net Income / Net Sales), also referred to as Return on Sales or Net Income Margin, measures the earnings generated by sales of each dollar.

- **Return on Total Assets** (= Net Income / Total Assets) measures the earning power of assets. However, it does not take account of asset composition or the debt/equity mix. This ratio is not applicable when a loss is reported.

4. Different Types of Security for Loan

When both the client's appraisal and specific project assessment are finished, a bank will begin to consider the security.

A bank has different kinds of security as cover for advance to his customers. There are several ways in which a bank may take security for an advance by lien, pledge, mortgage and hypothecation.

In the case of an ordinary **lien**, the borrower is still the owner of the property, but the creditor (bank) is in actual or constructive possession of the property, without as a rule having a right to sell it. The securities subject to the bank's lien are those which come into a bank's hands in the ordinary course of his business, for example, bills, checks and other negotiable instruments deposited with him in order that he may collect the proceeds.

Pledge is the characteristic model of taking goods as security. It arises when goods (or documents of title thereto) or bearer securities are delivered by one person (called the "pledger") to another person (called the "pledgee") to be held as a security for the payment of a debt or for the discharge of some other obligation, upon the express or implied undertaking that the subject matter of the pledge is to be restored to the pledger as soon as the debt or other obligation is discharged. The pledgee is entitled to the exclusive possession of the property until the debt is discharged, and the pledgee, in certain circumstances, has the power of sale, but the ownership remains with the pledger, subject to the pledger's right. Securities subject to pledge are goods and chattel and fully negotiable securities. Delivery of possession may be either actual or constructive.

Essentially, **mortgage** is an assignment or charge of some interest in land or other property, as security for the payment of a debt or for the discharge of some obligation. Mortgagee has a special interest in the property, and also a power of sale, but the possession of the property usually remains with the mortgagor unless and until there is a default and the mortgagee enters into possession, which is rare, or exercises any of his other remedies. Securities subject to mortgage are title deeds, life policies, and stocks and shares and others chosen in action.

Hypothecation is a transaction whereby goods may be made available as security for a debt without transferring either the property or the possession to the lender. There is risk of lending against the hypothecation of goods. Since the lender does not obtain actual or constructive possession of the goods, his measure of control over them is often very limited, giving the borrower an easy opportunity of dealing with them fraudulently.

5. Main Clauses of Loan Agreement

A bank will begin to negotiate and sign a loan agreement with its clients when all the above-mentioned four steps are taken. A loan agreement is a legally-binding document reached by both a bank and a client. It stipulates both parties' rights and obligations and also states what are events of default. The following are the major or commonly used clauses in a typical international term loan agreement:

General Clauses: including the denomination of loan currency, maturity, the available amount, interest rates and fees and the drawdown period, grace period, etc.

Conditions Precedent: The lender's obligation to lend would be subject to satisfaction of specified condition precedent. These are intended to ensure that all legal matters are in order and that any security required by the lender has been given. Conditions precedent usually include: necessary authorizations and governmental consents, legal opinions, true representations and warranties, no event of default, etc. Conditions precedent are only for the benefit of the lenders and may be waived by the lender to enable the borrowing to be made.

Interest: Loan agreements invariably state a rate of interest or a method for determining the rate, and the time payment of interest. Banks generally require borrower to pay a higher interest rate (**Penalty Interest**) on overdue sums than the normal rate and may charge compound interest.

Prepayment: Except rare absolute prohibition, prepayments are usually permitted on payment of a premium or fee calculated on the amount prepaid. The premium compensates the lender for the loss of its investment (i. e. the loan which yields interest).

Payments: Loan agreement usually states the place and currency of payment which are important matters to international lenders.

Calculations of Time: The clause specifies the meaning of term "year" (may mean a calendar year, any period of 12 months, or a financial year), "month", "week", or "day", calculating a period (commencement and end), etc. .

Taxation: The standard tax provisions require the borrower to pay all taxes due with respect to the loan, other than income taxes imposed upon the lending bank by its home jurisdiction. If the borrower is required to deduct or withhold taxes from any payment to the lending bank, then the sum due to the lending bank is increased ("gross up") to the extent necessary to ensure that the lending bank receives a net sum equal to the amount it would have received had the deduction or withholding not been made.

Representations and Warranties: These usually cover (a) the legality of the agreement, including, the borrower's status, and power to enter the agreement; authorizations and due execution; non-conflict with law; the validity and enforceability of the borrower's obligations under the agreement; exchange control and other governmental consents; filings and registrations; taxes and stamp duties and (b) the financial and commercial position of the borrower, including, the correctness of the borrower's most recent accounts and any information memorandum; the absence of material adverse changes in the financial conditions, defaults under other contracts, or material litigation involving the borrower. These representations and warranties may be required to be correct as of certain dates or "evergreen", i. e. , true so long as the loan is outstanding.

Covenants: Covenants relate to the management of the borrower's business and restricting its freedom of action.

- **Negative Pledge**: restriction on the grant by the borrower of security interests in favor of other creditors. A simple form states: "So long as any principal or interest is outstanding under this agreement, the borrower will not create or permit to subsist any mortgage, charge, pledge, lien or other encumbrance on its assets or revenues." Since an absolute negative pledge will interfere with the borrower's normal commercial operations, there is some relaxations.

- **Pari Passu (ranking equally) Clause** which may be stated as follows: The obligations of the borrower under this agreement are its direct, unsecured, general and unconditional obligations and rank pari passu with all its other present and future unsecured and unsubordinated obligations.

- **Disposals** Clause which may be written as follows: The borrower will not sell, transfer, lease or otherwise dispose of all or a substantial part of its business or assets whether by one transaction or a series of transactions related or not.

Events of Default: This provision enables the lender to take action to collect the entire amount of the loan or cease lending new funds if certain event occurs which makes it unlikely that the borrower will be able to pay the loan according to the agreed terms if the borrower does not comply with the agreement. Common events of default include:

- **Non-payment** i. e. , failure to pay principal, interest or other amounts when due.
- **Non-compliance** with the borrower's other obligations under the agreements.
- **Breach of warranty**.
- **Cross-default**: the borrower fails to perform obligations contained in other agreements entered into by him.

Governing Law and Jurisdiction: The loan agreement will specify what body of law will govern it and which jurisdiction in which lawsuits to enforce the loan agreement may be brought.

Waiver of Sovereign Immunity: Sovereign immunity refers to the general rule that a sovereign state, its political sub-divisions, agencies and instrumentalities are immune from jurisdiction of a country's court. However, exceptions exist for claims arising from commercial activities of the foreign state and situations where the foreign state has waived its rights of sovereign immunity. The waiver gives the lender an assurance that he can invoke the legal system of the country involved with the loan to assist him to obtain repayment of the loan.

III. Post-Disbursement Management

1. Credit Review

Credit review refers to a bank's on-going monitoring and analysis of its credit clients and the relevant factors that can influence safety of the clients' credit asset. Through credit review a bank can find out early warning signals as early as possible and take remedial measures. The process of credit review includes collecting clients' credit information, reviewing clients' current status, credit business progress, and security status in line with the information. After reviewing, the bank should know whether its clients are still qualified borrowers, whether their financial, operation and credit statuses have been deteriorated, whether there are any events that may incur material and negative impacts on clients' repayment capabilities. After credit review, the bank will find out early warning signals and take remedial measures to mitigate risks. At the same time, relevant reports should be prepared to record the review process.

Credit review consists of client review, credit risk review and security review.

A. *Client review*

i. For corporate clients, client review includes the review of:

- A client's basic status. Is the client still a qualified borrower? It is a precondition for the client to borrow from a bank.
- A client's operation status. Analyze the client's current profitability and repayment and their trends via understanding the client's internal enterprise development as well as its industry's development.
- A client's internal management level.
- Information of how a client uses its loans and the client's credit history.
- A client's financial status. Credit officers should take the client's industry and region's average financial status levels into consideration when analyzing the client's historical financial data. Based on it, credit officers can measure and forecast the client's repayment capabilities.
- Progress of material events. If a client involves itself with some material events, such as restructuring, foreign investment, fixed asset investment, and litigation, its operation, management, profits, loan repayment capabilities will be materially affected. Therefore, a bank must pay close attention to those events.

ii. For personal clients, when reviewing personal credit businesses like housing mortgage, auto consumption and CD pledge, credit officers should firstly monitor the client to see whether his repayment is in time, proactive and sufficient. Then they should pay attention to the relationship between the borrower and the sales merchant.

B. *Credit risk review*

In the process of credit review, a bank should not only pay attention to a borrower's qualification and overall financial status of operation and management, but also notice particularities of different credit products. Strict supervision and monitoring must be in place to produce early warning for particular risks of different products.

- Credit risk review of fixed asset loans.
- Credit risk review of working capital loans.

- Credit risk review of foreign currency loans and RMB packing loans. Because foreign exchange rate risk may be involved in these loans, a bank must monitor the risks and take preemptive measures.
- Credit risk review of L/C business without 100% security.
- Credit risk review of guarantee products. The focus is to review whether under the guaranteeing conditions, the client can carry out the obligations (responsibilities) or not.
- Credit risk review of acceptance products. The focus is to review the truthfulness of a trade between a client and its counterpart and whether a client has sufficient funds for repayment on maturity.

C. Security review

Security is the credit support for a client and is the secondary source of repayment. Credit associates and officers should often review the status of guarantor and security and analyze the guarantor's repayment capabilities and the level of liquidity of security. A bank should review and forecast that once the primary source of repayment cannot serve its obligation, it can effectively exercise the right.

2. Early Warning Signals

Early warning system or procedure is designed to warn of a potential or an impending problem. Early warning signals are omens or symptoms that a client may not be able to repay the principal and interest in time or service the loan. When the early warning system sends out signals, situations may be that a client has an undue loan in interest and part of its principal, or that there are no arrears from a client yet, or that a bank has not issued advance to its client yet. But signals show that risks might exist or risks might be extended. Therefore, in the process of credit review, credit associates must identify those early warning signals showing that the asset quality of a client has already or is about to be influenced. Credit associates should report their findings to credit officers as early as possible, take relevant measures and try to eliminate the potential risks of credit loss.

A. Early Warning Signals (Financial)

- Increase in sales volume but decrease in profit.
- Rapid increase in debt, in particular, abnormally rapid increase of short-term bank credit.
- Unexplainable increase of receivables and inventory.
- Shift from profit to loss, loss volume increases gradually.
- Abnormal fund transfer in large amount between related enterprises.

- Increase of non-performing loan loss.
- Dramatic decrease of net cash flow volume or even negative net cash flow volume, which cannot support normal business operation.
- Payment crisis.

B. Early Warning Signals (Non-Financial)

i. Early warning signals of management (or external policy)

- Great fluctuations in its stock price.
- Security accidents or leakage of secrets that inflict heavy losses or great personnel changes.
- Merge unfamiliar business, new business or start business in unfamiliar regions.
- New laws or regulations promulgated by government, which are disadvantageous to a client.
- Be involved in significant lawsuits, arbitration, and economic disputes and normal operation and repayment are adversely influenced.
- Plan to undergo Merger & Acquisition, de-merger, shareholding restructuring and asset restructuring.
- Dispose of security without bank's permission.
- Do not submit financial statement in time and after many times of warning, the client still doesn't submit financial statement.
- Be penalized for violation of laws and regulations by the taxation, customs, industry and commerce administrations.
- Disclosed by news media because of misconducts.
- The loan certificate, legal person business license, production certificate have been revoked. The client is ordered to stop production and its asset has been frozen.
- On the "black list" of regulating authorities.
- Provide large amount guarantee for another party.

ii. Early warning signals of operation (project construction)

- Over-concentration of clients, suppliers and products.
- Overstock of products and production has been stopped for a long time.
- Plan to apply for bankruptcy or liquidation or is applying for bankruptcy and liquidation.
- The enterprise is selling or liquidating its major fixed assets for production and operation.
- Plan to implement significant operation strategy.
- The industry's or the related industry's operation strategy has been adjusted signifi-

cantly.

- Most of its asset has been mortgaged.
- Great changes in project's construction conditions, technical conditions and product market. The project in construction has been cancelled or postponed.
- The client's credit risk rating has been lowered.

iii. Early warning signals of the relationship between the enterprise and the bank

- The enterprise is in arrears with repayment of principal and interest to the bank.
- The enterprise refuses the bank to inspect and review and is indifferent to the problems found out in the reviews.
- Sudden withdrawal of other financial institutions, especially those banks that have had long-term relationship with it and provided large credit lines.
- The bank cannot have normal communication with borrowers.
- The enterprise continuously provides false financial statements, balance sheets and profit and loss statements.
- The borrower uses the loan not in accordance with the loan agreement, and shirks the bank's monitoring.
- The bank acceptance bills, L/Cs and letters of guarantee issued by the bank are without trade basis.
- The borrower continuously asks banks to issue large amount bank acceptance bills, L/Cs and letters of guarantee.
- When an L/C arrives, the borrower refuses acceptance responsibilities with various excuses.
- After a packing loan is granted and disbursed, the borrower delays goods delivery or intentionally refuses to deliver goods, which leads to the expiry of the L/C.

3. Loan classification by risk

There is still no uniform standard for loan classification throughout the world. For example, Germany adopts four-category loan classification, the U. S. five-category one, Spain six-category one, and Brazil nine-category one. Nowadays, the five-category loan classification is a popular way for banks to rank loans based on their internal risks. In the past, the "old" system loosely classified loans as overdue (loans overdue up to 3 months), doubtful (loans overdue for more than 3 months but less than 24 months) and bad (loans overdue for more than 24 months). Under the system, undue loans could still be classified as "performing" even when an enterprise ceased operation due to financial difficulties. No provisions were required to be made against the undue loans. This lack of provisioning leads to bulk of

NPLs of many banks. Implementing a risk-based loan classification system to replace the one based on the overdue period is an advance in capital risk management.

China's wholly state-owned commercial banks (SCB) and joint shareholding commercial banks (JSCB) adopted the international five-category loan classification system as of 2004. According to the CBRC, the then existing parallel four-category loan classification system phased out by that time. The four-category system categorized loans into pass, past-due, idle and loss.

The five-category system classifies bank loans according to their inherent risks as pass (normal), special-mention, substandard, doubtful and loss.

"**Pass (Normal)**" indicates that borrowers are able to honor the terms of the contracts and there is no reason to doubt their ability to repay the principal and interest of loans in full and in a timely manner.

"**Special-mention**" means that borrowers are able to serve their loans currently, although repayment may be adversely affected by specific factors.

"**Substandard**" means that borrowers' abilities to service their loans are in question. Borrowers cannot depend on their normal business revenues to pay back the principal and interest so that losses may ensue, even when guarantees are invoked.

"**Doubtful**" indicates that borrowers cannot pay back the principal and interest in full and significant losses will be incurred, even when guarantees are invoked.

"**Loss**" means that the principal and interest of loans cannot be recovered or only a small portion can be recovered after taking all possible measures and resorting to necessary legal procedures.

Loan Provisioning Policy

Banks will need to make provision against a loan according to the category it is in. A fair level of provisions on non-performing loans is an essential input in mark-to-market accounting, and in the calculation of bank capital and solvency. Fair provisioning on non-performing loans is of great importance for bank regulators. If there has been intense discussion on the merits of BASEL 2, the revised capital accord that would much better capture the actual risks taken by banks (Basel Committee, 2003), it is quite evident that this accord will not have much relevance if the measurement of bank capital is not satisfactory. A key input in the measurement of bank capital is the amount of loan-loss provisions on non-performing loans. We can see that the loan provisioning of a bank is really essential for regulators and outsiders to view its asset quality.

Currently, Chinese banks are subject to a general provisioning requirement of 1% of total loans calculated at the beginning of the year. According to the PBOC, China's central bank, provisioning ratios for the five categories of loans (pass, special mention, sub-stand-ard, doubtful and loss) are 0, 2%, 25%, 50% and 100% respectively. But loan provision requirement ratios vary among countries, either for general provisioning or loan loss provisio-ning against non-performing loans. You can see the difference in the following chart:

Summary of provisioning policy in Asia

Loan category	Singapore	Thailand	Korea	Indonesia	Philippines
General provision	Up to 3% of total gross loans and investment portfollo	0. 25% of total loans	0. 5% on normal loans	0. 5% on current loans	Up to 2% of total gross loans
Specil mention	–	–	1%	–	–
Special provisions					
Substandard loans	10% at MAS's special request	15%	20%	10%	25%
Doubtful loans	50%	100%	75%	50%	50%
Loss loans	100%	100%	100%	100%	100%

source: http://www.bis.org/publ/plcy07d.pdf, Page 4.

The following example is the loan classification and its provisioning rates of the second largest commercial bank and the leading retail bank in Estonia.

Category	Loan Category Description	Provisioning rate
Pass	All necessary repayments (both interest and principal) have been made as specified in agreement. Either there is no overdue interest or principal, or it is not significant (nothing more than five days and not more often than six times during the year). Furthermore, no capitalization or re-scheduling of interest or principal has occurred.	2%
Special Mention	There have been minor disturbances in repayments of interest or princi-pal, interest has been capitalized or rescheduling of interest and principal has taken place. Delays in repayments have been 5 – 30 days and have not occurred more than three times during a year.	5%
Sub-standard	There have been disturbances in repayments of interest or principal, inter-est has been capitalized or rescheduling of interest and principal has taken place as per the difficulties of the customer. Delays in repayments have been 30 – 60 days and have not occurred more than three times during a year.	20%
Doubtful	There have been disturbances in repayments of interest or principal, inter-est has been capitalized or rescheduling of interest and principal has taken place as per the difficulties of the customer. Delays in repayments have been 60 – 90 days and have not occurred more than once during a year.	50%
Loss	There have been major disturbances in repayments of interest or principal, interest has been capitalized or rescheduling of interest and principal has taken place. Delays in repayments are more than 90 days.	100%

（http：//files. ee. omxgroup. com/bors/prospekt/ehp/eng/lending. htm）

And we can also see the difference again in the following example：

QCB（Qatar Central Bank）'s policy on loan loss provisioning is based on building up provisions against non-performing loans, which include substandard, doubtful, and bad loans. The following table shows the level of provisions（as percentage of loans）that banks must build up after excluding suspended interests and blocked deposits against loans.

Nonperforming Loans Classification	Provision level
Substandard loans	5% ~25%
Doubtful loans	25% ~60%
Bad loans	60% ~100%

Moreover, QCB requires all banks to build up general loans provisions, with a minimum level of 0. 2% and a maximum level of 1. 0% of the total credits facilities granted to the private sector. Banks wishing to increase the level of general provision by more than 1. 0% must obtain a prior approval from QCB.

（http：//www. qcb. gov. qa/QCB's%20Role. asp）

4. Non-performing Loans Management and Recovery

Under the five-category loan classification, substandard, doubtful and loss loans are defined as non-performing loans. Because the reasons behind non-performing loans formation are different, credit associates must take effective measures to manage, recover and dispose of these parts of asset according to their different characteristics. The bank should first find out the responsibilities of the guarantor and dispose of the security in time. Only when they confirm that the guarantor has lost the guarantee abilities and the security is not sufficient to pay off the loan, can they begin to dispose of the non-performing loans.

There are many reasons why banks have poorly performing loan portfolios. Irrespective of these causes, banks have an obligation to shareholders, depositors and creditors to maximize cash flow from assets, the most troublesome aspect of which has been the poor record of banks in recovering loans. It is this factor that has contributed the most to bank insolvency, and liquidity constraints.

There are several complementary options available to banks to restructure problem loans and portfolios, including：

- Exercise of collateral（liens against property, inventories）through judicial or extra-judicial means.
- Out-of-court settlement that may focus exclusively on debt negotiation, restructuring

and repayment, or lead to the financial, physical and operational restructuring of the enterprise.

- Bankruptcy/liquidation procedures through formal court proceedings. This may involve liquidation, reorganization or privatization of an enterprise to enforce partial or total loan repayment.

(Besides the bank itself, sometimes government also leads a restructuring program to help the bank to solve the problem of NPL in order to stabilize the banking industry or the whole economy. For example, Asset Management Company (AMC), a special purpose company, buys or exchanges NPL from bank and disposes of them).

A. Work-Out Unit

With aggregate loan portfolios universally troubled by delinquencies and defaults, some banks have opted to develop work-out units to improve loan portfolio quality. When work-out units are established, they are usually set up to deal with most of a bank's problem loans, effectively sectioning off non-performing loans from the broader bank portfolio of performing loans. The benefits expected from work-out units include:

- Concentrated focus on the recovery of problem loans;
- More developed banking expertise and credit risk evaluation skills;
- Improved internal bank system (early warning systems, collateral requirements, credit information needs).

Work-out units can make a significant difference in restructuring loan portfolios, particularly when supported by effective technical assistance.

B. Loan Restructuring and Loan "Rollover"

Case-by-case loan restructuring is common in market-oriented economies, particularly when borrowers are unable to meet the original terms of the loan agreement due to external factors. These restructuring invariably changes in the amount, terms and/or schedule of interest rates, principal repayment, and collateral values. Loan covenants (ratios, report requirements) often change to facilitate compliance. In some cases, radical measures such as replacing management are involved.

This approach is similar to what work-out units attempt to do: recover portions of loan portfolios which have deteriorated and are non-performing. However, work-out units are often organized on the basis of sector, location or bank exposure. Case-by-case loan restructuring is conducted on an individualized basis. The benefits of individual case-by-case loan restructurings include:

- Reinforcement of the bank-client relationship.
- Retention of the loan by the bank on its balance sheet, even if provisions are made

for possible losses.

- Preservation of the firm's relations with other parties (trade creditors, other banks, buyers, employees), thereby maintaining its reputation without embarrassing and costly bankruptcy/liquidation procedures.

As with debt-equity swaps, the risk to the bank is that it is overly optimistic about prospects, and that additional resources are committed to the borrower adding to bank losses and reduced loanable funds at a future date. This has occurred frequently in transition economies (such as China, East European countries, former Soviet Union).

In transition economy banks, the closest approximation to the Western loan restructuring has been the loan "rollover" which has been a common practice. Rollovers generally involve the following two techniques:

- Simple rollover of principal on/before the due date, with the enterprise meeting interest obligations.
- Rollover of principal on/before due date, with interest added back to the principal amount ("interest capitalization").

The first technique is legitimate and rational unless the enterprise is unable to repay principal, and likely to remain impaired in the future. The second technique often reflects a troubled loan and enterprise, and has been typically practiced in transition economy banking systems. Further more, the latter technique has been accompanied by accounting treatment which mistakenly recognizes these assets as performing loans, artificially inflating income statements and balance sheet book values.

C. *Debt-equity Swaps and Loan Sales/Asset Swap*

Debt-equity swap results in bank ownership of enterprises occur with differing frequencies in different countries. In some countries, bank ownership of enterprises is common (German interlocking directorates), while in other countries it is strictly regulated (USA) or strictly prohibited (In China, debt-equity swap is done through asset management company). By swapping NPL for equity, banks can exercise more direct control/supervision over enterprise management while the enterprise benefits from increased debt capacity. The risk to bank is excess exposure to a risky investment which may jeopardize deposit safety and bank capital, and demand scarce management time and resources.

Debt-equity swap represents nascent venture capital operation. Perhaps only one in 10 of these investments may succeed, but this should be sufficient to cover the risk of the other nine losing investment. Given existing low book values and the currently thin market that is likely to improve in the coming years, banks are prudent to allocate a small percentage of assets to enterprises they believe will generate significant profit at a later date. At that point, banks can sell their shares, and reap significant profit to bolster capital. All of this makes more sense given the current downside risk, which is limited, as most of these transactions are paper transactions that do not further impair bank liquidity.

But bank equity swap may be indicative of the failure of banks in some countries to properly define bank's roles as financial intermediaries, streamline their operations, special-ize in a few key areas within the limit of their current managerial and staffing capabilities, write down their assets to more accurate values, and progress toward a more stable and pru-dently-managed system devoid of excess risk. Investment in losing enterprises raises the risk of future liquidity being drained to prop up these enterprises in the hope of eventual profit-ability, which puts depositors and shareholders at risk.

In addition to debt-equity swaps, loan sales swaps are an option that could be used to restructure bank balance sheets. However, this option has not been commonly found in tran-sition economy due to absence of secondary market development.

D. *Securitization of Non-performing Loan*

Non-performing loan securitization is a pooling of non-performing loans packaged and issued as securities to investors through arrangements of legal structure, cash flow, and credit rating mechanisms. Non-performing Loans are also known as bad loans, overdue loans, receivables under collection, and loans still under normal payment statuses, but with circulating bonds rated lower than CCC level. During the securitization period, the originator (seller) will select the most ideal portfolio based on a set of eligibility criteria, such as debtors' locations, credit period, currency, and overdue ratings from all available non-per-forming loans.

After the screening process, bank will proceed with the risk assessment, cash flow sim-ulation and credit tranche. The securities are then offered to investors after confirmation from credit rating agencies and regulatory approval obtained. The asset management agency is particularly important to a non-performing loan securitization since the asset management agency's expertise is instrumental to increasing collection rates of these non-performing loans. Investors' risks are minimized through credit enhancement techniques; default risks, prepayment risks, etc. are also emphasized to evaluate the risk profile of non-performing loans.

E. *In-court Bankruptcy/Liquidation Proceedings*

Resorting to legal procedures to collect the repayment of non-performing loans is the last defense line. In practice, banks should grasp the timing of litigation. Because blind lawsuits will involve banks' time, energy, money and people. In addition, they could have negative impact on the relationship between banks and their clients.

Firstly, before litigation, banks should investigate the borrowers' income resources and asset categories and prevent them from hiding or transferring asset in this period of time. Banks can apply to the court for asset preservation. Secondly, banks should try their best to correct the deficiencies of credit documents and win themselves advantageous conditions in litigation. Thirdly, banks should also prepare themselves for the results of reconciliation or failure.

Bankruptcy/liquidation is an effective complement to out-of-court approaches, and serves as a last stage of debt collection, providing creditors with control over debtors in financial distress and prompting their restructuring. For this reason, many countries (transition economies) have developed and are seeking to expand the use of formal bankruptcy to broaden the array of dispute resolution mechanisms, provide banks with long needed recourse, and instill greater financial discipline on enterprises.

F. Exercise of Collateral

When a debt matures or is going to mature and the debtor has encountered serious operation difficulties, the debtor cannot repay the loan in cash and the guarantor cannot repay the loan in cash either. Maybe after negotiation, the two parties (the bank and the borrower) or three parties (the bank, the borrower and the guarantor) can reach a consensus. In line with the consensus or the ruling by the court, the debtor or the guarantor can make in-kind repayment of debts, which is one of the important means to dispose of non-performing loans.

G. Writing-off Bad Loans

In accordance with relevant state rules and regulation, if the principal of a loan is identified as unrecoverable, the bad loan can be written off. Writing-off of bad loans is the internal activity of a bank. So the bank still enjoys the recourse right and should continue to demand the repayment of the fund.

Notes

1. **Past due**: later than or after
2. **Portfolio** [ˌpɔːtˈfəuliəu] *n.* a group of investments
3. **Collateral** [kɔˈlætərəl] *n.* property acceptable as security for a loan or other obligation
4. **Maturity** [məˈtjuəriti] *n.* ①the time at which a note or bond is due②the state of a note or bond being due

Questions for discussion

1. How many kinds of loans could be offer to the company if all the requirements were

satisfied?

2. How many parties in BOT, and what are the responsibilities of the parties?

3. How could the lender find the problems of the loan before the due date?

4. Which items are necessary at the contract of home mortgage loan? And why?

5. What are the basic requirements of oversea funding in China?

6. What is the five-category system in China, do you think it is helpful?

Part Seven

International Settlement

I. Instruments

1. Bill of Exchange

A. *Definition*

A bill of exchange (draft) is an unconditional order in writing, addressed by one person to another, signed by the person giving it, requiring the person to whom it is addressed to pay on demand, or at a fixed or determinable future time, a sum certain in money, to or to the order of a specified person, or to the bearer.

A typical bill of exchange is drawn in this manner:

Bill of Exchange

(h)
Amount   USD100,000.00   (j)
                                   London,1st August 2005

(g) (a)(f)   (i)
At 30 days sight pay Bank of CCC,Hangzhou or order
                          (h)
The sum of Say United States Dollars One Hundred thousand only

For value received

(c, e)   (b, d)
To Vivian Wu   Clarence David
18 Tamper Road,
New York   TTT Co. Ltd.,London

(a) An unconditional order in writing.

(b) Addressed by one person (the drawer).

(c) To another (the drawee).

(d) Signed by the person giving it.

(e) Requiring the person to whom it is addressed.

(f) To pay.

(g) On demand or at a fixed or determinable future time.

(h) A sum certain in money.

(i) To or to the order of a specified person or to the bearer.

(j) Issue date and place.

B. Demand and Usance Bills

When a bill is payable on demand or at sight, the drawee is required to pay immediately when the bill is presented to him. A bill is payable on demand if it is so specified or if time for payment is not expressed.

A bill may be payable within a fixed period after the date of the bill. For example, "pay three months after date…"

A bill may be payable within a fixed period after an event which is certain to happen, e. g. , "one month after shipment" .

A bill may be expressed as being payable within a fixed period after sight; sight means the presentation of the bill to the drawee for acceptance.

2. Cheques

A. Definition

A cheque is an unconditional order in writing, addressed by a person to a bank, signed by the person making it, requiring the bank to pay on demand a sum certain in money to or to the order of a specified person or to the bearer.

B. Parties to a Cheque

Three parties are essentially involved:

(a) The Payee. A person to whom a cheque is expressed to be payable.

(b) The Drawer. The person who writes the cheque.

(c) The Drawee. The bank on whom the cheque is drawn and to whom the order to pay is given.

(c)
AABBCC BANK LIMITED
CH. NO. 12345   18 June 2005
(a)
Pay Clarence David ********** or bearer   USD1,000.00
The sum of Say United States Dollars one thousand only
(b)
Helen Cheng
A/C No. 000–54321–888

C. Traveller's Cheque

A traveller's cheque is a draft of a bank or travel agency which is self-identifying and may be cashed at banks, hotels and etc. , either throughout the world or in particular areas only. The self-identification is provided by obtaining the signature of the customer on the instrument at the time of issuance, with a second space for his signature being left blank until presentation for cashing, when the encashing agent will require signature in his presence. This gives reasonable safety, both for the traveller and for the party cashing the item. It is, naturally, of prime importance that the cheque not be signed in the second space until it is to be cashed, and then actually before the person cashing it.

Traveller's cheques are in fixed, round, convenient amounts. Their wider range of acceptability makes them suitable for persons taking comparatively smaller amounts or travelling from place to place and likely to require cash over weekends or holidays when banks are not open to negotiate drawings under Traveller's Letter of Credit.

3. Promissory Notes

A promissory note is an unconditional promise in writing made by one person (the maker) to another (the payee or the holder) signed by the maker engaging to pay on demand or at a fixed or determinable future time a sum certain in money to or to the order of a specified person or to the bearer.

A promissory note is a promise, and a bill is an order. There is no need to protest a dishonoured note. As the maker of a promissory note is the person primarily liable on it, there can be no acceptance.

A typical promissory note is made in this manner:

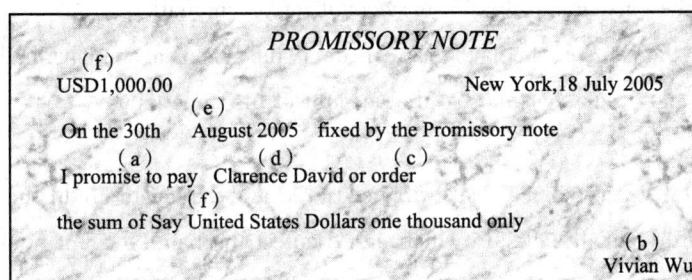

```
                    PROMISSORY NOTE
    (f)
USD1,000.00                           New York,18 July 2005
                    (e)
On the 30th    August 2005   fixed by the Promissory note
       (a)            (d)              (c)
I promise to pay   Clarence David or order
                    (f)
the sum of Say United States Dollars one thousand only
                                           (b)
                                        Vivian Wu
```

(a) An unconditional promise in writing.

(b) The maker.

(c) The payee or the holder.

(d) Engaging to pay.

(e) On demand or at a fixed or determinable future time.

(f) A sum certain in money.

II. Means of International Settlement

1. Remittance

A. *M/T and T/T*

i. Nostro and Vostro Accounts

From the point of view of a Chinese bank, a nostro account is our bank's account in the book of an overseas bank. A vostro account is an overseas bank's account with our bank.

ii. Bookkeeping for Transfers of Funds

When a customer wishes to transfer funds to the bank account of a beneficiary abroad, the bookkeeping is as follows, assuming that an account relationship exists between the respective banks:

- Debit the customer's account with the amount to transfer, plus banking charges, and credit the account of the overseas bank under advice to it. This is a vostro account from the customer's bank's point of view.

- On receipt of the advice, the overseas bank will withdraw the amount from the vostro account, and credit the beneficiary's account, less its charges.

Or,

- Debit the customer's account with the amount to transfer, plus banking charges, and credit the currency to the nostro account for reconciliation.

- Advise the overseas bank that it can debit the nostro account with the requisite amount and credit the funds to the account of the beneficiary.

iii. Procedures of M/T and T/T

First of all, the customer's bank will need to know whether to credit the account of the beneficiary with a named bank (in which case request the bank account number).

On receipt of the customer's instructions, the book keeping will be applied. The customer's bank will advise the overseas bank of the transaction by airmail, and the payment instruction must be signed by authorised signatories. This is so-called M/T, mail transfer.

If T/T, a telegraphic transfer, is used, the same procedure as for mail is adopted. However, the instructions to the overseas bank are sent by telex or SWIFT, and in case of telex, the overseas bank will require a special authenticating code word, which is called "test key", before it will act.

B. *D/D*

D/D, a demand draft, is in effect a bill of exchange drawn by one bank on another payable on demand. Like T/T and M/T, the draft will be drawn on either the vostro account or the nostro account.

The customer will forward the draft to the beneficiary who will pay it into his bank for credit to his account. Ultimately, the draft will be debited to either the appropriate nostro or vostro account. Sometimes, the bank will collect the draft to the issuing bank. The bank will not credit the customer's account until it is paid.

There are major disadvantages to the use of drafts for large transfers:

- The remitter is debited at the time the draft is issued, but there is a delay before the beneficiary can pay the draft into his bank account and obtain cleared funds.
- If the beneficiary does not bank at the bank on whom the draft is drawn, the funds will be treated as uncleared.
- The draft could be lost or stolen, and banks are reluctant to "stop" a bank draft because it amounts to dishonour of the bank's own paper.

C. Open Account and Cash in Advance

i. Open Account

Open account is an arrangement between the buyer and seller whereby the goods are manufactured and delivered before payment is required.

Open account provides for payment at some stated specific future date and without the buyer's issuing any negotiable instrument evidencing his legal commitment. The seller must have absolute trust that he will be paid at the agreed date.

Advantages to the buyer are as follows:

- He pays for the goods or services only when they are received and /or inspected; and
- Payment is conditioned on such issues as political, legal and economic issues.

Disadvantages to the seller are as follows:

- It releases the title to the goods without having assurance of payment;
- There is a possibility that political events will impose regulations which defer or block the movement of funds to it; and
- Its own capital is tied up until the goods are received and /or inspected by the buyer or until the services are found to be acceptable and payment is made.

ii. Cash in Advance

Cash in advance means that the buyer places the funds at the disposal of the seller prior to shipment of the goods or provision of services.

While this method of payment is expensive and involves risks, it is not uncommon when the manufacturing process or services delivered are specialized and capital intensive. In such circumstances the parties may agree to fund the operation by partial payments in advance or by progress payments.

This method of payment is used:

- when the buyer's credit is doubtful;
- when there is an unstable political or economic environment in the buyer's country; and /or,
- if there is a potential delay in the receipt of funds from the buyer, perhaps due to events beyond his control.

Advantage to the seller is its immediate use of funds.

Disadvantages to the buyer are as follows:

- It pays in advance, tying up its capital prior to receipt of the goods or services;
- It has no assurance that what he contracted for will be supplied; received in a timely fashion; and/or, received in the quality or quantity ordered.

2. Collection

A. *Outward Collection*

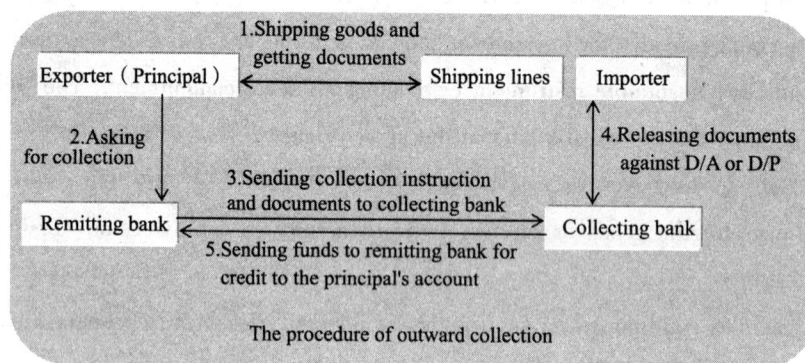

The procedure of outward collection

i. *Operation of a Collection*

Let us assume that an exporter and an importer agree on the transaction on the basis of collection.

- The exporter ships goods and obtains documents of title from the shipping line.
- The exporter , who is known as the principal, hands in the following documents to his bank (the remitting bank) :

—bill of exchange drawn on the importer;

—documents of title (i. e. a complete set of clean, shipped on board bills of lading, made out to order and blank endorsed) , and other relevant documents (commercial invoice, insurance policy or certificate of origin, etc.) ; and

—a collection order which contains the exporter's instructions to the remitting bank.

- The remitting bank completes its own collection order addressed to the importer's bank (the collecting bank).

- This collection order, which contains the same instructions as the exporter's original collection order, is then sent to the importer's bank, along with the other documents.

- If the instructions are D/P (documents against payment) , the importer's bank will release the documents to the importer only against payment.

- If the instructions are D/A (documents against acceptance) , the importer's bank will release the documents only against acceptance of the bill of exchange by the importer.

- If and when the bill of exchange is paid, the importer's bank will send the funds to the remitting bank for credit to the principal's account.

The importer will require a full set of bills of lading in order to obtain the goods from the overseas port. The bills of lading can only be obtained by payment of the bill of exchange (D/P) , or by acceptance (D/A). Therefore, the importer cannot obtain the goods without paying or accepting the bill of exchange, and conversely an exporter retains control of the goods until payment or acceptance of the bill of exchange. When goods are sent by air, the airway bill could show the importer's bank as consignee. Once again the importer must pay or accept a bill of exchange to be able to obtain the goods. Once the importer has paid or accepted the bill of exchange, the importer's bank will issue a delivery order. The delivery order is an authority, signed on behalf of the bank, authorizing the airport to release the goods to the named importer. An exporter should obtain the prior agreement of the importer and the importer's bank before he consigns goods to that bank. In practice, the importer's bank will not agree to be named as consignee, unless its own customer is of major importance.

When D/P terms are used, it is unnecessary to include a bill of exchange, since the overseas bank can release documents on payment of the invoice amount. However, sight drafts are usually included.

ii. *The Collection Instruction*

The specimen collection instruction is a standard form of authority, which enables the exporter/remitting bank to include specific instructions to his bank/collecting bank regarding the documentary collection.

You will see that specific instructions are required on the following points:

- Release documents to the importer against payment (D/P) or against acceptance (D/A). Normally D/P will apply with sight drafts and D/A with term drafts. It is, however, possible to arrange for D/P instructions to be given with term drafts and this can often arise in trade with the Far East.

X   X   X   **Bank**

Collection Instruction

ORIGINAL

Date _____

Our Ref No._____

Dear Sirs:

We send you herewith the under-mentioned item(s)/documents for collection.

Drawer:							Draft: No. : Date:		Due Date/Tenor
Drawee(s) :							Amount:		
Goods:				From				To	
By Par				On					
Documents	Draft	Invoice	B/L	Ins. Policy/Cert.		W/M	C/O		
1st									
2nd									

Please follow instructions marked "×":

☐ Deliver documents against payment/acceptance.

☐ Remit the proceeds by airmail/cable.

☐ Airmail/cable advice of payment/acceptance.

☐ Collect charges outside _____ from drawer/drawee.

☐ Collect interest for delay in payment _____ days after sight at_____ %P. A.

☐ Airmail/cable advice of non-payment/non-acceptance with reasons.

☐ Protest for non-payment/non-acceptance.

☐ Protest waived.

☐ When accepted, please advise us giving due date.

☐ When collected, please credit our account with _____.

☐ Please collect and remit proceeds to _____ Bank for credit of our account with them under their advice to us.

☐ Please collect proceeds and anthorize us by airmail/cable to debit your account with us.

Special Instructions

This collection is subject to

Uniform Rules for Collection

(1995 Revision) ICC Publication No.522

For X X X Bank

Authorized Signature(s)

- The collection order will state whether bank and other charges have to be collected in addition to the face value of the bill of exchange. The exporter should complete the clause in accordance with the details agreed in the sales contract.
- Specific instructions are required on whether or not to protest in the event of dishonour by either non payment or non acceptance.
- Advice of dishonour, with reasons, should be given by airmail or cable. Cable is most desirable, but again the cost will ultimately be borne by the exporter.
- Instructions as to the method of settlement are required. Obviously urgent SWIFT would be best from the exporter's point of view, but this is a more costly method than mail transfer.
- In the case of D/A, maturity date should be indicated if it is available.
- Drawer——exporter. Drawee——importer. Collecting bank.
- Documents enclosed.
- Finally, this collection is subject to URC (ICC Publication No. 522).

B. *Inward Collection*

i. *General Rules for the Handling of Inward Collections*

The handling of inward collections received by banks from their correspondents (banks) is considered to be a very important service which, if not taken seriously, can result in monetary loss and also damage a banking relationship.

A collection can be:

Clean—a bill of exchange or cheque unsupported by documents, or

Documentary—documents with (or without) a bill of exchange.

All documents sent for collection must be accompanied by a collection order giving complete and precise instructions. Banks are only permitted to act upon the instructions given in such collection orders and in accordance with these rules.

Any deviation from these instructions at the request of the drawee will be at the responsibility of the collecting bank.

The instructions of the remitting bank override the banking relationship, if any, between drawee and collecting bank.

Banks will act in good faith and exercise reasonable care and must verify that the documents received appear to be as listed in the collection order. Banks have no further obligation to examine the documents.

In the case of documents payable at sight, the collecting bank acting as presenting bank must make presentation for payment without delay. And in the case of documents payable at a tenor other than sight, the presenting bank must, where acceptance is called for, make presentation for acceptance without delay.

In respect of a documentary collection including a bill of exchange payable at a future date, the collection order should state whether the commercial documents are to be released to the drawee against acceptance (D/A) or against payment (D/P). In the absence of such statement, the commercial documents will be released only against payment.

ii. Procedures for Obtaining Acceptance of a Bill of Exchange

Acceptance of a bill of exchange is an unconditional undertaking to pay the bill on maturity. The drawee should not, therefore, when accepting the bill, impose any conditions on payment.

Acceptances citing for instance: (a) lesser amount, (b) payable at a different date are referred to as "unqualified acceptances" and would not be acceptable to the remitting bank.

. The presenting bank is responsible for seeing that the form of the acceptance of a bill of exchange appears to be complete and correct, but is not responsible for the genuineness of any signature nor for the authority of any signatory to sign the acceptance.

However, when the drawee is a customer, good banking practice dictates that the signature must be checked against the mandate.

iii. Actions to be Taken in the Event of Dishonour

A bill of exchange is dishonoured when a sight draft is unpaid on presentation or when a tenor draft is unaccepted on presentation or unpaid at maturity.

When an inward collection is dishonoured, the presenting bank must examine the collection order to see whether the bill is to be protested. Protesting a bill provides legal evidence of dishonour acceptable to a court of law.

If protest is to be carried out, a Notary Public will personally call upon the drawee/acceptor and demand payment or acceptance. If the payment/acceptance is not forthcoming, the Notary Public will draw up a deed of protest which will state the reasons for dishonour.

3. Documentary Credit

A. Definition

A documentary credit is any arrangement, however named or described, whereby a bank (the "Issuing Bank") acting at the request and on the instructions of a customer (the "Applicant") or on its own behalf

- is to make a payment to or to the order of a third party (the "Beneficiary"), or is to accept and pay bills of exchange (Draft (s)) drawn by the Beneficiary, or
- authorizes another bank to effect such payment, or to accept and pay such bills of

exchange (Draft (s)) , or

- authorizes another bank to negotiate, against stipulated document (s) , provided that the terms and conditions of the credit are complied with.

ISSUE OF A DOCUMENTARY CREDIT (BY SWIFT)

APPLICATION HEADER	700 × × × × × × × × × ×
USER HEADER	× × × × × × × × × × × × ×
SEQUENCE OF TOTAL	*27: 1/1
FORM OF DOC. CREDIT	*40A: IRREVOCABLE
DOC. CREDIT NUMBER	*20: LCM100XXX
DATE OF ISSUE	31 C: 080707
EXPIRY	*31 D: DATE 081215 PLACE GERMANY
APPLICANT	*50: AAA (ADDRESS SEE FIELD 47A ITEM 4)
BENEFICIARY	*59: BBB (ADDRESS AND TEL NO.)
AMOUNT	*32 B: CURRENCY EUR AMOUNT
AVAILABLE WITH/BY	*41 D: ANY BANK IN GERMANY
	BY NEGOTIATION
DRAFTS AT⋯	42 C: AT SIGHT
	FOR 100 PCT OF INVOICE VALUE
DRAWEE	42 A: BKCHCNBJXXX
	BANK OF CHINA BEIJING (HEAD OFFICE)
PARTIAL SHIPMENTS	43 P: NOT ALLOWED
TRANSSHIPMENT	43 T: PROHIBITED
LOADING IN CHARGE	44 A:
	ANY EUROPEAN PORT
FOR TRANSPORT TO⋯	44 B:
	MUSCAT PORT, OMAN
LATEST DATE OF SHIP	44 C: 081125
DESCRIPT. OF GOODS	45 A:
	DESCRIPTION QUANTITY TOTAL AMOUNTC
	CC1 SETEUR600,000.00
	CONTRACT NO. : DDD
	TOTAL CONTRACT VALUE: EUR600,000.00
	PRICE TERMS: CIF MUSCAT PORT, OMAN
	MANUFACTURER AND COUNTRY OF ORIGIN:
	EEE, GERMANY
	SHIPPING MARKS: FFF/FFF
DOCUMENTS REQUIRED	46 A:
	A: 90 PERCENT OF THE TOTAL CONTRACT VALUE, I.E. EUR540,000.00 SHALL BE PAID AGAINST THE PRESENTATION OF THE FOLLOWING DOCUMENTS:
	1. SIGNED COMMERCIAL INVOICE IN 5 ORIGINALS AND 1 COPY, SHOWING 100 PERCENT OF THE TOTAL CONTRACT VALUE AND CLAIMING FOR 90 PERCENT OF SUCH VALUE I.E. EUR540,000.00, INDICATING CONTRACT NO. , SHIPPING MARKS, L/C NO. AND TOTAL GOODS AMOUNT.
	2. FULL SET (INCLUDING 3 ORIGINALS AND 3 NON-NEGOTIABLE COPIES) OF "CLEAN ON BOARD" OCEAN BILLS OF LADING MARKED "FREIGHT PREPAID", MADE OUT TO ORDER, BLANK ENDORSED, INDICATING L/C NO. , CONTRACT NO. , SHIPPING MARKS AND SHOWING NOTIFY PARTY AS FOLLOWING MENTIONED IN FIELD 47A ITEM 3.

Continue

3. PACKING LIST/WEIGHT MEMO IN 3 ORIGINALS AND 1 COPY ISSUED BY THE BENEFICIARY INDICATING L/C NO. , CONTRACT NO. , SHIPPING MARKS, GROSS AND NET WEIGHT.

4. CERTIFICATE OF INSPECTION FOR QUANTITY/QUALITY IN 2 ORIGINALS AND 1 COPY ISSUED BY THE MANUFACTURER CERTIFYING THAT THE GOODS ARE BRAND NEW AND IN CONFORMITY WITH SPECIFICATION AND PERFORMANCE IN ALL RESPECTS.

5. FULL SET (INCLUDING 1 ORIGINAL AND 1 COPY) OF INSURANCE POLICY FOR 110 PERCENT OF SHIPPED GOODS VALUE, MARKED WITH "PREMIUM PAID", IN FAVOR OF APPLICANT, COVERING OCEAN MARINE TRANSPORTATION ALL RISKS AND WAR RISKS.

6. CERTIFICATE OF ORIGIN IN 2 ORIGINAL AND 1 COPY ISSUED BY THE MANUFACTURER.

7. PERFORMANCE GUARANTEE IN 1 COPY IN FAVOR OF THE APPLICANT ISSUED BY THE BENEFICIARY'S BANK WITH RECEIPT SIGNATURE AND SEAL BY AAA OMAN BRANCH, FOR 5 PERCENT OF THE TOTAL CONTRACT VALUE WHICH REMAINS VALID TILL NO LATER THAN 12 MONTHS FROM THE DATE OF COMMISSION.

B: 10 PERCENT OF THE TOTAL CONTRACT VALUE, I. E. EUR60, 000. 00 SHALL BE PAID AGAINST THE PRESENTATION OF THE FOLLOWING DOCUMENTS:

1. SIGNED COMMERCIAL INVOICE IN 3 ORIGINALS AND 3 COPIES, SHOWING 100 PERCENT OF THE TOTAL CONTRACT VALUE AND CLAIMING FOR 10 PERCENT OF SUCH VALUE I. E. EUR60, 000. 00, INDICATING CONTRACT NO. , SHIPPING MARKS, L/C NO. AND TOTAL GOODS AMOUNT.

2. CERTIFICATE IN 1 ORIGINAL ISSUED BY THE BENEFICIARY CERTIFYING THAT THE GOODS HAVE BEEN SUPPLIED AS PER THE CONTRACT.

ADDITIONAL COND

47 A:

1. A FEE OF USD56. 00 OR ITS EQUIVALENT IN THE L/C CURRENCY SHALL BE DEDUCTED FROM THE PROCEEDS FOR EACH PRESENTATION OF DISCREPANT DOCUMENTS UNDER THIS CREDIT.

2. IN CASE THE BENEFICIARY FAILS TO EFFECT SHIPMENT IN TIME, THE LATE DELIVERY PENALTIES SHALL BE DEDUCTED FROM PAYMENT AGAINST THE APPLICANT'S STATEMENT, SHOWING THE RATE AND CALCULATION OF PENALTIES AS FOLLOWS:

THE LATE DELIVERY PENALTY SHALL BE CALCULATED AFTER THE LATEST SHIPMENT DATE SHOWN IN THE L/C UNTIL THE ACTUAL SHIPMENT DATE AT THE RATE OF 0. 7 PERCENT OF THE LATE DELIVERY GOODS VALUE FOR EVERY ONE WEEK. LESS THAN ONE WEEK SHALL BE COUNTED AS ONE WEEK. THE TOTAL LATE DELIVERY PENALTY SHALL NOT EXCEED 5 PERCENT OF THE LATE DELIVERY GOODS VALUE.

3. THE DETAILS OF THE NOTIFY PARTY ARE AS FOLLOWS:
NOTIFY PARTY: SINOHYDRO CORPORATION OMAN BRANCH
ADDRESS: × × × × × ×
TEL: × × ×
FAX: × × ×

Continue

	4. APPLICANT'S ADDRESS: ROOM NO. 202, × × × BUILD-ING, XUANWU DISTRICT, BEIJING, 100761 P. R. CHINA.
	5. BENEFICIARY'S FAX: × × × × × ×
	6. ALL DOCUMENTS TO BE FORWARDED IN ONE COVER, ADDRESS: BANK OF CHINA, HEAD OFFICE, NO. 1, FUXINGMEN NEI DAJIE, BEIJING, 100818, CHINA.
DETAILS OF CHARGES	71 B: ALL BANKING CHARGES OUTSIDE THE OPENING BANK ARE FOR BENEFICIARY'S ACCOUNT.
PRESENTATION PERIOD	48: DOCUMENTS MUST BE PRESENTED WITHIN 21 DAYS AFTER THE DATE OF ISSUANCE OF THE TRANSPORT DOCUMENTS BUT WITHIN THE VALIDITY OF THE CREDIT.
CONFIRMATION	*49: WITHOUT
INSTRUCTIONS	78:
	UPON OUR RECEIPT OF DRAFT (S) AND DOCUMENTS IN ORDER, WE SHALL REIMBURSE THE PROCEEDS OF DRAFTS TO THE NEGOTIATING BANK AS INSTRUCTED. WE HEREBY ISSUE THE DOCUMENTARY CREDIT IN YOUR FAVOUR, IT IS SUBJECT TO ICC UCP 600 AND ENGAGES US IN ACCORDANCE WITH THE TERMS THEREOF. THE NUMBER AND THE DATE OF THE CREDIT AND THE NAME OF OUR BANK MUST BE QUOTED ON ALL DRAFTS REQUIRED. IF THE CREDIT IS AVAILABLE BY NEGOTIATION, EACH PRESENTATION MUST BE NOTED ON THE REVERSE OF THIS L/C BY THE BANK WHERE THE CREDIT IS AVAILABLE.
"ADVISE THROUGH"	57 A: × × × × × ×

Application for L/C Amendment

To: Bank of China, Head Office
   Banking Department, Beijing.   Date: 20080814
                               Our Ref. No. _____
This is our amendment No. _____ Contract No. _____

Re: L/C No. × × × × ×
  For amount of EUR600,000.00
  Beneficiary: × × × × × ×

We hereby request to amend the above-mentioned L/C as follows:
Clause 46A: A
6. Amend to "Certificate of origin in 1 original and 2 copies issued by the Chamber of Commerce of Germany."
7. Amend to "···which remains valid till May 31, 2010."
              All other terms and conditions remain unchanged

---

Applicant: × × ×
Name of businessman: × × ×   Telephone No. : × × ×
Any charges and commissions under this amendment should be borne by (A/C No.)
This amendment should be issued by SWIFT.

                    Applicant: × × ×
                    Signature and authorized stamp

B. *Parties to a Documentary Credit*

i. *Applicant*

This is the party on whose request the credit is issued.

ii. *Beneficiary*

This is the party who under the terms of a letter of credit is entitled to have its complying presentation honoured.

iii. *Issuing Bank*

This is the bank that issues a letter of credit in favour of beneficiary.

iv. *Advising Bank*

This is the bank who, at the request of an issuing bank, a confirming bank, or another advising bank, notifies or requests another advising bank to notify the beneficiary that a letter of credit has been issued, confirmed, or amended.

v. *Confirming Bank*

This is a nominated bank who undertakes, at the request or with the consent of the issuing bank, to honor a presentation directly under a letter of credit issued by another, or to honour a presentation to the issuing bank when the bank fails to pay.

vi. *Nominated Bank*

This is the bank whom the issuing bank designates or authorizes to pay, accept, negotiate, or otherwise give value under a letter of credit or undertakes by agreement or custom and practices to reimburse.

C. *How a Documentary Credit Operates*

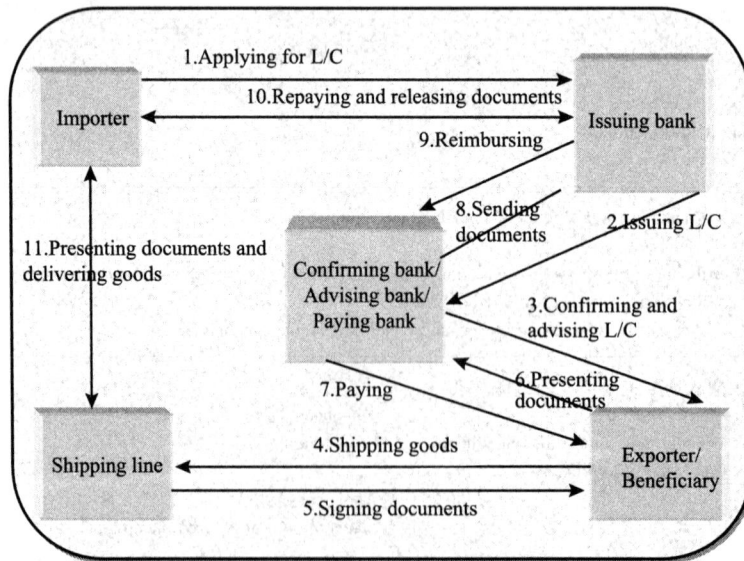

Let us assume that an importer and an exporter have agreed that payment terms will be by way of an irrevocable, confirmed documentary credit.

The procedures are as follows (chart attached):

(a) The importer asks their banker (issuing bank) to issue an irrevocable credit (1) and to request confirmation by another bank (confirming bank). And their banker agrees (2).

(b) The issuing bank requests a bank (advising bank) to advise the beneficiary (2), the exporter, of the details. Meanwhile the advising bank is asked to confirm the credit. The advising bank agrees to this (3).

(c) The advising bank, now writes to or notifies by other means the beneficiary the details of the credit (3).

(d) After consignment, the beneficiary obtains the shipping documents (4 \ 5) and presents the documents to confirming bank (6) through their banker (presenting bank). Confirming bank pays the beneficiary provided that the documents are in full compliance with the terms and conditions of the credit (7).

(e) The confirming bank sends the documents to the issuing bank (8) and gets reimbursement from the bank (9).

(f) The issuing bank settles the payment with the importer, and then the importer is given the documents (10) for taken delivery of the goods (11).

D. Some Important Notes on the Operation of a Documentary Credit

i. Review of the Documentary Credit Application and Security Agreement by the Issuing Bank

The issuing bank should:

- review the terms and conditions of the proposed documentary credit to ensure that they are in compliance with the policies of the bank and in accordance with the legal requirements or regulations of the issuing bank's country, and

- review whether the applicant's instructions, as to the method of notifying the beneficiary, are acceptable or whether the bank is authorized to choose its own correspondent for advising the documentary credit.

Applicants, at times, request the issuance of documentary credits containing excessive details for the beneficiary to comply with under the documentary credit. Unfortunately, banks may not encourage this practice as they are concerned that certain applicants may include excessive details for fear that the beneficiary may overlook certain conditions or present documents with discrepancies which would cause the documents to be refused if the applicant so desired.

Moreover, the issuing bank should carefully review the documentary credit application to determine if the documentary credit would require the beneficiary to submit a document, the performance or production of which is totally dependent on the performance by a third party not controlled by the beneficiary (other than a transport document, an insurance document or an inspection certificate etc.). In addition, the issuing bank should also carefully review the documentary credit application to determine that there are no "non-documentary conditions" stated in the application. If such conditions are required, it is the responsibility of the issuing bank to inform the applicant that these conditions must be transformed into a distinct documentary requirement.

ii. Utilization of the Documentary Credit

Upon receipt of the documentary credit, the beneficiary should review it to see that:

- the documentary credit is a valid,

- the type of documentary credit and its terms and conditions are in accordance with the sales contract,

- the documentary credit does not contain any conditions which are unacceptable or impossible to comply with,

- the documents required by the documentary credit are obtainable and presentable under the documentary credit,

- the goods description or unit prices, if any, are as stated in the sales contract,

- there are no conditions indicated in the documentary credit requiring payment of interest, charges, or expenses not contracted for in the sales contract,

- the shipping and expiry dates indicated in the documentary credit and the period for presentation of the documents are sufficient to enable the beneficiary to comply with them in order to obtain payment thereunder,

- the port of loading, taking in charge, or place of dispatch and the port of discharge or delivery correspond to the sales contract,

- the insurance requirement (whether to be covered by the beneficiary or the buyer) is declared in the documentary credit, and

- the bank's obligation under the documentary credit is conditioned in total compliance with its terms and conditions and subject to the Uniform Customs and Practice for Documentary Credits ICC Publication No. 600.

iii. Common Sense Rules for the Beneficiary

- Although considerable time may elapse between the receipt of a documentary credit and its utilization, the beneficiary should study it immediately and request any necessary changes.

- The beneficiary should assure himself that his company's name and address details are exactly as they appear in the documentary credit.

- A documentary credit should always describe, in a very clear and definitive manner, the documents that the beneficiary must present to obtain payment. A documentary credit should not be issued if it declares a condition which is not supported by the presentation of a stated document (s).

- The beneficiary should satisfy himself that the terms, conditions and documents called for in the documentary credit are in agreement with the sales contract.

- When making presentation of the documents to the bank, the beneficiary should present the required documents exactly as called for by the documentary credit and not, on their face, inconsistent with one another and present the documents to the bank as quickly as possible, and in any case within the validity of the documentary credit and within the period of time after date of shipment specified or applicable under UCP600 Article 6.

- The beneficiary should remember that non-compliance with the terms and conditions stipulated in the documentary credit, or irregularities in the documents, obliges the bank to refuse settlement.

iv. Honouring the Obligation Under the Documentary Credit

Once the documents have been examined by the bank, which has verified that the terms and conditions of the documentary credit have been complied with, documents should be delivered by the confirming bank to the issuing bank and by the issuing bank to the applicant against reimbursement of the sums owed, or against other methods of settlement indicated in the documentary credit or the application.

In certain instances, the documents presented under the documentary credit may not comply with its terms and conditions. If so, the nominated bank (s) may only act as follows:

- return the documents to the beneficiary so that the beneficiary can correct them and represent them during the period of validity under the documentary credit and in accordance with UCP600 Article 14, or

- remit under approval, with reference to the documentary credit and with the consent of the beneficiary, the unpaid documents to the respective issuing bank or confirming bank, if any, for settlement under the credit, or

- return the discrepant documents to the beneficiary with instructions that he remit the documents directly to the issuing bank or confirming bank, if any, for their approval and settlement under the credit, or

- request by tele-transmission, with the beneficiary's consent, the issuing bank's, or confirming bank's, if any, authorization to proceed with the payment, negotiation, or acceptance against the discrepant documents presented, or

- require a beneficiary's guarantee or indemnity or his banker's undertaking to reimburse the bank for any payment, acceptance, or negotiation it may undertake, despite the fact that the terms and conditions of the documentary credit were not complied with if the respective issuing bank or confirming bank, if any, refuses to accept such discrepant documents and refuses to reimburse for settlement.

The obligation of the issuing bank and the confirming bank, if any, is to examine documents in order to determine if there is compliance with the terms and conditions of the documentary credit. For this reason it is important to recognize the conditions associated with UCP600 Article 14 and 16 which address the standard for examination of documents and the actions to be taken relative to discrepant documents and notice thereof.

E. *Four Types of Documentary Credit*
i. *Payment Credit*

The meaning of the term "payment" is self-evident. The nominated bank will pay the beneficiary on receipt of the specified documents and on fulfillment of all the terms of the credit.

Sometimes the issuing bank nominates itself as paying bank, in which case payment will be made on receipt of the correct documents at the bank's counter. On other occasions, usually with confirmed credits, the issuing bank will nominate the advising bank to pay.

The term "payment" only applies to sight drafts, and sometimes, fixed time drafts (deferred payment).

ii. *Negotiation Credit*

Sometimes the issuing bank will nominate the advising bank to negotiate a credit, or it may even make the credit freely negotiable, in which case any bank may be a nominated bank.

If a bank negotiates a credit, it will advance money to the beneficiary on presentation of the required documents and will charge interest on the advance from the date of the advance until such time as it receives reimbursement from the issuing bank.

Such negotiation advances are said to be with recourse, so that if payment is not ultimately forthcoming from the issuing bank, the negotiating bank will be able to claim repayment from the beneficiary of the advance, plus interest. If the negotiating bank has confirmed the credit, the advance will be on a "without recourse" basis.

iii. *Acceptance Credit*

The term "acceptance" can only apply when the credit calls for usance bills (term bills), i. e. , bills of exchange payable at a specified time after acceptance by the drawee.

And bills should be drawn on a bank.

The acceptance credit is also referred to as a "term credit" or "usance credit", which means that the seller draws a draft on the nominated bank demanding payment at some determinable future date, e. g. , at 30 days sight instead of at sight.

In practice, this means that instead of receiving immediate payment on presentation of the documents (at sight), the seller's draft is returned to him accepted on face by the nominated bank.

iv. Deferred Payment Credit

Normally the terms of a documentary credit will include an instruction to the beneficiary to draw bills of exchange, and the issuing bank will guarantee that such bills will be honoured, provided all the other terms of the credit are met.

However, in deferred payment credits, there is no need for the exporter to draw a bill of exchange. The issuing bank simply guarantees that payment will be made on a fixed or determinable future date, provided the other conditions have been fulfilled. Although the exporter does not draw a bill of exchange, in practice some banks will negotiate the documents provided.

One benefit of deferred credits is that they avoid the need for payment of stamp duty on bills of exchange. In some countries stamp duty is set at a low rate, or there may not be any stamp duty at all, whereas in other countries stamp duties can be much higher.

F. Transferable Letters of Credit and Back- to-Back Letters of Credit

i. Transferable Letters of Credit

A transferable credit is defined in Article 38 of UCP600. Under UCP a credit is only transferable if it is expressly designated transferable by the issuing bank. Terms such as "divisible", "assignable" and "fractionable" do not render a credit transferable.

The transferable credit will be used when the supplier of goods sells them through a middleman and does not deal directly with the ultimate buyer. If the supplier is in a strong bargaining position, he may insist that a documentary credit be set up in his favour.

The middleman may not wish to arrange a documentary credit by himself, and his bankers in any case may not be willing to issue a credit on his behalf. Thus the middleman will approach the ultimate buyer and ask him to arrange a transferable documentary credit in his (the middleman's) favour. The middleman is known as the first beneficiary of the credit.

The credit will be designated transferable, and will allow the first beneficiary to request the bank authorized to pay, incur a deferred payment undertaking, accept or negotiate, or in the case of a freely negotiable credit, the bank specifically authorized as the transferring bank to make the credit available to one or more third parties who are known as "second beneficiaries" . Thus the original supplier of the goods is known as the second beneficiary.

ii. *Back-to-Back Credits*

Back-to-Back credits consist of two entirely separate documentary credits, but one credit may act as security for the other. They apply in transactions when original suppliers and ultimate buyers deal through a middleman. In fact back-to-back credits are used in the same situations as transferable credits, but the rights and obligations of the parties differ between the two types of credit.

If the supplier insists on a documentary credit, the middleman may apply to his bankers to issue one on his behalf. If the middleman's bankers are satisfied with his creditworthiness, they will issue the credit in the normal way and no other formalities will apply. However, the "back-to-back" aspect comes into play if the middleman's bankers insist that the middleman obtain a documentary credit in his favour from the ultimate buyer as security for one which the middleman has applied for in favour of the seller.

Only the middleman and his banker need to know of the back-to-back aspect, and only they are concerned with the back-to-back aspect. The other parties, the ultimate buyer, the original supplier and their bankers, are not affected in any way whatsoever by the back-to-back aspect.

iii. *Differences Between Transferable and Back-to-Back Credits*

With transferable credits, the ultimate buyer is aware that he is dealing with a middleman; with back-to-back credits, he is not. With transferable credits the middleman and his bankers have no liability, but with back-to-back credits, they are fully liable on the second credit.

G. *Irrevocable Documentary Credit*

An irrevocable documentary credit constitutes a definite undertaking of the issuing bank, provided that the stipulated documents are presented to the nominated bank or to the issuing bank and that the terms and conditions of the documentary credit are complied with, to pay, accept drafts and/or document (s) presented under the documentary credit. (See UCP600 Article 7, for a full description of the obligations of the issuing bank under this kind of documentary credit.)

An irrevocable documentary credit gives the beneficiary greater assurance of payment; however, he remains dependent on an undertaking of foreign issuing bank. The issuing bank irrevocably commits itself to honour the exporter's draft and/or documents provided that the stipulated documents are presented and all the stipulations of the documentary credit are complied with. The irrevocable documentary credit cannot be cancelled/modified without the express consent of the issuing bank, the confirming bank (if any) and the beneficiary.

H. Confirmed Documentary Credit

i. Definition

A confirmation of an irrevocable documentary credit by a bank (the confirming bank) upon the authorization or request of the issuing bank constitutes a definite undertaking of the confirming bank, in addition to that of the issuing bank, provided that the stipulated documents are presented to the confirming bank or to any other nominated bank on or before the expiry date and the terms and conditions of the documentary credit are complied with, to pay, to accept draft (s) or to negotiate.

ii. A Double Assurance of Payment

An irrevocable confirmed documentary credit gives the beneficiary a double assurance of payment, since it represents the undertaking of both the issuing bank and the confirming bank. The second obligor (the confirming bank) engages that drawings under the documentary credit will be duly honoured in accordance with the terms and conditions of the documentary credit.

Normally, one considers the classification of the credit and the financial standing of the issuing bank. If an issuing bank is considered to be a first class bank, there may not be any need to have its documentary credit confirmed by another bank. Nevertheless, the beneficiary may desire that the documentary credit and payment thereunder be guaranteed by a bank located in his own country. In such a situation, such confirming bank becomes legally liable to the beneficiary to the same extent that the issuing bank does. The beneficiary should review the confirmation of a documentary credit given by a branch or a subsidiary of the issuing bank to see whether it is indeed another separate and distinct bank obligation under the documentary credit.

iii. Silent Confirmation

Silent confirmation represents an agreement between a bank and the beneficiary for that bank to "add its confirmation" to the documentary credit despite not being so authorized by the issuing bank.

The beneficiary wishes to obtain the security of "the confirming bank" and is willing to pay the "confirmation commission", but does not wish to request the applicant to instruct the issuing bank to authorize another bank to confirm its documentary credit.

Under UCP600 sub article 8, the documentary credit may only be confirmed if it is so authorized or requested by the issuing bank. Therefore, the documentary credit may not be confirmed when it has not been authorized or requested by the issuing bank. Nevertheless, the fact that such an unauthorized "confirmation" may have been effected extends the responsibility of the bank which "confirmed" the documentary credit against the beneficiary, without recourse as a "confirming bank" to the issuing bank which clearly did not request or authorize the bank to "add its confirmation" . In effect, there has not been a "confirmation" but a separate arrangement between the beneficiary and the "confirming bank" which "confirmed" the documentary credit under which the said bank is irrevocably obligated, subject to compliance, to purchase or discount the draft (s) and/or document (s) drawn and presented by the beneficiary, and usually without recourse.

I. Revolving Documentary Credit

A revolving documentary credit is one by which, under the terms and conditions thereof, the amount is renewed or reinstated without specific amendments to the documentary credit being required. The revolving documentary credit may be revocable or irrevocable, and may revolve in relation to time or value.

In the case of a documentary credit that revolves in relation to time, e. g. which is initially available for up to USD15,000.00 per month during a fixed period of time, say, six months, the documentary credit is automatically available for USD15,000.00 each month irrespective of whether any sum was drawn during the previous month. A documentary credit of this nature can be cumulative or non-cumulative. If it is stated to be "cumulative", any sum not utilized during the first period carries over and may be utilized during a subsequent period. If it is "non-cumulative", any sum not utilized in a period ceases to be available, that is, it is not carried over to a subsequent period. It must be remembered that under this kind of documentary credit and following this example, the obligations of the issuing bank would be for USD90,000.00, i. e. six revolving periods each for USD15,000.00. Thus while the face value of the documentary credit is given as USD15,000.00 the total undertaking of the issuing bank is for the full value that might be drawn.

In the case of a documentary credit that revolves in relation to value, the amount is reinstated utilization within a given overall period of validity. The documentary credit may provide for automatic reinstatement immediately upon presentation of the specified documents, or it may provide for reinstatement only after receipt by the issuing bank of those documents or another stated condition. This kind of documentary credit involves the buyer and the banks in an incalculable liability. For that reason, it is not in common use. To maintain a degree of control, it would be necessary to specify the overall amount that may be drawn under the documentary credit. Such amount would have to be decided by the buyer and the seller to meet their requirements, and would have to be agreed to by the issuing bank.

Specimen

APPLICATION FOR A STANDBY LETTER OF CREDIT

DATE: Jan. 1st, 2008

TO: BANK OF CN, HEAD OFFICE, BANKING DEPARTMENT

FROM: Cony Import and Export Corp. , Beijing, China

We request that you issue on our behalf and for our account your irrevocable Standby Letter of Credit in accordance with the following (and any attached) instructions.

Beneficiary Name and Address: E-bay Co. Ltd. , New York, USA

Amount (specify currency): USD100,000.00

Expiry Date: June 1st, 2010

Place of Expiry: USA

Sent by: Tele-transmission

Advising Bank: Bank of CN, New York Branch

Confirmation of the Credit: No confirmation requested

Available by: The beneficiary's draft (s) drawn at sight on issuing bank accompanied by the beneficiary's signed statement stating that default has been made by the buyer in due performance of its obligations to make payment according to the contract terms.

Partial Drawing: Permitted

The letter of credit shall be subject to ISP98 of the International Chamber of Commerce in effect as of the date the letter of credit is issued.

For Applicant By

(signature)

Specimen

IRREVOCABLE STANDBY LETTER OF CREDIT

Advised through: Bank of CN, New York Branch

Issued by: Bank of CN, Head Office

Date of Standby Letter of Credit: Jan. 1st, 2008

On Account of: Cony I/E Corp. , Beijing, China

Addressed to Beneficiary: E-bay Co. Ltd. , New York, USA

Expires: June 1st, 2008 in USA

We hereby open our Irrevocable Standby Letter of Credit Number SLC1, 001/00 in an amount of Say U. S. Dollars One Hundred Thousand only available for payment at sight by your draft drawn on issuing bank accompanied by the following documents:

Beneficiary's signed statement stating that default has been made by the applicant in due performance of its obligations to make payment according to the contract terms.

Special Conditions:

(1) Draft (s) drawn under this Letter of Credit may not be presented prior to May 1st, 2008.

(2) All banking charges, including any advising bank charges are for the account of beneficiary.

(3) Partial drawings are permitted.

(4) In no event may drawings under this Letter of Credit exceed the value of this Letter of Credit.

(5) The amount available for drawings under this Letter of Credit will be reduced by the amount of any payment (s) that the beneficiary receives outside this Letter of Credit if such payment (s) are made by issuing bank and make reference to this Letter of Credit number SLC1, 001/00.

We hereby engage with you that drafts accompanied by documents drawn under and in compliance with the terms of this credit will be duly honoured upon presentations specified. This Letter of Credit sets forth in full the terms of our undertaking, and such undertaking shall not in any way be modified, amended, or amplified by reference to any document, instrument, or agreement referred to or in which this Letter of Credit is referred to or to which this Letter of Credit relates and any document, instrument, or agreement.

This Letter of Credit shall be subject to the International Standby Practices, ISP98.

(signature)

For and on behalf of

Bank of CN, H. O.

4. Standby Letters of Credit

A. *General introduction*

A standby letter of credit, like a commercial letter of credit, is a promise by the issuer to honor the beneficiary's presentation of the document or documents specified in the letter of credit.

The standby letter of credit, however, is not typically used as a payment mechanism. In a standby letter of credit, the parties do not normally expect that the presentation of documents will occur. The issuer is merely "standing by", just in the case that the obligation in the underlying transaction is not performed by the obligor.

A standby letter of credit anticipates the possibility that something will go wrong or a negative event will occur, such as the failure of the applicant to perform a payment pursuant to a loan agreement or the failure of the applicant to perform some other kind of obligation. A commercial letter of credit, by contrast, is a method of payment that anticipates a positive event, the consummation of the underlying transaction. Thus commercial letters of credit are a means of implementing the performance of the buyer and the seller while standby credits envision the possibility of non-performance by the applicant in the underlying transaction.

B. *Documents under a Standby Letter of Credit*

The documents presented to the issuer under a standby letter of credit are typically very different from the documents presented under a commercial letter of credit. Documents presented under a commercial letter of credit are invoices, transport documents, insurance documents, weight certificates, packing lists, and other documents customarily delivered in transaction for the sale of goods. These documents must be examined carefully by the bank to ensure that they are in compliance with the requirements of the credit.

The documents presented under a standby letter of credit, by contrast, usually indicate in a relatively perfunctory manner that the applicant has defaulted in its obligations to the beneficiary. For example, the underlying obligation in a standby letter of credit might be a loan. In the standby letter of credit, the issuer would undertake to pay the lender the amount specified by the lender upon presentation by the lender of a draft or a demand for payment and a document certifying that "the Borrower is in default under the Loan". If a standby letter of credit is used to secure payment of a purchase and sale transaction, additional documents required for presentation may be a copy of a commercial invoice and a copy of a document showing that the beneficiary effected delivery of the goods.

Standby letters of credit can be used to provide payment in lieu of the performance of non-monetary obligations as well as to assure the payment of monetary obligations. The underlying obligation, for example, might be an obligation to construct a building. The documents presented might be a draft or a demand for payment of a specified sum of money and a statement such as "the Contractor has failed to perform its obligations under the Construction Contract".

The positions of the parties could be reversed. The contractor might be the party seeking assurance of the payment of the construction price under a standby letter of credit. In that event the documents presented by the contractor might be a demand for payment of the balance due under the construction contract and a statement that "the Contractor has performed all its obligations under the Construction Contract and the said sum is due and unpaid".

Standby letters of credit have been used for a wide variety of purposes and are available for use in virtually all circumstances in which the applicant owes a payment or performance obligation to the beneficiary.

Standby letter of credit could be used subject to UCP600 as well as to the International Standby Practices (ISP98, ICC Publication No. 590). In the latter the term "standby" is adopted instead of "standby letter of credit".

5. Bonds

A. *The Roles of Bonds in International Trade*

A bond is issued by a guarantor, usually a bank or an insurance company, on behalf of the principal. It is a guarantee to the beneficiary that the principal will fulfill his contractual obligations. If these obligations are not fulfilled, the guarantor undertakes to pay a sum of money to the beneficiary in compensation. This sum of money can be anything from 1% to 100% of the contract value.

If the bond is issued by a bank, then the principal is asked to sign a counter indemnity which authorizes the bank to debit his account with any money paid out under the bond.

Bonds are usually required in connection with overseas contract, or with the supply of capital goods and services. When there is a buyer's market, the provision of a bond can be made an essential condition of the granting of the contract. Bonds are commonly required by Mid-Eastern countries, but nowadays many other countries and international aid agencies also require them.

B. *Types of Bonds*
i. *Tender or Bid Bonds*

A tender or bid bond, usually from 2% to 5% of the contract value, guarantees that the principal will take up the contract if it is awarded. Failure to take up the contract results in a penalty for the amount of the bond. In addition, the tender bond usually commits the principal and his bank to joining in performance bond if the contract is awarded. Tender bonds serve to prevent the submission of frivolous tenders.

ii. Performance Bonds

Performance bonds guarantee that the goods or services will be of the required standard and a stated penalty is payable if they are not. The amount payable will be a stated percentage of the contract price, often 10% but sometimes more.

iii. Advance Payment Bonds

Advance payment bonds undertake to refund any advance payments if the goods or services are unsatisfactory.

iv. Warranty or Maintenance Bonds

Warranty or maintenance bonds undertake that the exporter will maintain the equipment for a period of time.

v. Retention Bonds

Retention bonds enable retention monies, which would otherwise be held by the buyer beyond the completion of the contract, to be released early. These bonds guarantee the return to the buyer of these retention monies in the event of non-performance of post-completion obligations by the exporter.

C. "On Demand" Bonds and Conditional Bonds

i. "On Demand" Bonds

These bonds, sometimes known as "unconditional bonds", can be called at the sole discretion of the beneficiary. The bank must pay if called upon to do so, even in circumstances where it may be clear to the principal that the claim is wholly unjustified.

If the bank has to pay under the bond, it will debit the customer's account under the authority of the counter indemnity. The principal will then be left with the unenviable task of claiming reimbursement in the courts of the beneficiary's country.

It must be stressed that banks never become involved in contractual disputes. If payment called for conforms to the terms of the bond, the bank must pay.

ii. Conditional Bonds

There are two types of conditional bonds:

- conditional bonds requiring documentary evidence; and
- conditional bonds which do not require documentary evidence.

Conditional bonds requiring documentary evidence give maximum protection to the principal. Payment can only be called for by the beneficiary against production of a specified document, such as a certificate of award by an independent arbitrator. Unfortunately, this type of conditional bond is often unacceptable, particularly in the case of Middle East buyers.

On the other hand, conditional bonds which do not require documentary evidence are a bit better than "on demand" bonds from the principal's point of view. Such bonds often specify that payment must be made in the event of default or failure on the part of the contractor to perform his obligations under the above-mentioned contract. This terminology is so vague that banks are often obliged to pay a simple "on demand" claim if one is received.

D. *The Procedures for Issuing Bonds*

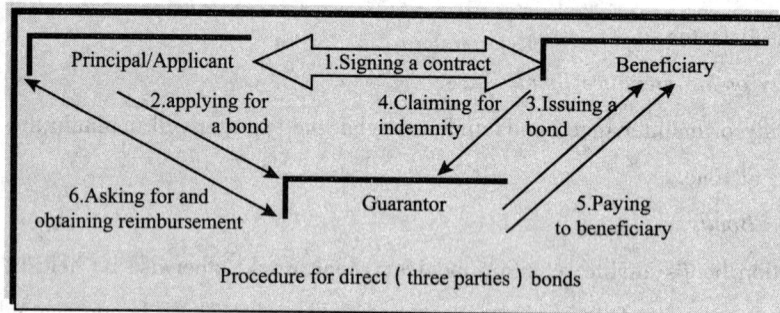

Procedure for direct (three parties) bonds

If a bank is satisfied that joining in a bond is justified, it would prefer to issue its own bond direct to the beneficiary.

However, if in the beneficiary's country, local laws or customs prevent the importer from accepting bonds issued directly by banks in the exporter's country, the exporter's bank will instruct a bank domiciled in the importer's locality to issue a bond against the exporter's bank's own indemnity.

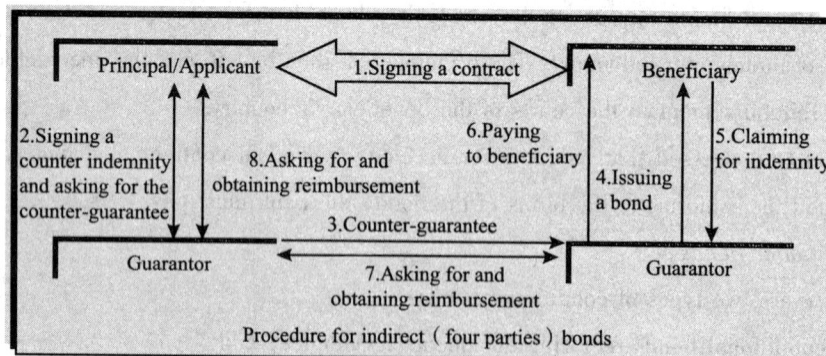

Procedure for indirect (four parties) bonds

At the same time in the case, as the bond is issued, the exporter will complete the counter indemnity to authorize the bank to debit the account with the cost of any payments under the bond. The bank will make a suitable charge for the service, usually a stated annual percentage of the bond's value.

Specimen Tender Guarantee

GUARANTEE NUMBER LG001/00

Advised Through: Bank of CN, New York Branch

Issued By: Bank of CN, Head Office

Date: Jan. 1st, 2005

Please advise our following letter of guarantee number LG001/00 to the beneficiary without any obligation on your part.

Quote:

Beneficiary: E-bay Co. Ltd. , New York, USA

We do understand that Cony Import and Export Corp. , Beijing ("the applicant") are tendering for the Goods under your invitation to Tender No. 100/00 and that a Bank Guarantee is required for 10% of the amount of their tender.

We, Bank of CN, H. O. , Beijing hereby guarantee the payment to you on demand of up to USD100,000.00 (SAY US DOLLARS ONE HUNDRED THOUSAND ONLY) in the event of your awarding the relative contract to the Applicant and of its failing to sign the contract in the terms of its tender, or in the event of the Applicant withdrawing its tender before expiry of this guarantee without your consent.

This guarantee shall come into force on Jan. 1st, 2005 being the closing date for tenders, and will expire at close of banking hours at this office on June 1st, 2005 (expiry).

Our liability is limited to the sum of USD100,000.00 and your claim hereunder must be received in writing at this office before Expiry accompanied by your signed statement that the Applicant has been awarded the relative contract and has failed to sign the contract awarded in the terms of its tender or has withdrawn its tender before Expiry without your consent, and such claim and statement shall be accepted as conclusive evidence that the amount claimed is due to you under this guarantee.

Upon expiry this guarantee shall become null and void, whether returned to us for cancellation or not and any claim or statement received after expiry shall be ineffective.

This guarantee shall be governed by and construed in accordance with the Laws of People's Republic of China.

Unquote

Regards

Specimen Performance Guarantee

GUARANTEE NUMBER LG002/00

Advised Through: **Bank of CN, New York Branch**

Issued By: **Bank of CN, Head Office**

Date: **Jan. 1st, 2005**

Please advise our following letter of guarantee number LG002/00 to the beneficiary without any obligation on your part.

Quote:

Beneficiary: E-bay Co. Ltd. , New York, USA

We do understand that you have entered a Contract no. 100/00 ("the Contract") with Cony Import and Export Corp. , Beijing ("the applicant") for the Goods and that under such Contract the Applicant must provide a Bank Performance Guarantee for an amount of USD100, 000. 00 being 10% of the value of the contract.

We, Bank of CN, H. O. , Beijing hereby guarantee the payment to you on demand of up to USD100, 000. 00 (SAY US DOLLARS ONE HUNDRED THOUSAND ONLY) in the event of the Applicant's failing to fulfill the said Contract, provided that your claim hereunder is received in writing at this office accompanied by your signed statement that the Applicant has failed to fulfill the Contract. Such claim and statement shall be accepted as conclusive evidence that the amount claimed is due to you under this guarantee.

This guarantee shall expire at close of banking hours at this office on June 1st, 2006 (expiry).

Upon expiry this guarantee shall become null and void, whether returned to us for cancellation or not and any claim or statement received after expiry shall be ineffective.

This guarantee shall be governed by and construed in accordance with the Laws of People's Republic of China.

Unquote

Regards

Specimen Advance Payment Guarantee

GUARANTEE NUMBER: LG003/00

Advised Through: Bank of CN, New York Branch

Issued By: Bank of CN, Head Office

Date: Jan. 1st, 2005

Please advise our following letter of guarantee number LG003/00 to the beneficiary without any obligation on your part.

Quote:

Beneficiary: E-bay Co. Ltd. , New York, USA

We do understand that you have entered a Contract No. 200/00 (the Contract) with Cony Import and Export Corp. , Beijing ("the applicant") for the Goods and that under such Contract you must provide advance payment for an amount of USD100,000.00 being 10% of the value of the contract.

In consideration of your making an advance payment of USD100,000.00 (the advance payment) to the Applicant, we, Bank of CN, H. O. Beijing hereby guarantee the payment to you on demand of up to USD100,000.00 (SAY US DOLLARS ONE HUNDRED THOUSAND ONLY) in the event of the Applicant's failing to fulfill the said Contract. Such claim and statement shall be accepted as conclusive evidence that the amount claimed is due to you under this guarantee.

This guarantee shall expire at close of banking hours at this office on June 1st, 2005 (expiry).

Upon expiry this guarantee shall become null and void, whether returned to us for cancellation or not and any claim or statement received after expiry shall be ineffective.

This guarantee shall be governed by and construed in accordance with the Laws of People's Republic of China.

Unquote

Regards

III. Documents Used in International Trade

1. Commercial Invoice

A commercial invoice gives details of the goods, details of the payment and delivery terms, and a detailed breakdown of the monetary amount due. Invoices are usually prepared/made by the seller.

If we study the specimen document, we can see the following main details appeared on invoices:

```
specimen          SHANGHAI X X X IMPORT AND EXPORT CO LTD

                  2TH/FL, 2000 ZHONGSHAN ROAD (N),SHANGHAI 200063,CHINA


                         COMMERCIAL INVOICE          DATE: MAR.4,2002

                                                     INVOICE NO.2XC4059

TO: AHLENS FAR EAST LIMITED SUITES 908-9, TOWER 1, CHINA HK CITY, CANTON ROAD, T.S.T. KLN, HONGKONG


L/C NO.: LCADV-SEB/30275 DATE: MAR.08, 2002

SHIPMENT FROM SHANGHAI TO ICD PATPARGANJ, NEW DELHI VIA NAVA SHEVA PORT.


MARKS & NUMBERS          QUANTITY AND DESCRIPTIONS          AMOUNT


POLYESTER TROLLEY CASE   600D POLYESTER TROLLEY CASE   FOB SHANGHAI

ART. NO.23381242           ITEM #R069

C/NO.1-500               SIZE: 46CM      COLOUR:RED

                         200PCS       @USD16.00/PC           USD3,200.00

                         SIZE:46/56/70CM   COLOUR: NAVY

                         200SETS      @USD58.00/SET          USD11,600.00

                         SIZE:56/70CM      COLOUR: BLACK

                         200SETS      @USD42.00/SET          USD8,400.00

                                                       _____

                                                             USD23,200.00


                         ORDER NO.1436249-163    1444801-163


                         PACKED IN 500CARTONS

                         G.WT.:6500KGS

                         N.WT.:6000KGS

                         MEASUREMENT: 48.8CBM


                         SHANGHAI X X X I/E CO.LTD.SHANGHAI CHINA

                                          陈大光
```

1) Name and address of the exporter.

2) Name and address of the importer.

3) Reference number, (place and) date of issue.

4) Terms of delivery (sometimes called Incoterms, sometimes called shipment terms).

5) Shipping marks. Note how these tie up with the marks on the bill of lading.

6) Description of goods.

7) Breakdown of the cost of freight and insurance, but it is not always necessary for the seller to supply this information.

8) Quantity of goods.

9) Total amount payable by the importer.

10) Signature of the exporter. Under a documentary letter of credit, it is not necessary for the invoice to be signed, unless it is called for in L/C terms.

2. Transport Documents

A. *Bills of Lading*

i. The Functions of a Bill of Lading

There are four main functions:

- The bill of lading is evidence of the contract for carriage between the shipper and the carrier. The full contract details appear on the bill of lading (except for the short form/blank back bill of lading).

- Bill of lading acts as a receipt of the goods from the shipping company to the shipper. When there is no indication of damage to the goods, a bill of lading is said to be clean.

- A bill of lading is a quasi negotiable document. Any transferee for value who takes possession of an endorsed bill of lading obtains a good title to it, provided the transferor had a good title in the first place.

- A bill of lading acts as a document of title to goods being shipped. The goods will be released from the port only against production of one of the original bills of lading. Original bills of lading are usually issued in sets of two or three (the number of originals will be indicated on the bill of lading). As any one original bill of lading will enable the possessor to obtain the goods, possession of a complete set is required before the control of the goods is assured. Shipping companies often issue unsigned copies of the bill of lading for record purposes. These unsigned copies are not documents of title.

ii. Different Types of Bill of Lading

There are many different types of bills of lading, but the main ones we need to consider are:

- Combined Transport Bills of Lading and Similar Documents

A combined transport bill of lading may evidence that goods have been collected from a named inland place and have been dispatched to a port or inland container depot in the importer's country.

Depending on the terms of the sales contract, the importer may have to make separate arrangements to have the goods collected from the port or inland container depot in his country and delivered to his factory or warehouse.

A through bill of lading is a similar document which may evidence dispatching of goods to a named destination, for example the importer's warehouse. When a through bill of lading is used, there must be one part of the journey covered by a sea voyage.

```
specimen                            BILL OF LADING
              FOR COMBINED TRANSPORT SHIPMENT OR PORT TO PORT SHIPMENT

SHIPPER:                            B/L NO.: SUHD92FC055        ORIGINAL

SHANGHAI LIGHT INDUSTRIAL PRODUCTS CORP. LTD.   CHINA SHIPPING CONTAINER LINES CO., LTD.

CONSIGNED TO ORDER OF HABIB BANK LIMITED.   CABLE:0001    TELEX: 33200 CSCO CN

                                    PORT-TO-PORT OR COMBINED TRANSPORT BILL OF LADING
NOTIRY PARTY/INTERMEDIATE CONSIGNEE   RECEIVED IN EXTERNAL APPARENT GOOD ORDER AND CONDITION. EXCEPT
                                    OTHERWISE NOTEDTHE TOTAL NUMBER OF CONTAINERS OR OTHER PACKAGES
1.HUSSAIN JUMA BAQIR TRADE EST.,      OR UNITS SHOWN IN THIS BILL OF LADING RECEIPT, SAID BY THE SHIPPER
                                    TO CONTAIN THE GOODS DESCRIBED ABOVE. WHICH DESCRIPTION THE
P.O.BOX 2630,P.C.112, RUWI, SULTANATE OF OMAN.   CARRIER HAS NO REASONABLE MEANS OF CHECKING AND IS NOT PART OF
                                    THE BILL OF LADING. ONE ORIGINAL B/L SHOULD BE SURRENDERED, EXCEPT
2.HABIB BANK LIMITED CENTRAL BRANCH P.O.BOX   CLAUSE 22PARAGRAPH 5, IN EXCHANGE FOR DELIVER OF THE SHIPMENT.
                                    SIGNED BY THE CONSIGNED OR DULY ENDORSED BY THE HOLDER IN DUE
NO.1326, RUWI P.C.112 SULTANATE OF OMAN.   COURSE. WHEREUPON THE OTHER ORIGINAL(S) ISSUED SHALL BE VOID. IN
                                    ACCEPTING THIS B/L. THE MERCHANTS AGREE TO BE BOUND BY ALL THE TERMS
PRE-CARRIAGE BY        PLACE OF RECEIPT   ON THE FACE AND BACK HEREOF AS IF EACH HAD PERSONALLY SIGNED THIS
                                    B/L.

                                    WHEN THE PLACE OF RECEIPT OF THE GOODS AN INLAND POINT AND IS SO
VESSEL VOYAGE          PORT OF LOADING   NAMED HEREIN, ANY NOTATION OF "SHIPPED ON BOARD" OR WORDS TO LIKE
UNI ASSURE             SHANGHAI           EFFECT ON THIS B/L SHALL BE DEEMED TO MEAN ON BOARD THE TRUCK, TRAIL
                                    CAR, AIR CRAFT OR OTHER INLAND CONVEYANCE (AS THE CASE MAY
PORT OF DISCHARGE      FINAL DESTINATION   BE), PERFORMING CARRIAGE FROM THE PLACE OF RECEIPT OF THE GOODS TO
PORT SULTAN QABOOS                        THE PORT OF LOADING. SEE CLAUSE 4 ON THE BACK OF THIS B/L (TERMS
MUSCAT OMAN                               CONTINUED ON THE BACK HEREOF READ CAREFULLY).

 MARKS AND NO.   NO. OF PKGS   DESCRIPTION OF PACKAGES AND GOODS    G.W.      MEASUREMENT
                               (PARTICULARS FURNISHED BY SHIPPER)   (KGS)      (CBM)
                 290 CARTONS
                                  MANTLES                         5,400KGS   27.88CBM
HUSSAIN JUMA                    SPARE PARTS FOR PRESSURE LANTERNS
PORT SULTAN QABOOS             L/C NO. CBZ/483/01
MUSCAT                         FREIGHT PREPAID
                               SHIPPER'S LOAD & COUNT SAID TO CONTAIN
                               290 CARTONS
                               SHIPMENT FROM SHANGHAI TO PORT SULTAN QABOOS MUSCAT OMAN
EISU3475479/20'/8638           WITH TRANSHIPMENT AT HONGKONG
                               SHIPMENT EFFECTED IN 20' CONTAINER ON CY TO CY BASIS. ALL FCL AND CONTAINER HANDLING
                                  CHARGES AT THE PORT OF LOADING AND FCL THC. PORT HANDLING CHARGES, DELIVERY ORDER
                                  CHARGES AT THE PORT OF DESTINATION ARE PREPAID. BILL OF LADING ALSO EVIDENCE
                                  BREAK-UP OF THESE CHARGES PAID AT THE PORT OF LOADING.
                               THE NAME, THE ADDRESS OF THE CARRYING VESSEL'S LOCAL AGENT IN SULTANATE OF OMAN:SOHAR
                                  SHIPPING TRANSPORT AND TRADING AGENCIES L.L.C.P.O.BOX 284-MUTTRAH, OMAN
                               TEL:968-711719/711762 FAX:714478

TOTAL NUMBER OF CONTAINERS     SAY TWO HUNDRED AND NINETY CARTONS ONLY
OR PACKAGES (IN WORDS)

FREIGHT & CHARGES    REVENUE    ROTE           PREPAID           COLLECT
USD850.-             TONS       PER

NUMBER OF ORIGINAL B(S)/L   PLACE OF B(S)/L ISSUE/DATE   SIGNED FOR THE CARRIER
        3                   SHANGHAI, MAR.6, 2002        CHINA SHIPPING AGENCY CO., LTD.
SERVICE TYPE/MODE           SHIPPED ON BOARD THE VESSEL   王刚    GENERAL MANAGER
FCL/FCL O/O                 ON BOARD DATE: MAR.05, 2002   AS AGENT FOR CARRIER CSCL
(TERMS OF BILL OF LADING ARE CONTINUED ON THE BACK HEREOF AND ENLARGED VERSION OF BACK CLAUSE IS AVAILABLE UPON REQUEST)
```

- Transhipment Bills of Lading

These are used when the goods have to be transferred from one ship to another at a named transhipment port. Once again the carrier has full responsibility for the whole journey, and these documents are usually considered to be documents of title if the appropriate negotiable wording appears.

- Container Bills of Lading

When goods are packed in containers, shipping companies will issue bills of lading simply acting as receipts for a container. Container bills of lading can be issued to cover goods being transported on a traditional port-to-port basis, or they can cover transport from an inland container depot in exporter's country to an inland container depot in the importer's country.

Once again the shipping company is responsible for the whole journey, and these bills of lading are considered to be documents of title, provided they contain the appropriate negotiable wording.

- Marine /Ocean Bills of Lading

These bills of lading are issued when the goods are being transported from one port to another by ship.

- Short Form Bills of Lading

These bills of lading do not contain the full details of the contract of carriage on the back. However, they fulfill all the other functions of bills of lading, and in particular they are considered to be documents of title.

- Liner Bills of Lading

These documents fulfill all the normal functions of a bill of lading, including that of document of title. The liner bill of lading indicates that goods are being transported on a ship which travels on a scheduled route and has a reserved berth at destination; thus the exporter can reasonably assume that his goods will reach the buyer's country by a set date.

An alternative name for these documents is "bill of lading (liner)".

- Charter Party Bills of Lading

A charter party bill of lading is issued by the hirer of a ship to the exporter. The terms of the bill of lading are subject to the contract of hire between the ship's owner and the hirer. Such bills are usually marked subject to charter party.

Because of the legal complexity involved, charter party bills of lading are not usually considered to be documents of title.

B. Sea Waybills

A sea waybill is a transport document which can be issued by the shipping company as an alternative to a bill of lading.

The functions of a sea waybill are similar to those of a bill of lading, except that a sea waybill is not negotiable and it is not a document of title. On arrival at their destination, the goods would be released by the shipping company to the named consignee against identification.

When exporters agree to sell on open account terms, it follows that the exporter should ask the shipping company for sea waybills rather than for bills of lading.

The objective of open account is for the goods to reach the importer with the minimum formality, and sea waybills can meet that objective. As soon as the goods reach their destination, the shipping company notifies the consignee, who is the importer. The importer can then collect the goods, without the need to produce the waybill.

If bills of lading go astray, there are problems for the importer in collecting the goods, whereas it is immaterial to the importer whether or not he has possession of a waybill.

Sea waybills are very similar in scope to air waybills.

C. *Air Waybills*

Air waybills are issued by airlines when goods are sent by air freight. There is no such thing as a bill of lading with air transport, and the only transport document which can be issued is an air waybill.

D. *Other Transport Documents*

i. *Rail/Road Transport Documents*

When goods are sent by rail or road haulage the transport documents will be rail or road consignment notes, or truck/carrier receipts. These are not documents of title, and goods are released to the consignee on application and identification.

ii. *Parcel Post Receipt*

When goods are sent by post, the document evidencing postage is a parcel post receipt. And in the case of courier service, the courier's receipt will meet the need.

All forms of waybill/consignment note/parcel post receipt/courier's receipt fulfill two of the functions of a bill of lading. They act as a receipt of the goods by the carrier, and give some evidence of the contract of carriage. However, these documents are not negotiable and are not documents of title. Usually the words "not negotiable" will appear on these documents to indicate that they are not documents of title, but that the goods will be released to the named consignee.

3. Insurance Documents

A. *Insurance of Goods*

It is a matter for negotiation between the exporter and the importer as to who is responsible for insuring the goods during their journey from the exporter's hands to the importer's hands. In some transactions, it may be agreed that the seller will insure the whole journey and in others it may be on the buyer, it is also possible for the agreement to say that the seller must cover part of the journey, and the buyer must cover the rest.

For the moment let us consider the position of an exporter who is responsible for insurance of goods.

When an exporter sells goods on a regular basis, he will normally arrange an open policy of insurance to cover all his exports during a specific period. This provides insurance cover at all times within agreed terms and conditions. Each time a shipment is made, the exporter will declare the details and pay a premium to the insurer. A certificate of insurance is then issued by the exporter, who sends one copy to the insurance company for their record.

The benefit of the open cover system is that it avoids the need to negotiate insurance terms each time a shipment is made, and it avoids the necessity of issuing a separate policy for each individual shipment.

If an exporter sells goods on a one-off basis, then he will negotiate terms with the insurers and an insurance policy will be issued.

In many countries, an insured person must have a policy before he can take legal action against an insurer. A certificate alone is insufficient evidence on which to base a legal action. This legal problem is only important if the buyer needs to go to court because the insurance company has challenged a claim.

B. *The Risks Covered by an Insurance Policy*

The insurance cover is often based on the standard clauses of the Institute of London Underwriters, which is called Institute Cargo Clause (ICC). In China, China Insurance Clause (CIC) is used in many cases and accepted by importers abroad.

Three main standard clauses of the Institute of London Underwriters refer to risk. Clause A begins: "This clause covers all risks of loss or damage to the subject matter below, except as provided in clauses 4, 5, 6 and 7 below."

This clause provides the fullest available cover against risks, and it should not be misunderstood that the exception clause is detrimental. Buyers and sellers are generally satisfied that institute clause A is perfectly acceptable cover against all risks.

Institute cargo clauses B and C also cover risks, but the extent of cover they provide is less than that provided by clause A.

4. Other Shipping Documents

A. *Certificate of Origin*

Some countries require certificates of origin for customs clearance. The exporter inserts the relevant details, and the form has then to be authenticated by an independent body, such as a chamber of commerce.

Specimen

THE X X X INSURANCE COMPANY OF CHINA
HEAD OFFICE, BEIJING

INSURANCE POLICY   ORIGINAL

POLICY NO. : SH02/PYCK200231010700000794

THIS POLICY OF INSURANCE WITNESSES THAT THE xxx INSURANCE COMPANY OF CHINA (HEREIN AFTERCALLED "THE COMPANY"), AT THE REQUEST OF <u>SHANGHAI LIGHT INDUSTRIAL PRODUCTS CORP. LTD.</u> (HEREIN AFTER CALLED"THE INSURED") AND IN CONSIDERATION OF THE AGREED PREMIUM PAID TO THE COMPANY BY THE INSURED UNDERTAKES TO INSURE THE UNDERMENTIONED GOODS IN TRANSPORTATION SUBJECT TO THE CONDITION OF THIS POLICY AS PER THE CLAUSES PRINTED OVERLEAF AND OTHER SPECIAL CLAUSE ATTACHED HEREON.

MARKS AND NUMBERS 标记	QUANTITY 包装及数量	DESCRIPTION OF GOODS 保险货物项目	AMOUNT INSURED 保险金额
HUSSAIN JUMA PORT SULTAN QABOOS MUSCAT	290CTNS	BUTTERFLY BRAND MANTLES, SPARE PARTS FOR PRESSURE LANTERNS SHIPMENT FROM SHANGHAI TO PORT SULTAN QABOOS MUSCAT OMAN WITH TRANSHIPMENT AT HONGKONG	USD20,735.00

TOTAL AMOUNT INSURED: US DOLLARS TWENTY THOUSAND SEVEN HUNDRED THIRTY FIVE ONLY

<u>PREMIUM</u> AS ARRANGED, RATE AS ARRANGED, PER UNI-ASSURE & OR STEAMER

<u>SAILING</u> ON OR ABOUT 20020306

<u>FROM</u> SHANGHAI <u>TO</u> PORT SULTAN QABOOS MUSCAT OMAN WITH TRANSHIPMENT AT HONGKONG

CONDITIONS:

COVERING ALL RISKS AND WAR RISKS AS PER OCEAN MARINE CARGO CLAUSES AND WAR RISKS CLAUSES (1/1/1981) OF THE PEOPLE'S INSURANCE COMPANY OF CHINA (ABBREVIATED AS C.I.C.-ALL RISKS & WAR RISKS). (WAREHOUSE TO WAREHOUSE CLAUSE IS INCLUDED).
INCL. S.R.C.C.

IN THE EVENT OF LOSS OR DAMAGE WHICH MAY RESULT IN A CLAIM UNDER THIS POLICY,IMMEDIATE NOTICE MUST BE GIVEN

TO THE COMPANY'S AGENT AS MENTIONED HEREUNDER.CLAIMS,IF ANY, ONE OF THE ORIGINAL POLICY WHICH HAS BEEN

ISSUED IN **TWO** ORIGINALS TOGETHER WITH THE RELEVENT DOCUMENTS SHALL BE SURRENDERED TO THE COMPANY. OF ONE

OF THE ORIGINAL POLICY HAS BEEN ACCOMPLISHED. THE OTHERS TO BE VOID.

CLAIMS AGENT: OMAN INSURANCE CO.RUWI,SULTANATE OF OMAN

CLAIM PAYABLE: OMAN

DATE: MAR.6,2002. SHANGHAI.   THE X X X INSURANCE COMPANY OF CHINA

                                              SHANGHAI BRANCH, CHINA.

ADDRESS: B500 ZHONGSHAN ROAD,

SHANGHAI 200010, CHINA.   XYZ

B. Black List Certificate

A black list certificate certifies that the goods have no connection with certain countries. Many countries in the Middle East require such a document before allowing goods to be imported.

C. *Third Party Inspection Certificate*

This is a certificate, issued by an independent third party resident in the exporter's country, stating that the goods conform to a certain standard.

Sometimes the buyer will insist that such a document is issued and this stipulation can form part of the sales contract.

D. *Packing List/ Weight List*

This gives details of the goods packed and may also list the weight of individual items, together with a total weight.

IV. Trade Finance

1. Negotiation of Documentary Collections

When a customer sells on documentary collection terms, he may be able to arrange a negotiation facility with his bank. A negotiation facility is a lending facility, and normal lending criteria apply.

Such a facility works as follows:

- The exporter submits the normal documentary collection items to his bank, but instead of signing a collection order, he signs a negotiation request which is very similar to the collection order. This form requests a negotiation facility and gives the exporter's bank the right to deal with the documents in any way it thinks fit to ensure repayment. By negotiating, the bank is in fact buying the bill of exchange and documents from the exporter and therefore collects the proceeds in its own name. The advance is therefore for 100% of the bill amount.

- If the bank agrees to the facility, it will immediately credit the customer's account with the full face value.

- The exporter's bank then sends the collection to the collecting/presenting bank in the usual way. The standard customer authority gives the exporter's bank the right to vary the customer's instructions on the collection order, should it so wish. Generally speaking, the collecting bank will wish to include protest instructions, even if the customer prefers not to do so. As far as the collecting/presenting bank is concerned, the collection is received and dealt with in the same way as any other documentary collection. The exporter's bank completes its own standard collection order, so the collecting/presenting bank will not know of the negotiation facility.

- On receipt of the proceeds, the negotiation account is cleared. Interest is calculated, and then debited to the customer's account.

- If the bill of exchange is dishonoured, the exporter's bank has right against: the exporter, since this finance is with recourse; the drawee, provided he has accepted the bill of exchange; the goods provided they have not been released to the importer. Under a D/P collection, goods will not have been released, but under D/A terms, the goods will have been released to the importer on acceptance.

- The bank's basic considerations when asked to grant a negotiation facility are: creditworthiness of exporter; creditworthiness of importer; existence of exchange control regulations in importer's country; sale ability of goods if on D/P terms; whether the terms are D/P or D/A, D/P being much more secure; whether credit insurance is held, and if so whether it is assigned to the bank; whether there is an agreement for acceptance on D/A terms; whether the documents give full control of the goods.

2. Facilities Available in Connection with Documentary Credits

A. *Negotiation of Bills of Exchange Drawn under Documentary Credits*

This facility operates in the same way as in the case of Documentary Collection except that the bill of exchange is always drawn on the issuing bank. Provided the issuing bank is sound and the credit terms have been fulfilled, the bill will be accepted by the issuing bank and honoured at maturity. Thus the exporter's bank will look upon such facilities as being risk free.

Such finance named as negotiation or bill purchase is with recourse, unless the lending bank has confirmed the credit. When the credit is confirmed by the negotiating bank before, recourse can never be effected even if the issuing bank fails to accept or honour the bill for reasons other than discrepancies being found in the documents.

B. *Acceptance and Discount of Bills of Exchange Drawn under Documentary Credits*

Bills of exchange which have been drawn on and accepted by banks and are drawn for a period of less than 180 days are called eligible bills. The rates of discount are much lower on eligible bills. The terms "fine rate of interest" is used to indicate that a bill is an eligible one which qualifies for lower rates.

The exporters should remember that it may be possible to persuade the importer to pay the costs of negotiating/discounting bills of exchange drawn under documentary credits. If such an agreement is made, the details should be incorporated in the credit at the time of issue.

C. *Packing Loan*

Packing loan is a pre-shipment financing facility. The exporter can obtain a packing loan from a bank when it receives the letter of credit issued in its favour. The money required is to finance the business between the commencement of the manufacturing process and the dispatch of goods. Usually, the finance available will not exceed 90% of the L/C amount. After shipment, the exporter can present the documents to a bank for negotiation, and repay the packing loan.

For the security, the lending bank must keep in touch with the exporter, and urge them to dispatch the goods and present document in time. If the exporter fails to present documents after the expiry of the L/C, the bank will ask them to repay according to the terms of the loan agreement.

D. *Assignment of the Proceeds of a Documentary Credit*

This is a means of obtaining pre-shipment credit with the co-operation of the exporter's bank. The exporter's bank, acting on its customer's authority, issues a letter of comfort to the exporter's local suppliers indicating:

- that the exporter is the beneficiary of a documentary credit; and
- that the bank is authorized to pay, direct to the supplier, a certain sum from the proceeds (if any) of the credit when received.

Banks will always accept their customer's application for assignment, but will not issue such a letter.

E. *Red Clause Documentary Credits as a Form of Pre-Shipment Finance*

A red clause documentary credit contains an instruction from the issuing bank for the advising bank to make an advance to the beneficiary prior to shipment. When the exporter subsequently presents the documents, the amount of the advance and interest will be deducted from the full amount of the credit.

Such advance can be in two forms:

- conditional, whereby the beneficiary must sign an undertaking to use the money to help him assemble the goods referred to in the credit; or
- unconditional, whereby the beneficiary merely signs a receipt for the money.

In either case, the issuing bank will be responsible for reimbursing the advising bank if the exporter should subsequently fail to present the documents called for under the credit. (The issuing bank will then seek reimbursement from its customer, the applicant.)

In this case, the bank releases its facilities at the request of the issuing bank instead of the beneficiary itself, not as in the case of packing loan.

F. *Usance Drafts Paid at Sight*

In some cases of usance letters of credit, the beneficiary (the exporter) can be paid at sight, although it issues usance draft (s). The discounting fee and charges are borne by the importer. Actually it is a finance facility offered by the L/C issuing bank or paying bank to the importer.

Usually, the terms of L/C for this facility are:

- Usance draft (s) negotiated at sight, discounted by the issuing bank, the discounting and acceptance charges are for account of the applicant. Or
- Usance draft (s) discounted by the negotiating bank, interest is borne by the buyer.

3. Other Facilities

A. *Loan or Overdraft to be Repaid from the Export Proceeds*

These facilities can be secured or unsecured, and the bank's considerations are the ones which apply to any lending proposition.

The customer benefits of an overdraft facility are its simplicity and flexibility. Interest is charged only on the debt balances actually outstanding on a day-to-day basis.

B. *Loan or Overdraft Secured by an Assignment of a Credit Insurance Policy*

This is a traditional type of facility which has formed the basis of many of the specialist schemes in Short Term Export Finance Schemes below.

The exporter signs a standard assignment form which instructs the insurance company to allow the lending bank to take over the exporter's rights to:

- any claim against the policy; or
- any claim against a particular buyer; or
- any claim against any buyer from a particular country.

This assignment is useful backing to the bank if an exporter cannot repay because a particular buyer has defaulted. The bank will be able to stand in the shoes of the exporter, and eventually will be able to receive the proceeds (if any) of the claim from the insurance company.

Some students mistakenly believe that this form of security is absolutely safe, but this is not the case. The bank's rights are no better than the exporter's. Thus, if the exporter's claim is refused by the insurance company, then the bank's assignment will be worthless.

An exporter's claim under his credit insurance could fail because:

- The exporter did not fulfill the commercial contract;
- The exporter did not declare the shipment and pay the premium; and
- The amount outstanding from the buyer who defaulted exceeded the credit insurance limit for that buyer.

Nevertheless, for a commercially reliable exporter, such an assignment is a very useful security for a lending bank, and some banks would rather charge a slightly lower rate of interest than meet an ordinary unsecured overdraft.

V. Incoterms 2000

1. Purpose and Scope of Incoterms

The purpose of Incoterms is to provide a set of international rules for the interpretation of the most commonly used trade terms in foreign trade. Thus, the uncertainties of different interpretations of such terms in different countries can be avoided or at least reduced to a considerable degree.

Frequently, parties to a contract are unaware of the different trading practices in their respective countries. This can give rise to misunderstandings, disputes and litigation, with all the waste of time and money that this entails. In order to remedy these problems, the International Chamber of Commerce first published in 1936 a set of international rules for the interpretation of trade terms. These rules were known as "Incoterms 1936". Amendments and additions were later made in 1953, 1967, 1976, 1980, 1990 and presently in 2000 in order to bring the rules in line with current international trade practices.

It should be stressed that the scope of Incoterms is limited to matters relating to the rights and obligations of the parties to the contract of sale with respect to the delivery of goods sold (in the sense of "tangibles", not including "intangibles" such as computer software).

It appears that two particular misconceptions about Incoterms are very common. First, Incoterms are frequently misunderstood as applying to the contract of carriage rather than to the contract of sale. Second, they are sometimes wrongly assumed to provide for all the duties which parties may wish to include in a contract of sale.

As has always been underlined by ICC, Incoterms deal only with the relation between sellers and buyers under the contract of sale, and, moreover, only do so in some very distinct respects.

While it is essential for exporters and importers to consider the very practical relationship between the various contracts needed to perform an international sales transaction where not only the contract of sale is required, but also contracts of carriage, insurance and financing, Incoterms relate to only one of these contracts, namely the contracts of sale.

Nevertheless, the parties' agreement to use a particular Incoterm would necessarily have implications for the other contracts. To mention a few examples, a seller having agreed to a CFR or CIF contract cannot perform such a contract by any other mode of transport than carriage by sea, since under these terms he must present a bill of lading or other maritime document to the buyer, which is simply not possible if other modes of transport are used. Furthermore, the document required under a documentary credit would necessarily depend upon the means of transport intended to be used.

Further, they deal with the obligations to clear the goods for export and import, the packing of the goods, the buyer's obligation to take delivery as well as the obligation to provide proof that the respective obligations have been duly fulfilled. Although Incoterms are extremely important for the implementation of the contract of sale, a great number of problems which may occur in such a contract are not dealt with at all, like transfer of ownership and other property rights, breaches of contract and the consequences following from such breaches as well as exemptions from liability in certain situations. It should be stressed that Incoterms are not intended to replace such contract terms that are needed for a complete contract of sale either by the incorporation of standard terms or by individually negotiated terms.

Generally, Incoterms do not deal with the consequences of breach of contract and any exemptions from liability owing to various impediments. These questions must be resolved by other stipulations in the contract of sale and the applicable law.

Incoterms have always been primarily intended for use where goods are sold for delivery across national boundaries, hence, international commercial terms. However, Incoterms are in practice at times also incorporated into contracts for the sale of goods within pure domestic markets.

2. Structure of Incoterms

In 1990, for ease of understanding, the terms were grouped in four basically different categories: namely starting with the term whereby the seller only makes the goods available to the buyer at the seller's own premises (the "E" -term Ex works); followed by the second group whereby the seller is called upon to deliver the goods to a carrier appointed by the buyer (the "F" -terms FCA, FAS and FOB); continuing with the "C" -terms where the seller has to contract for carriage, but without assuming the risk of loss of or damage to the goods (CFR, CIF, CPT and CIP); and, finally, the "D" -terms whereby the seller has to bear all costs and risks to bring the goods to the place of destination (DAF, DES, DEQ, DDU and DDP). The following chart sets out this classification of the trade terms.

Group E	EXW, Ex Works (…named place)	Departure
Group F	FCA, Free Carrier (…named place)	Main Carriage Unpaid
	FAS, Free Alongside Ship (…named port of shipment)	
	FOB, Free On Board (…named port of shipment)	
Group C	CFR, Cost and Freight (…named port of destination)	Main Carriage Paid
	CIF, Cost, Insurance and Freight (…named port of destination)	
	CPT, Carriage Paid To (…named place of destination)	
	CIP, Carriage and Insurance Paid To (…named place of destination)	
Group D	DAF, Delivered At Frontier (…named place)	Arrival
	DES, Delivered Ex Ship (…named port of destination)	
	DEQ, Delivered Ex Quay (…named port of destination)	
	DDU, Delivered Duty Unpaid (…named place of destination)	
	DDP, Delivered Duty Paid (…named place of destination)	

Further, in the 1990 revision of Incoterms, the clauses dealing with the seller's obligation to provide proof of delivery permitted a replacement of paper documentation by EDI messages provided the parties had agreed to communicate electronically. Needless to say, efforts are constantly made to improve upon the drafting and presentation of Incoterms in order to facilitate their practical implementation.

Appendix: Customs and Practice of International Trade

1. UCP 600

A. Introduction

UCP 600 are the latest revision of the Uniform Customs and Practice that govern the operation of letters of credit. UCP 600 comes into effect on 01 July 2007.

In May 2003, the International Chamber of Commerce authorized the ICC Commission on Banking Technique and Practice (Banking Commission) to begin a revision of the Uniform Customs and Practice for Documentary Credits, ICC Publication 500.

As with other revisions, the general objective was to address developments in the banking, transport and insurance industries. Additionally, there was a need to look at the language and style used in the UCP to remove wording that could lead to inconsistent application and interpretation.

When work on the revision started, a number of global surveys indicated that, because of discrepancies, approximately 70% of documents presented under letters of credit were being rejected on first presentation. This obviously had, and continues to have, a negative effect on the letter of credit being seen as a means of payment and, if unchecked, could have serious implications for maintaining or increasing its market share as a recognized means of settlement in international trade. The introduction by banks of a discrepancy fee has highlighted the importance of this issue, especially when the underlying discrepancies have been found to be dubious or unsound. Whilst the number of cases involving litigation has not grown during the lifetime of UCP 500, the introduction of the ICC's Documentary Credit Dispute Resolution Expertise Rules (DOCDEX) in October 1997 (subsequently revised in March 2002) has resulted in more than 60 cases being decided. One of the structural changes to the UCP is the introduction of articles covering definitions (article 2) and interpretations (article 3). In providing definitions of roles played by banks and the meaning of specific terms and events, UCP 600 avoids the necessity of repetitive text to explain their interpretation and application. Similarly, the article covering interpretations aims to take the ambiguity out of vague or unclear language that appears in letters of credit and to provide a definitive elucidation of other characteristics of the UCP or the credit.

This revision of the UCP represents the culmination of over three years of extensive analysis, review, debate and compromise amongst the various members of the Drafting Group, the members of the Banking Commission and the respective ICC national committees. Valuable comment has also been received from the ICC Commission on Transport and Logistics, the Commission on Commercial Law and Practice and the Committee on Insurance.

B. *Some of the Main Provisions*

Article 2 Definitions For the purpose of these rules:

Advising bank means the bank that advises the credit at the request of the issuing bank.

Applicant means the party on whose request the credit is issued.

Banking day means a day on which a bank is regularly open at the place at which an act subject to these rules is to be performed.

Beneficiary means the party in whose favour a credit is issued.

Complying presentation means a presentation that is in accordance with the terms and conditions of the credit, the applicable provisions of these rules and international standard banking practice.

Confirmation means a definite undertaking of the confirming bank, in addition to that of the issuing bank, to honour or negotiate a complying presentation.

Confirming bank means the bank that adds its confirmation to a credit upon the issuing bank's authorization or request.

Credit means any arrangement, however named or described, that is irrevocable and thereby constitutes a definite undertaking of the issuing bank to honour a complying presentation.

Honour means: a. to pay at sight if the credit is available by sight payment; b. to incur a deferred payment undertaking and pay at maturity if the credit is available by deferred payment; c. to accept a bill of exchange ("draft") drawn by the beneficiary and pay at maturity if the credit is available by acceptance.

Issuing bank means the bank that issues a credit at the request of an applicant or on its own behalf.

Negotiation means the purchase by the nominated bank of drafts (drawn on a bank other than the nominated bank) and/or documents under a complying presentation, by advancing or agreeing to advance funds to the beneficiary on or before the banking day on which reimbursement is due to the nominated bank.

Nominated Bank means the bank with which the credit is available or any bank in the case of a credit available with any bank.

Presentation means either the delivery of documents under a credit to the issuing bank or nominated bank or the documents so delivered.

Article 4 Credits v. Contracts

a. A credit by its nature is a separate transaction from the sale or other contract on which it may be based. Banks are in no way concerned with or bound by such contract, even if any reference whatsoever to it is included in the credit. Consequently, the undertaking of a bank to honour, to negotiate or to fulfil any other obligation under the credit is not subject to claims or defences by the applicant resulting from its relationships with the issuing bank or the beneficiary.

A beneficiary can in no case avail itself of the contractual relationships existing between banks or between the applicant and the issuing bank.

b. An issuing bank should discourage any attempt by the applicant to include, as an integral part of the credit, copies of the underlying contract, proforma invoice and the like.

Article 5 Documents v. Goods, Services or Performance

Banks deal with documents and not with goods, services or performance to which the documents may relate.

Article 6 Availability, Expiry Date and Place for Presentation

a. A credit must state the bank with which it is available or whether it is available with any bank. A credit available with a nominated bank is also available with the issuing bank.

b. A credit must state whether it is available by sight payment, deferred payment, acceptance or negotiation.

c. A credit must not be issued available by a draft drawn on the applicant.

d. (i) A credit must state an expiry date for presentation. An expiry date stated for honour or negotiation will be deemed to be an expiry date for presentation. (ii) The place of the bank with which the credit is available is the place for presentation. The place for presentation under a credit available with any bank is that of any bank. A place for presentation other than that of the issuing bank is in addition to the place of the issuing bank.

e. Except as provided in sub-article 29 (a), a presentation by or on behalf of the beneficiary must be made on or before the expiry date.

Article 7 Issuing Bank Undertaking

a. Provided that the stipulated documents are presented to the nominated bank or to the issuing bank and that they constitute a complying presentation, the issuing bank must honour if the credit is available by: i. sight payment, deferred payment or acceptance with the issuing bank; ii. sight payment with a nominated bank and that nominated bank does not pay; iii. deferred payment with a nominated bank and that nominated bank does not incur its deferred payment undertaking or, having incurred its deferred payment undertaking, does not pay at maturity; iv. acceptance with a nominated bank and that nominated bank does not accept a draft drawn on it or, having accepted a draft drawn on it, does not pay at maturity; v. negotiation with a nominated bank and that nominated bank does not negotiate.

b. An issuing bank is irrevocably bound to honour as of the time it issues the credit.

c. An issuing bank undertakes to reimburse a nominated bank that has honoured or negotiated a complying presentation and forwarded the documents to the issuing bank. Reimbursement for the amount of a complying presentation under a credit available by acceptance or deferred payment is due at maturity, whether or not the nominated bank prepaid or purchased before maturity. An issuing bank's undertaking to reimburse a nominated bank is independent of the issuing bank's undertaking to the beneficiary.

Article 8 Confirming Bank Undertaking

a. Provided that the stipulated documents are presented to the confirming bank or to any other nominated bank and that they constitute a complying presentation, the confirming bank must: i. honour, if the credit is available by (a) sight payment, deferred payment or acceptance with the confirming bank; (b) sight payment with another nominated bank and that nominated bank does not pay; (c) deferred payment with another nominated bank and that nominated bank does not incur its deferred payment undertaking or, having incurred its deferred payment undertaking, does not pay at maturity; (d) acceptance with another nominated bank and that nominated bank does not accept a draft drawn on it or, having accepted a draft drawn on it, does not pay at maturity; (e) negotiation with another nominated bank and that nominated bank does not negotiate. ii. negotiate, without recourse, if the credit is available by negotiation with the confirming bank.

b. A confirming bank is irrevocably bound to honour or negotiate as of the time it adds its confirmation to the credit.

c. A confirming bank undertakes to reimburse another nominated bank that has honoured or negotiated a complying presentation and forwarded the documents to the confirming bank. Reimbursement for the amount of a complying presentation under a credit available by acceptance or deferred payment is due at maturity, whether or not another nominated bank prepaid or purchased before maturity. A confirming bank's undertaking to reimburse another nominated bank is independent of the confirming bank's undertaking to the beneficiary.

d. If a bank is authorized or requested by the issuing bank to confirm a credit but is not prepared to do so, it must inform the issuing bank without delay and may advise the credit without confirmation.

Article 9 Advising of Credits and Amendments

a. A credit and any amendment may be advised to a beneficiary through an advising bank. An advising bank that is not a confirming bank advises the credit and any amendment without any undertaking to honour or negotiate.

b. By advising the credit or amendment, the advising bank signifies that it has satisfied itself as to the apparent authenticity of the credit or amendment and that the advice accurately reflects the terms and conditions of the credit or amendment received.

c. An advising bank may utilize the services of another bank ("second advising bank") to advise the credit and any amendment to the beneficiary. By advising the credit or amendment, the second advising bank signifies that it has satisfied itself as to the apparent authenticity of the advice it has received and that the advice accurately reflects the terms and conditions of the credit or amendment received.

d. A bank utilizing the services of an advising bank or second advising bank to advise a credit must use the same bank to advise any amendment thereto.

e. If a bank is requested to advise a credit or amendment but selects not to do so, it must so inform, without delay, the bank from which the credit, amendment or advice has been received.

f. If a bank is requested to advise a credit or amendment but cannot satisfy itself as to the apparent authenticity of the credit, the amendment or the advice, it must so inform, without delay, the bank from which the instructions appear to have been received. If the advising bank or second advising bank selects nonetheless to advise the credit or amendment, it must inform the beneficiary or second advising bank that it has not been able to satisfy itself as to the apparent authenticity of the credit, the amendment or the advice.

Article 10 Amendments

a. Except as otherwise provided by article 38, a credit can neither be amended nor cancelled without the agreement of the issuing bank, the confirming bank, if any, and the beneficiary. b. An issuing bank is irrevocably bound by an amendment as of the time it issues the amendment. A confirming bank may extend its confirmation to an amendment and will be irrevocably bound as of the time it advises the amendment. A confirming bank may, however, choose to advise an amendment without extending its confirmation and, if so, it must inform the issuing bank without delay and inform the beneficiary in its advice.

c. The terms and conditions of the original credit (or a credit incorporating previously accepted amendments) will remain in force for the beneficiary until the beneficiary communicates its acceptance of the amendment to the bank that advised such amendment. The beneficiary should give notification of acceptance or rejection of an amendment. If the beneficiary fails to give such notification, a presentation that complies with the credit and to any not yet accepted amendment will be deemed to be notification of acceptance by the beneficiary of such amendment. As of that moment the credit will be amended.

d. A bank that advises an amendment should inform the bank from which it received the amendment of any notification of acceptance or rejection.

e. Partial acceptance of an amendment is not allowed and will be deemed to be notification of rejection of the amendment.

f. A provision in an amendment to the effect that the amendment shall enter into force unless rejected by the beneficiary within a certain time shall be disregarded.

Article 11 Teletransmitted and Pre-Advised Credits and Amendments

a. An authenticated teletransmission of a credit or amendment will be deemed to be the operative credit or amendment, and any subsequent mail confirmation shall be disregarded. If a teletransmission states "full details to follow" (or words of similar effect), or states that the mail confirmation is to be the operative credit or amendment, then the teletransmission will not be deemed to be the operative credit or amendment. The issuing bank must then issue the operative credit or amendment without delay in terms not inconsistent with the teletransmission.

b. A preliminary advice of the issuance of a credit or amendment ("pre-advice") shall only be sent if the issuing bank is prepared to issue the operative credit or amendment. An issuing bank that sends a pre-advice is irrevocably committed to issue the operative credit or amendment, without delay, in terms not inconsistent with the pre-advice.

Article 12 Nomination

a. Unless a nominated bank is the confirming bank, an authorization to honour or negotiate does not impose any obligation on that nominated bank to honour or negotiate, except when expressly agreed to by that nominated bank and so communicated to the beneficiary.

b. By nominating a bank to accept a draft or incur a deferred payment undertaking, an issuing bank authorizes that nominated bank to prepay or purchase a draft accepted or a deferred payment undertaking incurred by that nominated bank.

c. Receipt or examination and forwarding of documents by a nominated bank that is not a confirming bank does not make that nominated bank liable to honour or negotiate, nor does it constitute honour or negotiation.

Article 13 Bank-to-Bank Reimbursement Arrangements

a. If a credit states that reimbursement is to be obtained by a nominated bank ("claiming bank") claiming on another party ("reimbursing bank"), the credit must state if the reimbursement is subject to the ICC rules for bank-to-bank reimbursements in effect on the date of issuance of the credit.

b. If a credit does not state that reimbursement is subject to the ICC rules for bank-to-bank reimbursements, the following apply: i. An issuing bank must provide a reimbursing bank with a reimbursement authorization that conforms with the availability stated in the credit. The reimbursement authorization should not be subject to an expiry date. ii. A claiming bank shall not be required to supply a reimbursing bank with a certificate of compliance with the terms and conditions of the credit. iii. An issuing bank will be responsible for any loss of interest, together with any expenses incurred, if reimbursement is not provided on first demand by a reimbursing bank in accordance with the terms and conditions of the credit. iv. A reimbursing bank's charges are for the account of the issuing bank. However, if the charges are for the account of the beneficiary, it is the responsibility of an issuing bank to so indicate in the credit and in the reimbursement authorization. If a reimbursing bank's charges are for the account of the beneficiary, they shall be deducted from the amount due to a claiming bank when reimbursement is made. If no reimbursement is made, the reimbursing bank's charges remain the obligation of the issuing bank. c. An issuing bank is not relieved of any of its obligations to provide reimbursement if reimbursement is not made by a reimbursing bank on first demand.

Article 15 Complying Presentation

a. When an issuing bank determines that a presentation is complying, it must honour.

b. When a confirming bank determines that a presentation is complying, it must honour or negotiate and forward the documents to the issuing bank.

c. When a nominated bank determines that a presentation is complying and honours or negotiates, it must forward the documents to the confirming bank or issuing bank.

Article 16 Discrepant Documents, Waiver and Notice

a. When a nominated bank acting on its nomination, a confirming bank, if any, or the issuing bank determines that a presentation does not comply, it may refuse to honour or negotiate.

b. When an issuing bank determines that a presentation does not comply, it may in its sole judgement approach the applicant for a waiver of the discrepancies. This does not, however, extend the period mentioned in sub-article 14 (b).

c. When a nominated bank acting on its nomination, a confirming bank, if any, or the issuing bank decides to refuse to honour or negotiate, it must give a single notice to that effect to the presenter. The notice must state: i. that the bank is refusing to honour or negotiate; and ii. each discrepancy in respect of which the bank refuses to honour or negotiate; and iii. a) that the bank is holding the documents pending further instructions from the presenter; orb) that the issuing bank is holding the documents until it receives a waiver from the applicant and agrees to accept it, or receives further instructions from the presenter prior to agreeing to accept a waiver; or c) that the bank is returning the documents; or d) that the bank is acting in accordance with instructions previously received from the presenter.

d. The notice required in sub-article 16 (c) must be given by telecommunication or, if that is not possible, by other expeditious means no later than the close of the fifth banking day following the day of presentation.

e. A nominated bank acting on its nomination, a confirming bank, if any, or the issuing bank may, after providing notice required by sub-article 16 (c) (iii) (a) or (b), return the documents to the presenter at any time.

f. If an issuing bank or a confirming bank fails to act in accordance with the provisions of this article, it shall be precluded from claiming that the documents do not constitute a complying presentation.

g. When an issuing bank refuses to honour or a confirming bank refuses to honour or negotiate and has given notice to that effect in accordance with this article, it shall then be entitled to claim a refund, with interest, of any reimbursement made.

Article 18 Commercial Invoice

a. A commercial invoice: i. must appear to have been issued by the beneficiary (except as provided in article 38); ii. must be made out in the name of the applicant (except as provided in sub-article 38 (g)); iii. must be made out in the same currency as the credit; and iv. need not be signed.

b. A nominated bank acting on its nomination, a confirming bank, if any, or the issuing bank may accept a commercial invoice issued for an amount in excess of the amount permitted by the credit, and its decision will be binding upon all parties, provided the bank in question has not honoured or negotiated for an amount in excess of that permitted by the credit.

c. The description of the goods, services or performance in a commercial invoice must correspond with that appearing in the credit.

Article 19 Transport Document Covering at Least Two Different Modes of Transport

a. A transport document covering at least two different modes of transport (multimodal or combined transport document), however named, must appear to: i. indicate the name of the carrier and be signed by: the carrier or a named agent for or on behalf of the carrier, or the master or a named agent for or on behalf of the master. Any signature by the carrier, master or agent must be identified as that of the carrier, master or agent.

Any signature by an agent must indicate whether the agent has signed for or on behalf of the carrier or for or on behalf of the master. ii. indicate that the goods have been dispatched, taken in charge or shipped on board at the place stated in the credit, by: pre-printed wording, or a stamp or notation indicating the date on which the goods have been dispatched, taken in charge or shipped on board.

The date of issuance of the transport document will be deemed to be the date of dispatch, taking in charge or shipped on board, and the date of shipment. However, if the transport document indicates, by stamp or notation, a date of dispatch, taking in charge or shipped on board, this date will be deemed to be the date of shipment. iii. indicate the place of dispatch, taking in charge or shipment and the place of final destination stated in the credit, even if (a). the transport document states, in addition, a different place of dispatch, taking in charge or shipment or place of final destination, (b) the transport document contains the indication "intended" or similar qualification in relation to the vessel, port of loading or port of discharge. iv. be the sole original transport document or, if issued in more than one original, be the full set as indicated on the transport document. v. contain terms and conditions of carriage or make reference to another source containing the terms and conditions of carriage (short form or blank back transport document). Contents of terms and conditions of carriage will not be examined. vi. contain no indication that it is subject to a charter party.

b. For the purpose of this article, transhipment means unloading from one means of conveyance and reloading to another means of conveyance (whether or not in different modes of transport) during the carriage from the place of dispatch, taking in charge or shipment to the place of final destination stated in the credit.

c. (i) A transport document may indicate that the goods will or may be transhipped provided that the entire carriage is covered by one and the same transport document. (ii) A transport document indicating that transhipment will or may take place is acceptable, even if the credit prohibits transhipment.

Article 20 Bill of Lading

a. A bill of lading, however named, must appear to:

i. indicate the name of the carrier and be signed by: the carrier or a named agent for or on behalf of the carrier, or the master or a named agent for or on behalf of the master. Any signature by the carrier, master or agent must be identified as that of the carrier, master or agent. Any signature by an agent must indicate whether the agent has signed for or on behalf of the carrier or for or on behalf of the master. ii. indicate that the goods have been shipped on board a named vessel at the port of loading stated in the credit by: pre-printed wording, or an on board notation indicating the date on which the goods have been shipped on board. The date of issuance of the bill of lading will be deemed to be the date of shipment unless the bill of lading contains an on board notation indicating the date of shipment, in which case the date stated in the on board notation will be deemed to be the date of shipment. If the bill of lading contains the indication "intended vessel" or similar qualification in relation to the name of the vessel, an on board notation indicating the date of shipment and the name of the actual vessel is required. iii. indicate shipment from the port of loading to the port of discharge stated in the credit. If the bill of lading does not indicate the port of loading stated in the credit as the port of loading, or if it contains the indication "intended" or similar qualification in relation to the port of loading, an on board notation indicating the port of loading as stated in the credit, the date of shipment and the name of the vessel is required.

This provision applies even when loading on board or shipment on a named vessel is indicated by pre-printed wording on the bill of lading. iv. be the sole original bill of lading or, if issued in more than one original, be the full set as indicated on the bill of lading. v. contain terms and conditions of carriage or make reference to another source containing the terms and conditions of carriage (short form or blank back bill of lading). Contents of terms and conditions of carriage will not be examined. vi. contain no indication that it is subject to a charter party.

b. For the purpose of this article, transhipment means unloading from one vessel and reloading to another vessel during the carriage from the port of loading to the port of discharge stated in the credit.

c. (i) A bill of lading may indicate that the goods will or may be transhipped provided that the entire carriage is covered by one and the same bill of lading. (ii) A bill of lading indicating that transhipment will or may take place is acceptable, even if the credit prohibits transhipment, if the goods have been shipped in a container, trailer or LASH barge as evidenced by the bill of lading.

d. Clauses in a bill of lading stating that the carrier reserves the right to tranship will be disregarded.

Article 27 Clean Transport Document

A bank will only accept a clean transport document. A clean transport document is one bearing no clause or notation expressly declaring a defective condition of the goods or their packaging. The word "clean" need not appear on a transport document, even if a credit has a requirement for that transport document to be "clean" on board.

Article 29

a. If the expiry date of a credit or the last day for presentation falls on a day when the bank to which presentation is to be made is closed for reasons other than those referred to in article 36, the expiry date or the last day for presentation, as the case may be, will be extended to the first following banking day.

b. If presentation is made on the first following banking day, a nominated bank must provide the issuing bank or confirming bank with a statement on its covering schedule that the presentation was made within the time limits extended in accordance with sub-article 29 (a).

c. The latest date for shipment will not be extended as a result of sub-article 29 (a).

Article 38 Transferable Credits

a. A bank is under no obligation to transfer a credit except to the extent and in the manner expressly consented to by that bank.

b. For the purpose of this article: Transferable credit means a credit that specifically states it is "transferable" . A transferable credit may be made available in whole or in part to another beneficiary ("second beneficiary") at the request of the beneficiary ("first beneficiary"). Transferring bank means a nominated bank that transfers the credit or, in a credit available with any bank, a bank that is specifically authorized by the issuing bank to transfer and that transfers the credit. An issuing bank may be a transferring bank.

Transferred credit means a credit that has been made available by the transferring bank to a second beneficiary.

c. Unless otherwise agreed at the time of transfer, all charges (such as commissions, fees, costs or expenses) incurred in respect of a transfer must be paid by the first beneficiary.

d. A credit may be transferred in part to more than one second beneficiary provided partial drawings or shipments are allowed. A transferred credit cannot be transferred at the request of a second beneficiary to any subsequent beneficiary. The first beneficiary is not considered to be a subsequent beneficiary.

e. Any request for transfer must indicate if and under what conditions amendments may be advised to the second beneficiary. The transferred credit must clearly indicate those conditions.

f. If a credit is transferred to more than one second beneficiary, rejection of an amendment by one or more second beneficiary does not invalidate the acceptance by any other second beneficiary, with respect to which the transferred credit will be amended accordingly. For any second beneficiary that rejected the amendment, the transferred credit will remain unamended.

g. The transferred credit must accurately reflect the terms and conditions of the credit, including confirmation, if any, with the exception of: the amount of the credit; any unit price stated therein; the expiry date; the period for presentation, or the latest shipment date or given period for shipment, any or all of which may be reduced or curtailed.

The percentage for which insurance cover must be effected may be increased to provide the amount of cover stipulated in the credit or these articles. The name of the first beneficiary may be substituted for that of the applicant in the credit.

If the name of the applicant is specifically required by the credit to appear in any document other than the invoice, such requirement must be reflected in the transferred credit.

h. The first beneficiary has the right to substitute its own invoice and draft, if any, for those of a second beneficiary for an amount not in excess of that stipulated in the credit, and upon such substitution the first beneficiary can draw under the credit for the difference, if any, between its invoice and the invoice of a second beneficiary.

i. If the first beneficiary is to present its own invoice and draft, if any, but fails to do so on first demand, or if the invoices presented by the first beneficiary create discrepancies that did not exist in the presentation made by the second beneficiary and the first beneficiary fails to correct them on first demand, the transferring bank has the right to present the documents as received from the second beneficiary to the issuing bank, without further responsibility to the first beneficiary.

j. The first beneficiary may, in its request for transfer, indicate that honour or negotiation is to be effected to a second beneficiary at the place to which the credit has been transferred, up to and including the expiry date of the credit. This is without prejudice to the right of the first beneficiary in accordance with sub-article 38 (h).

k. Presentation of documents by or on behalf of a second beneficiary must be made to the transferring bank.

2. URC522

A. *Introduction*

For many years, this practical set of rules help banks, buyers and sellers in their collections process. The first revision coming out in 1971 and the newest revision becoming effective from January 1st, 1996, it describes the conditions governing collections, including those for the presentation, payment and acceptance terms. The articles also specify the responsibility of the bank regarding protest, case of need and actions to protect the merchandise.

B. *Some of the Main Provisions*

Article 4:

The principal should insert the complete address of the drawee in the collection order. If the complete address is not shown, the collecting bank may try and ascertain the information, but it is under no obligation to do so. Any loss or delay caused by an incomplete drawee's address will rest with the principal. In practice the remitting bank should check that the full address appears on the collection order.

Article 7:

The collection order should indicate D/A or D/P. In the absence of such a statement, documents can only be released on payment.

Articles 9 and 10:

These two articles state that bank will act in good faith and exercise reasonable care. Banks must check that they appear to have received the documents which are specified in the collection order, but they have no obligation to examine the documents any further.

Article 11:

Where the principal specifies a collecting bank, the remitting bank will use that bank. Where no collecting bank is specified, the remitting bank will choose a collecting bank. In practice, it is better for the choice to be left to the remitting bank. Not all overseas banks can be relied upon, and it is much safer for the remitting bank to select one of the collecting overseas banks, which it knows will carry out instructions properly.

Articles 12 and 14:

Banks have no liability for any delay or loss caused by postal or telecommunication failure.

Article 21:

A collection order must state whether charges and interest can be waived if refused.

Article 24:

The collection order should give specific instructions about whether or not to protest in the event of non-payment or non-acceptance. In the absence of such instructions no protest need to be made. Any legal fees incurred by the presenting bank in a protest will be charged to the remitting bank who will debit the principal's account.

Article 25:

Where the collection order indicates a case of need, an agent of the exporter who is resident in the importer's country, his powers must be clearly stated. In the absence of such indication banks will not accept any instruction from the case of need.

C. *Some Official Comments of the ICC Working Party for Uniform Rules for Collections*

Article 1:

As indicated, these Rules apply where they are shown to be incorporated into the text of the Collection Instruction.

Banks understand the distinction between a collection which is made up of the actual documents themselves and the instruction from the party who sends the collection. Every collection must be accompanied by such a collection instruction and the application of these Rules must be shown on this document.

In order that all parties are aware of the possibility that these Rules and collection instructions can be overridden by requirements of individual countries, the Rules should make reference to national, state and /or local law.

Sub Article 1b is stated as simply and as unambiguously as possible, to dispel any instruction related to a collection is received, an obligation is automatically imposed on the recipient of the collection or instruction. This is not so and the simplicity of sub-Article 1b is intended to this.

Sub Article 1c makes it obligatory for the bank that receives the collection to advise the sender if it is unable either to handle a collection as a whole or to handle any instruction. Failure to carry out this obligation may jeopardize the position of the bank subsequently and, therefore, this requirement must not be forgotten. It is important to stress that once the bank sends out an advice that it is unable to handle the collection or cannot carry out an instruction, it may at its discretion return the documents to the sender without any further action.

Article 2:

The layout of sub-Article 2a is designed to show clearly the various steps in the collection process. It is to be noted that the definition indicates clearly that collections covered by these Rules are those that are handled by banks.

This includes those items where the seller/the principal uses a collection form from his bank as the basis of the collection instruction to send the documents to the buyer's bank, while at the same time a copy of the collection order is sent to his own bank. The collection form is a bank form and should have an indication to show that a) the collection is subject to URC Rules No. 522 , and b) the collection is to be treated by the collecting bank as though it was received from the remitting bank.

Article 3:

The following points should be noted:

In view of the fact that the "principal" has been included as one of the parties it was agreed that a separate definition for the "drawer" is not really necessary.

It has been noted that in sub-Article 3a, the definition of collecting bank appears to exclude the remitting bank. This is not necessarily so as in local collections, the remitting bank may also be the collecting bank and therefore a practical and pragmatic approach should be adopted in this respect in order to facilitate the collection operation.

Although the drawee eventually may become involved in the collection operation he is not one of the initial parties and accordingly the definition of the drawee is shown separately from the other parties.

Article 4:

The principles are:

(a) All collections must have a separate collection instruction attached.

(b) Collecting banks will only be guided by the instructions on the collection instruction itself.

(c) Collecting banks will not look elsewhere for instructions and will not be obliged to examine documents for instructions; no instructions are to be shown on individual documents and if they are, they may be ignored.

Particular mention must be made of sub-Article 4a, the purpose of which was to discourage the imposition of additional responsibilities on the collecting bank by so called "Global Collections".

This term is used to describe the practice prevalent in certain parts of the world where the progress of a collection sent by a bank in, say, the Far East, is to be monitored by, for example, a bank in the US, and the collecting bank receives instructions/queries from the latter bank.

3. ISP98

A. *Introduction*

The International Standby Practices (ISP98 ICC Publication No. 590) reflects generally accepted practice, custom, and usage of standby letters of credit. It provides separate rules for standby letters of credit in the same sense that the Uniform Customs and Practice for Documentary Credits (UCP) and the Uniform Rules for Demand Guarantee (URDG) do for commercial letters of credit and independent bank guarantees.

The formulation of standby letter of credit practices in separate rules evidences the maturity and importance of this financial product. The amounts outstanding of standbys greatly exceed the outstanding amounts of commercial letters of credit. While the standby is associated with the United States where it originated and where it is most widely used, it is truly an international product. Non-U. S. bank outstanding have exceeded those of U. S. banks in the United States alone. Moreover, the standby is used increasingly throughout the world.

For convenience, standbys are commonly classified descriptively (and without operative significance in the application of these Rules) based on their function in the underlying transaction or other factors not necessarily related to the terms and conditions of the standby itself. For example:

- A "Performance Standby" supports an obligation to perform other than to pay money including for the purpose of covering losses arising from a default of the applicant in completion of the underlying transactions.
- An "Advance Payment Standby" supports an obligation to account for an advance payment made by the beneficiary to the applicant.
- A "Bid Bond/Tender Bond Standby" supports an obligation of the applicant to execute a contract if the applicant is awarded a bid.
- A "Counter Standby" supports the issuance of a separate standby or other undertaking by the beneficiary of the counter standby.
- A "Financial Standby" supports an obligation to pay money including any instru-

ment evidencing an obligation to repay borrowed money.

- A "Direct Pay Standby" supports payment when due of an underlying payment obligation typically in connection with a financial standby without regard to a default.
- An "Insurance Standby" supports an insurance or reinsurance obligation of the applicant.
- A "commercial Standby " supports the obligations of an applicant to pay for goods or services in the event of non-payment by other methods.

In the past, many standbys have been issued subject to the UCP even though it was intended for commercial letters of credit. The UCP reinforced the independence and documentary character of the standby. It also provided standards for examination and notice of dishonor and a basis to resist market pressures to embrace troublesome practices such as the issuance of standbys without expiration dates.

Despite these important contributions, it has been apparent that the UCP was not fully applicable. Even the least complex standbys (those calling for presentation of a draft only) pose problems not addressed by the UCP. More complex standbys (those involving longer terms or automatic extensions, transfer on demand, requests that the beneficiary issue its own undertaking to another, and the like) require more specialized rules of practice. The ISP fills these needs.

The ISP differs from the UCP in style and approach because it must receive acceptance not only from bankers and merchants, but also from a broader range of those actively involved in standby law and practice corporate treasurers and credit managers, rating agencies, government agencies and regulators, and indenture trustees as well as their counsel. Because standbys are often intended to be available in the event of disputes or applicant insolvency, their texts are subject to the degree of scrutiny not encountered in the commercial letter of credit context. As a result, the ISP is also written to provide guidance to lawyers and judges in the interpretation of standby practice.

Differences in substance result either from different practices, different problems or the need for more precision. In addition, the ISP proposes basic definitions should the standby permit or require presentation of documents by electronic means. Since standbys infrequently require presentation of negotiable documents, standby practice is currently more conducive to electronic presentations, and the ISP provides definitions and rules encouraging such presentations. The development of SWIFT message types for the ISP is anticipated.

The ISP, like the UCP for commercial letters of credit, simplifies, standardizes, and streamlines the drafting of standbys, and provides clear and widely accepted answers, because standby and commercial practices are fundamentally the same. Even where the rules overlap, however, the ISP is more precise, stating the intent implied in the UCP rule, in order to make the standby more dependable when a drawing or honor is questioned.

Like the UCP and the URDG, the ISP will apply to any independent undertaking issued subject to it. This approach avoids the impractical and often impossible task of identifying and distinguishing standbys from independent guarantees and, in many cases, commercial letters of credit. The choice of which set of rules to select is, therefore, left to the parties as it should be. One may well choose to use the ISP for certain types of standbys, the UCP for others, and the URDG for still others. While the ISP is not intended to be used for dependent undertakings such as accessory guarantees and insurance contracts, it may be useful in some situations in indicating that a particular undertaking which might otherwise be treated as dependent under local law is intended to be independent.

For the ISP to apply to a standby, an undertaking should be made subject to these Rules by including language such as (but not limited to) :

This undertaking is issued subject to the International Standby Practices 1998; or subject to ISP98.

Although the ISP can be varied by the text of a standby, it provides neutral rules acceptable in the majority of situations and a useful starting point for negotiations in other situations. It will save parties (including banks that issue, confirm, or are beneficiaries of standbys) considerable time and expense in negotiating and drafting standby terms.

The ISP is designed to be compatible with the United Nations Convention on Independent Guarantees and Stand-by Letters of Credit (which represents a useful and practical formulation basis for standby and independent guarantee law) and also with local law, whether statutory or judicial, and to embody standby letter of credit practice under that law. If these rules conflict with mandatory law on issues such as assignment of proceeds or transfer by operation of law, applicable law will, of course, control. Nonetheless, most of these issues are rarely addressed by local law and progressive commercial law will often look to the practice as recorded in the ISP for guidance in such situations, especially with respect to cross border undertakings. As a result, it is expected that the ISP will complement local law rather than conflict with it.

The ISP is intended to be used also in arbitration as well as judicial proceedings (such as the export based letter of credit arbitration system developed by the International Center for Letter of Credit Arbitration (ICLOCA) Rules or general commercial ICC arbitration) or with alternative methods of dispute resolution. Such a choice should be made expressly and with appropriate detail. At a minimum, it can be made in connection with the clause relating to ISP98 e. g. This undertaking is issued subject to ISP98, and all disputes arising out of it or related to it are subject to arbitration under ICLOCA Rules (1996).

Although translations of the ISP into other languages are envisioned and will be monitored for integrity, the English text is the official text of the ISP in the event of disputes.

The ISP is drafted as a set of rules intended for use in daily practice. It is not intended to provide introductory information on standbys and their uses.

B. Some Principles

i. Nature of Standbys

- A standby is an irrevocable, independent, documentary, and binding undertaking when issued and need not so state.

- Because a standby is irrevocable, an issuer's obligations under a standby cannot be amended or cancelled by the issuer except as provided in the standby or as consented to by the person against whom the amendment or cancellation is asserted.

- Because a standby is independent, the enforceability of an issuer's obligations under a standby does not depend on:

—the issuer's right or ability to obtain reimbursement from the application;

—the beneficiary's right to obtain reimbursement from the applicant;

—a reference in the standby to any reimbursement agreement or underlying transaction; or

—the issuer's knowledge of performance or breach of any reimbursement agreement or underlying transaction.

- Because a standby is documentary, an issuer's obligations depend on the presentation of documents and an examination of required documents on their face.

- Because a standby or amendment is binding when issued, it is enforceable against an issuer whether or not the applicant authorised its issuance, the issuer received a fee, or the beneficiary received or relied on the standby or the amendment.

ii. Independence of the Issuer-Beneficiary Relationship

An issuer's obligations toward the beneficiary are not affected by the issuer's rights and obligations toward the applicant under any applicable agreement, practice, or law.

iii. Limits to Responsibilities

An issuer is not responsible for:

- performance or breach of any underlying transaction;

- accuracy, genuineness, or effect of any document presented under the standby;

- action or omission of others even if the other person is chosen by the issuer or nominated person; or

- observance of law or practice other than that chosen in the standby or applicable at the place of issuance.

Notes

1. **Usance** [ˈjuːzəns] the period of time allowed by law or commercial practice for the payment of a bill of exchange

2. **Traveller's Letter of Credit**: a letter of credit is issued by a bank to a customer preparing for an extended trip. The customer pays for the letter of credit, which is issued for a specific period of time in the amount purchased. The bank furnishes a list of correspondent banks or its own foreign branches at which drafts are drawn against the letter of credit

3. **Dishonour** [disˈɔnə] refusal by a drawee bank to accept a promissory note, or to pay a cheque or draft, as might happen if the cheque writer's account has insufficient funds. 2. refusal by a check writer or maker to pay a cheque or other negotiable instrument

4. **Vostro account**: "your account"; used by a depository bank to describe an account maintained with it by a bank in a foreign country

5. **Nostro account**: "our" account; an account maintained by a bank with a bank in a foreign currencies of the country in which the monies are held, with the equivalent dollar value listed in another column

6. **Open account**: credit extended that is not supported by a note, mortgage, or other formal written evidence of indebtedness (e. g. , merchandise for which a buyer is billed later)

7. **Acceptance** [əkˈseptəns] a time draft (bill of exchange) on the face of which the drawee has written "accepted" over his signature. The date and place payable are also indicated. The person accepting the draft is known as the acceptor

8. **Protest** [prəˈtest] a written statement by a notary public, or other authorized person, under seal for the purpose of giving formal notice to parties secondarily liable that an instrument has been dishonoured, either by refusal to accept or by refusal to make payment

9. **Notary public**: a person commissioned by a state for a stipulated period to administer certain oaths and to attest and certify documents, thus authorized to "protest" negotiable instruments for non-payment or nonacceptance

10. **Transferable credit**: a documentary credit under which a beneficiary has the right to give instructions to the paying or accepting bank or to any bank entitled to effect negotiations, to make the credit available to one or more third parties

11. **Back-to-Back credit**: two letters of credit with identical documentary requirements, except for a difference in the price of merchandise as shown by the invoice and the draft

12. **Confirmed letter of credit**: a foreign bank wishing to issue a letter of credit to a local concern may request a local bank in the city in which the beneficiary is located to con-

firm this credit to the beneficiary. The purpose of this confirmation is to lend the prestige and responsibility of the local bank to the transaction because the status of the foreign bank may be unknown to the beneficiary. The confirming bank assumes responsibility for the payment of all drafts drawn under the credit and usually charges a fee for doing so.

13. **Recourse** [ri'kɔːs] the rights of a holder in due course of a negotiable instrument to force prior endorsers on the instrument to meet their legal obligations by making the payment of the instrument if dishonored by the maker or acceptor

14. **Standby letter of credit**: a letter of credit or similar arrangement that represents an obligation on the part of the issuing bank to a designated third party (the beneficiary) contingent upon the failure of the issuing bank's customer (account party) to perform under the terms of the underlying contract with the beneficiary, or obligates the bank to guarantee or stand as surety for the benefit of a third party to the extent permitted by law or regulation

15. **Indemnity** [in'demniti] ① *n.* protection against loss, esp. in the form of a promise to pay ②payment for loss or money, goods, etc.

16. **Quasi** ['kwɑːzi (ː)] seeming like

17. **Charter party**: a written contract, usually on a special form, between the owner of a vessel and a charter who rents use of the vessel or a part of its freight space. The contract generally includes the freight rates and the ports involved in the transaction.

18. **Freight forwarder**: an independent business that handles export shipments for compensation or that acts as the shipper's appointed agent

19. **Stamp duty**: ① an actual tax collected ② a tax imposed on the importation, exportation, or consumption of goods, usually of the foreign goods

20. **Certificate of insurance**: a document issued to the insured certifying that insurance has been effected. It contains the same details as an insurance policy except that the version of the provisions of the policy is abbreviated.

21. **Open policy of insurance**: ①an insurance policy that applies to all shipment made by an exporter over a period of time rather than one shipment only. ② an insurance term for a continuous, open-term contract designed to insure automatically all cargo moving at the insured's risk.

22. **Eligible bill**: a negotiable instrument, having met certain requirements, that is eligible for rediscounting at a special rate by member banks of the Federal Reserve System

23. **Negotiation** [niɡəuʃi'eiʃən] the act by which a negotiable instrument is place into circulation, by being physically passed from the original holder to another person

24. **Assignment** [ə'sainmənt] ① the transfer in writing of property title from one individual to another. ② the transfer in writing of the legal right in a policy to another party.

③ the transfer of stock title

25. **Discount** ['diskaunt] ① the amount of money deducted from the face value of a note. ② in foreign exchange, a margin by which the forward rate drops below spot

Questions for discussion

1. What are the essentials of a draft?

2. Please tell the difference between crossed cheque and open cheque?

3. What is the difference between TT and MT?

4. How do you understand "by open account business"?

5. What is the most satisfactory arrangement to the exporter of goods as far as payment is concerned?

6. What's the function of the collection service offered by banks?

7. What's the advantage of a documentary collection to the exporter?

8. Explain the difference between a documentary collection and a clean collection.

9. What responsibilities do the banks take in a documentary collection?

10. What is meant by documents against payment and documents against acceptance?

11. What are the parties involved in a letter of credit arrangement?

12. Describe briefly the procedure in the credit operation?

13. Why is it imperative for a bank to make certain that the documents submitted are in strict compliance with the credit terms?

14. Explain the advantages of a letter of credit for the exporter and for the importer?

15. A bank is not responsible if goods do not conform to documents, what's the bank's responsibility under a letter of credit?

16. Why does a confirmed LC give the beneficiary a double assurance of payment?

17. When is a transferable LC normally used? What is the difference between a transferable letter of credit and back-to-back credit?

18. Most commercial letters of credit are documentary. What documents must be included together with any drafts drawn under the terms of the credit, then?

19. What are functions of the bill of lading?

20. What is the difference between the packing loan and red clause credit?

Part Eight

Securities and Futures Markets

I. Overview

1. Impressive Growth

Following years of dynamic economic growth, China's securities and futures markets have been advancing with an improved market capacity, improved market structure, better legal framework, and diversified market functions. The offering and trading of stocks, listed bonds and close-end securities investment funds are all dematerialized and executed by centralized trading and settlement systems nationwide.

As of June 2006, a total of 1,376 companies had been listed in Shanghai and Shenzhen Stock Exchanges with a total market capitalization of RMB 4,420 billion. **Market capitalization** refers to the total value at market prices of the shares in issue for a company (or a stock market, or a sector of the stock market). The accumulated proceeds of both A-share and B-share offerings amounted to RMB 956 billion. The monthly turnover of June 2006 was RMB 899 billion, with an average daily turnover of RMB 41 billion. Additionally, a total number of 132 Chinese companies had listed H-shares in Hong Kong and other overseas stock exchanges, raising USD 68.9 billion. In 2005, the futures trading volume reached 323 million lots with the turnover amounting to RMB 13,450 billion. More financial derivatives like stock index futures and T-bond futures are expected to emerge, as the first financial futures exchange is now in the pipeline.

There were about 110 securities companies and 183 futures brokerage firms in China. The number of opened securities investment accounts exceeded 75 million, including 0.38 million institutional accounts. 57 funds management companies were managing 257 funds with a total asset of RMB 511 billion. The Social Security Fund, insurance funds and corporate annuities are all permitted to be invested in the securities market.

Meanwhile, a multi-tier trading market for bonds has taken shape in China including on-exchange bond market, inter-bank bond market and over-the-counter (OTC) market. In July 1981, the issuance of T-bonds was resumed in China and six years later, a secondary market for T-bonds was established and thereafter it has been growing rapidly. The inter-bank bond market is the most important platform for block trading of bonds among financial institutions as well as for open market operations by the PBOC. The major participants in the inter-bank bond market are: the PBOC, commercial banks, securities companies, insurance companies, securities investment funds and credit cooperatives. Non-financial institutions may entrust commercial banks with the task to trade on their behalf in the inter-bank bond market. The traded instruments include T-bonds, financial bonds, corporate bonds, convertible bonds, short-term corporate notes and international bonds.

The exchange-traded bond market refers to the bond markets on the two domestic stock exchanges. It is an order-driven market, where the major participants are: securities companies, insurance companies, securities investment funds, trust and investment companies, credit cooperatives, other non-financial institutional investors and individual investors. The commercial banks have no access to this market. Available at the market are cash T-bonds, T-bonds repurchase, cash corporate bonds, corporate bonds repurchase and convertible bonds.

In the year 2005, the total issuance of bonds reached a value of RMB 704. 2 billion, a significant increase compared with the RMB 4. 9 billion in 1981, while the turnover of on-exchange bonds reached RMB 2, 836. 7 billion.

2. Opening up to the Outside World

A. *Opening-up of the Markets*

As aforementioned, the B-shares have been available since 1992 and H-shares since 1993. And starting from November 2001, foreign-invested companies registered in China can issue stocks and get listed in China.

In December 2002, China launched the Qualified Foreign Institutional Investor (QFII) scheme, which opened up China's domestic A-share market to international investors at a time when there was the non-convertibility of Renminbi under the capital account. Under such a scheme, a QFII can remit into China an approved amount of foreign capital which is then exchanged into Renminbi under a designated account. The QFII uses it to invest in A-shares. The outbound remittance of QFII principal and dividend are subject to controls. **Dividend** is money divided among shareholders, based on the companies underlying earnings.

Since November 2002, the state-owned shares and legal-person shares can be transferred to international investors. Besides, starting from January 2006, international investors have been allowed to become medium to long-term strategic investors of listed companies with their initial investment being no less than 10% of the outstanding shares for a lockup period of 3 years.

Table 1   Summary of China's Securities and Futures Markets (1992–2005)

Indicator \ Year	1992	1993	1994	1995	1996	1997	1998	1999	2000	2001	2002	2003	2004	2005
No. of domestic listed companies (A-shares, B-shares)	53	183	291	323	530	745	851	949	1,088	1,160	1,224	1,287	1,377	1,381
No. of B-shares companies	18	41	58	70	85	101	106	108	114	112	111	111	110	110
No. of H-shares companies		6	15	18	25	42	43	46	52	60	75	93	111	122
Total shares issued (100 million shares)	68.87	387.73	684.54	848.42	1,219.54	1,942.67	2,526.79	3,088.95	3,791.71	5,218.01	5,875.45	6,428.46	7,149.43	7,657.50
Tradable shares (100 million shares)	21.18	107.88	226.04	301.46	429.85	671.44	861.94	1,079.65	1,354.26	1,813.17	2,036.90	2,269.92	2,577.18	2,941.77
Total stock market cap. (100 million yuan)	1,048.13	3,531.01	3,690.61	3,474.28	9,842.38	17,529.24	19,505.64	26,471.17	48,090.94	43,522.20	38,329.12	42,457.72	37,055.57	32,430.28
Market cap. of tradable shares (100 million yuan)	—	861.62	968.89	938.22	2,867.03	5,204.42	5,745.59	8,213.97	16,087.52	14,463.17	12,484.55	13,178.52	11,688.64	10,630.53
Total stock trading volume (100 million shares)	3,795.39	23,422.17	201,333.91	70,547.06	253,314.06	256,079.12	215,411.00	253,238.88	475,840.00	315,228.76	301,619.49	416,308.40	582,773.29	662,354
Total stock turnover (100 million yuan)	681.25	3,667.02	8,127.63	4,036.47	21,332.16	30,721.84	23,544.25	31,319.60	60,826.65	38,305.18	27,990.46	32,115.27	42,333.95	31,663.16
Shanghai Stock Exchange Composite Index (close price)	780.39	833.80	647.87	555.29	917.01	1,194.10	1,146.70	1,366.58	2,073.48	1,645.97	1,357.65	1,497.04	1,266.50	1,161.06
Shenzhen Stock Exchange Composite Index (close price)	241.2	238.27	140.63	113.24	327.45	381.29	343.85	402.18	635.73	475.94	388.76	378.62	315.81	278.74

Continue

Indicator \ Year	1992	1993	1994	1995	1996	1997	1998	1999	2000	2001	2002	2003	2004	2005
Securities accounts (10 thousand)	216.65	835.17	1,107.76	1,294.19	2,422.08	3,480.26	4,259.88	4,810.63	6,154.53	6,965.90	7,202.16	7,344.41	7,215.74	7,336.07
Amount issued of T-bonds (100 million yuan)	460.78	381.31	1,137.55	1,510.86	1,847.77	2,411.79	3,808.77	4,015.00	4,657.00	4,884.00	5,934.30	6,280.10	6,923.90	5,042.00
Amount issued of enterprise bonds (100 million yuan)	683.71	235.84	161.75	300.80	268.92	255.23	147.89	158.20	83.00	147.00	325.00	358.00	327.00	654.00
Cash T-bonds turnover (100 million yuan)	7.1276	61.02	468.37	775.20	5,029.24	3,582.75	6,059.95	5,300.87	4,157.49	4,815.59	8,708.68	5,756.11	2,966.46	2,779.05
Repurchase T-bonds Turnover (100 million yuan)	0.00	0.42	75.78	1,248.52	13,008.64	12,876.06	15,540.84	12,890.53	14,733.68	15,487.63	24,419.64	52,999.85	44,086.61	23,621.18
No. of Securities investment funds							6	22	34	51	71	95	161	218
Amount issued of securities investment funds (100 million yuan)							120.00	510.00	562.00	804.23	1,318.85	1,614.67	3,308.79	4,714.00
Turnover of securities investment funds (100 million yuan)							555.33	1,623.12	2,465.79	2,561.88	1,166.58	682.65	728.58	773.13
Futures transaction volume (10,000 lot)		890.69	12,110.72	63,612.07	34,256.77	15,876.32	10,445.57	7,363.91	5,461.07	12,046.35	13,943.37	27,992.43	30,569.76	32,287.07
Futures turnover (100 million yuan)	5,521.99	31,601.41	100,565.00	84,119.16	61,170.66	36,967.24	22,343.01	16,082.29	30,144.98	39,490.28	108,396.59	146,935.32	134,462.71	

B. *Opening up of the Industry*

When joining the WTO in December 2001, China made the following commitments regarding securities and futures industry: (1) foreign securities institutions may directly engage (without Chinese intermediary) in B-share business. (2) representative offices of foreign securities institutions in China may become Special Members of all Chinese stock exchanges. (3) foreign service suppliers are permitted to establish joint ventures with foreign investment up to 33 per cent to conduct domestic securities investment fund management business. Within three years after China's accession to the WTO, foreign investment can be increased to 49 per cent. (4) within three years after China's entry to the WTO, foreign securities institutions will be permitted to establish joint ventures, with foreign minority ownership not exceeding 1/3, to engage directly in underwriting A-shares and in underwriting and trading B-shares and H-shares as well as government and corporate bonds. All these commitments have been fully fulfilled.

In addition, the Chinese mainland has special arrangements with the Hong Kong SAR and Macao SAR in the field of financial services, which allows a wider opening-up of Chinese markets to these two regions. According to the Closer Economic Partnership Arrangement (CEPA): (1) Since January 1, 2004, there has been no need for the licensed professionals for securities and futures businesses from Hong Kong and Macao to take professional exams in order to practice in the Chinese mainland, what they need to do is only to take exams on the relevant laws, rules and regulations; (2) Since January 1, 2005, Hong Kong and Macao services providers meeting the CSRC's requirements have been allowed to hold a stake in Chinese futures brokerage houses; (3) Since January 1, 2006, high-quality Chinese securities firms have been allowed to set up subsidiaries in Hong Kong, and qualified Chinese futures brokerage houses have been allowed to do businesses in Hong Kong and set up their subsidiaries there.

II. Securities Market

1. Securities Offering

A. *Stocks*

i. *A-share market*

A company applying for a public offering of A-shares has to submit its application to the CSRC for approval. An issuer can choose either a public or non-public offering. Below are several kinds of public offerings:

- A public offering of securities to unspecified investors;
- A public offering of securities to accumulatively more than 200 specified investors;
- A public offering as prescribed by any law or administrative regulations.

The public offering of stocks may be used to initiate a joint stock limited company, to make initial public offerings (IPOs) of established companies or follow-on offerings of listed companies. To initiate a joint stock limited company means to establish such a company via public issuance of stocks. The promoter subscribes a significant portion of the shares while the rest are offered to the public. Such a public offering shall meet the following requirements:

- No less than 2 but no more than 200 promoters, of whom half or more shall have domiciles in China;
- The shares subscribed by the promoters shall be no less than 35 % of the total shares issued.

An IPO applicant shall meet the following requirements:

- Owning a well-functioning organizational structure;
- Capable of making profits continuously with a sound financial condition;
- No record of false financial statements over the previous 3 years or other wrongdoings.

Listed companies can issue additional shares to the public by placing them to their existing shareholders (hereinafter referred to "rights issue") or to the general public (hereinafter referred to as "follow-on offering").

The review and approval procedures are as follows:

- The issuers are required to make public their application documents after being accepted by the CSRC;
- The Public Offering Supervision Department of the CSRC conducts preliminary reviews on the application documents;
- The application documents are subject to the review and examination of the Public Offering Review Committee[1], which comprises both the CSRC staff and external experts. The Review Committee members vote by majority;
- After taking into consideration the recommendation of the Review Committee, the CSRC finally decides whether to approve it or not.

The current pricing mechanism for a public offering, introduced on January 1, 2005, is

---

① The Committee is composed of 25 members, five of whom are the CSRC staff and the rest are industry experts. The tenure of a committee member is one year and the consecutive tenure shall be no more than 3 terms. Some of them are full-time members.

in essence a market-oriented book-building pricing process which generally involves two stages. First, the issuer and its sponsor propose an initial price range to solicit price offers from institutional investors. After receiving the first round of feedback, the issuer and the lead underwriter will adjust the price range and offer it to the institutional investors for a second-round feedback which sets the final price of the offering.

ii. B-share market

B-share issuers shall meet the following requirements:

- The capital raised shall be used in a manner consistent with state industrial policy;
- They shall comply with regulations regarding fixed-asset investments and foreign investments;
- The promoters must hold at least 35% of the issued shares and pay up no less than RMB 150 million when the company is set up;
- The company must float at least 25% of its total shares; in the case of a total share capital exceeding RMB 400 million, the public floating requirement may be reduced to no less than 15%;
- Neither any predecessor entity (entities) of which the joint-stock company is a part nor any major promoter who is a state-owned enterprise, has committed any significant breaches against laws over the previous 3 years.

B. Bonds

The issuance of bonds such as T-bonds, financial bonds and corporate bonds are subject to the approval of the relative government authorities other than the CSRC. The issuance of convertible bonds and bonds of securities companies are subject to the approval of the CSRC and shall meet the following requirements:

i. Convertible bonds

The issuance of convertible bonds shall meet the requirements in Articles 13 and 16 of the *Securities Law* of China which are listed below:

- The net asset of a joint stock limited company is no less than RMB 30 million and the net asset of a limited liability company is no less than RMB 60 million;
- The accumulated outstanding bonds constitute no more than 40% of the net assets of the issuer;
- The average annual distributable profits over the previous 3 years are sufficient to pay 1-year interests of the bonds;
- The raised funds are invested in a manner consistent with the state industrial policies;
- The interest rate of bonds does not exceed the ceiling set by the State Council.

ii. Bonds issued by securities companies

Such bonds can be issued to the public or to qualified investors by private placement. Aside from complying with the requirements as prescribed in the *Securities Law*, the securities company issuing bonds shall also comply with the following requirements:

a) The latest un-audited assets shall be no less than RMB 1 billion;

b) The company made profits in the preceding year;

c) All risk control indicators have met the requirements;

d) No material violation of laws or wrongdoing has been committed during the past 2 years;

e) The shareholders' meetings and the Board of Directors are in sound operation and internal control systems are working effectively with proper business firewalls and internal control mechanism;

f) Assets of the company have not been misappropriated by any controlling person/party.

Securities companies that apply to issue bonds by private placement should comply with the above-mentioned requirements numbered a), b), c), d), e), f) and the *Securities Law*. Meanwhile, the securities companies shall have no less than RMB 500 million of un-audited net assets.

2. Listing and Trading of Securities

A. *Listing of Shares*

According to the *Securities Law*, publicly issued stocks, corporate bonds or other securities shall be listed on a stock exchange or other approved securities marketplaces subject to the exchange's review and approval.

i. Listing of stocks

An applicant for listing its securities shall meet the following requirements:

- publicly issued shares;
- no less than RMB 30 million of total share capital;
- ensuring that the publicly issued shares shall exceed 25% of the total shares; where the total share capital exceeds RMB 400 million, the publicly issued shares shall be no less than 10% thereof; and
- no material violation of laws and regulations over the previous three years.

A listing agreement shall be signed by a stock exchange and a listing applicant which mainly covers: the code of conducts requirement on the listed company, listing fees, suspending or terminating the listing, services from the exchange, etc.

ii. Listing of corporate bonds

An applicant for listing corporate bonds shall meet the following requirements:

- more than 1 year of maturity;
- no less than RMB 50 million for the actual issuance.

The applicant for listing convertible bonds shall meet the requirements for public offering of stocks in addition to the above parameters.

B. *Trading of Securities*

i. *Trading instruments.*

Currently the financial instruments traded on the stock exchanges are: shares (both A-shares and B-shares), bonds (cash T-bonds, T-bonds repurchase, cash corporate bonds, corporate bonds repurchase and convertible bonds) securities investment funds (close-ended funds, open-ended funds, ETF, LOF) and warrants.

ii. *Market participants.*

The major participants include: securities companies, insurance companies, securities investment fund management companies, trust and investment companies, non-financial institutional investors, and retail investors.

iii. *Means of trading.*

Securities are traded on stock exchanges where an open, centralized and computerized matching method is adopted based on the principle of "price precedence and then time precedence". Other means of trading include collective bidding and block trading bidding. **Block trading** refers to large-volume stock transactions (no less than half a million shares for A-shares).

iv. *Trading fees.*

Investors purchase or sell securities through the brokerage of securities companies which charge commissions no higher than 3‰ of the trading value (but no less than the total amount of the trading regulatory fee and the charges by the stock exchanges). Furthermore, both buyers and sellers are levied a stamp duty of 1‰ of the trading value.

v. *Daily caps on the stock fluctuations.*

At present, except Specially Treated Shares (shares of listed companies in poor financial or operational conditions) which are subject to the daily price fluctuation limit of $\pm 5\%$, all other shares are subject to the daily price limit of $\pm 10\%$ based on the previous day's closing price.

vi. *Registration and clearing.*

The registration and clearing of securities are centralized through China Securities Depository and Clearing Corporation Ltd. (CSDCC). **Clearing** is the centralized process whereby transacted business is recorded and positions are maintained while **settlement** refers to the completion of a transaction. Before trading, an investor must place all the securities into an account opened with the CSDCC (fully dematerialized). Currently, the settlement for A-shares is T + 1 and the settlement for B-shares is T + 3.

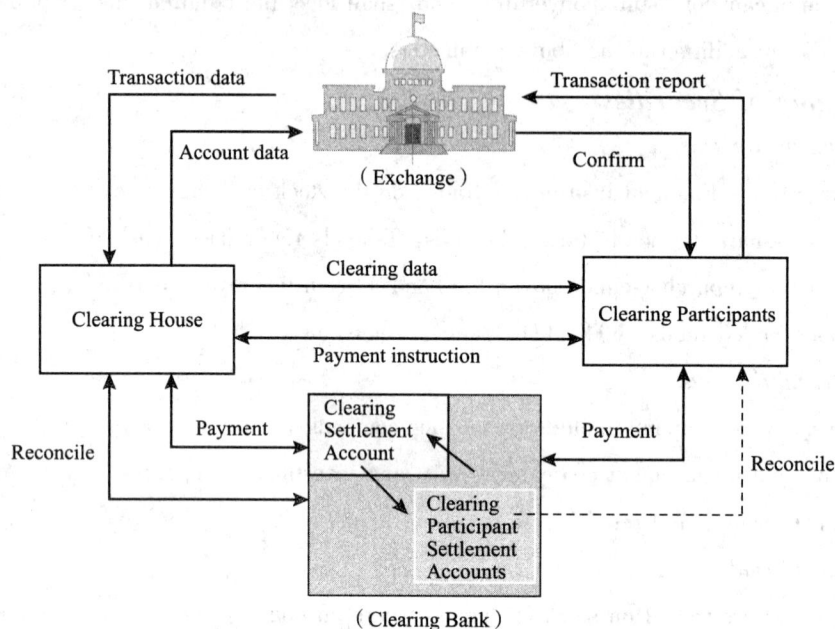

Figure 1   A-share Clearing and Delivery Flow Chart

vii. Market indices.

They are samples of shares used to represent a share (or other) markets level and movements. The commonly cited stock indices include Shanghai Composite Index, Shanghai 50 Index, Shanghai 180 Index, Shenzhen Component Index, Shenzhen Composite Index and SME Index.

C. Delisting of Securities

i. De-listing of shares

Where a listed company is under any of the following circumstances, the stock exchange shall suspend the listing of its shares:

- The share capital or shareholding structure of the company changes and thus failing to meet the listing requirements;
- The company fails to disclose its financial statements or provides false information in its statements;
- The company has committed serious wrongdoings;
- The company has been losing money for the latest 3 consecutive years.

Where a listed company is under any of the following circumstances, the stock exchange shall terminate the listing of its stocks:

- The total share capital or shareholding structure of the company changes and thus fails to meet the listing requirements, and still unable to meet the listing requirements following the rectification period set by the stock exchange;
- The company fails to disclose its financial statements or provides false information in its statements, and yet refuses to rectify;
- The company has been making losses for the latest 3 consecutive years with a failure to make profits in the fourth year;
- The company is disbanded or declared bankrupt.

ii. De-listing of corporate bonds

After the listing, where the bond issuer is under any of the following circumstances, the stock exchange shall suspend the listing of its corporate bonds:

- The company has committed a wrongdoing;
- A major change takes place in the company which disqualifies it for the listing;
- The proceeds raised are used for purposes other than the verified;
- The company has failed to fulfill its obligations in the covenant; or
- The company has been losing money for the latest 2 consecutive years.

Where a company is under any of the circumstances in item (1) or (4) committing serious violations, or where a company is under any of the circumstances as described in item (2), (3), or (5) and fails to rectify within a specified timeframe, or where a company is disbanded or declared bankrupt, the stock exchange shall terminate its listing of corporate bonds.

3. Listed Companies

A. *Domestically-listed Companies*

The share capital of domestically listed companies is mostly between RMB 100 million and RMB 1 billion, with less than 10% listed companies having more than RMB 1 billion of share capital. Listed companies are located in different parts of the mainland of China and cover various industrial sectors (mainly machinery, metallurgy, chemicals, electronics, infrastructure, transportation and energy).

The supervisions over listed companies focus on information disclosure, corporate governance, related party transactions, M&A activities, etc.

i. Information disclosure

The information disclosed by issuers and listed companies shall be authentic, accurate and complete. There are 3 categories of information: public offering information, periodic reports, and ad hoc reports. The public offering information includes prospectus, stock listing announcement, bonds issuance scheme and bond listing announcement, etc. Periodic reports include annual reports, interim reports and quarterly reports. In the case of a material event, the listed company shall immediately submit an ad hoc report to the CSRC. Routine reports like notification of shareholders' meeting and its decision can also be regarded as ad hoc reports.

ii. Corporate governance

The *Code of Corporate Governance for Listed Companies*, issued in January 2002, sets forth the following basic requirements:

- **Independent Directors**. In a domestically listed company, independent directors shall account for no less than one-third of the board. Related party transactions must be endorsed by independent directors.

- **Independence of Listed Company**. A listed company shall be separate from its controlling shareholders in such matters as human resources, assets and financial affairs, and independent in organization, business and accounting issues.

- **Specialized Committees**. The board of directors may establish a strategy committee, an audit committee, a nomination committee, a remuneration committee and an appraisal committee pursuant to the resolutions of shareholders' meetings. The audit committee shall have at least one independent director with accounting expertise.

iii. Related party transactions

Related party transactions refer to the issues regarding resources or obligations transfers between a listed company or its subsidiary under its control and its related party. Timely information disclosure is required when:

- the transaction value between a listed company and its related natural person exceeds RMB 300 thousand; or

- the transaction value between a listed company and its related legal person exceeds RMB 3 million and accounts for 0.5% or above of the latest audited net assets of the listed company.

The director (s) representing a related party shall withdraw when the board or the shareholders' meeting is deliberating and voting on a related party transaction.

iv. Mergers & Acquisitions

Investors can acquire a listed company by a public offer, agreement-based offer and other legitimate ways. The stocks of the target company held by an acquirer cannot be transferred within 12 months following the acquisition.

B. *Overseas-listed Companies*

Initially the overseas listed companies were primarily large SOEs that were critical to the national economy. Recently, with the increasing overseas listing of small and medium-sized enterprises (SMEs), particularly privately-owned enterprises, these companies have exhibited truly diversified ownership structures and industrial sectors with a higher degree of transparency and compliance.

After restructuring into joint-stock companies, all eligible enterprises are entitled to apply for overseas listing. A listing on overseas main boards shall meet the following requirements:

- The proceeds raised shall be no less than USD 50 million dollars and used in a manner consistent with the state industrial policy as well as regulations on fixed-asset investments and foreign investment;
- The company must own a net capital of no less than RMB 400 million, with no less than RMB 60 million of post-tax profits and demonstrate great potentials for growth via its P/E ratio;
- The company must have a sound corporate governance and internal control regime, and capable senior executives with sufficient management skills;
- The company must have sufficient foreign exchange resources for dividends.

4. Securities Intermediaries and Service Providers

A. *Securities Companies*

Securities companies are the leading intermediaries on China's stock market. By the end of 2005, there were 116 securities companies with 3,090 retail branches nationwide. They are often termed "investment banks" in the United States, and "merchant banks" in the United Kingdom.

i. Establishment requirements

A securities company can apply for a license if it meets the following requirements:

- Its major shareholders are able to make profits continuously, have a good reputation with a net asset of no less than RMB 200 million, and commit no serious violation of laws or wrongdoings over the past 3 years;
- It has a sound risk control and internal control regime.

ii. Business scope

A securities company may undertake some or all of the following business activities subject to the approval of the CSRC:

- Securities brokerage;

- Securities investment consultation;
- Financial advising relating to securities trading or securities investment;
- Underwriting and sponsorship of securities;
- Securities proprietary trading;
- Securities asset management.

iii. Registered capital

Where a securities company engages in the business activities as prescribed in the above-mentioned item (1), (2) or (3), its registered capital shall be no less than RMB 50 million; where a securities company engages in one of the business activities as prescribed in item (4), (5), (6) or (7), its minimum paid-in capital shall be RMB 100 million; where a securities company engages in two or more business activities as prescribed in item (4), (5), (6) or (7), its minimum registered (paid-in) capital shall be RMB 500 million.

iv. Internal control

A securities company shall have a sound internal control system, and build up effective Chinese "fire walls" to prevent any conflict of interest between the company and its clients or among different clients.

v. Funds of the clients

The clients' funds in a securities company shall be deposited in a commercial bank and managed through separate accounts under the clients' names. Where a securities company is under bankruptcy or liquidation procedures, the funds or securities of its clients shall not be defined as its insolvent assets or liquidation assets. Unless for the purpose of paying the liabilities of its clients or prescribed by laws, such funds or securities shall not be sealed up, frozen, deducted or enforced compulsorily.

B. Securities trading service providers

Such providers refer to the entities that render securities services to issuers and investors, such as depository and clearing house, investment advisers, credit rating agencies, financial advisory companies, accounting firms, asset appraisal agencies and law firms.

i. Securities depository and clearing house

From October 1, 2001 onwards, the CSDCC has taken charge of all depository and clearing services for listed securities, which marks the establishment of a unified securities depository and clearing system. Headquartered in Beijing, the CSDCC has two subsidiaries located respectively in Shanghai and Shenzhen.

In addition, the CSDCC is responsible for the depository and clearing of other exchange-listed instruments as well as the open-ended funds.

ii. Other securities trading service institutions

Investment consulting institutions, financial advisors, credit rating agencies asset appraisal institutions, or accounting firms engaging in securities service are subject to ex ante licensing, ongoing supervision and afterwards sanctions.

The employees of investment consulting institutions, financial advisory institutions or credit rating agencies who engage in securities services shall possess sufficient professional expertise as well as more than 2 years of work experience.

An investment consulting institution and its practitioners shall not have any of the following acts:

- Engaging in any securities investment on behalf of its entrusting party;
- Signing with any party an agreement on sharing the gains or bearing the loss of securities investments;
- Purchasing or selling any share of a listed company, for which the consulting institution provides services;
- Providing or disseminating any false or misleading information to investors through media or by any other means.

5. Investors

China's securities market has been traditionally dominated by individual investors, so vigorous efforts have been made in recent years to nurture the institutional investors.

A. *Institutional Investors*

i. *Securities investment funds*

In 1998, the first five contractual closed-ended funds were launched, marking the inception of China's securities investment fund industry. In 2001, the first contractual open-ended fund was set up. As of June 2006, there had been 54 closed-end and 201 open-ended funds under the management of 57 fund management companies.

Besides equity funds, there are bond funds, index funds, monetary market funds, umbrella funds, principal guaranteed funds, exchange traded funds and listed open-ended funds.

Fund management shall be assumed by fund management companies while custodians are acted by qualified commercial banks. A fund manager is required to be licensed by the CSRC, while a custodian needs to be jointly licensed by the CSRC and the CBRC. A fund custodian and a fund manager cannot be the same party or invest in each other's share or cross-hold each other's shares. The following requirements shall be met in order to establish a fund management company:

- having a registered capital of no less than RMB 100 million;

- principal shareholders demonstrating a good track record and reputation in the securities business, securities investment consultation, trust assets management or other financial assets management, committing no violation of law within the preceding 3 years, and having a registered capital of no less than RMB 300 million; and
- meeting the statutory requirement for the number of licensed fund professionals.

In managing its assets, a fund manager shall invest in listed shares, bonds and other permitted instruments. The fund assets shall not be used in any of the following ways:

- Underwriting securities;
- Providing loans or guarantees to others;
- Engaging in investment with unlimited liability;
- Trading other fund units, unless otherwise approved by the State Council;
- Paying capital to the fund manager and custodian, or trading the shares or bonds issued by the aforesaid manager and custodian;
- Trading the securities issued or underwritten by the shareholders controlling the fund manager or custodian, or by companies with other significant interests with the aforesaid manager or custodian;
- Insider dealing, market manipulation or other wrongdoings.

ii. Qualified Foreign Institutional Investors (QFII)

Up to the approved investment quota, a QFII can invest in such financial instruments as A-shares, treasuries, convertible bonds and corporate bonds listed on the Chinese stock exchanges. A QFII applicant should meet the following criteria:

- It is in a sound financial and credit status, being able to meet the requirements of assets and other indicators; and its risk control indicators meet the requirements of its home jurisdiction;
- Its employees meet the qualification requirements in its home jurisdiction;
- With a sound management and internal control system, and a good track record without any substantial penalties imposed by its home regulators over the previous three years;
- Its home jurisdiction has a sound legal and regulatory regime, and its regulator has signed Memorandum of Understanding with the CSRC for an efficient co-operative regulatory relationship.

iii. Other major institutional investors

There are other institutional investors such as National Social Security Fund, insurance companies, corporate annuity funds as well as securities firms authorized for proprietary trading and assets management, etc.

B. Securities Investor Protection Fund

The Securities Investor Protection Fund (SIPF) was launched in 2005 with a paid-up capital of RMB 6. 3 billion in order to protect the interests of securities investors against the losses from failing securities companies. The SIPF revenues primarily come from five sources: (1) 20% of the transaction fees submitted by Shanghai and Shenzhen Stock Exchanges when their risk reserves reach the stipulated upper limits; (2) 0. 5% to 5% of operating revenues of securities companies; (3) the interest income from the "locked" funds subscribing for stocks or convertible bonds; (4) proceeds from the compensation of liable parties and the liquidation of securities companies; (5) donations of domestic and foreign institutions, organizations and individuals as well as other legitimate incomes.

III. Futures Market

1. Market Overview

China's commodity futures market started almost simultaneously with the stock market. In October 1990, as the first commodity futures market in China, Zhengzhou Grain Wholesale Market introduced its first futures contract. However, the following years saw disorders and other problems in the market. From 1994 onwards the market has undergone a consolidation process. Today, the market has 3 exchanges and 183 brokerage firms, compared with 50 exchanges and 1, 000 brokerage firms at the peak time in 1994. The traded products have now been downsized from 35 to 12 products.

China's financial derivatives market is still in its infancy. At present there is only warrant traded on stock exchanges. To meet the demands of market participants for price discovery and risk control, financial derivatives as stock index futures and Treasury futures are about to emerge.

Both Zhengzhou Commodity Exchange (ZCE) and Dalian Commodity Exchange (DCE) trade for agricultural products, such as wheat, cotton, corn, soybean, mung bean, bean oil and sugar, while Shanghai Futures Exchange (SHFE) offers futures contracts on copper, aluminum, rubber, fuel oil, etc.

2. Futures Brokerage Companies

Futures brokerage companies are the leading intermediaries in the futures market. The regulatory requirements concerning a future brokerage company's establishment, business scope and risk control are as follows:

A. *Establishment*

Besides the relevant provisions in the *Company Law*, an applicant shall also fulfill the following requirements:

- with a registered capital of no less than RMB 30 million;
- qualified senior executives and principal employees for futures business;
- a physical business venue and sufficient trading facilities;
- a well-functioning management system.

B. *Business scope*

A futures brokerage company may engage in the following futures business activities:

- futures brokerage;
- consultation and training services in relation to futures.

Currently futures brokerage companies are prohibited to openly or disguisedly engage in futures proprietary trading.

C. *Risk control*

A futures brokerage company shall set up a specific department or positions for risk control which will check its own financial condition, business operation and compliance with the relative regulations as well as drafting risk control reports. It shall also recruit qualified accounting firms to audit its financial and operating statements annually.

IV. Legal Framework

The establishment of a sound regulatory framework has been the cornerstone as well as the basis for China's securities and futures markets. The revised *Company Law* and *Securities Law* came into effect on January 1, 2006. The revision, based on the accumulated past experience and in-depth studies, made a number of significant changes and laid out a series of wide-ranging and far-sighted mechanisms, which marked a new era for securities-and-futures legal framework.

Such a legal framework is contained mainly in three pieces of legislation: *Company Law*, *Securities Law*, and *Securities Investment Fund Law*, supplemented by 13 additional regulations and administrative rules such as *Provisional Regulations on Public Offering & Trading* and *Provisional Regulations on Futures Trading* in addition to over 300 departmental rules, guidelines and codes.

1. Securities Offering, Listing, and Disclosure

The Articles 2 and 3 of *Securities Law* govern public offering and listing of shares. And the Articles 238 of *Securities Law* authorizes the State Council to issue rules regarding a Chinese enterprise directly or indirectly issuing and listing securities overseas for trading. Chapter 5 of *Company Law* also sets forth a number of principles on the issuance of a joint stock company's shares. Meanwhile, other rules and regulations in this area include: *Provisional Regulations on Public Offering and Trading*; *State Council's Special Rules on Overseas Offering and Listing of Joint Stock Companies*; *The CSRC Public Offering Approval Procedures*; *Interim Measures on the Sponsor System for Securities Public Offerings*; *Guidelines on Approval and Supervision of Chinese Companies Listing on Hong Kong Growth Enterprise Market*; and *Standards for Content and Format of Information Disclosure of Public Companies*.

2. Securities and Futures Trading

Articles 3 of the *Securities Law* sets forth the principles for securities trading, which fall into two categories:
- general regulations on trading, including trading venue, modes, commissions, eligible participants, etc.
- regulations on prohibited behaviors such as insider dealing, market manipulation, forging and circulating false information, etc.

Other relevant rules and regulations include the *Measures on the Administration of Stock Exchanges*, *Measures on the Administration of Futures Exchanges*, and *Notice on Tightening Control over Members' Settlement Risks*.

3. Corporate Governance, Mergers and Acquisitions of Listed Companies

Article 4 of the *Securities Law* governs the M & A activities in addition to provide general principles on organizational structure, independent directors, board secretary and related party transaction of listed companies.

There are a number of other rules and regulations governing this area, such as the *Guidelines for Establishing Independent Directors of Listed Companies*, *Code of Corporate Governance for Listed Companies*, *Measures on the Merger and Acquisition of Listed Companies*, etc.

4. Securities and Futures Intermediaries

A. *Regarding Securities Companies*

Article 6 of the *Securities Law* lays out principles for securities firms on their establishment criteria, business scope, capital requirements, nomination of senior management, internal control system, and penalties for wrongdoings. Other related rules and regulations include the *Measures on the Administration of Securities Companies*, *Provisional Measures on Clients' Asset Management by Securities Companies*, *Administration Measures on Senior Management of Securities Companies* and *Administration Measures on Clients' Settlement Fund Management*.

B. Regarding Futures Brokerage Houses

The *Provisional Regulations on Futures Trading* enacted on September 1, 1999 for governing the futures brokerage houses in the areas of their establishment criteria, approval procedure, business scope, liquidation, etc. Other rules and regulations include: *Administration Measures on Futures Brokerage Houses*, *Administration Measures on Senior Management of Futures Brokerage Houses*, *Code of Governance of Futures Brokerage Houses* (*provisional*).

C. Regarding Other Service Providers

Articles 7 and 8 of the *Securities Law* set forth the principles for investment advisors, financial advisors, credit rating agencies, assets evaluation institutions and accounting firms engaging in securities services. Besides, *Administration Measures on Stock Exchanges* also lays out details on the establishment, organizational structure and functions of securities registration and settlement institutions. The *Provisional Measures on Securities and Futures Investment Consultancy* and the corresponding implementation rules give details on how to govern securities and futures investment consultancy business.

5. Supervision of Securities Investment Funds

The *Securities Investment Fund Law* has provisions regarding fund managers, custodians, placement and trading of funds, subscription and redemption of funds, operations and information disclosure, modification and termination of contracts, liquidation of funds, rights and interests of fund holders and their ways of exercising these rights, supervision and administration of funds, and legal liabilities.

In line with the *Securities Investment Fund Law*, the CSRC formulated 6 *Measures* for regulating respectively the information disclosure, operation and sales of securities investment funds in 2004.

6. Securities and Futures Markets Supervision and Legal Liabilities

The *Securities Law* has specific provisions regarding stock exchanges, securities industry association and securities regulators.

The *Securities Law*, *Company Law*, *Securities Investment Fund Law* and *Criminal Law* expressly lay out the civil, administrative and criminal liabilities of a party guilty of securities and futures offenses and crimes, including fraudulent practices, insider dealings and market manipulations. Meanwhile, the Supreme Court has issued a number of legal explanations which set rules on handling civil liability lawsuits in relation to securities and futures markets. In addition, the SROs including stock and futures exchanges, securities and futures associations, have established their own legal system disciplining their members and activities.

Notes

1. **categorize** [ˈkætigəraiz] *vt.* ① to put in a category ②to classify

2. **tandem** [ˈtændəm] *n.* ① a two-wheeled carriage drawn by horses harnessed one before the other ② a team of carriage horses harnessed in single file ③ an arrangement of two or more persons or objects placed one behind the other

   adj. having two identical components arranged one behind the other

3. **pen-end fund**: *n.* ①A fund, from which shares can be redeemed at any time at a price that is tied to the asset value of the fund ② a mutual fund that accepts investments and allow investors to redeem shares at any time. The value of the shares is tied to the value of investment assets of the fund

4. **close-end fund**: *n.* ①A fund in which a fixed number of non-redeemable shares are sold at an initial offering and are then traded in the over-the-counter market like common stock ②A fund that sells a fixed number of shares of stock and does not continue to accept investments

5. **legal person**: *n.* legal entity or artificial person

6. **shareholder**: *n.* one that owns or holds a share or shares of stock; a stockholder in AmE. Also called shareowner

7. **listing** [listiŋ] *n.* having a quotation for securities on a recognized stock exchange

8. **stamp duty**: *n.* tax on specific transactions collected by stamping the legal documents giving rise to the transactions.

9. **closing price**: *n.* buying or selling prices recorded at the end of a day's trading on a commodity market on stock exchange

10. **securities**: *n.* financial assets like shares, government stocks, debentures, bonds, unit trust and rights to money lent or deposited. Securities do not include insurance policies

11. **delist**: *v.* to remove from a list, especially from a list of securities that may be traded on a stock exchange

12. **ad hoc**: *adv.* for the specific purpose, case, or situation at hand and for no other

    adj. ① formed for or concerned with one specific purpose ② improvised and often impromptu

13. **interim** ['intərim] *adj.* ① temporary② time between

14. **M&A ·** *abbr* *n.* Merger and acquisition

15. **intermediary** [ˌintə (ː) 'miːdjəri] *n.* an organization or person that acts as an agent or broker between the parties to a transaction

16. **paid-in capital**: *n.* capital contributed by stockholders and assigned to accounts other than capital stock

17. **jurisdiction** [dʒuəris'dikʃən] *n.* right or power to give out justice

18. **penalty** ['penlti] *n.* punishment imposed by law

19. **liquidation** [ˌlikwi'deiʃən] *n.* distribution of a company's assets among its creditors and members prior to its dissolution, so bringing the life of the company to an end

20. **enact** [i'nækt] *vt.* to make or pass a law

21. **futures** ['fjuːtʃəs] *n.* the commodities, currencies, or securities to be sold or bought at a fixed price for delivery at a fixed date in the future

22. **private placement**: *n.* this is another way of issuing securities. In such way the seller contacts a large investor and negotiates a price for the issue

23. **clearing house**: *n.* place where bills of exchange, cheques, etc are exchanged and settled

24. **index** ['indeks] *n.* measure of stock market performance used to monitor the behavior of a group of stocks. It serves as an indicator of both stock prices and the investor's confidence in the securities markets by enabling them to gain some insight as to how a broad of stocks may have performed

25. **systematic risk**: *n.* the component of an asset's risk that can not be eliminated by diversification

26. **financial statements**: *n.* any statement made by an individual, a proprietorship, a partnership, a corporation, an organization, or an association, regarding the financial status of the legal entity. Main financial statements include: balance sheet, income statement and profit and loss statement

27. **right issue**: issue of new shares to existing shareholders, who must be offered the new shares in proportion to their holding of old shares

28. **brokerage** ['broukridʒ] *n.* ① the business of a broker ② a fee or commission paid to a broker③ a firm engaged in buying and selling stocks and bonds for clients

29. **umbrella fund**: *n.* offshore fund consisting of a fund of funds that invests in other offshore funds

30. **prospectus** [prəs'pektəs] *n.* document that gives details about a new issue of shares and invites the public to buy shares or debenture in the company

31. **warrant** [ˈwɔrənt] *n.* finance security that offers the owner the right to subscribe for the ordinary shares of a company at a fixed date, usually at a fixed price. Warrants are themselves bought and sold on stock exchanges and are equivalent to stock options

32. **subscribe** [səbˈskraib] to pledge or contribute (a sum of money)

33. **investment banker**: *n.* a securities dealer who facilitates the transfer of securities from the original issuer to the public

34. **over-the-counter markets (OTC)**: *n.* they are markets in which dealers at different locations have an inventory of securities and stand ready to buy and sell securities "over-the-counter" to anyone who comes to them and is willing to accept their prices. In the U.S. many common stocks are traded over-the-counter, although the largest corporations have their shares traded in organized stock exchanges, such as the New York Stock Exchange

35. **stock exchange**: *n.* an organization that provides a market for the trading of bonds and stocks

36. **insider dealing/trading**: *n.* dealing in company securities with a view to making a profit or avoiding a loss by using inside information that is not generally known

37. **audit** [ˈɔːdit] *vt.* an independent examination of, and the subsequent expression of opinion on, the financial statements of an organization, such as a bank, a company or a government agency, etc.

38. **manipulation** [məˌnipjuˈleiʃən] *n.* ① the act or practice of manipulating; the state of being manipulated ② shrewd or devious management, especially for one's own advantage

Questions for discussion

1. What is meant by M&A?

2. What requirements must be met if a Chinese company wants to get listed overseas?

3. Can you name some of the securities intermediaries in China? And the main services provided by a securities company?

4. What is meant by QFII? What requirements must be fulfilled if a QFII wants to invest in Chinese securities?

5. How do you define the term of futures?

6. How many ways of issuing securities do you know?

7. Can you explain the difference between public issue of securities and private placement?

8. How many kinds of investors are active participants in China's securities market?

Why in recent years vigorous efforts have been made to nurture institutional investors?

9. Name as many as possible the laws and regulations for supervising and regulating securities market in China.

10. What is systematic risk? Is it possible to eliminate it?

11. Please give definitions of the following terms: warrants, rights issue, insider dealing, prospectus, umbrella fund, financial statements.

12. What is the main function performed by an investment bank?

13. Can you tell the two ways in which secondary markets are organized?

14. How do you distinguish between a capital market and a money market?

15. What government body in China regulates and supervises the securities and futures markets?

16. When did China start to open its capital markets to the outside world?

17. What are the usual punishments for violating China's securities law?

18. Can you tell all the important rules governing the Chinese securities markets?

Part Nine

Fundamental Insurance

I. Principles and Contracts

1. Principles

A. *Principle of indemnity*

This principle is commonly incorporated into all insurance contracts. In general, the "principle of indemnity" serves as a legal foundation for all parties to an insurance contract, the Insurance Company and the policyholder, so that in the event of a covered cause of loss, the policyholder will not recover more than the actual cash value of loss. In simple terms, the policyholder should be restored to the original financial condition prior to the loss event. Keep in mind that the value of a policyholder's loss is generally determined "at the time of the loss". This principle prevents the insured from making a profit on an insurance claim.

B. *Principle of insurable interest*

In order for an insurance policy to be considered a legally enforceable insurance contract, entities to be insured, individual, families or businesses should possess an "Insurable Interest" with the risk (s) that are being protected, the subjects of insurance found within the insurance policy and the insured entities should face the possibility of financial loss or harm resulting from the various covered "causes of loss" that are found within the insuring agreements, terms and conditions of the insurance policy. This is known as the "Principle of Insurable Interest". In other words, entities to be insured should face the possibility or potential for loss. The "principle of insurable interest" and the "principle of indemnity" support each other in that the insurance policy will only provide for indemnification of its policyholder as long as the insured entity suffers a financial loss or is harmed, as a direct result of a covered cause of loss found within the insurance policy. The purpose of this principle is to prevent the insured from "gambling" with the insurance company. This principle serves as a means by which the insurance company will be able to "objectively" establish the amount of a covered loss at the time of an insured's loss or financial harm.

C. *Principle of subrogation*

Most insurance policies permit the insurance company to recover the financial value of the loss to their insured policyholder, from a liable or negligent entity that caused the financial loss or harm to their insured policyholder. This "Principle of Subrogation" permits the insurance company to take the place of the insured, or become a "substitute" for the insured, to recover the financial damages from the negligent party. The purpose of this principle is to encourage responsibility and accountability by holding the negligent party responsible for the financial burdens of a covered loss. Without this principle, insurance rates would increase in an unpredictable and inequitable fashion, resulting in higher risk costs for all members of the "risk pool".

D. *Principle of utmost good faith*

All insurance policies are contracts of "utmost good faith", in which there exists a higher standard of honesty that is expected by all parties to the insurance policy. The "Principle of Utmost Good Faith" demands that the insured or applicant for insurance provide factual and relevant material representations for underwriting suitability and acceptance by an insurance company. If it is determined that the insured or applicant for insurance misrepresented the truth about the material facts of the insured risk, the insurance policy can be declared "null and void", as if the policy never existed, thus leading to a denial of coverage, no claim payment or remedy for the insured.

2. Insurance Contracts

An Insurance contract determines the legal framework under which the features of an insurance policy are enforced. Insurance contracts are designed to meet very specific needs and thus have many features not found in many other types of contracts. Many features are similar across a wide variety of different types of insurance policies.

A. *General Features*

The insurance contract is a contract whereby the insurer will pay the insured (the person whom benefits would be paid to, or on his/her behalf), if certain defined events occur. Subject to the "fortuity principle", the event must be uncertain. The uncertainty can be either as to when the event will happen (i. e. in a life insurance policy, the time of the insured's death is uncertain) or as to if it will happen at all (i. e. a fire insurance policy).

- Insurance contracts are generally considered contracts of adhesion because the insurer draws up the contract and the insured has little or no ability to make material changes to it. This is interpreted to mean that the insurer bears the burden if there is any ambiguity in any terms of the contract.

- Insurance contracts are aleatory in that the amounts exchanged by the insured and insurer are unequal and depend upon uncertain future events.

- Insurance contracts are unilateral, meaning that only the insurer makes legally enforceable promises in the contract. The insured is not required to pay the premiums, but the insurer is required to pay the benefits under the contract if the insured has paid the premiums and met certain other basic provisions.

- Insurance contracts are governed by the principle of utmost good faith which requires both parties of the insurance contract to deal in good faith and in particular it imparts to the insured a duty to disclose all material facts which relate to the risk to be covered.

B. *Parts of an insurance contract*

- Definitions.

- Insuring agreement—the part of the contract where the insurer agrees to pay the insured for covered losses.

- Declarations—section that notes the identifying information about the insured and/or the insured property, such as name and address.

- Exclusions—section where certain perils that are not covered under the policy are enumerated.

II. Types of Insurance

1. Life Insurance

Life insurance provides compensation against unforeseen contingencies affecting human life. Unlike other types of insurance, the insured event (survival or death) must occur at some time: the risk concerns only the timing of the event. Early death may deprive dependants of a breadwinner and leave an estate encumbered with unpaid debts. Unforeseen longevity, on the other hand, may cause equivalent problems if resources cannot provide an adequate income on retirement.

There are two forms of life insurance:

- Industrial life insurance is the business of effecting insurances upon human life, where premiums are paid to collectors at intervals of less than two calendar months.

- Ordinary life insurance is simply a life insurance that is not "industrial".

The major types of ordinary life policy are:

- Temporary or term life insurance

This is the simplest and oldest form of life insurance. Policies provide for the payment of the sum insured to the policyholder's estate if he or she dies within a pre-specified period or term. If the life insured survives to the end of the policy term, then the contract ceases and no payment is made. There is therefore no savings element.

- Whole life insurance

The benefits in whole life insurance are paid on death, whenever that occurs. The cover is therefore provided for the whole of the policyholder's life.

- Endowment life insurance

Like temporary policies, endowment contracts are issued for a prespecified term and benefits are paid if the insured dies within that period. The difference is that benefits are also paid if the policyholder survives to the end of the policy term. Endowment policies are therefore equivalent to term insurance plus a lump-sum benefit paid on survival.

2. Non-Life Insurance

Any risk that can be quantified probably has a type of insurance to protect it. Besides life insurance, there are different types of non-life insurance, and the major ones are:

- Automobile insurance, also known as auto insurance, or car insurance and in the UK as motor insurance, is probably the most common form of insurance and may cover both legal liability claims against the driver and loss of or damage to the vehicle itself.

- Boiler insurance (also known as Boiler and Machinery Insurance or Equipment Breakdown Insurance).

- Casualty insurance insures against accidents, not necessarily tied to any specific property.

- Credit insurance pays some or all of a loan back when certain things happen to the borrower such as unemployment, disability, or death.

- Financial loss insurance protects individuals and companies against various financial risks. For example, a business might purchase cover to protect it from loss of sales if a fire in a factory prevented it from carrying out its business for a time. Insurance might also cover failure of a debtor to pay money it owes to the insured. Fidelity bonds and surety bonds are included in this category.

- Health insurance covers medical bills incurred because of sickness or accidents.

- Liability insurance covers legal claims against the insured. For example, a homeowner's insurance policy provides the insured with protection in the event of a claim brought by someone who slips and falls on the property, and brings a lawsuit for her injuries. Similarly, a doctor may purchase liability insurance to cover any legal claims against him if his negligence (carelessness) in treating a patient caused the patient injury and/or monetary harm. The protection offered by a liability insurance policy is two-fold: a legal defense in the event of a lawsuit commenced against the policyholder, plus indemnification (payment on behalf of the insured) with respect to a settlement or court verdict.

- Marine Insurance covers the loss or damage of goods at sea. Marine insurance typically compensates the owner of merchandise for losses sustained from fire, shipwreck, etc. , but excludes losses that can be recovered from the carrier.

- Property insurance provides protection against risks to property, such as fire, theft or weather damage. This includes specialized forms of insurance such as fire insurance, flood insurance, earthquake insurance, home insurance, inland marine insurance or boiler insurance.

- Travel insurance is an insurance cover taken by those who travel abroad, which covers certain losses such as medical expenses, loss of personal belongings, travel delay, personal liabilities, etc.

- Workers' compensation insurance replaces all or part of a worker's wages loss and accompanying medical expense incurred due to a job-related injury.

3. Reinsurance

Reinsurance is a means by which an insurance company (called the reinsured, ceding company or the direct insurer) shares the risk of loss with another insurance company (called the reinsurer).

A. *Functions of reinsurance*

There are many reasons an insurance company will choose to buy reinsurance as part of its responsibility to manage a portfolio of risks for the benefit of its policyholders and investors. The main uses of reinsurance are to allow the ceding company to assume individual risks greater than its size would otherwise allow, and to protect the direct insurer against catastrophic losses.

Reinsurance allows an insurance company to offer larger limits of protection to a policyholder than its own capital would allow. If an insurance company can safely write only USD 5 million in limits on any one policy, it can reinsure (or cede) the amount of the limits in excess of USD 5 million to reinsurers.

Reinsurance can help to make an insurance company's results more predictable by absorbing larger losses and reducing the amount of capital needed to provide coverage.

Reinsurance can improve an insurance company's balance sheet by reducing the amount of net liability thereby increasing Surplus. Surplus is roughly the same as shareholders' equity on a balance sheet (assets less liabilities) of a non-insurance company.

The insurance company may be motivated by arbitrage in purchasing reinsurance coverage at a lower rate than what they believe the cost is for the underlying risk.

B. How reinsurance works

Reinsurance can take place in several stages, making insured risks spread more widely among a large number of insurers and reinsurers. The following figure illustrates such spreading in the case of an individual large risk. The fire insurance on a large plant is usually coinsured (that is, shared among several insurers or coinsurers). Insurance company A normally accepts a larger share of this insurance than the maximum it would wish to retain for its own account and will therefore cede part of the risk to one or more reinsurers (companies 1, 2, 3, and so on). In turn, all or some of company A's reinsurers may pass on part of the risk they have accepted: reinsurance purchased by a reinsurer is known as a retrocession contract. If fire damages the plant, the manufacturer will present his claim against the original coinsurers. Company A is responsible for paying its share, but can then recover the reinsured part of that loss from its reinsurers, and company 1 will in turn look to company (1) and the other retrocessionaires to recover a part of its loss.

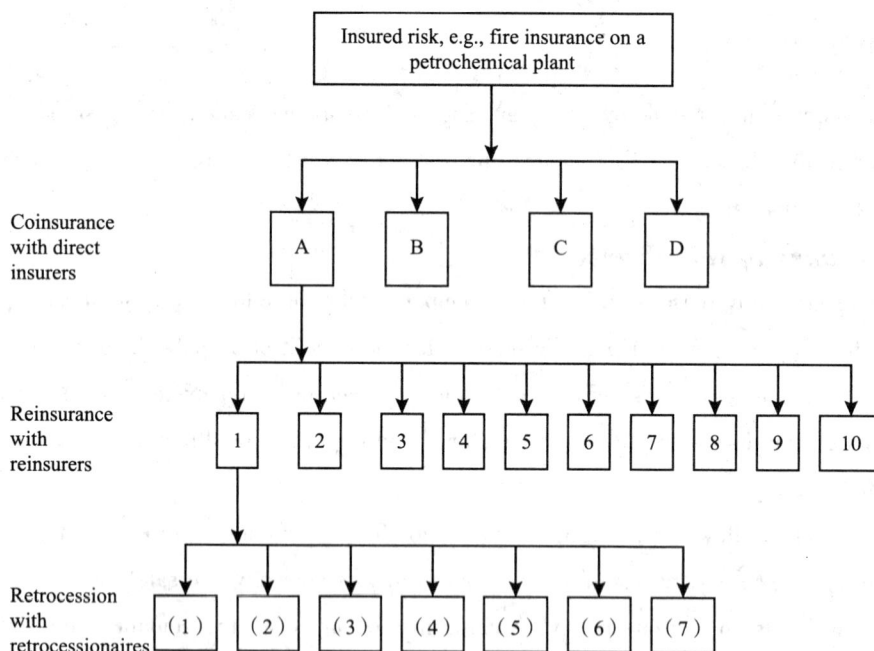

Figure 1   How reinsurance works

Coinsurance and reinsurance differ fundamentally. With coinsurance, there is a contractual relationship between the policyholder and the coinsurer, so that in the event of a loss each coinsurer is directly and separately responsible to the policyholder for paying its share of the loss. A reinsurance contract, on the other hand, is between the ceding company and the reinsurer—the original policyholder is not a party to that contract. By the principle of privity of contract, the original policyholder thus neither enjoys any benefit nor incurs any liability under a contract of reinsurance. So, if for some reason a policyholder is unable to recover a loss from his insurer, he cannot look to any reinsurers for payment of their share of that loss.

4. Government Sponsored Insurance

Government insurance may be discussed under two general headings: social insurance and all others. Social insurance includes Social Security, workers' compensation insurance, unemployment insurance and temporary disability insurance. Other government programs include veterans' life insurance, various property-liability insurance programs and different insured-loan programs.

Social insurance is that type of government insurance, usually compulsory in nature, designed to benefit persons whose incomes are interrupted by an economic or social problem or condition, or who are faced with personal losses from these conditions.

Social insurance plans tend to be introduced when a social problem exists that requires governmental action for solution and where the insurance method is deemed most appropriate as a solution. A social problem is a condition or set of circumstances that society as a whole finds undesirable, and for which the solution is generally beyond the control of the individual.

The justification for social insurance, then, lies in the fact that some insurance tasks either cannot be or are not accomplished by private insurers without assistance from a government. These tasks concern social problems that are deemed too important to ignore.

An understanding of social insurance coverages can be facilitated by an appreciation of the basic differences between these and privately sponsored insurance devices:

A. *Compulsion*

Most social insurance plans are characterized by an element of compulsion. Because social insurance plans are designed to solve some social problems, it is necessary that everyone is involved in cooperation. Thus, if an employer qualifies under the law, this employer and all employees must be covered by workers' compensation and unemployment insurance.

B. *Set level of benefits*

In social insurance plans, little choice is given as to what level of benefits is provided. Thus, even if so desired, an employee cannot purchase more or less unemployment insurance than is offered under the plan. In private individual insurance, of course, one may usually buy any amount of coverage desired.

C. *Floor of protection concept*

A basic principle of social insurance in a system of private enterprise is that it aims to provide a minimum level of economic security against perils that may interrupt income. This principle is known as the floor of protection concept.

D. *Subsidy concept*

All insurance devices have an element of subsidy in that the losses of the unfortunate few are shared with the fortunate many who escape loss. In social insurance it is anticipated that an insured group may not pay its own way but will be subsidized either by other insured groups or by the taxpayers generally.

E. *Unpredictability of loss*

For several reasons the cost of benefits under social insurance cannot usually be predicted with great accuracy. Therefore, the cost of some types of social insurance is unstable. For example, in a general depression unemployment may rise to unusual heights, causing tremendous outlays in unemployment benefits.

Attaching conditions to the right to receive payments is not a feature of private insurance, as it is in social insurance. In a life insurance contract the worker may elect to use cash values at retirement to purchase a life annuity of a definite promised amount, regardless of employment status or whether the worker meets a retirement test.

F. *Contributions required*

In order to qualify as social insurance a public program should require a contribution, directly or indirectly, from the person covered or the employer or both. Thus, social insurance does not include public assistance programs wherein the needy person receives outright gifts and must generally prove the inability to personally pay for the costs involved. This does not mean that the beneficiary in social insurance must pay all of the costs, but the beneficiary must make some contributions or the program is not really an insurance program, but rather a form of public charity.

G. *Attachment to labor force*

While it is not a necessary principle of social insurance, most social insurance plans cover only groups that are or have been attached to the labor force. Private insurance contracts, of course, are issued to individuals regardless of their employment status. The basic reason for this is that nearly all social insurance plans are directed at those perils that interrupt income.

III. Insurance Market

1. Insurance Companies

The business of any insurance company is to pay claims in return for the payment of premiums. But running such a business is, of course, a great deal more complex than this. Every insurance company undertakes certain essential activities:

A. *Underwriting*

This is the procedure by which an insurer evaluates the risk of a proposal and decides whether or not to enter into contract, and if so on what terms.

B. *Deciding a price*

An important part of underwriting is deciding what price to charge for the insurance, a process known as premium rating.

C. *Generating new business*

Like all other businesses, insurance companies want to increase the amount of business that they undertake and attempt to do this in various ways.

D. *Paying claims*

E. *Maintaining a fund*

Insurers cannot pay all claims out of revenue received from premiums and investment income. Because the timing of these payments and receipts cannot be coordinated they must therefore maintain a fund that can be used to pay claims.

F. *Investing the fund to earn investment income*

In many classes of insurance, substantial funds are accumulated. Careful investment of these funds allows insurers to earn investment income and make capital gains.

G. *Buying reinsurance*

The insurer may be aware that certain potential claim payments may exceed his financial resources. He will therefore wish to pass on part of the liability for these claims to another insurer by purchasing reinsurance.

H. *Providing additional services*

As part of their operations, insurers may provide additional services and advice to their customers.

I. *Drawing up accounts*

Like other trading enterprises, insurers make payments to creditors and receive money from debtors. They must then compile accounts for internal management, shareholders, and the taxation and supervisory authorities.

J. *Paying tax*

Insurance companies, like other trading enterprises, must pay corporation tax, value-added tax, and capital gains tax.

K. *Distributing profits and surpluses*

The shareholders of proprietary companies must be paid a dividend as a reward for risking their capital.

2. Reinsurance Companies

Reinsurance companies are insurance companies that sell policies to other insurance companies, allowing them to reduce their risks and protect themselves from very large losses. The reinsurance market is dominated by a few very large companies, with huge reserves.

In most countries reinsurance markets cannot be divided neatly into buyers and sellers because the same institutions operate in both capacities.

The main buyers of reinsurance are the direct insurance companies, but in turn many direct insurers themselves undertake reinsurance business. Although many direct insurers confine themselves largely to the reciprocal exchange of reinsurances (i. e. reinsuring each other), some major companies write a substantial volume of reinsurance business either through their reinsurance departments or through specialist reinsurance subsidiaries. Some companies employ underwriting agents to write reinsurance accounts.

The main sellers of reinsurance business are the specialist reinsurance companies, often known as professional reinsurers. The major companies operate internationally, but many developing countries have established State reinsurance corporations primarily to handle the reinsurance of the local direct insurance companies, which are often required by law to make cessions to the corporation. The specialist reinsurance companies act as buyers of reinsurance in order to control their own exposures and also, to some extent, to provide reciprocity to their ceding companies.

3. Insurance Intermediaries

The primary role of an independent intermediary is to bring buyers and sellers together so that they can complete their transactions efficiently. In a market where every buyer knows about every seller and every type of product sold, there would be little need for intermediaries. But in many areas, potential buyers and sellers know little about what is for sale or who is selling or buying and are prepared to pay an intermediary to provide such information.

Auctioneers, estate agents, stockbrokers, and insurance brokers are all intermediaries who provide information and bring buyers and sellers together.

In insurance, an intermediary is someone who brings a potential policyholder into contact with the insurers for the purpose of effecting a contract of insurance, and who is not employed solely by one insurer. There are several types of insurance intermediary, and many of them do more than just bring buyer and seller together: they also provide services to both the insurer and the insured. They may, for example, advise on the type of insurance to purchase, recommend an insurer, help the proposer fill in proposal forms, advise on making a claim, and so on.

The intermediary's overall duty is to act with the reasonable skill and care expected of him and in accordance with the terms of his agreement with the insured. Higher standards are expected of insurance brokers because of their assumed expertise.

Intermediaries should try to comply exactly with any instructions issued by the insured and tell him promptly if they cannot. No secret payments should be accepted from anybody else. Intermediaries must also account to the insured for any monies received on his behalf.

4. Insurance Associations

Insurers sometimes encounter exposures that they are unwilling to insure individually because the losses either occur too frequently or are potentially too large. Pools or associations can be formed to handle such exposures, either voluntarily or to meet statutory requirements.

A pool or an association consists of several insurers that have joined together to insure risks that the individual members are not willing to cover alone. For example, the losses from an accident at a large nuclear power plant might reach several billions of dollars for liability and property damage combined. Since no single insurer is willing to assume such tremendous liability, nuclear energy associations were formed with many member insurers to absorb the losses when they occur. In addition, the associations buy reinsurance from non-members to increase their capacity.

Associations operate either as a syndicate or through reinsurance. A syndicate association issues a joint policy to the insured, listing all association members and specifying the part of the insurance for which each member is responsible. Under such policies, the insured has a contractual relationship with each member of the association and may sue any or all of them directly if a disagreement arises.

Under a reinsurance association, one member of the association issues the policy to the insured, and the other association members reinsure an agreed proportion of each risk insured. In this kind of arrangement, the insured only has a direct contractual relationship with the company that issued the policy. The policyholder has no direct legal rights against the other members of the association and may not even know that they exist.

IV. Insurance Business

1. Product Development

A product may be defined as anything that can be offered to someone to satisfy a need or want. All products have elements of tangibility and intangibility. A tangible product is one that can be seen and touched. In insurance, the tangible product is a legal contract represented by words on paper and known as an insurance policy. Other dimensions of tangibility may include a product name, endorsements, and packaging. Insurance products also have elements of intangibility. The intangible product is the promise to satisfy prospective customers who are asked to buy.

Insurers introduce new products at all stages of the product development life cycle. The steps in the product development process for insurance products are as follows:

A. *Opportunity assessment*

The first step, opportunity assessment, consists of monitoring the marketplace to identify potential opportunities.

B. *Development of contract, underwriting and price fixing*

Once approval is secured to continue the process, the next phase is to develop the policy forms, underwriting guidelines, and fixing price. Cooperation among various insurer functions—including underwriting, actuary, claims, reinsurance, premium audit, and loss control—is essential to the process.

C. *Business forecast*

The business forecast phase establishes benchmarks for evaluating the success of the program. Such measures include the number of policies expected to be issued, the premium volume expected to be generated, the number of producers who will be expected to participate, and the loss ratio expected to develop.

D. *Regulatory requirements*

After the business forecast is approved, the development process enters the regulatory arena. Regulators require, at a minimum, notification of new policy forms, rating plans, and policy writing rules.

E. *Distribution requirements*

Following regulatory approval, the insurer completes the distribution requirements, including training and promotional materials for the sales force.

F. Introduction

The product is introduced with advertising and sales promotion. Management must also make tough decisions about eliminating weak products. Many insurers carry products that do not contribute to profitability objectives. Management must be able to identify such products, determine whether the continued existence of the product line is appropriate, and take action to improve the product performance, or to phase it out, or to eliminate it altogether.

2. Distribution Channels

There are many arrangements that may be made for the distribution of the insurance contract. These arrangements are comparable to the channels taken by physical goods. For example, life insurance generally takes a short, direct channel, while property insurance normally uses a long, indirect channel with one or more independent middlemen involved.

A. Direct distribution in life insurance

In a direct distribution channel, a sales person, called an agent or underwriter, contacts the ultimate consumer and reports directly to the insurer or to an intermediary, commonly called a general agent, who in turn reports to the insurer. The authority of the underwriter or agent is limited; the underwriter cannot be called an independent middleman, since he or she is actually an employee working on contract under the guidance of the insurer or the insurer's representative.

A general agent is an individual employed to hire, train and supervise the agents at a lower level. The general agent sometimes collects premiums and remits them to the home office of the insurer. Usually the general agent represents only one insurer, and works on a salary plus commission plan, or sometimes on commission only. The general agent is not an independent middleman like a typical wholesaler, for the general agent does not exercise final control over the issuance and the terms of the contract. The company normally is not bound by the general agent in putting a contract in force. The general agent exercises no control over the amount of the premium with no investment in inventory and does not own any business written, and legal right to exercise any control over policyholders once he or she leaves the employment of the company.

B. Direct writing in property-liability insurance

In some lines of property insurance, independent middlemen have been dispensed with and the contract is marketed directly from the insurer to the insured, with or without an intermediary. Small amounts of insurance are sold directly by mail and no agent of any kind is employed; all negotiations are made between the insurance company and the consumer. In most cases, however, the insurer employs a representative called an exclusive agent to handle its business, to solicit prospects, to take care of paper work, and, in general, to serve as the insurer's direct contact with the insured. Insurers who employ this type of distribution are called direct writers. In general, direct writers have been able to sell insurance at lower cost to the final consumer and this, plus a vigorous advertising campaign, has contributed greatly to their success. The lower cost has been achieved by the insurer largely through stricter underwriting and smaller allowances to the agent for the production and servicing of business.

C. Indirect distribution (Agency system)

The channel of distribution for a majority of property insurance lines is indirect. A system of middlemen, comparable to the wholesaler-retailer system in tangible-goods marketing, is used. This system has been termed Agency System.

In property insurance, the middleman most comparable to the wholesaler is called the general agent, while the retailer is called the local agent or broker. These terms should not be confused with those that are applied in the field of life insurance.

Often an insurer will not use a general agent, but will work directly through local agents, or set up a branch office to deal with local agents. This plan is known as the branch office system. It corresponds to a manufacturer's sales branch in the tangible-goods field. This system gives the insurer more control over the distribution of its contracts than when a general agent is employed.

3. Underwriting

Underwriting is the process by which the insurer decides whether or not to accept a proposal of insurance, on what conditions, in what proportion, and at what price. People fulfilling this duty are underwriters.

Objective underwriting almost always contains certain well-defined elements:

- An evaluation of the major underwriting factors affecting claims experiences for the particular type of insurance. These factors must be identifiable and serve to divide up potential policyholders into distinctly recognizable groups, with people in the same group having similar claims experiences. For example, we would expect the relevant underwriting factors for life insurance to include age, sex, health, and type of contract.

- An assessment of the claims experiences of the "average" member of each group. The underwriter needs to estimate the annual claims consisting in this "average" member and also some breakdown of the annual frequency and average size of claims. This average claims experience is then reflected in an "average" premium rate. For example, a life insurance underwriter considering an application from a 45-year-old man will first find out the mortality experience and appropriate premium rate for the "average" healthy man of 45.

- An assessment of the effect of the different underwriting factors on claims experience, which the underwriter can reflect in varying premium rates. For example, life insurance underwriters know fairly accurately how age affects mortality rates.

- A comparison of the proposer's characteristics with those of the "average" group member, in order to see whether the proposer represents a better or worse claims experience than average. For the 45-year-old applicant for life insurance, the underwriter will check the medical evidence to see whether the proposer has any condition that could affect his chances of premature death. The premium rate is then fixed above or below the "average" rate to reflect the particular anticipated claims experience.

- A comparison of the premium to be charged with the amount to be paid in the event of a claim. If they are similar in size the underwriter may well turn down the proposal since the insurance has then very little significance.

4. Reinsurance

As we have mentioned reinsurance in part Ⅲ3, here we would introduce methods of reinsuring and forms of reinsurance.

A. *Methods of reinsuring*

i. Reinsurance treaty

This method accounts for by far the largest part of reinsurance business. Strictly speaking, most types of treaty are not contracts of reinsurance: they are agreements between a ceding company and one or more reinsurers whereby the former agrees to cede and the reinsurer agrees to accept automatically any reinsurances falling within the terms of the treaty.

ii. Facultative reinsurance

These are reinsurances arranged on an individual risk basis. Facultative means "optional" —the ceding company is free to decide whether to offer the risk to the reinsurer, who in turn is not obliged to accept. Like an original insurer, a facultative reinsurer can exercise his judgement in deciding whether to accept and, if so, how much and on what terms.

B. *Forms of reinsurance*

i. Proportional

Proportional reinsurance (mostly known as quota share reinsurance) is where the reinsurer takes a stated percent share of each policy the insurer writes and then shares in the premiums and losses in that same proportion. The size of the insurer might only allow it to write a risk with a policy limit of up to USD 1 million, but by purchasing proportional reinsurance it might double or triple that limit. Premiums and losses are then shared on a pro rata basis. For example an insurance company might purchase a 50% quota share treaty; in this case they would share half of all premium and losses with the reinsurer. In a 75% quota share, they would share (cede) 3/4 of all premiums and losses. The reinsurance company usually pays a commission on the premiums back to the insurer in order to compensate them for costs incurred in sourcing and administering the business. This is known as the ceding commission.

The other (lesser known) form of proportional reinsurance is surplus share. In this case, a "line" is defined as a certain policy limit— say USD 100,000. In a 9 line surplus share treaty the reinsurer could then accept up to USD 900,000 (9 lines). So if the Insurance Company issues a policy for USD 100,000, they would keep all of the premiums and losses from that policy. If they issue a USD 200,000 policy, they would give (cede) half of the premiums and losses to the reinsurer (1 line each). If they issue a USD 500,000 policy, they would cede 80% of the premiums and losses on that policy to the reinsurer (1 line to the company, 4 lines to the reinsurer 4/5 = 80%). If they issue the maximum policy limit of USD 1,000,000 the reinsurer would then get 90% of all of the premiums and losses from that policy.

ii. Non-proportional

Non-Proportional Reinsurance (or Excess of Loss) only responds if the loss suffered by the insurer exceeds a certain amount (retention). An example of this form of reinsurance is where the insurer is prepared to accept a loss of USD 1 million for any loss which may occur and purchases a layer of reinsurance of USD 4 million in excess of USD 1 million—if a loss of USD 3 million occurs the insurer pays the USD 3 million to the insured (s), and then recovers USD 2 million from their reinsurer (s). In this example, the insurer will retain any loss exceeding USD 5 million unless they have purchased a further excess layer (second layer) of say USD 10 million excess of USD 5 million.

5. Loss Settlement

One basic purpose of insurance is to provide for the indemnification of those members of the group who suffer losses. This is accomplished in the loss-settlement process, but it is sometimes a great deal more complicated than just pass out money. The payment of losses that have occurred is the function of the claims department. Life insurance companies refer to employees who settle losses as claim representatives or benefit representatives. The nature of the difficulties frequently encountered in the property and liability field is evidenced by the fact that employees of the claims department in this field are called adjusters.

It is obviously important that the insurance company pay its claims fairly and promptly, but it is equally important that the company resist unjust claims and avoid overpayment of them. The view is rapidly increasing among insurers that prompt, courteous, and fair claim service is one of the most effective competitive tools available to a company.

A. *Courses of action in claim settlement*

Two basic courses of action are open to the company when confronted with a claim: pay or contest. In most cases there is little question concerning coverage, and payment of the loss This is the most common procedure, but in those instances where the company feels that a claim should not be paid, it will deny liability and thereby contest the claim. The company might deny payment on two basic grounds: either because the loss did not occur or because the policy does not cover the loss. A loss might not be covered under the policy because it does not fall within the scope of the insuring agreement, it is excluded, it happened when the policy was not in force, or the insured had violated a policy condition.

B. *Adjustment process*

In determining whether to pay or contest a claim, the adjuster follows a relatively set settlement procedure with four main steps: (1) notice of loss, (2) investigation, (3) proof of loss, and (4) payment or denial of the claim. The details of these steps vary with the type of insurance.

i. *Notice*

The first step in the claim process is the notice by the insured to the company that a loss has occurred. The requirements differ from one policy to another, but in most cases the contract requires that the notice be given "immediately" or "as soon as practicable" . Some contracts stipulate that notice be given in writing, but even in these, the requirement is not strictly enforced. Normally, the insured gives notice saying that a loss has occurred by informing the agent, and this satisfies the contract.

ii. *Investigation*

The investigation is designed to determine if there was actually a loss covered by the policy, and if so, the amount of the loss. In deciding whether there was a covered loss, the adjuster must determine first that there was in fact a loss, and then whether the loss is covered by the policy. Determination as to whether there was a loss is the simpler of the two. There are instances in which the claimant attempts to defraud the insurer, and in some instances payment is undoubtedly made where there has not in fact been a loss. Once it has been determined that a loss has occurred, the adjuster must determine whether the loss is covered under the policy. First, was the policy in effect at the time of the loss? If the policy is newly issued, did the loss take place before the policy became effective? Or at the other end of the time spectrum, did the policy expire before the loss took place? Once it has been established that the loss took place during the policy period, there is still the possibility that the insured might have violated a condition that caused the suspension or voidance of the contract. If it appears that the policy was in effect at the time of the event and that there was a loss, then the next question to be dealt with is: was the peril causing the loss insured against in the policy? In the case of property insurance, does the property damaged or loss meet the definition of the property insured? The location of the property is still another question, because some contracts cover property only at a specific location, or are applicable only in certain jurisdictions. Finally, the adjuster must decide if the person making the claim is entitled to payment under the terms of the policy.

If the answer to all these questions is yes, the loss is covered. Yet to be determined is the amount of the loss, which in most cases can be far more complicated than the determination of whether or not coverage applied.

iii. Proof of loss

Within a specified time after giving notice, the insured is required to file a proof of loss. This is a sworn statement that the loss has taken place and gives the amount of claim and the circumstances surrounding the loss. The adjuster normally assists the insured in the preparation of this document.

iv. Payment or denial

If all goes well, the insurance company draws a draft reimbursing the insured for the loss. If not, it denies the claim. The claim may be disallowed because: there was no loss, the policy did not cover the loss, or the adjuster feels that the amount of the claim is unreasonable.

C. Difficulties in loss settlement

It is inevitable that there will be disagreements regarding loss settlements. In some instances, the insured will mistakenly feel that a loss should have been covered under the policy when in fact it is not. Adjusters, being human, also err, and there are occasions when a legitimate claim is denied. In addition to the question of whether the loss is covered, the amount of the loss is a continuing source of trouble. Value in most instances is matter of opinion, and we should therefore not be surprised that the insured and the adjuster may differ regarding the amount of the loss. For these reasons the role of the adjuster is a delicate one. He or she must be fair, and yet must try not to leave the insured disgruntled. This is difficult when a loss is not covered.

On the surface, it would seem that and insured is relatively powerless against the insurance company in the event of a dispute. This is not the case. In those cases there the disagreement is over the amount of the loss, most policies provide for compulsory arbitration on the request of either party. In the case of a denial based on an alleged lack of coverage, the insured who feels unfairly treated may appeal to the state regulatory authority, which is charged with the protection of the consumer's interest. Finally, the insured has recourse through the courts. In some instances, the only alternative remaining to the insured is to bring suit against the insurer.

6. Reserve

Insurance companies, particularly life insurance companies, have substantial funds at their disposal. Such funds are a necessary part of insurance operations and are split into two broad types:

A. *Policyholders' funds or technical reserves*

These are necessary to cover outstanding liabilities to policyholders.

i. Technical reserves in non-life insurance

Technical reserves necessary to meet non-life insurance liabilities have six components:

Unearned premium reserves

Unexpired risk reserves

Outstanding claims reserves

IBNR reserves (Incurred But Not Reported reserves)

Catastrophe reserves

Claims equalization reserves

ii. Technical reserves in life insurance

A life insurance policy's level of premium is more than sufficient to pay for expected claims in the early years of the contract but insufficient later on. A reserve of the excess of premium in the early years must therefore be built up in order to cover subsequent claims. This reserve value is particularly important in savings-based policies where the policy monies must eventually be paid.

B. *Shareholders' funds, free reserves, or surplus*

These constitute the remaining funds, and are not tied to any specific liabilities to policyholders. They can therefore be used as the insurer wishes, although part must be maintained to fulfill the solvency requirements of the statutory authorities. The use of these funds depends on the type of business underwritten:

- In life insurance they are known as surplus and are used primarily to provide bonuses with profits for policyholders and dividends to shareholders.
- In non-life insurance they are known as shareholders' funds or free reserves, and are used to provide dividends to shareholders and an additional cushion against an unexpected proliferation of claims.

7. Investment

The substantial funds held by insurers are invested so as to earn interest and capital gains. In most classes of insurance, particularly in long-term business-life insurance, annuities and pensions, investment income makes a vital contribution to an insurer's profits. In the investment of insurance company funds, the overall aim is to be able to meet liabilities when they fall due, while earning the highest possible yield without incurring too great a risk.

In non-life insurance, the major problem for an insurer is the unexpectedly large claim that might force him to sell investments at short notice, possibly at a loss. Insurers therefore hold cash deposits and assets like quoted securities that can be easily sold at short notice and avoid those like property and land that cannot. But these investments must also produce a satisfactory yield so that shareholders can be paid good dividends and any underwriting losses can be balanced by investment gains.

In long-term insurance business, the major concern is to earn a rate of interest greater than that used to calculate premium: failure to do so will lead to insolvency. Moreover, since the vast bulk of life insurance business is savings-based, insurers must earn an interest rate that allows them to compete with other forms of savings. The longer-term nature of their liabilities allows life insurers to concentrate on longer-term investments, which they are less concerned about the possibility of selling assets at short notice to pay claims, and they therefore invest much of their assets in long-dated or undated government securities, equities and property.

Notes

1. **toss** [tɔs] *vt. & vi.* : ① throw up into or through the air; jerk, toss (up) a coin, send a coin spinning up in the air and guess which side (head or tails) will be on top when it falls② (cause to) move restlessly from side to side or up and down

2. **"heads" or "tails"** : that side of a coin on which the "head" of a ruler appears, the other side being "tail"

3. **fortuitous** [fɔːˈtjuːitəs] *adj.* happening by chance

4. **death benefit**: one of the benefits under the (British) National Insurance (Industrial Injuries) Act (1946), where an employee suffers death as a result of an accident at work. It is not to be confused with Funeral Expenses

5. **amass** [ə'mæs] *vt.* pile or heap up, collect (esp. riches)

6. **replenish** [ri'pleniʃ] *vt.* fill up (sth.) again (with...)

7. **by-pass**: *n.* road joining two parts of an older road

8. **marathon** ['mɑːrəθən] *n.* (the Marathon, usu. Marathon race) long-distance race on foot (about 26 miles at modern sports meetings)

9. **treacherous** ['tretʃərəs] *adj.* ① false or disloyal (to a friend, cause, etc.) ②deceptive; not to be relied upon

10. **rapid** ['ræpid] *adj.* ①quick; (of action) done quickly② (of a slope) steep; descending steeply

n. (usu. pl.) part of a river where a steep slope causes the water to flow fast.

11. **capsize** [kæp'saiz] *vt. & vi.* (esp. of a boat in the water) (cause to) overturn, upset

12. **jettison** ['dʒetisn] *vt.* throw (goods) overboard in order to lighten a ship (e. g. during a storm)

13. **haunt** [hɔːnt] *vt.* ①visit, be with, habitually or repeatedly② return to the mind repeatedly

n. place frequently visited by the person (s) named

14. **underwrite** ['ʌndə'rait] vt. ① to agree to pay the cost of making or doing something ②to guarantee a person against commercial loss ③to accept liability for loss under a contract of insurance

15. **devour** [di'vauə] *vt.* ① eat (fig. look at, hear, read) hungrily or greedily②be devoured by (curiosity, anxiety, etc.) be filled with, have all one's attention taken up by

16. **pecuniary** [pi'kjuːnjəri] *adj.* of money

17. **insurable interest**: a direct monetary interest in an object or person being insured. It is a ruling condition of insurance that the person who benefits from an insurance contract must himself be liable to suffer a loss that can be valued in units of money if the insured object is damaged or lost, or the insured person is injured or dies. If this condition is not met, the interest is not insurable and the contract would not be supported in a court of law

18. **subrogation** [ˌsʌbrə'geiʃən] *n.* the legal right of an insurer to receive any money obtained by the insured as a result of his making use of his rights against third parties; this reduces the cost of the loss to the insurer and prevents the insured from obtaining more than

his full indemnity. Sometimes the conditions of the policy give the insurer the right to bring a legal action against a third party who is liable for any loss suffered by the insured

19. **null and void**: *adj.* without legal effect; invalid

20. **fortuity** [fɔːˈtju (ː) iti] *n.* an accident; any chance event causing loss or damage which was not inevitable, i. e. which was not certain to happen

21. **adhesion** [ədˈhiːʒən] *n.* ① adhering; being or becoming attached or united ② support ③ joining together of tissues in the body (e. g. after an injury); insurance of this

22. **impart** [imˈpɑːt] *vt.* give, pass on (a share of something, a quality, a secret, news etc. to somebody)

23. **encumber** [inˈkʌmbə] *vt.* ① get in the way of , hamper, be a burden to ② crowd; fill up

24. **fidelity bond**: *n.* an insurance contract protecting an employer against loss caused by any act of dishonesty or failure to perform duties by an employee, e. g. a cashier

25. **surety bond**: *n.* a formal agreement by a person (called a guarantor) to pay a stated sum of money if a certain party fails to perform a duty he owes to another party, e. g. to pay a debt by a stated date. Such bonds often take the form of an insurance contract, the insurance company being the guarantor

26. **cede** [siːd] *vt.* give up (right, land, etc. to somebody, to another state, etc.)

27. **motivate** [ˈmoutiveit] *vt.* give a motive to; be the motive of . (motive [məutv] *n.* that which causes somebody to act)

28. **arbitrage** [ˈɑːbitridʒ] *n.* a form of speculation more particularly found in foreign exchange markets, where it is sometimes possible to purchase markets, where it is sometimes possible to purchase currency in one centre and immediately sell it at a profit in another. Arbitrage in foreign currencies is possible only because of the ease and speed of telegraphic transfers between commercial centers throughout the world. So ① the business of buying some currency, bill of exchange (or even commodity) in one market centre and selling it in another almost at the same time, thus taking advantage of any difference in exchange rate or price between the two centers. When dealing takes place in several centers, arbitrage is said to be indirect or compound ② in the U. S. A, the difference in market price between two securities that are closely related, e. g. the stock of a holding company and of a subsidiary

29. **retrocession** [ˌretrouˈseʃən] *n.* moving backward; a ceding back

30. **retrocessionaire** [retrouseʃəˈnɛə] *n.* the person who exercises retrocession

31. **vest** [vest] *vt. & vi.* : ① furnish or supply (somebody with) ② (with, in) (of

property, etc.) be vested in③ (old use or poet) clothe

32. **fiduciary** [fi'djuːʃjəri] *n.* a person holding a position formally recognized by law as being one of special confidence, usu. a person such as trustee or executor to whom property has been given to hold and manage, not for his own profit, but for the benefit (advantage) of someone else. Such a person is said to hold the property in a fiduciary capacity

33. **vie** [vai] (present participle: vying) *vi.* rival or compete (with)

34. **indulge** [in'dʌldʒ] *vt. & vi.* gratify; give way to and satisfy (desires, etc.)

35. **actuarial** [ˌæktjuː'ɛəriəl] *adj.* of an actuary (['æktjuəri] *n.* expert who calculates rate of insurance—by studying rates of mortality, frequency of fires, accidents, etc.)

36. **pro rata** [prou'reitə] *adv.* in proportion; according to the share, etc. , of each

37. **disgruntled** [dis'grʌntid] *adj.* discontented; in a bad temper (at something, with somebody)

38. **allege** [ə'leiʒ] *vt.* put forward as a fact, excuse, reason, or argument

n. alleging; statement, esp. one made without proof

39. **proliferation** [prouˌlifə'reiʃən] the noun for proliferate— [prou'lifəreit] *vt. & vi.* grow, produce, by multiplication of cells, new parts, etc. ; reproduce (cells, etc.)

40. **synchronize** ['siŋkrənaiz] *vt. & vi.* (cause to) happen at the same time, agree in time, speeds, etc

Questions for discussion

1. Please point out the main principles in preparing an insurance contract.

2. What is a policy in insurance business and what is a policy-holder?

3. What are the main types of insurance?

4. Please explain the following: Insurance, Coinsurance and Reinsurance. What is a retrocession contract?

5. Which organizations and persons are involved in insurance industry? And what are their respective functions?

6. How is a settlement made after a loss has happened?

7. Why do the insurance companies usually have big amount of fund and how do they make use of the funds?

Part Ten

Bank Letters and Telecommunications

This part aims at helping readers to have a good understanding and mastery of the format and application of bank letters, telex and SWIFT messages through explanation and illustration in banking situations. All the sample letters are chosen from actual banking transactions with names of persons, institutions and date (if there is any) being changed. Most of them contain just the Subject and the Body of Letter, leaving out the other parts to save space.

Readers should be aware that the contents in the Sample Letters can be applied in telex messages; some of them can also be used in SWIFT messages. Readers should also know that these three types of correspondence are different in FORM, but as to the LANGUAGE, the difference can be blurred. For instance, a telex message can be prepared in the sentences totally the same as those in a letter, or with abbreviated words and phrases or shortened sentences.

I. Bank Letters

The alarming development of internet and E-mail has brought a great leap forward in bank correspondence. To a certain degree, bank letters, nowadays, are giving way to telex and SWIFT messages. Nevertheless, bankers are still aware of the importance of effective letter writing. Bankers cannot have a good relationship with their customers if they do not know how to communicate with them by letters. The services of a bank can hardly be marketed if a prospective customer is discouraged by a poorly written letter. Letter writing, therefore, is still crucial to the success of bankers.

1. Main Parts of a Bank Letter

- Letter Head: Name and address of the sender.
- Date: The name of month is officially in full spelling.
- Inside Address: Name and address of receiver of the letter.
- Salutation: It usually ends with a comma. The usual Salutation is either "Dear Sirs" / "Gentlemen" or "Mr. ×××" / "Madam ×××".
- Subject/Caption: It indicates the central idea of the letter and is usually short but clear.
- Body of Letter: The most important part of the whole letter. It usually contains three

(or more) paragraphs, i. e. the opening paragraph, the purpose paragraph (s) and the closing paragraph.

- Complimentary Close: It can be one of the following: "Truly yours" / "Yours truly", "Sincerely yours" / "Yours sincerely", and "Faithfully yours" / "Yours faithfully" or their variations such as "Truly", "Sincerely", "Faithfully", etc.

- Signature and Designation: Name of writer (name both in handwriting and in print) with or without professional title, and name of the institution sending the letter. Note that in many banks senior management members usually use personal stationery with the name and title pre-printed. In such case, only the signature in handwriting is needed when letters are made.

- Enclosure: This part is not indispensable, depending on the actual situation. Usually it is in the abbreviation of "Enc." / "Encl." indicating one single enclosure, or "Encs." / "Encls." representing two or more enclosures.

You are advised to refer to SAMPLE LETTERS in the part of Printing Styles.

Full-block style (the most popular style):

- Letter head;
- Date;
- Inside Address;
- Salutation;
- Subject/Caption;
- Body;
- Complimentary close;
- Signiture;
- Name and title of the sender;
- Enclosure.

2. Printing Styles

Bank letters are usually printed in three different styles, but the following two are most popular.

A. *Semi-block Style*

The Semi-block Style is the traditional style printed with an indention of 4 to 6 spaces at the beginning of each paragraph in the Body of Letter. In this style, the Date Line is typed flush with the right margin while the Inside Address, the Salutation and the Enclosure (if there is any) are typed flush with the left margin. The Complimentary Close, the Signature and Designation are typed in the center about 6 spaces towards the right, while the Caption is typed in the center of the page above the Body of Letter.

December 23, 2005

ABC Bank

Guangdong Branch

Guangzhou, China

Gentlemen,

Documentary Credit No. 3728306

Issued by Fuji Bank Ltd. , Tokyo, Japan

Originally in favor of T & G Co. , Ltd, Hong Kong

Without any engagement on our part and under the instructions from the original beneficiary of the captioned credit, we transfer the documentary credit to you, with terms and conditions as per attached certified copy of the original credit and amendment (if any) except the following:

Transferred amount: USD 28, 230. 00 (United States Dollars Twenty Eight Thousand Two Hundred and Thirty Only).

Expiry date and place: March 1, 2006, Hong Kong.

Latest date of shipment: February 15, 2006.

Value of the goods must not be shown on documents, with the exception of the following:

Draft, if required.

Commercial invoices.

Export license and GSP Form A.

Please note that this transfer is not valid unless it is accompanied by the aforesaid photostatic copy of the original credit and amendment, if any. Drawing under this transferred credit must be endorsed on the reverse hereof by the presenting bank.

We shall advise you of further amendment only upon and in accordance with instructions from the original beneficiary.

Your early attention to this matter is highly appreciated.

Truly yours,

Davi Malvin

Managing Director

XYZ Bank

Hong Kong Branch

Encl.

CC. T &G CO. , Ltd. Hong Kong

B. Full-block Style

In this style all parts of the letter are typed flush with the left margin.

BANK, NA

Hong Kong Branch

13th Floor, Jardine House

I Connaught Place

Hong Kong

January 10, 2006

ABC Bank

Guangdong Provincial Branch

4/F, 338 Huanshidong Road

Guangzhou, China.

Attn: Mr. So-and-so

Deputy General Manager

Dear Sir,

This letter serves as a follow-up to the recent meeting we had before the end of 1999, when Mr. Eric Yuen of our Beijing branch and I met with you and Mr. Song. Due to heavy workload at year-end we could not get back to you at an earlier time, we apologize for the delay. As agreed at the meeting, I have attached herewith a list of Latin America and Middle East/ Africa banks, of which Bank One is willing to confirm letters of credit. We must emphasize the fact there is no implied commitment to confirm and all transactions will be subject to final credit approval. The name printed in red is our preferred bank with which we used to do business. Please do not hesitate to check with us on any potential business opportunity and we will give you our quotations upon request.

Bank One values the cordial relationship maintained with Agricultural Bank of China and we would very much like to expand it in the trade finance area. We look forward to servicing you in the near future.

Yours truly,

John Savithson

Vice President Operating Products Group

3. Writing Principles

If you want to produce a well written letter you are advised to follow the following seven principles (or 7C principles):

- Completeness. This means when writing a letter you should include whatever details needed to produce the response you want. Only a thoughtless writer leaves the reader at loose ends.

- Conciseness. To carry out this principle, you have to write in the fewest possible words, by avoiding wordiness and very long sentences. Wordy expressions cost money—the writer's time and the readers' time. Businessmen are always busy. Time to them means money.

- Consideration. As a writer of bank letters, you should think of the reader's interest first. To observe this principle, you have to emphasize your reader's interest rather than your own concern; you should emphasize what you can do, not what you can not. Remember, if you always think of yourself first, you may end up last. In other words, when your letter is one-sided—when your letter seeks an advantage for you without offering any to the readers or when it expresses your view and feelings without regard for those of the reader – your letter cannot be considered entirely successful even if the reader eventually takes the action you want.

- Clarity. Simplicity and conciseness lead to clarity. To achieve this purpose, you must try your best to avoid ambiguity and needless commercial jangons like "We beg to remain yours sincerely". Just "sincerely" will be good enough for the complementary close of your letter.

- Concreteness. If you want your letter to be concrete you have to use specific expressions rather than general language, more active voices not passive ones.

- Courtesy. Courtesy means politeness and good manner in writing a business letter, it means you must treat your reader with respect and friendly human concern. Very often courtesy can be cultivated through the following techniques:

—showing sincerity

—basing your tone on a positive attitude

—softening your request: For example, a request can be softened if it is phrased as a question. Instead of using harsh sentence like "take care of this matter at once", you can say: "Will you please take care of this matter at once?" or "May we ask you to take care of this matter at once?"

- Correctness. By correctness we mean your grammar, punctuation, spelling, sentence structure, phrases etc. must be all correct. The figures and information stated in your letter must be correct and accurate.

4. Sample Letters in Different Banking Transactions

A. *Letters concerning bank relationship*

March 10, 2006

John A. Renyi

Chairman and Chief Executive Officer

AAA Bank

Wall Street, New York

N. Y. 10286, U. S. A.

Dear Mr. Renyi,

It was a great pleasure to host you and your colleagues during your recent visit to China, which gave us the opportunity to show our appreciation for the friendly and mutually beneficial relationship we have over the years.

We will be delighted to see the business growth of AAA Bank in China and to find more opportunities where we could work together. With more convenient communication and ready resources in place, we are convinced that cooperation between our two banks will be expanded in possible areas.

Thanks for your kind invitation and looking forward to meeting you on some other occasion.

Yours sincerely,

(Handwriting Signature)

Aug. 25, 2006

Li Ping, Senior Executive Vice President

AAA Bank

No. 5 Jinrong Street

Xicheng District, Beijing

Dear Mr. Li,

On August 24, BBB Bank announced that it had signed an agreement to sell its retail and commercial franchise in Hong Kong and Macau to CCC Bank. This sale will have no impact on your relationship with us or on the services we provide to you.

Our wholesale banking franchise will continue to be an integral part of the bank's global aspirations. BBB Bank has had a long history in Asia for more than 50 years and operates in twelve Asian countries with over 2,100 associates. Our commitment to the corporate banking and wholesale franchise remain unaffected by the transaction and our associates will continue to provide premier service across treasury services, capital markets, investment banking, corporate lending and other businesses conducted through BBB Bank and other related entities.

The company's philosophy is to have significant market share or presence where we choose to do business. The Hong Kong and Macau retail business, BBB Bank, ranks 17th in assets in Hong Kong, a local market dominated by a few top players. We concluded, after an extensive review, that we did not have the economies of scale to remain competitive in that market.

However, BBB Bank will continue to invest in and is committed to building out its wholesale banking businesses in Asia, to better serve and to grow with valued customers such as yourself.

Please contact me or your usual BBB representative if you have any questions about the sale.

We look forward to continuing being of service to you.

Your sincerely,

(Handwriting Signature)

B. Letters concerning Credit Inquiry

Private & Confidential

We shall appreciate your providing us with an opinion as to credit standing, respectability and financial responsibility of the following firm:

East Trading Co. , Ltd. Hong Kong

Any information you give us will be kept strictly private and confidential. We shall, of course, be happy to reciprocate your courtesy whenever you allow us the opportunity to do so.

C. *Letters concerning Bank Account and Bank Accounting*

Transfer of Sam Gray's Account # A01357

Enclosed are savings passbook # A01357 and customer's draft # B 3682 in the name of Sam Gray. Please close the account and forward the principal balance plus any accrued interest to OVERSEAS CHINESE BANK CORP. , LTD. A postage-paid envelope is enclosed for your convenience.

We thank you for your assistance in this matter.

Your Unused Cheques No. 33478

& 33479 for Closing Your A/C

Reference is made to your captioned cheques.

According to our regulations, our customers should return all the unutilized blank cheques to us for cancellation before closing their checking accounts in our books. We shall appreciate it if you will send back to us the unused cheques in connection with your account No. 33671 so that we can remit the balance to your account with ABC Bank, New York.

Thank you for your cooperation.

Opening a Renminbi Account

In recent months, we have been asked to open an increasing number of letters of credit denominated in Renminbi by our clients.

In this regard, we feel that rather than asking you to draw in USD on our New York correspondent in reimbursement of each negotiation, it may be simple for us to open a Renminbi account with you and to give you the authority to fund the account by drawing on the FIRST SAUDI BANK, New York in certain amount of U. S. currency when funds are required. Negotiations under our Renminbi letters of credit can then be debited to the account in your books.

If you deem this arrangement acceptable to you, we will give you the necessary authority to draw on the said FIRST SAUDI BANK, New York, whom we shall authorize to honor your drawings.

We anticipate to receive your early favorable reply.

Statement of Our A/C No. 46437

As your statement of our captioned account ending November 30 does not indicate particulars for the amounts USD 7, 360 and USD 6, 830 of November 17 and 23 respectively on the debit side, we are not able to trace them in our records.

We shall be much obliged if you will advise us of the nature of these transactions and our reference numbers so that we can do the needful on our part.

Our Debit Advice No. 12345
for USD66, 500. 00

With reference to the captioned debit advice claiming cable charges from you through City Bank, we regret to state that owing to an oversight on our part the above claim was lodged with you by mistake. Now that City Bank has reversed the entry at our request, you may consider our said debit advice as null and void.

We apologize for the inconvenience caused to you in the matter.

D. Letters concerning Credit Loan

Offer of a Credit Line

In view of the excellent relations between our two banks, at your request, we are pleased to offer you a trade-oriented credit line of up to USD150, 000. 00 to be used to finance your clients for importing goods from our country. This credit line is made available at any time subject to your 5 day prior notice to us and remains valid for a period of one year.

If you are interested, please write to us for further discussion on the terms and conditions. Please be mindful that our offer is available for half a year.

Your early reply will be appreciated.

Proposed Credit Line

In response to your recent request, we have drawn up a credit proposal that would meet part of your financial needs. If this proposal is acceptable, we shall begin the formal approval process necessary to convert it to a commitment.

The credit line we offer is USD300, 000. 00 which is unsecured, and will give you tremendous flexibility. The line may be used for:

- Direct borrowings priced at the prime rate;
- Acceptance financing with a 1% commission rate; and
- Fixed rate borrowing priced at LIBOR plus 1%.

A five percent balance would be required on the line.

If you feel it is appropriate we would like to meet you for further discussion on it.

We anticipate your early reply.

Mortgage Loan

On behalf of ABC BANK, I take pleasure in informing you that your application for a mortgage loan has been approved. The terms stated below are firm, and we hope to know whether you accept them or not within 15 days.

The loan will be secured by a good and sufficient first mortgage on the house. We reserve the right to withdraw this commitment if the title or other conditions necessary to make the loan are not satisfactory.

Please complete the enclosed form to indicate your acceptance of our conditions for payment of all of ABC BANK's fees and costs.

Mortgage Loan Terms

Amount: USD800,000.00   Years: 20

Interest Rate: 9.5% for the first 36 months, then subject to adjustment and adjustable every three years.

Payment: USD6,870.33 monthly principal and interest for the first 36 months, then subject to adjustment.

Taxes: USD1,655 per year

Please contact me if you have any questions.

8th Commitment Fee
under L/A 01-367742

Reference is made to the captioned item.

In accordance with Clauses II and IV of the captioned Loan Agreement, we wish to inform you that the 8th commitment fee of USD48,000.00 will be due and payable on April 16, 2001. Please arrange to pay the aforesaid amount to us on the due date.

Your cooperation in this regard is highly appreciated.

E. *Letters concerning Letters of Credit*
L/C No. 03 353 for USD17,590.00
Issued by YYY Bank Ltd., Osaka
In favour of Dongfang Trading Co., Shenzhen

In accordance with the issuing banks instructions, we enclose herewith the original of the credit mentioned above, which please deliver to the beneficiary.

Please acknowledge receipt by returning to us the attached copy of this letter duly signed.

We thank you for your cooperation in this matter.

<u>Our BP No. 43551 for £ 921. 10</u>

<u>under Your L/C No. 03345/03</u>

We refer you to our letter of Nov. 3, 2005 and would inform you that our New York Office now advises us of having credited our account with the above amount against your Transfer Order dated November 12, 2005.

We wish to state that according to the credit terms, payment of the above item should have been made by you right upon your receipt of the documents. But now, as it is, the payment was effected 22 days late, excluding the time for normal postal voyage. Our clients claim compensation for the loss of interest for the 22 days.

We wish to have your favorable reply.

<u>Your L/C No. 6854</u>

<u>Our BP33048 921</u>

Upon claiming reimbursement of our negotiation under the captioned L/C on National Westminster Bank, London, we have been informed by our London Office that the payment was effected under reserve for the reason that the L/C is overdrawn by USD110. 00 according to their records.

In this regard, we would point out that the credit stipulates "Difference of about 2% in quantity and amount is acceptable". In view of the fact that the amount we claimed is within the said limit, we therefore request them to lift the reserve under advice to us.

Your early attention to this matter is highly appreciated.

F. *Letters concerning Bills for Collection*

<u>Your Collection No. 3456-02</u>

We are in receipt of your captioned collection along with the relative documents, which have been duly forwarded to the drawees.

In this connection, we have been today informed by our clients that they disagree to make payment for the reason that the bill of lading under the collection bears "tank at one end slightly rusty outside." They will, however, effect payment upon arrival of the goods according to their actual condition.

Please take note of the above and advise the drawers of it.

<u>New Documents under Our</u>

<u>Coll. No. 56708 Dated May 2, 2006</u>

Our client, G&T Co., Ltd., asks you to change the drawees of the captioned collection to BB Chemicals In. , New York. We accordingly enclose herewith the new documents made out in the name of the new drawees.

Draft—in duplicate

Invoice—in triplicate

Weight List—in triplicate

Inspection Cert. —in duplicate

Please return to us at your earliest convenience the documents previously sent to you.

We look forward to your early attention to this matter.

Return of Documents under

Our Coll. No. OC　03　6781

We thank you for returning the unpaid documents under the captioned collection along with your letter dated June 23 , 2006 which have been duly notified to the drawers.

To close this item, please arrange with the payers to return, at our expense, the relative parcel to the drawers under their advice to us. As instructed, we have today remitted your handling charges of USD116. 500 to AAA Bank, Hong Kong for your account.

We appreciate your kind assistance and look forward to your reply.

<u>Payment of Your Coll. No. 223372 through ABC Bank</u>

Referring to your enquiry dated May 21 , 2006, we take pleasure in informing you that the said collection was already paid and the proceeds were remitted to your account with Credit Lyonnais in Paris on June 13 , 2006.

Enclosed is a copy of our relative payment order for your reference. We consider this item as closed now. Please approach the above bank directly, if you still cannot trace receipt of payment.

We expect further cooperation with you in the future.

G. *Letters concerning Business Inquiry*

<u>Our T/T Claim for USD15, 630. 00</u>
<u>Under Your L/C No.　370860-T-63</u>

Reference is made to the credit advice No. R 45368 from our New York Office in settlement of the above claim. We have found that our account has been credited with a USD15, 510. 00 which is USD 450 less than our claim.

We would request you to kindly look into the matter and pay the difference of the said USD 450 to our account under advice to us.

We thank you for your kind cooperation in this regard.

<u>Our Documentary Collection No. DC5348</u>

for USD7,430.00 Drawn by P & T Co., Hong Kong

We wish to draw your attention to the fact that this collection remains outstanding in our records. You are requested to investigate the matter and inform us of the present status of this item.

If you have already sent report to us, which should reach us after the date of this tracer, please disregard this request.

We thank you in advance for your cooperation in this matter.

<u>Our BP No. 402471 For USD73,450</u>

<u>Under Your L/C No. 14-3165</u>

We acknowledge receipt of your Credit Advice under the captioned item. However, upon checking it, we found a difference between the amount of your credit advice and the amount of our payment as shown below:

Amount of your Credit Advice: USD71,450

Amount of our payment: USD73,450

We shall very much appreciate it if you will look into your records and give us any information on how the difference came about.

We anticipate to receive your early reply.

H. Others

<u>Request for Correspondent Relationship</u>

We are indeed pleased to notice that the volume of trade between our two countries has been increasing rapidly. In order to cope with the ever increasing transactions between our two banks, it is our pleasure to propose the establishment of correspondent relationship with your esteemed bank.

With this good wish, we enclose herewith a copy of our Annual Report for the fiscal year 2005 for your reference. We shall be pleased to dispatch to you our Control Documents upon receipt of your favorable reply.

We anticipate to receive a favorable reply from you.

<u>Report on XYZ</u> Company

We are informed:

Business: Polyester silk flowers, plastic products

Established: September 28, 1963

Capital: (Authorized): HKD800,000.00

（Paid）: HKD800, 000. 00

Number of Employees: 210

Head Office:... Hong Kong Bldg. ,... Queen's Rd, Hong Kong.

Associated/Subsidiary Companies:

TCD Enterprise Ltd. , Kowloon

FET Trading Co. , Ltd. , Hong Kong

We report:

They have maintained an active and well conducted current account in our books since January 1968. We negotiate their export bills under documentary credits.

We finance their import bills drawn both under and not under documentary credits. We find that they are reliable shippers, under a respectable and experienced board of directors, and considered good for their normal business engagement.

The information is for your reference. We assume no responsibility on our part.

Our Draft No. 364729

Further to our letter of October 22, 2006 in respect of our draft No. 364729 which was reported missing, we wish to advise you that our London Office has placed "stop payment" to the above mentioned draft as requested.

If you want the amount of the draft to be paid by our London Office, you may approach them direct with a Banker's Letter of Indemnity acceptable to them.

Your Mail Transfer dated May 10, 2006

With reference to your captioned mail transfer, we regret to inform you that we are unable to effect payment due to the absence of the name of the city in the address given. Therefore, we shall appreciate it if you will make the revision as soon as possible.

We look forward to your early reply.

Our Terms and Conditions

Thank you for your letter dated June 20, 2006, the contents of which have received our prompt attention.

Now, we take pleasure in informing you that we have today sent our new Terms and Conditions which is to take effect on July 1, 2006.

I believe that you will see from our new Terms and Conditions that we have made certain adjustment to some items mostly relating to telecommunication so as to offer more competitive rate to our clients.

We reassure you of our best services.

II. Telex

Telex is the abbreviation of one of the following three phrases "Teletypewriter Exchange", "Teletyprinter Exchange" and "Telegraph Exchange". The first use of telex can be traced back to the 1930s in Germany, the Netherlands and Belgium. It was not until the early 1970s that telex was introduced to China and has achieved remarkable development ever since the 1980s.

Telex is becoming more and more widely used in banking transactions because of its high speed, low cost and great convenience. However, it has gradually give way to SWIFT since 1990s, which will be covered in the next section.

1. Main Parts of a Telex Message

A. *Date*

It marks the date when the telex is sent.

Examples of the way of dating.

OCT. 12, 2005;   3RD APRIL, 2006

18/09/06; 06/27/05

B. *Name (and Address) of receiver headed by "To"*

e. g. TO: BANK OF CHINA, NEW YORK

   TO: HABIB BANK LTD. , NEW YORK

      42 ST. , NEW YORK

C. *Name (and Address) of sender headed by FM representing "From"*

e. g. FM: AGRICULTURAL BANK OF CHINA , SHENZHEN

FM: NANYANG COMMERCIAL BANK LTD. , HONG KONG

   151 DES VOEUX RD. , C. HONG KONG

D. *Reference*

It is usually shortened into REF or RE representing the subject of the telex message.

e. g. ● REF: YOUR BP No. 308543

  ● RE : OUR COLLECTION NO. 0C564320

E. *Body of Telex*

It is the most important part of a telex. It includes the ideas (contents) to convey, in one single paragraph or, two or more paragraphs. At the end of body of telex there is usually the Complimentary Close with the following expressions: THANKS/THKS; BEST RE-

GARDS/B RGDS; THANKS AND REGARDS/THKS N RGDS ···

NOTE:

A Test (Number/Word) is used when a telex message involves authorization or obligation, such as dispatch of letters of credit, credit/debit instruction/advice.

A Test can be placed: (1) in a separate line above the body of telex, or

(2) at the beginning of the body of telex.

e. g. (1) TEST: 038942; TEST: DT464781

(2) TEST 6334610 IN REPLY TO YOUR TLX DD 09/18/01

MON 2436703 RE YR BP NO. 33086 WE LEARNT FM BENEF TT ···

2. Language

- All the letters composing the words and sentences in the telex should be capitalized.
- All the sentences in the body of telex can be totally the same as those in a letter including spelling and punctuation.
- The following particularities, which mark the difference of telex messages from letters, merit attention.

—Abbreviations of words or phrases are very often used.

e. g. BEN-BENEFICIARY; YTLX-YOUR TELEX

PYT-PAYMENT; RYL-REFERRING TO YOUR LETTER; ASAP-AS SOON AS POSSIBLE

—Structural words such as "a (n)", "the", "at", "in", and auxiliary verbs such as "may", "be", etc. in the sentences can be omitted.

e. g. FRESH INVOICES (HAVE BEEN) DISPATCHED

LC (WAS) AIRMAILED (ON) 23RD OCT.

—In the body of telex, punctuation can either remain the same as in a letter, or be omitted. (You can refer to some Sample Telex Messages in the following part.)

3. Sample Telex Messages

A. *Inter bank Borrowing*

DATE: MAY 19, 2006

TO: AAA BANK, NEW YORK

FM: BBB BANK, HONG KONG

RE: USD2,000,000 SHORT TERM BORROWING

PLEASE BE ADVISED THAT INTEREST RATE FOR THE BORROWING IS SET AT 4.6250% (LIBOR 3.375 PLUS 1.250 PERCENT). INTEREST FOR THE BORROWING

PERIOD (MAY24, 2001 TO NOV. 24, 2001) IS USD47, 277. 28.

WE'LL REMIT USD2, 000, 000 TO CCC BANK'S ACCOUNT WITH DDD BANK NEW YORK A/C NO. 10-0-202252-2-001 IN FAVOUR OF YOUR BRANCH VALUE MAY 24, 2006.

BEST REGARDS

B. *Foreign Exchange Dealing*

Buying Foreign Exchange

DATE: 07/22/05

TO: AAA BANK, SHENZHEN

FM: BBB BANK, LTD. , HONG KONG

RE: CONFIRMATION ON FOREX DEALING

TRANSACTION NO. FX-01-47191

CODE/COMMON REF. AMOUNT BOUGHT: USD4, 000, 000

EXCHANGE RATE: 1. 3761 VALUE DATE: JULY 24, 2005.

WE CONFIRM THE ABOVE DEAL AND WIIL PAY DM5, 504, 400 TO YOUR AC-COUNT WITH CCC BANK NEW YORK ON DUE DATE.

PLS REMIT USD4, 000, 000. 00 TO OUR ACCOUNT WITH CHASE MANHATTAN NEW YORK ON THAT DATE.

Buying Foreign Exchange

OUR REF NO. 445566

TEST: 1011

FX CONFIRMATION

WE BUY USD1, 000, 000. 00 AGAINST RMB8, 322, 600. 00 AT RATE 8. 3226 VAL-UE 11/14/06

AFTER PAYMENT, PLS CREDIT OUR USD A/C NO. 35678 WITH YOU ON VAL-UE DAY. WE WILL PAY RMB TO AAA GUANGDONG BR AND AUTHORIZE THEM TO CREDIT YOUR RMB A/C.

BEST REGARDS

C. *Letters of Credit*

Pre advice of L/C

FROM: BBB BANK, CAIRO

TO: CCC BANK GUANGDONG

PREADVICE OF IRREVOCABLE LC NO. 0035 OPENED ON 4TH MAY, 2005

ACCOUNTEE IMAG CO FAVOURING CHINA NATIONAL METALS I/E CORPORA-TION

SHENZHEN BRANCH FOR AMOUNT USD50,000 COVERING SUNDRY METAL-WARES SHIPMENT LATEST MAY 2005 VALIDITY 15TH JUNE, 2005 YOUR CONFIRMATION TO BE ADDED THERETO.

Delivery of L/C

RE YOUR L/C NO. GDBFS93022 FOR USD644,290DD 230993

FAVOUR BVK ONGROTRADE BUDAPEST

HAVING RECEIVED YOUR ABOVE L/C WE HANDED OVER TO CENTRAL EUROPEAN INTERNATIONAL BANK LTD. BUDAPEST FOR FURTHER CONTINUATION PLS CONTACT THEM IN FUTURE.

BEST REGARDS

Amendment to L/C

AMEND OUR CREDIT 0054-01-187-0102 FVG. CHINA NATIONAL MEDICAL MEDICINE AND HEALTH PRODUCTS IMPORT AND EXPORT CORP. SHANGHAI BR

SANYU HOTEL, CAST ERN BLDG. NO. 23 NANJING ROAD SHANGHAI CHINA

UNIT PRICE OF MERCHANDISE NOW TO READ "USD14.19 PER 100 SETS

C AND F KARACHI AS PER REVISED INDENT DATED 17/04/2001" INSTEAD OF EXISTING.

OTHER TERMS UNCHANGED

Amendment to L/C

OUR AMENDMENT REF NO. 101345

RE OUR CREDIT NO. 232401 FOR USD 940,440.00

DD: 12/08/05

THE CREDIT IS AMENDED AS FOLLOWS:

- EXPIRY DATE OF L/C: 01/20/06
- TIME OF SHIPMENT: BEFORE 12/30/05

OTHER TERMS AND CONDITIONS UNCHANGED

SUBJECT TO UCP 500

KINDLY ADVISE BENEFICIARY SOON.

THIS IS AN OPERATIVE AMENDMENT NO MAIL CONFIRMATION TO FOLLOW

D. Payment

Payment Instruction

PLS DEBIT OUR A/C NO. 01-1-1-16035 WITH USD555,229.75 (CABLE CHGS USD2,000 DEDUCTD) VALUE TODAY UNDER OUR L/C NO. OX 19310 AND P/O NO. CP93207 AND PAY THE SUM TO BANKERS TRUST CO., H.O., NEW YORK FOR CREDIT OF AAA BANK LTD HEAD OFFICE ACCT NO. 042769 FAVOURING AAA

BANK LTD. OSAKA QUOTING THEIR REF. BB300-01-412 RGDS

<u>Payment Instruction</u>

PLS PAY VIA "CHIPS" TO BBB BANK, NEW YORK FOR OUR ACCOUNT (NO. 158762) WITH THEM UNDER THEIR AND YOUR CABLE ADVICE TO US QUOTING OUR BP NO. 4040694

<u>Advice of Payment</u>

YOUR REF. BPFS 93015 OUR REF. 1799714

BILL AMOUNT HKD518, 955. 65 LC NO. 16316663

THE ABOVE BILL HAS BEEN PAID. PROCEEDS ARE AS FOLLOWS:

BILL AMOUNT HKD518, 955. 65

LESS DISCREPANCY FEE 200. 00

TELEX CHARGES 170. 00

NET HKD518, 585. 65

WE HAVE REMITTED THE ABOVE AMOUNT AS INSTRUCTED ON YOUR COVERING SCHEDULE THROUGH CLEARING HOUSE AUTOMATED TRANSFER SYSTEM-74716.

DHBFE HX.

<u>Urging Payment</u>

YUR LC NO. 12346-011 FOR USD1, 012, 500. 00

OUR BP96103 ON 15 NOV 2001

FUNDS NOT YET RECEIVED

PLS FOLLOW OUR SETTLEMENT INSTRUCTIONS IN OUR COVER LETTER AND CABLE CONFIRM US YOUR EXECUTION WE RESERVE RIGHT TO CLAIM ON YOU FOR ANY UNDUE DELAY PAYMENT INTEREST CAUSED AT YOUR END.

REGARDS.

<u>Inquiry about Reasons for Non-Payment</u>

RE: OUR REF BP367789. FOR USD32, 600. 00 UNDER YR LC NO. 123651

RE: OUR TLX DD940609 INDICATING TT YR REFUSAL OF OUR DOCS BASED ON "LATE PRESENTATION" CANNOT BE ACCEPTED AND CLEARLY SHOWING OUR OPINION BUT UP TO NOW NO RESPONSE FROM YOU RECEIVED. WE WOULD APPRECIATE IT IF YOU COULD REVIEW AND SETTLE THIS MATTER IN ACCORDANCE WITH USUAL BANKING PRACTICE. YR PROMPT ATTENTION IS HIGHLY APPRECIATED. BEST RGDS.

E. Discrepancies

<u>Discrepancies and Non Payment</u>

YOUR BP NO. 40167708

DOCUMENTS FOR USD42, 230. 00

DRAWN UNDER OUR DOC. CREDIT NO. LC94050892

DOCUMENTS RECEIVED AND FOUND TO CONTAIN THE FOLLOWING DISCREP-
ANCIES:

- INV SHOWING DESCRIPTION OF GOODS DIFFERS FROM L/C
- INS POLICY NOT SHOW L/C NO
- PACKING LIST NOT SEPARATELY SHOW EACH QUANTITY AND SIZE OF
  GOODS

THIS ADVICE CONSTITUTES OUR REFUSAL OF DOCUMENTS. WE HAVE HOW-
EVER REFERRED SAME TO THE APPLICANT. MEANWHILE WE ARE HOLDING
DOCUMENTS AT YOUR PRINCIPAL'S DISPOSAL AND THIS SWIFT CHARGES WILL
BE FOR YOUR PRINCIPAL'S A/C.

PLEASE ADVISE THEM ACCORDINGLY AND INSTRUCT BY SWIFT/TELEX FOR
ATTN: I/E DEPT QUOTING OUR I/E DEPT.

Discrepancies Accepted

RE OUR TLX DD93/02/09

YR REF NO. BPFS 93011

BILL AMT FOR HKD221, 630. 00

UNDER OUR REF NO. BOIK00173 01

DISCREPANCIES ACCEPTED.

WE HAVE TODAY PAID THE NET PROCEEDS OF HKD221, 215. 00 ONLY (OUR
TLX FEE FOR HKD150. 00 AND DISCREPANCY FEE FOR HKD 235. 00 AND CHITS
FEE FOR HKD30. 00 DEDUCTED) TO KINGCHENG BANKING CORP. H. K. VIA CHI-
TS AS PER YR INSTRUCTIONS.

III. SWIFT

SWIFT is the abbreviation of Society for Worldwide Inter-bank Financial Telecommunication. It is a non-profitable worldwide inter-bank organization with its headquarters in Brus-
sels. As early as in 1973, 240 large European and North American banks founded this inter-
bank communication network. The system enables member banks to transit among themselves international payments, statements and other transactions relating to international
banking. The use of the network is more convenient and reliable than the past methods (letter, telex and cable), and enables banks to offer better services to their customers. Nowa-

days SWIFT is the most frequently used method of bank communications.

SWIFT's worldwide community not only includes banks, but also broker/dealers and investment managers, as well as their market infrastructures in payments, securities, treasury and trade. Up to the present, there are 7,800 SWIFT members in more than 200 countries all over the world. Over the past ten years SWIFT message prices have been reduced by over 70%, system availability approaches 5 ×9's reliability—99.999% of uptime. [1]

In China, Bank of China took the lead in joining SWIFT in 1983, and its Head Office began using the SWIFT system in 1985, followed by other Chinese financial institutions.

The essential element of SWIFT is to develop and release "SWIFTS standards" among its community. All SWIFT messages are formated and standardized so as to be readily and easily processed by computers. The most recent Standards Release 2006 became effective on November 18, 2006.

1. Category and Message Type

By SWIFTS standards all messages are grouped into 9 categories, based on basic classification of different financial transactions:

Cat. 1: Customer Transfers and Checks

Cat. 2: Financial Institution Transfers

Cat. 3: Treasury Markets or Foreign Exchange, Money Markets and Derivatives

Cat. 4: Collections and Cash Letters

Cat. 5: Securities Markets

Cat. 6: Precious Metals and Syndications

Cat. 7: Documentary Credits and Guarantees

Cat. 8: Travellers Cheques

Cat. 9: Cash Management and Customer Status

In each category, there are some Message Type (MT) s, representing different types of specific transactions. Each Message Type (MT) consists of three digits indicating actual transactions of the same type. MTs of the most frequently used three categories are listed as follows:

Category 1: Customer Transfers

MT 101: Request for Transfer

MT 102: Mass Payments Message

---

[1] See http://www.swift.com.

MT 102 + : Mass Payments Message

MT 103 : Single Customer Credit Transfer

MT 103 + : Single Customer Credit Transfer

MT 104 : Customer Direct Debit

MT 105 : Edifact Envelope

MT 106 : Edifact Envelope

MT 107 : General Direct Debit Message

MT 110 : Advice of Cheque

MT 111 : Request for Stop Payment of a Cheque

MT 112 : Status of a Request for Stop Payment of a Cheque

MT 121 : Multiple Inter-bank Funds Transfer (EDIFACT FINPAY Message)

MT 190 : Advice of Charges, Interest, and Other Adjustments

MT 191 : Request for Payment of Charges, Interest, and Other Expenses

MT 192 : Request for Cancellation

MT 195 : Queries

MT 196 : Answers

MT 198 : Proprietary Message

MT 199 : Free Format Message

Category 2 : Financial Institution Transfers

MT 200 : Financial Institution Transfer for Its Own Account

MT 201 : Multiple Financial Institution Transfer for Its Own Account

MT 202 : General Financial Institution Transfer

MT 203 : Multiple General Financial Institution Transfer

MT 204 : Financial Markets Direct Debit Message

MT 205 : Financial Institution Transfer Execution

MT 206 : Cheque Transition Message

MT 207 : Request for Financial Institution Transfer

MT 210 : Notice to Receive

MT 256 : Advice of Non-Payment of Cheques

MT 290 : Advice of Charges, Interest, and Other Adjustments

MT 291 : Request for Payment of Charges, Interest, and Other Expenses

MT 292 : Request for Cancellation

MT 295 : Queries

MT 296 : Answers

MT 298: Proprietary Message

MT 299: Free Format Message

Category 7: Documentary Credits and Guarantees

MT 700: Issue of a Documentary Credit

MT 701: Issue of a Documentary Credit

MT 705: Pre-Advice of a Documentary Credit

MT 707: Amendment to a Documentary Credit

MT 710: Advice of a Third Bank's Documentary Credit

MT 711: Advice of a Third Bank's Documentary Credit

MT 720: Transfer of a Documentary Credit

MT 721: Transfer of a Documentary Credit

MT 730: Acknowledgement

MT 732: Advice of Discharge

MT 734: Advice of Refusal

MT 740: Authorisation to Reimburse

MT 742: Reimbursement Claim

MT 747: Amendment to an Authorization to Reimburse

MT 750: Advice of Discrepancy

MT 752: Authorization to Pay, Accept or Negotiate

MT 754: Advice of Payment/Acceptance/Negotiation

MT 756: Advice of Reimbursement or Payment

MT 760: Guarantee

MT 767: Guarantee Amendment

MT 768: Acknowledgement of a Guarantee Message

MT 769: Advice of Reduction or Release

MT 790: Advice of Charges, Interest, and Other Adjustments

MT 791: Request for Payment of Charges, Interest, and Other Expenses

MT 792: Request for Cancellation

MT 795: Queries

MT 796: Answers

MT 798: Proprietary Message

MT 799: Free Format Message

Besides, under each Message Type there is a Common Group (MTn/Category n), including the following:

    N 90 ADVICE OF CHARGES, INTEREST AND OTHER ADJUSTMENT

    N 91 REQUEST FOR PAYMENT OF CHARGES, INTERST AND OTHER EX-
PENSES

    N 92 REQUEST FOR CANCELLATION

    N 93 INFORMATION SERVICE MESSAGE

    N 95 QUERIES

    N 96 ANSWERS

    N 98 PROPRIETARY MESSAGE

    N 99 FREE FORMAT

2. Fields

There are different fields subordinating to each Message Type. Each field is preceded by a field tag. The following shows some field descriptions:

20: Transaction Reference Number

21: Related Reference

32A: Value Date, Currency Code, Amount

50: Ordering Customer

52: Ordering Institution

53: Sender's Correspondent (Preferred Option A)

54: Receiver's Correspondent (Preferred Option A)

57: Account with Institution (Preferred Option A)

58: Beneficiary Institution (Preferred Option A)

59: Beneficiary Customer

70: Details of Payment

71A: Details of Charges

72: Sender to Receiver Information

Examples:

MT 202

20: YOUR REFERENCE

21: FXDEAL 34178

32A: SEPT 18, 2002 GBP3,000.00

53B: /002 90224 001/

57A: BKCHHKHH

58A: BKCHCNBJ300

3. Structure of a SWIFT Message

A SWIFT message consists of the following five parts usually termed BLOCKS.

A. BASIC HEADER BLOCK

B. APPLICATION HEADER BLOCK

C. USER HEADER BLOCK

D. TEXT BLOCK

E. TRAILER BLOCK

SAMPLE:

BASIC HEADERF01BKCHCNBJAHZUI062 837371

APPLICATION HEADER01001738 920701 BOKF JZAXXX 0206

020053 9207071 1638 U

KYOTO

USER HEADER BANK PRIORITY113:

TEXT BLOCK

TRN 20: 101 1943 301

DATE/CUR/AMOUNT 32A: DATE 920701 CURRENCY USD

AMOUNT 19,450.93

ORDER. CUSTOMER 50: DOKOH SHOJI CO., LTD.

SENDER'S CORR. 53 A: BOTKUS33

BANK OF TOKYO LTD., NEW YORK, NY

BENEFIC. CUSTOMER 59: /ZHEJIANG SILK IMP/EXP CORP.

55 TIYUCHANG RD., HANGZHOU

DETAILS OF PAYMENT70: INV. NO. RS9220050 RS9260046

DETAILS OF CHARGES   71A: BEN

SEND. TO REC. INFO   72: /REC/ COVER PAID TO YOUR H. O.

BEIJING A/C WITH BANK OF TOKYO

LTD., NEW YORK IN FAVOUR OF YOU

TRAILEREND OF MSG

MAC/B5DD937B

CHK/4D7372C2CE063

4. Sample SWIFT Messages

A. *Narrative*

Benjamin Tsai orders Industrial & Commercial Bank of China, Beijing (ICBKCNBJ) to pay, on November 12, 2002, JPY1, 500, 000, to James Tsai (a/c #12345678) with Amsouth Bank of Alabama (AMSBUS44). AMSBUS44 keeps all of its foreign currency accounts with CITIUS33

The Sakura Trust and Banking Co., Tokyo (SKTRJPJT) services a JPY account for both ICBKCNBJ and CITIUS33

Charges are shared. The beneficiary customer wants to be notified by phone at number 9142552586

    SENDER'S BIC : ICBKCNBJ

      MT: 103

    RECEIVER'S BIC : SKTRJPJT

    20: FT1240

    23B: CRED

    23E: PHOB/9142552586

    32A: 021112JPY1500000

    50K: BENJAMIN TSAI

        NO. 7 JIANGUOMEN NEI AVE

        BEIJING, P. R. CHINA

    56A: CITIUS33

    57A: AMSBUS44

    59: /12345678

      JAMES TSAI

      23 STATE STREET

      ALABAMA, USA

    71A: SHA

B. Narrative

Your branch maintains an A/C with Hang Seng Bank in Hong Kong. Instructions to pay HKD2, 000 to standard Chartered Bank, Hong Kong (SWIFT Address: SCBLHKHH) for account of Standard Chartered Bank, London Treasury (SWIFT Address: SCBLGBILTSY).

    RECEIVER: HASEHKHH

      MT 202

      20: YOUR REFERENCE

      21: DEAL NO. 3456

      32A: 020723 HKD2, 000. 00

      57A: SCBLHKHH

58A: SCBLGBQLTSY

C. *Narrative*

Algemene Bank Nederland, Amsterdam, asked Hang Seng Bank in Hong Kong to stop payment of a cheque (No. 02 23763) in the amount of USD12,300, which was issued by Chase Manhattan Bank, Singapore Branch on November 6, 2002 in favour of TST CO. in Hong Kong for the reason that the cheque was found to have been lost.

RECEIVE: HASEHKHH

MT 111

20: ABNANLQA

21: 0223763

30: NOVEMBER 6, 2002

32A: USD12,300.00

52A: CHASE MANHATTAN BANK, SINGAPORE BR

59: TST COMPANY, HONGKONG

75: /21/ CHEQUE HAS BEEN LOST

END OF MESSAGE TEXT

D. *Narrative*

On May 27, 2001 Oester Reichische Laender Bank, Vienna requested Algemene Bank Nederland, Amsterdam to consider cancellation of the following customer's transfer, sent on May 27, 2001.

MT N 92

OELBATWWA 00072

100 02

ABNANLZA

20: 494932/DEV

32A: 010527NLG1958,47

50: FRANZHOLZAPFEL GMBH VIENNA

53B: /219 4290555 81

59: H. F. JANSSEN

LEDEBOERSTRAAT 27

QMSTERDAM

70: /RFB /INV 18042 010412

END OF MESSAGE TEXT...

E. *MT S400 ADVICE OF PAYMENT*

BASIC HEADERF01BKCHCNBJAXXX 9918 342250

APPLICATION HEADER04001846 001115 MNGBTRISA007 0564

039873 001116 0046 N M. N. G. BANK A. S. ISTANBUL

(BAKIRKOY BRANCH)

USER HEADERSERVICE CODE   103：

              BANK. PRIORITY   113：

              MSG USER REF.   108：

              INFO. FROM CI   115：

SENDING BANK'S TRN20：ZVA 00700008

RELATED REFERENCE21：BP10000010196

AMOUNT COLLCTED 32A：DATE 001115 CURRENCY USD AMOUNT 12. 766 32

PROCEEDS REMITTED 33A：DATE 001115 CURRENCY USD AMOUNT 12. 766 32

SENDER'S CORR. 53A：IRVTUS3N, BANK OF NEW YORK

          NEW YORK, NY

RECEIVER'S CORR. 54A：BKCHUS33

              BANK OF CHINA

       NEW YORK, NY

TRAILER ORDER IS ＜MAC：＞ ＜PAC：＞ ＜ENC：＞ ＜CHK：＞ ＜TNG：＞

＜PDE：＞

          MAC：F02F2A1A

          CHK：2CA564958EU6

F. MT S734 *ADVICE OF REFUSAL*

BASIC HEADERF01SKCHCNBJAXXX 9767 467158

APPLICATION HEADER0734 1008 000429 HSBCHKHHCHKH 3270738926

    000429 1008 N

    HONG KONG AND SHANGHAI BANKING CORPORATION LTD. ,

    HONG KONG (ALL HK OFFICES AND HEAD OFFICE)

USER HEADERSERVICE CODE 103：

    BANK. PRIORITY 113

    MSG USER REF. 108 120038890

    INFO. FROM CI 115

SENDING BANK'S TRN20：DC LCK104031

CORR. BANK'S REF.   2：BP10000004138

CURRENCY/AMOUNT 32A：DATE 000429 CURRENCY USD AMOUNT 305, 745. 00

SEND. TO REC. INFO. 72：WE HAVE REFERRED DISCREPANCY TO APPLI-

             CANT AND WILL

REVERT AS SOON AS WE HEAR FROM THEM. MEANWHILE WE

HOLDDOCUMENTS AT YOUR DISPOSAL IN ACCORDANCE

WITH ART. 140 OF CP500. PLS FORWARD YOUR DISPOSAL INST.

DISCREPANCIES77J: PHOTOCOPIES OF FORWARDERS CARGO RECEIPT SHOWING:

—SHIPMENT EFFECTED ON 20APR00

—SUPPLIER'S INV. NOS AND DATES DIFFER FROM INVOICES.

—PHOTOCOPY FC/R NO. WCL 0286/00 SHOWING ITEM NUMBER
  DIFFERED.

—PHOTOCOPIES I/O ORIGINAL CERT. OF ORIGIN PRESENTED WHICH ISSUED BY MANUFACTURER "NINGBO FURNITURE INDUSTRIES LTD" WHEREAS INVOICES SHOWING NAME SHOULD BE "NINGBO NO. 1 WOODEN FURNITURE FACTORY".

—APPLICANT'S INSPECTION CERTIFICATE SHOWING ADDRESS SLIGHTLY DIFFERED.

SUBJECT TO ANY WAIVER OF DISCREPANCIES BEING RECEIVED FROM APPLICANT GIVEN TO OUR SATISFACTION, WE SHALL EFFECT SETTLEMENT AND RELEASE DOCS TO APPLICANT WITHOUT FURTHER NOTICE TO YOU UNLESS WE RECEIVE CONTRARY INSTRUCTION FROM YOU.

REFUSAL OF DOC. 77B: WE HOLD DOCS AT YR DISPOSAL. PLS FORWARD YR INST. BY SWIFT.

QUOTING OUR REF. BP COR120036LCK.

TRAILER ORDER IS < MAC: > < PAC: > < ENC: > < CHK: > < TNG: > < PDE: >

MAC: DB4C6AC5

CHK: 1B1ED1D41777

G. MT S742 *REIMBURSEMENT CLAIM*

BASIC HEADERF01BKCHCNBJAXXX 9765 294461

APPLICATION HEADERI 742   BOTKUS33XXX N 2

BANK OF TOKYO MITSUBISHI, LTD. NEW YORK, NY

(NEW YORK BRANCH)

USER HEADER   SERVICE CODE 103:

BANK. PRIORITY 113:

SG USER REF   108：EX317353

CLAIM. BANK'S REF   20：   BP10000004160

DOC. CREDIT NUMBER 21：   U 086 2000566

DATE OF ISSUE   31C：   991019

ISSUING BANK   52A：   BOTKJBJTXXX

BANK OF TOKYO MITSUBISHI, LTD. ,

TOKYO (HEAD OFFICE)

AMOUNT CLAIMED   32B：   CURRENCY USD AMOUNT15, 971. 60

TOTAL AMOUNT CLAIM34B：   DATE CURRENCY USD AMOUNT15, 971. 60

BENEFICIARY BANK   58A：   BKCHCNBJXXX

BANK OF CHINA, BEIJING

SEND. TO REC. INFO. 72：   DOCS NEG AND SENT AS PER LC TERM.

TERMS COMPLIED WITH.

PLS QUOTE OUR REFBP10000004160.

TRAILER   ORDER IS ＜MAC：＞ ＜PAC：＞ ＜ENC：＞ ＜CHK：＞ ＜TNG：＞

＜PDE：＞

MAC：506AC098

H. MT S795 QUERIES

BASIC HEADERF01BKCHCNBJAXXX 9761 298844

APPLICATION HEADERO7951912 00421AEIBUS33AXXX 8518 61844

AMERICAN EXPRESS BANK,

NEW YORK, NY

USER HEADER   SERVICE CODE103

BANK. PRIORITY113

MSG USER REF. 108

INFO. FROM CI 115

TRN20：   RB4149 000101／01

RELATED REFERENCE 21：1030753

QUERIES75 ：   DEPARTMENT ATTENTION：MANAGERL/C SUBJECT：

NONRECEIPT OF REIMBURSEMENT AUTH.

L/C NUMBER：CTGRBL9967CFER

OPENING BANK：

NARRATIVE77A：RUOALI BANK DHAKA

YOUR REF NO. : BP10000004149

AMOUNT：US DOLLARS 686, 386. 00

OUR REF NO. : 1030753

PLS BE ADVISED THAT WE ARE UNABLE TO HONOR YOUR CLAIM FOR REIM-BURSEMENT AT THIS TIME AS WE HAVE NOT YET RECEIVED ISSUING BANK AU-THORIZATION. WE WILL NOTIFY ISSUING BANK OF YR CLAIM AND SEEK AU-THORIZATION TO REIMBURSE. IN THE INTEREST OF TIME WE SUGGEST YOU CONTACT THEM AS WELL. ALSO, PLS RECHECK THE INFO. THAT YOU HAVE PROVIDED IN YR CLAIM AND MAKE CERTAIN THAT YOU ARE QUOTING THE L/C NUMBER CORRECTLY. THKS AND RGDS.

TRAILERORDER IS < MAC: > < PAC: > < ENC: > < CHK: > < TNG: > < PDE: >

MAC: 5BAAE7C1

CHK: A5EDEA03B4B4

I. MT S910 *CONFIRMATION OF CREDIT*

BASIC HEADERF01BKCHCNBJAXXX 9918 391070

APPLICATION HEADER0910 0117 001117 IRVTUS3NAXXX 617182

001117 1418

BANK OF NEW YORK, NEW YORK, NY

USER HEADER	SERVICE CODE 103
	BANK. PRIORITY 113
	MSG USER REF. 108 RCS001103889900
	INFO. FROM CI 115

TRN	20: RCS0011103889900
RELATED REFERENCE	21: BP10000010506
ACCOUNT IDENT	25: 8033412224
DATE/CUR/AMOUNT	32A: DATE 001117 CURRENCY USD AMOUNT 13, 255. 00
ORDERING INST	52A: ABKKKWKW ALAHLI BANK OF KUWAIT K. S. C. KUWAIT
SEND. TO REC. INFO.	72: /REC/NB REF: BP10000010506 /NB: BANK OF CHINA /CR: BNY COMM
TRAILER ORDER IS	< MAC: > < PAC: > < ENC: > < CHK: > < TNG: > < PDE: >

CHK: 49EC0B7704DB

J. MT S999 *FREE FORMAT*

Sender: GOLDUS33XXX

GOLDMAN, SACHS AND CO.

NEW YORK, NY US

Receiver: × × × × × × × × ×

AAA BANK

(HEAD OFFICE)

BEIJING CN

20: Transaction Reference Number

GTOS05241055236

79: Narrative

ATTN: SWIFT ADMINSISTRATOR

REF: BKE REQUEST

WE WISH TO ESATABLISH AUTHENTICATION BETWEEN OUR INSTITUT-
IONS. PENDING YOUR AGREEMENT WE PROPOSE

OUR SWIFT ID: GOLDUS33

OUR KMA ID: GOLDUS33

TYPE OF KEY: BI-DIRECTIONAL

INITIATOR OF EXCHANGE: GOLDUS33

FREQUENCY OF EXCHANGE: 12 MONTHS

ACTIVATION DATE: ASAP

PLEASE CONFIRM ACCEPTANCE OF OUR TERMS BY RETURN MT999 TO
OUR ATTENTION ADVISING US OF YOUR SWIFT ID AND KMA DETAILS.

KEY MANAGEMENT AUTHORITY

REGARDS,

GOLDMAN, SACHS CO.

K. *MT* 094 *Broadcast*

Sender: MEME × × × × × × × ×

Receiver: × × × × × × × × ×

AAA BANK

(HEAD OFFICE)

BEIJING CN

135: broadcast priority

U

136: broadcast nb for ALL

B62870

129: section number nn of nn

01/01

130: heading code

/06/WARNING LOST OF STOLEN

/02/DRAFTS

134: brdcst requestor BIC Name City

BOTKGB2L

BANK OF TOKYO-MITSUBISHI UFJ, LTD. , THE

(LONDON BRANCH)

LONDON GB

BANK OF TOKYO-MITSUBISHI UFJ, LTD. ,

THE (LONDON BRANCH) LONDON GB

312: broadcast text

ATTN CHEQUE COLLECTION DEPARTMENT

THIS IS TO ADVISE THAT TWO DRAFT CHEQUES, IN BLANK FORMAT, HAVE BEEN LOST.

THE DRAWEE IS THE BANK OF TOKYO-MITSUBISHI UFJ LTD (BTMU).

DRAT NUMBERS 001066 AND 001067.

PLEASE EXERCISE UTMOST CARE TO NOT HONOUR SAID CHEQUES IF PRESENTED TO YOU.

WE HAVE REQUESTED ALL BTMU BRANCHES WORLDWIDE TO CONFIRM THESE INSTRUCTIONS WITH THEIR CORRESPONDENTS. SHOULD YOU HOLD AN ACCOUNT FOR A BRANCH OF BTMU AND HAVE NOT BEEN CONTACTED BY THAT BRANCH WITHIN THREE WORKING DAYS KINDLY CONTACT BTMU LONDON.

CONTACT DETAILS…

OR BY SWIFT MESSAGE TO BOTKGB2L FOR THE ATTENTION OF THE ABOVE.

KIND REGARDS

BTMU LONDON

L. *MT* 094 *Broadcast*

Sender: MEME × × × × × × ×

Receiver: × × × × × × × ×

AAA BANK

(HEAD OFFICE)

BEIJING CN

135: broadcast priority

N

136 : broadcast nb for ALL

    B62792

129 : section number nn of nn

    01/01

130 : heading code

    /01/ BANK

    /02/ CLOSURE

134 : brdcst requestor BIC Name City

    BOFCUS33

    UNION BANK OF CALIFORNIA INTERNATIONAL

    NEW YORK, NY US

    UNION BANK OF CALIFORNIA INTERNATIONAL

    NEW YORK

312 : broadcast text

    TO : OPERATIONS MANAGER

UNION BANK OF CALIFORNIA HAS LARGELY COMPLETED THE SALE AND TRANSFER OF ITS INTERNATIONAL CORRESPONDENT BANKING BUSINESS TO WACHOVIA. THE FINAL STAGES OF THIS TRANSFER WILL BE COMPLETED OVER THE NEXT SEVERAL WEEKS. TO MINIMIZE ANY POTENTIAL INCIDENCIES OF MISROUTING PAYMENTS AND OTHER TRANSCTIONS, PLEASE NOTE THE DATES BELOW WHICH CONSTITUTE SIGNIFICANT MILESTONES IN OUR EXITING THIS BUSINESS:

MARCH 31, 2006 ALL USD ACCOUNTS WITHIN THE INTERNATIONAL BANKING GROUP HAVE BEEN CLOSED.

APRIL 7, 2006 AT THE CLOSE OF BUSINESS, UNION BANK OF CALIFORNIA INTERNATIONAL (UBOCI), CHIPS ABA 0505, WILL TERMINATE CHIPS PARTICIPATION. PLEASE DO NOT SEND PAYMENTS TO UBOCI AFTER THIS DATE.

PLEASE REVISE YOUR PAYMENT INSTRUCTIONS TO DIRECT YOUR UBOCI-RLEATED TRANSACTIONS TO WACHOVIA BANK, EFFECTIVE IMMEDIATELY, OR ALTERNATIVELY CONTACT THE REMITTER FOR AMENDED INSTRUCTIONS.

UBOC BRANCHES IN SEOUL, HONG KONG AND TAIPEI HAVE CEASED OPERATIONAL ACTIVITY, AND TOKYO IS EXPECTED TO CEASE OPERATIONAL ACTIVITY, TO BE CONFIRMED BY SUBSEQUENT BROADCAST, BY THE END OF APRIL.

UNION BANK OF CALIFORNIA

INTERNATIONAL BANKING GROUP

IV. Memos

1. Meaning

Memo is the oral form of memorandum, which is a usual brief communication written for interoffice circulation or a kind of short report typewritten on interoffice stationary.

2. Structure

A memo will include the date and the name of the receiver. It may also include the name of the sender, and the subject. A memo ends with a signature, but the name is not preceded by complementary closing like "very truly, yours."

3. Rules for Writing A Memo

The following rules are usually followed when producing a memo:
- Avoid the stereotyped in favor of a natural style.
- Use trade or professional jargons only when it represents a common language between you and the reader.
- Be restrained from (but do not necessarily avoid) using the personal pronoun "I" or in otherwise referring to yourself.
- Unless your personal opinions are desired, concentrate as objectively as you can on the conditions you are reporting.
- Avoid superlatives and other extremes of language.
- Write as simply and as clearly as you can, no matter what your subject or your audience is.

4. Functions of A Memo

Memo writing is regarded as a part of daily routine of office work. The chief functions performed by memos are as follows:
- providing information to the people concerned,
- Analyzing situations the office workers are faced with, and
- Making recommendations to the superior or the subordinate.

5. Example of A Memo

To: Mr. Hotchkiss Date: May 10, 20--

From : T. Cady Subject : Cost analysis

of DLB 750

Terminals

In response to a memorandum dated May 4 , 1998 , from Mr. Jones , Manager of the In-formation Processing Department , a cost examination was undertaken in the Teleprocessing Division. The purpose of this study was to determine whether it will be more efficient to lease or purchase the six DLB 750 terminals now in use.

After thorough investigation , it is recommended that the terminals be purchased instead of being leased.

The costs of the two proposals for the period June 1998 to June 1999 were examined. The results indicated that if the equipment is leased for the three years, and over-all cost of USD12, 960 will be incurred. If the equipment is purchased , the cost would be USD10, 212 including maintenance for three years. These figures show a cost advantage of USD2, 748. A breakdown of the costs is shown in Table I.

The USD2, 748 savings derived from purchasing the terminals indicate that it will be to the Company's advantage to take this alternative.

Attachment

TABLE I : COST ANALYSIS

	3 Year Cost
<u>Leasing cost</u>	
6 Terminals @ USD60 per month per terminal	USD12, 960
<u>Purchasing cost</u>	
6 Terminals @ USD1, 500 per terminal	USD9, 000
6 Terminals @ USD350 monthly main-tenance per terminal	756
6 Terminals@ USD19 repair service charge per terminal × estimated number of service calls	456
	USD10, 212
Monetary savings if terminals are purchased	USD2, 748

V. E-mail

1. Concept

E-mail means sending a letter or a piece of writing on the computer connected with internet, which is a system for linking computers around the world.

Today it has become perhaps the most inexpensive and the quickest way of communicating between businesses and individuals. On the web you can learn a lot about almost everything available online.

2. Comments on E-mailed Messages

E-mail offers numerous benefits. Because of its speed, relative inexpensiveness, and ease of use, it is rapidly replacing hard copy as a means of communication within and between business firms.

For all its benefits, however, E-mail can also lead to litigation nightmares when E-mailed documents are requested during discovery. The reasons for this include common misperceptions about the nature of E-mail and the sheer volume of E-mail messages being sent and received by firms today.

3. Common Misperceptions about E-mail

A common misperception about E-mail is that such message is private. Those sending E-mail thus tend to be more casual—and often more candid—in these communications than they would be if they were writing similar thoughts in interoffice memos or business correspondence using company letterhead. Informal comments made via E-mail, however, can come back to haunt the sender years late, as many firms are learning. For example, E-mail messages exchanged years ago by Microsoft Corporation executives became, for the Department of Justice (DOJ), evidence supporting the DOJ's position in the department's suit against Microsoft for anticompetitive business practices. The DOJ claimed that the E-mail tended to show that Microsoft deliberately tried to monopolize access to the Internet.

Another common misperception is that E-mail lacks permanence because it can be so easily deleted. In fact, the E-mail is not easily deleted from the computer's hard drive just by a click of the mouse; rather, the delete command clear space on the hard drive that can be overwritten when the computer needs that space. Until the message is overwritten, it can be retrieved by an opponent in a lawsuit during the discovery process.

Furthermore, copies of the E-mail message exist not only in the sender's hard drive but also in the hard drives of any recipients of the message, as well as in any servers through which the E-mail might have been routed.

Finally, many businesses routinely back up computer information, and back-up tapes may contain E-mail that has been sent to the electronic trash bin.

4. E-mail Management Policies

To curb potential litigation problems stemming from the use of E-mail, some firms simply delete E-mail after a specified period, such as two weeks or thirty days, and do not include E-mail on their routine back-ups. Other businesses keep back-up copies of their E-mail forever, in the event they may need access to those messages at some future time (to defend against a lawsuit, for example). Still other companies print out or make back-up copies of important E-mail and trash the rest, just as they do with paper documents; this is perhaps the most prudent approach.

Creating an effective E-mail management policy has now become a priority for many firms due to the sheer volume of their E-mail exchanges. According to a poll conducted in May 1998, the typical office worker in the U. S. sends and receives an average of sixty E-mail messages each day. That means that a company with, say, four thousand workers sends and receives, on average, a staggering 240, 000 E-mail messages per day, or 1. 2 million per week. If the company were to keep all E-mails on back-up storage devices, in the event of a lawsuit it could face a nightmare indeed. In one case, for example, the court ordered a defendant to review and produce about 30 million pages of E-mail stored on back-up tapes at a cost of between 50, 000 and 70, 000.

5. Illustration of Writing A Typical E-mail Message

FROM: Keith. Willis@ a-bglobal. com on 11/9/06

TO: All. staff@ a-bglobal. com

SUBJECT: Enterprise Wiki

I would like to inform all colleagues that our new Enterprise Wiki has today gone live. It's a secure, hosted solution that has content creation and communications as core functionality. Our Enterprise Wiki will completely replace our existing content management platforms. In today's fast-changing and highly competitive world, optimizing for seed and rich feedback will make us a truly collaborative environment.

Keith Willis, chief IT architect

Notes

1. **franchise** ['fræntʃaiz] *n.* special right givenby public authorities to a person or company

2. **confidential** [kɔnfi'denʃəl] *adj.* (to be kept) secret, given in confidence

3. **term** [təːm] *n.* words used to express an idea, esp. a specialized concept; (pl) conditions offered or agreed to

4. **discrepancy** [dis'krepənsi] *n.* (of statements and accounts) difference; absence of agreement

5. **infrastructure** ['infrə'strʌktʃə] *n.* the parts of a system composing the whole; installations for operations

6. **release** [ri'liːs] *n.* publishment, that is published or announced

7. **superior** [sjuː'piəriə] *n.* person of higher rank, authority, etc. than another

8. **subordinate** [sə'bɔːdinit] *n.* person of junior rank or position

9. **litigation** [,liti'geiʃən] *n.* suing or being sued, legal claims against or being brought to law

Questions for discussion

1. What's the difference between semi-block style and full-block style of bank letters?

2. Have you ever read another style which is not described in this part of book?

3. Which principle do people often break when writing bank letters? How does it happen?

4. How did telex get prosperous? What will its future going to be?

5. What's the basic principle for good telexes?

6. What's SWIFT?

7. What are the characteristics of Standards – Release – 2006 of SWIFT?

8. What do we need to do to write good memos?

9. What should be the length of memos?

10. What do we need to do to write good E-mails?